A Flock of Shepherds:
The National Conference of Catholic Bishops

Thomas J. Reese, S.J.

Sheed & Ward

Sheed & Ward™ is a service of The National Catholic Reporter Publishing Company.

Library of Congress Cataloguing-in-Publication Data

Reese, Thomas J., 1945-
    A flock of shepherds : The National Conference of Catholic Bishops / Thomas J. Reese
       p.   cm.
    Includes bibliographical references and index.
    ISBN: 1-55612-557-7 (alk. paper)
    1. Catholic Church. National Conference of Catholic Bishops--History.   I. Title
BX1407.B57R44   1992
262'.12--dc20   92-13530
                                               CIP

Published by: Sheed & Ward
                 115 E. Armour Blvd.
                 P.O. Box 419492
                 Kansas City, MO 64141-6492

To order, call: (800) 333-7373

Contents

Introduction:

A Conspiracy of Bishops

The conference offers the most effective vehicle nationally for our teaching office.[1]

—————CARDINAL JAMES HICKEY

As the bishops must surely recognize, their moral authority is visibly eroding.[2]

—————PATRICK BUCHANAN

Our national conference . . . provides a framework and a forum for us to share ideas, to teach and elucidate sound Catholic Doctrine, set pastoral directions and develop policy positions on contemporary social issues.[3]

—————CARDINAL JOSEPH BERNARDIN

From every corner of the United States, the conspirators, dressed in black, gather in Washington, D.C., to plot a radical transformation of America. From outward appearances, this mostly middle-aged, white, male assembly is not the stuff of conspiracies. But these are the American Catholic bishops, and their agenda is nothing less than capturing the soul of America.

Unlike other conspirators, they do not hide what they do. Their conspiracy is mostly open and public. They are truly conspirators as their classical training would tell them. "Conspiracy" comes from the Latin *"conspirare"* which means to breathe together, to harmonize, to agree together. For Christians, the root also conjures up the idea of the Spirit that dwells in the people of God. The goal of these conspirators is more revolutionary than that of any antiestablishment comrades for they want to transform American society by the power of the Gospel.

When the bishops gather in Washington, they do so as the National Conference of Catholic Bishops—the organization by which the American Catholic hierarchy speaks and acts on the national and international level. In the period since the Second Vatican Council, the conference has been active in making policy for the Catholic church in the United States. Its decisions have changed the face of American Catholicism by translating the liturgy into English, by allowing communion in the hand, by eliminating meatless Fridays, by modernizing the religious education of American Catholics, by making it easier for divorced Catholics to remarry, by authorizing the ordination of married deacons, and by making many other decisions that have affected the religious lives of American Catholics.

When the American Catholic bishops wish to speak or act on national issues they do so through the United States Catholic Conference, the public policy arm of the bishops' conference. The bishops' involvement in public policy has often been controversial. Through their conference, they have intervened in the public policy debate on many issues: abortion, AIDS, birth control, capital punishment, American foreign policy in Central America, child care, disarmament, education, health care, medical ethics, the Panama Canal treaty, prison reform, Third World debt, the Vietnam and Persian Gulf wars, welfare reform, and many other issues. They have influenced public policy in the United States through public statements, through their lobbyists on Capitol Hill, and through litigation in the courts.

The actions of the National Conference of Catholic Bishops (NCCB) and the United States Catholic Conference (USCC) have been criticized by both the left and the right of the political and religious spectrum. Political liberals have complained of the bishops' opposition to abortion and their support of public aid to parochial schools. Political conservatives have chastised the bishops for being naive about the Cold War and ignorant of economic reality. Liberal Catholics have complained of the bishops' opposition to artificial birth control and their insistence on a celibate male clergy. Conservative Catholics accuse the bishops of being too independent of Rome. Roman officials have questioned the teaching authority of episcopal conferences and accused them of infringing on the autonomy of local bishops.

Attacked from the right and the left, the bishops have sometimes been divided themselves. Meeting in public sessions, their disagreements have made headlines, but their ability to reach consensus on difficult matters has also been impressive, especially when compared with other churches.

This book examines the American bishops' conference. How did it come to be, who are its movers and shakers, how does it operate, what has it done, how does it make decisions, how do its decisions impact on local churches, how does it relate to the Vatican, and what has been its impact on American life?

To answer these questions, I will examine the NCCB/USCC as a legislative assembly using social science methods that have been applied to political legislatures for many years. This is not a work of theology, canon law, or spirituality, although sometimes these disciplines will be referred to. Rather the book is an examination of how the bishops' conference operates from a social science and journalistic perspective by someone who is a priest, a political scientist, and a journalist. No denial of the spiritual nature of the church or of the NCCB/USCC is intended. Social science cannot measure the activity of the Holy Spirit; it can only look at the external data. Nor is it the purpose of this book to defend or condemn specific decisions or actions of the conference. Rather it is an attempt to understand how the conference works and what it has done.

For those unfamiliar with the governmental structure of the Catholic church, a few terms need explanation. The church in the United States is divided into over 180 geographical units called dioceses or archdioceses, depending on whether they are headed by a diocesan bishop or an archbishop.[4] (There is also a military archdiocese that serves Catholics in the U.S. armed forces all over the world, and eleven Eastern rite dioceses serving Eastern rite Catholics in union with Rome). These separate and independent sees (a generic term for dioceses and archdioceses) cover every corner of the United States and are grouped into 33 provinces, each headed by an archbishop who is called the metropolitan of the province. These archbishops have very little power over the other bishops in their provinces.[5] A few of these archbishops are also cardinals who can vote in the election of a new pope. Some of these archbishops and diocesan bishops are assisted by auxiliary bishops. If an assistant bishop has the right of succession, he is called a coadjutor bishop. Each diocese has a chancery whose staff serves the bishop.[6]

All together the archbishops, diocesan bishops, and auxiliary bishops add up to about 290 bishops working in the United States,[7] plus another 80 or so retired bishops. These bishops are automatically members of the National Conference of Catholic Bishops (NCCB) and the United States Catholic Conference (USCC), although the retired bishops cannot vote in the conference. The NCCB is the assembly of bishops given certain duties and powers under church law, which is called canon law. The USCC is the body of bishops incorporated under civil law. Both work through committees and are served by a Washington-based staff or secretariat.[8] When the NCCB and the USCC were organized in 1966, the plan was for the NCCB to deal with church issues while the USCC would deal with public policy questions. As will be explained later, this distinction proved difficult to maintain. This book will refer to both as "the conference" or the NCCB/USCC.

The operations of the bishops' conference, like the operations of any organization, are affected by several variables whose interaction helps explain what the organization does and why. Every organization is affected by its members and those who work with them. Thus it will be important to look at who are the bishops, how they are selected, and who helps them in the conference.

Second, norms and procedures of the organization are important factors in determining outcomes. In political organizations, the ideological perspectives of the participants and the legal system are important considerations. In a bishops' conference, we must look at theological perspectives and canon law, the internal legal system governing the church. The organizational structure of the conference is also an important consideration in explaining how the conference works.

Third, the environment the organization operates in will affect it. War or peace, prosperity or depression, persecution or acceptance, all these can affect an organization. For the bishops' conference the religious environment is also important, whether it is a period of stability or reform, growth or decline, consensus or controversy. The conference responds and adapts to its environment.

No single variable is sufficient in explaining the actions of the NCCB/USCC. The conference is a complex organization attempting to attain many different goals in a changing environment.

Outline

Chapter 1 will look at the men who make up the bishops' conference. Who are they, what are their backgrounds, how did they become bishops and therefore members of the conference?

Chapter 2 will examine the ecclesial environment in which the episcopal conference operates. What is the theological and juridical status of episcopal conferences? What are their historical origins, their theological justification, and their canonical powers? How did the bishops' conference originate and evolve in the United States?

Chapter 3 will spotlight the presidents of the conference. Who are they, how are they elected, what have they done?

Chapter 4 will examine the NCCB/USCC staff that helps the bishops operate as a conference. This staff is overseen by a general secretary. Over the years, these general secretaries have been some of the most influential men in the operations of the conference. Conservative Catholics have attacked the staff, blaming it for leading the bishops astray.

Chapter 5 will look at the NCCB/USCC committees and chairs that are essential to the smooth operation of the conference. How are chairs chosen, what do they and their committees do? This chapter also will examine the role of the NCCB/USCC Administrative Committee/Board and the National Advisory Council.

Chapter 6 will deal with the full assembly of the conference which meets once or twice a year for three to four days with all the bishops present. How does this body of 290 bishops function? What procedures do they follow? What issues do they take up? What have they done? What has divided and united the bishops? How do they achieve consensus?

Chapter 7 will investigate how the conference interacts with political life in the United States. What issues does the conference take on and why? How does it influence American political life through statements, lobbying, and litigation? How and why has the conference gotten involved in various issues?

Relations between the conference and the church outside the United States, especially the Holy See, will be examined in Chapter 8. How do the conference and the Vatican interact and communicate? Where has there been conflict, how was it dealt with? Chapter 8 also considers the impact the conference has had on the life of the church outside the United States. What has been the U.S. bishops' interaction with other episcopal conferences?

Chapter 9 will look at the finances and budget of the conference. Where does its money come from and how is it spent? How does it plan and decide priorities?

The concluding chapter will put the conference in the context of political science literature on legislatures. It also will enumerate the strengths and weaknesses of the conference, evaluate the role of the American bishops' conference, and make recommendations for its improvement.

Methodology

The research for this book was done by examining the official minutes and press releases of conference meetings since its formation in 1966. I have also attended all the bishops' conference meetings since 1981.[9] Also helpful were the press files of Catholic News Service. All the living presidents, vice presidents, and general secretaries of the conference were interviewed, as were many committee chairs and staff. Also helpful were the interviews done for my book *Archbishop: Inside the Power Structure of the American Catholic Church.* Quotations in the text that are not footnoted are from my interviews.

Many people through their cooperation have made this book possible. They deserve my thanks but no blame for the contents of the book. I especially want to thank the presidents of the conference (Cardinals Joseph L. Bernardin and John J. Krol, Archbishops Daniel E. Pilarczyk, John L. May, John R. Quinn, John R. Roach, and Bishop James L. Malone) and the general secretaries (Archbishop Thomas Kelly, Msgr. Daniel Hoye, and Msgr. Robert Lynch). The NCCB/USCC staff was also most cooperative. Special thanks go to the staff of the USCC Office of Media Relations, the staff of the CNS library, and Dr. Warren Willis, archivist of the NCCB/USCC.

Exceedingly helpful also were my research assistant, Jelita McLeod, Eugene Rooney, S.J., of the Woodstock Theological Center Library, and Robert Hyer of Sheed and Ward. Nor could this book have been written without the support and encouragement of the Woodstock Theological Center director, James Connor, S.J., and other members of the Woodstock Theological Center and Jesuit community. Finally, I would like to thank those bishops who leaked me documents that I could not get from the NCCB/USCC staff. Especially helpful were some confidential minutes of NCCB/USCC Administrative/Board meetings and of executive sessions of the NCCB/USCC assembly. The documents of the June 1991 NCCB/USCC meeting were invaluable.

1. A Flock of Shepherds

> Episcopal candidates should be "priests who have already proven themselves as *teachers of the faith as it is proclaimed by the Magisterium of the church.*"
>
> ———JOHN PAUL II

> I try to get there [Rome] when an American appointment is under consideration.
>
> ———CARDINAL JOHN O'CONNOR

> This is the man who was the tradesman's son: the backstairs brat who was born in Cheapside.
>
> ———THE FOUR KNIGHTS[1]

The National Conference of Catholic Bishops is the most exclusive men's club in America. The club's size is currently limited to about 290 active members. To be eligible for membership one must be Catholic, male, unmarried, between 35 and 75 years of age.[2] Like many exclusive clubs, it is mostly white (42 percent of Irish ancestry, 20 percent German, 8 percent English, and 14 percent other European). In 1991, two Native Americans, 12 blacks, 20 Hispanics, and no Asians were in the club, which brings the minority membership to about 11 percent. Its members preside over numerous multi-million dollar corporations whose combined finances would dwarf most major corporations. They employ thousands of people and manage large properties.

In many ways, however, this group breaks company with other exclusive clubs in America. Not only are its members unmarried, they must be celibate and Catholic priests for at least five years before becoming a bishop. Celibacy is an impossible hurdle for most Americans. Nor docs the club cater to the upper class as do other exclusive clubs. Most members come from working-class backgrounds. Only 11 percent of the bishops had fathers who graduated from college. Sixty-two percent of their

1

fathers never graduated from high school. And despite their heavy responsibilities, the bishops are poorly paid. Considering the long hours they put in working, their take-home pay probably would equal that of someone on minimum wage.

To understand the NCCB/USCC, it is essential to understand who these bishops are and how they became members of the episcopal club. What happens in the NCCB/USCC is determined to a great extent by the makeup of its episcopal membership. Thus the NCCB/USCC cannot be understood without first examining how priests become bishops.

The NCCB is much more than a club, it is a flock of shepherds. A bishop is the leader or shepherd of his local church, his diocese. As a bishop, his primary responsibility is to his local flock, the diocese he ministers to and governs. The typical bishop spends most of his time worrying not about the episcopal conference but about his local church. Even those involved in the conference as presidents devote no more than a third of their time to conference business. For most bishops, NCCB/USCC work takes up fewer than a couple of weeks of their time each year. The NCCB/USCC is a group of shepherds who spend most of their time and energy with their sheep and not with one another.

Career Ladder

Who are these men and how did they become bishops and members of the bishops' conference? Each bishop is a unique individual, but some generalizations can be made that, though not true of all bishops, are true of most. Since their average age is 62, these are men whose earliest memories would be of the Great Depression and the New Deal. Their fathers were pro-union and often out of work so their families had to cut corners and scrape to make ends meet. Some families survived because of relief and WPA jobs that came from the New Deal. The bishops' parents vividly remembered the anti-Catholic propaganda that helped defeat Al Smith in the 1928 election. Not surprisingly, their parents voted Democratic.

As the sons of good Catholic families, most grew up in Catholic neighborhoods where the priest was one of the few educated and respected leaders of the community. As children they usually attended the parish grammar school, where they were taught the *Baltimore Catechism* as well as secular subjects by sisters from families like their own. They abstained from meat on Fridays. They went to church on Sundays with their families, and as altar boys recited the responses in Latin.

While they were in their early teens, America was pushed into World War II. Their Irish, German, and Italian parents were not eager for another European war, but Pearl Harbor turned them into staunch supporters of the Allies. They kept count of the number of Purple Hearts and Medals of Honor awarded to Catholic soldiers. Like their neighbors, they were patriotic Americans.

About two-thirds of the bishops began their ecclesiastical careers by entering a high school seminary where they lived under strict discipline in an all-male environment. They practiced an asceticism that stressed sacrifice, self-denial, and obedience. In the seminary, they studied Latin, philosophy, canon law, and theology along with the other humanities, but they learned little about business and the physical or social sciences. This seminary training imbued them with the values and norms of the clerical club they joined at ordination.

After the war, about a third were singled out from their classmates by their bishops to study theology or canon law in Rome, a third (with some overlapping) also studied at the bishops' Catholic University of America in Washington, D.C. Over 20 percent ended up with ecclesiastical doctorates in canon law or theology. As a group, the bishops are better educated than the clergy as a whole. They were among the church's best and brightest.

They were ordained to serve a growing and upwardly mobile church of the 1950s when their Catholic brothers and sisters were becoming part of the American mainstream. The GI Bill helped the Catholic laity get educated, and as they moved up the economic ladder they also moved out of ethnic neighborhoods into the suburbs. The priests followed them and built new churches and schools. Anti-Catholicism began to decline as America acknowledged the church's anti-Communism as a sure sign of its loyalty. They cheered the election of John F. Kennedy and saw overt anti-Catholicism die with him.

Like most American Catholics, they were caught unprepared for John XXIII and the Second Vatican Council. Their pope had always been the brilliant but austere Pius XII. Few of them, even those with doctorates, had read the authors (Yves Congar, Augustine Bea, Hans Küng, John Courtney Murray, Karl Rahner, Henri de Lubac, Joseph Ratzinger, Edward Schillebeeckx, and Joseph Jungmann) who were the leading minds behind the council. They had been taught with seminary textbooks that lacked historical depth, critical perspectives, or a sense of the development of doctrine. By the time of the council, they were holding high positions in diocesan chanceries or seminaries. They watched their bishops respond with uncertainty, confusion, and then enthusiasm to the council. They followed along, sometimes with conviction, sometimes as loyal churchmen who presumed the hierarchy knew what was best for the church.

Ultimately they embraced the reforms of the council, but the upheavals of the late 1960s and early 1970s taught them the importance of prudence and a nonauthoritarian style of leadership. They proved to be more adaptable to change and, at the same time, more stable than many of their clerical peers. In the late 1970s they began to take up the episcopal crozier to shepherd a flock in a church very different from the one they had been prepared for. They watched younger priests, and even some of their classmates, leave the priesthood. They had to close almost all their high school seminaries and some of their major seminaries as vocations plummeted. Where their predecessors had commanded and been obeyed, they were often met with nonnegotiable demands from parishioners, priests, sisters, minority groups, and women.

They supported civil rights and the social programs of the Great Society. They buried the dead who came home in body bags from Vietnam, a war they at first supported and then became disillusioned with. In the 1970s they watched a president forced out of office, and saw their financial plans destroyed by inflation and high interest rates. In the 1980s they tried to help the poor who were cast adrift by the Reagan revolution.

Meanwhile on the ecclesial front, they admired and respected Paul VI who appointed many of them. They watched as his encyclical *Humanae Vitae* divided the church. Their orthodoxy was questioned by right-wing Catholics who denounced them to Rome. And they trimmed their sails in response to changing winds and a new captain in Rome. The election of John Paul II was a significant event in their ecclesial lives. By 1991 about half the active bishops had been appointed by John Paul, and through his letters, papal visits, and Vatican officials he set the direction for their episcopal lives.

Secret Selection Process

How exactly did these men become bishops and therefore members of the National Conference of Catholic Bishops?[3] It should be stressed that those involved in the appointment process are primarily looking for someone who can be a pastoral leader in his diocese. Only secondarily would they consider the candidate's impact as a member of the bishops' conference. This is especially true of the candidate's bishop, who starts him off on his ecclesiastical career.

Almost all of the bishops were first advanced up the ecclesiastical ladder by their own bishops. At a young age, they were singled out as brighter, harder working, or more loyal than their classmates. Loyalty is a sine qua non for advancement in the church hierarchy. When the bishop is looking for a secretary, a chancellor, a vicar general, or other chancery official, he does not want someone who will publicly or privately criticize him. He wants a team player who might argue a point in private but will defend any decision of his boss in public.

After proving himself with years of loyal service, the priest's name would be proposed by his bishop as a possible episcopal candidate. This would be done at a meeting of the bishops of a province chaired by the local archbishop. The bishop would argue his protege's case, but a majority of the bishops would have to support him in a secret ballot before his name is passed on to the pro-nuncio, the pope's representative in Washington, D.C. These bishops would give some weight to how the priest would fit into the episcopal club.

The pro-nuncio (called an apostolic delegate before U.S.-Vatican diplomatic relations were established in 1984) plays a key role in the appointment of new bishops. The current pro-nuncio, Archbishop Agostino Cacciavillan, was appointed in 1990 after serving as pro-nuncio to India and Nepal. He followed Archbishop Pio Laghi (1980-90) and Archbishop Jean Jadot (1973-80). The pro-nuncio is responsible for investigating the backgrounds, character, and views of the candidates. This must be done secretly without consulting the candidates themselves. A questionnaire is sent to people who know the priest, asking about his views and his character. Those questioned are warned not to tell the priest or anyone else. "ANY VIOLATION OF THIS SECRET NOT ONLY CONSTITUTES A GRAVE FAULT, BUT IS ALSO A CRIME PUNISHABLE WITH A CORRESPONDING ECCLESIASTICAL PENALTY" warns the pro-nuncio in large bold print when requesting information on a candidate.[4]

The questionnaire sent by the pro-nuncio contains 14 items, including a request for additional names of persons who know the candidate.[5] Although the questionnaire is detailed, the covering letter indicates that it "is only to serve as an orientation . . ." and the respondent can answer in a discursive manner.

Most of the questions deal with the obvious physical, intellectual, moral, spiritual, social, and priestly characteristics that one would hope for in a bishop. The questions are more relevant to the work of a bishop in his diocese than to his work in the conference of bishops. The question on leadership qualities (item 9) suggests a desire for a pastor with "A fatherly spirit . . . the ability to lead others, to dialogue, to stimulate and receive cooperation . . . to direct and engage in team work; appreciation for the role and the collaboration of religious and laity (both men and women) and for a just share of responsibilities. . . ." The questionnaire asks about the administrative skills of the candidate (item 10) and his pastoral fitness and experience (item 8). Under this item are listed not only pastoral skills but also "a spirit of ecumenism" and "the promotion and defense of human rights," qualities that could impact on his conference work.

The questions on orthodoxy (item 6) indicate the Vatican is looking for priests who adhere "with conviction and loyalty to the doctrine and magisterium of the Church." It asks about "the attitude of the candidate toward documents of the Holy See on the Ministerial Priesthood, on the priestly ordination of women, on the Sacrament of Matrimony, on sexual ethics, and on social justice." The questions on church discipline also stress "Loyalty and docility to the Holy Father, the Apostolic See, and the Hierarchy; esteem for and acceptance of priestly celibacy . . . ; respect for and observance of the general and particular norms governing divine worship and clerical attire."

Correct thinking on doctrine and church discipline is desired not only for a bishop of a diocese but for a member of the bishops' conference. A priest supporting the ordination of women, optional priestly celibacy, or birth control would not be made a bishop. Neither would a priest opposed to the teaching of the church on social justice. It is no wonder then that the National Conference of Catholic Bishops has taken the positions it has. Its membership has been expertly vetted before appointment. Having an unorthodox bishop is even less likely than having a Communist in the CIA.

Auxiliary and Diocesan Bishops

When a vacancy occurs because of the death or retirement of a bishop, it can be for a diocesan bishop or an auxiliary bishop.[6] There are about 190 diocesan bishops heading dioceses in the United States who are helped by approximately 100 auxiliary bishops.[7] Auxiliary bishops are concentrated in populous dioceses and archdioceses, but a small diocese would have only a diocesan bishop.[8] Both kinds of bishops are members of the bishops' conference and theoretically have equal power in the conference, except on financial matters as will be explained later.

Usually a priest becomes an auxiliary bishop before he becomes a diocesan bishop. Fewer than one out of four bishops are given a diocese when they first become a bishop. The appointment processes for auxiliaries and diocesan bishops are different. If a diocesan bishop needs an auxiliary, he will prepare a list of three names called a ternus[9] that he submits to the pro-nuncio. Normally the names are of priests in his diocese. The bishop indicates his preferred candidate with the reasons for each candidate. After the pro-nuncio does his own investigation, he passes the names on to the Congregation for Bishops in Rome with his own evaluation of the candidates.

If the vacancy is for a diocesan bishop, the ternus is prepared by the pro-nuncio after gathering information about the diocese itself. The ternus might contain the names of priests and/or men who are already bishops. The pro-nuncio lists the candidates according to his preference and gives the reasons supporting each candidate.

All this preparatory work is done in secrecy. Although there can be a public discussion of the qualities needed for a bishop in a particular diocese, public discussion of names is strictly forbidden by church law. As part of the process, the pro-nuncio consults with some American bishops, especially the current and former bishops of the diocese, the bishops and archbishop of the province, the cardinals, and the officers of the National Conference of Catholic Bishops.

The NCCB Committee on Selection of Bishops

The role of the conference in the selection of bishops was discussed by the NCCB as early as 1967 when the bishops considered proposals from an ad hoc committee on nominations of bishops chaired by Archbishop John Krol, then vice president of the conference. The committee apparently wanted to have the NCCB Committee on the Selection of Bishops, rather than the bishops of a province, draw up the list of priests who were potential candidates for the episcopacy. Although Archbishop Krol argued that Vatican II required participation of the conference in the nomination process, the majority wanted to keep a role for provincial bishops.

The committee report was amended to keep the provincial meetings but to have the province bishops prepare a report on each candidate that would be sent to the NCCB Committee on the Selection of Bishops. In communications with the Vatican representative in Washington, the NCCB committee would be authorized to "signal out certain persons on these lists whom they recognize as having exceptional merit."[10]

The conference revisited the issue in November 1970 when it considered norms for the nomination of bishops that had been proposed by Rome. Regional discussions showed the bishops leaning against increasing the role of the conference in the nomination of bishops.[11] Arguments by Cardinals Krol and John Dearden swayed the bishops the other way. Cardinal Krol argued that Vatican II documents required conference participation in the nomination of bishops. Cardinal Dearden, the president, indicated that the NCCB Committee on the Selection of Bishops would not have exclusive control over the list of candidates. It would work in close cooperation with local bishops and the pope's representative in Washington. The bishops voted (150-43) in favor of having the list of provincial candidates sent to the NCCB Committee on the Selection of Bishops. They also voted (143-54) to have the NCCB committee review or draw up the ternus for a vacant diocese. The last recommendation was unacceptable to the Vatican.

The bishops were reluctant to give up their role on the province level in the nomination process. Although the role of the bishops in the 31 U.S. provinces is limited to compiling lists of possible episcopal candidates, they do not want to lose this power to a national committee that has little knowledge of local needs or local clergy.

After seven years reviewing provincial lists, the NCCB Committee on the Selection of Bishops concluded it was a waste of time. "We do not believe that it serves any useful purpose for all twelve regional representatives to meet to review twenty provincial lists containing the names of hundreds of potential candidates," reported Bishop Francis Mugavero in 1979, when he chaired an ad hoc committee to study the role of the committee.[12]

The committee "could not effectively function," says Bishop James W. Malone, NCCB/USCC president (1983-86). "It still exists, but it does not meet for the purpose in its title." In a conference the size of the United States, most members of the committee do not know the priests who are being considered for the episcopacy. As a result, they have little to contribute. "If the bishops of the nation knew more about the finest candidates for the episcopacy," said one bishop, "we might have more creative results."

On the other hand, some argue that when it is a question of advancing a bishop to a higher position, then regional or multiprovincial meetings are useful since the bishops know each other. For example, a bishop like Thomas Daily was first an auxiliary in Boston, than diocesan bishop in Palm Beach, Florida. Next he was assigned to Brooklyn.

Bishop Mugavero's committee recommended that the then 12 NCCB regional representatives on the selection committee be divided into four groups, each with three regions. Each group would meet once a year to review the provincial lists from its regions. A report, including any observations from the representatives, would be forwarded to the NCCB president who would forward it to the papal representative with his observations. This proposal was unacceptable to the Vatican.

Role of NCCB Officers

Although the NCCB Committee on the Selection of Bishops has functioned poorly, consultation by the pro-nuncio with the NCCB president and vice president has worked better. This consultation takes place in two stages. Archbishop John Roach, conference president from 1980 to 1983, recalls:

> The president receives notification from the pro-nuncio that a see will be opening up or that he is considering the appointment of an auxiliary for a particular diocese. The president is asked to give his impressions of the state of the diocese, the kind of leadership it needs.
>
> Each of the 13 regions of the United States elects a bishop to be on the Committee for the Selection of Bishops. I would consult with the regional representative. They would not get a list of names, but I would ask what the diocese is like and he would recount its story. I would forward that to the apostolic delegate.[13]

After the pro-nuncio narrows down the list of candidates to eight or ten names, he sends them to the officers of the NCCB for a second consultation. A typical list, said Archbishop John May, president of the conference from 1986 to 1989, "had maybe six bishops and then about four or five priests who had been proposed for that particular diocese." This second consultation is a special concession granted by the Holy See.[14] The president still does not see the final ternus or report submitted by the pro-nuncio.

Because of the size of the United States, often the NCCB officers do not know the priests who are being proposed. "A lot of times I don't know any of the priests," admits Archbishop May. "If I did not know them," Archbishop Roach explains, "I would say, 'Sorry.' If the person was already an auxiliary or a bishop I would know something about him."

According to Bishop Malone, "The pro-nuncio says, 'These are the names that have surfaced. Give me a list of three in order of your preference and give the reasons for your preference.'" Similarly, Archbishop May says, "These names have been proposed, and you are told, 'If you wish, will you comment on these names or, if you prefer, put in any different names, put in your own names. Then give us a terna and give your reasons for it.' So I usually come up with three names [and] tell why I think these three deserve consideration."

Some have criticized the NCCB leadership for not taking a more active role at this point in the process. One archbishop said:

> When the second consultation occurs, the conference leadership ought to contact whoever represents that region on the NCCB Committee on Appointments and find out what he thinks. If that bishop doesn't know, he ought to find out.
>
> But that step doesn't seem to occur, and whenever I hear the bishops complain about appointments, I feel that we have ourselves to blame for not using well what has been offered us.

In the past there were certain American bishops who were "kingmakers" in the hierarchy because they had unique influence in the choice of bishops. "There is no kingmaker among the American bishops today," reports the church historian Msgr.

John Tracy Ellis. Neither Archbishop Jadot nor Archbishop Laghi had one American prelate whom they listened to exclusively. Cardinals John O'Connor, Bernard Law, and James Hickey were said to be the members of the American hierarchy closest to Archbishop Laghi. But one archbishop explained, "In the long run, Laghi will do a couple of things to make people happy, but then he will shift off to some other force. He is a very skilled diplomat."

When the names arrive in Rome they are considered by the Congregation for Bishops, which is headed by Cardinal Bernardin Gantin, a Vatican official from the Benin Republic in West Africa who was named prefect of the congregation in 1984. The congregation in 1991 included 34 papal appointees who have five-year renewable terms—28 cardinals and six archbishops. Seventeen of the cardinals are permanently stationed in Rome as part of the Vatican curia.

Cardinals William Baum, Edmund Szoka, and John O'Connor are the only American members of the congregation. Cardinal Baum, formerly archbishop of Washington, D.C., resides in Rome as head of the Apostolic Penitentiary, a Vatican tribunal. Cardinal Szoka, formerly archbishop of Detroit, is in charge of Vatican finances. Both can therefore easily attend the congregation's weekly meetings. Cardinal O'Connor of New York gets to Rome about every other month for meetings of the congregation since his appointment in 1985. "I try to get there when an American appointment is under consideration," explains Cardinal O'Connor. He reports attending meetings that consider from 75 to 80 percent of the American appointments. When he cannot attend, he sends in his vote by mail or telephone. Also a member of the congregation is Cardinal Laghi who as a former pro-nuncio is very knowledgeable about the United States.

In December 1989, Archbishop Justin Rigali, a native of Los Angeles, became secretary to the Congregation for Bishops. As secretary, he is the only staff person in the room when the congregation meets. He can be very influential in the selection of American bishops. Thus, Cardinals Baum, O'Connor, and Szoka and Archbishop Rigali are positioned to be the most influential

Americans in deciding who becomes a member of the National Conference of Catholic Bishops.

After the Congregation for Bishops discusses the three candidates, it chooses one to pass on to the pope. It can reject all the candidates and tell the pro-nuncio to try again, but normally, at least one candidate is acceptable. The pope normally accepts the congregation's recommendation.

Before names are even submitted to him, the pope sets the criteria for selecting the candidates he wants. In an address to the American bishops visiting Rome in 1983, John Paul II stressed the importance of unity and fidelity to the magisterium. He said that the bishops should look for "priests who have already proven themselves as *teachers of the faith as it is proclaimed by the Magisterium of the church*, and, who, in the words of St. Paul's pastoral advice to Titus, 'hold fast to the authentic message.'"

He told the bishops,

> It is important for the episcopal candidate, as for the bishop himself, to be *a sign of the unity of the universal church*. . . . Never is the unity of the local church stronger and more secure, never is the ministry of the local bishop more effective than when the local church under the pastoral leadership of the local bishop proclaims in word and deed the universal faith, when it is open in charity to all the needs of the universal church and when it embraces faithfully the church's universal discipline.[15]

Results of Selection Process

Many people argue that the type of bishops appointed while Archbishop Jean Jadot (1973-80) represented the pope in Washington is different from the type appointed under Archbishop Pio Laghi (1980-90).[16] Archbishop Jadot was appointed by Paul VI who, it is argued, was looking for pastoral bishops. Archbishop Laghi was appointed by John Paul II, who emphasizes loyalty to church orthodoxy and discipline. "Laghi's mandate was to find men for the hierarchy who would put the Church back on track," says Archbishop Rembert Weakland, "men who would listen to and be obedient to Rome."[17]

The consensus among journalists and nonepiscopal experts is that the bishops appointed under Archbishop Laghi and John Paul II are more "conservative" than bishops appointed under Archbishop Jadot and Paul VI. E. J. Dionne, Jr., stated it succinctly in the *New York Times*: The Jadot bishops "tend to be liberal. . . . The Laghi bishops . . . tend to be more conservative."[18]

These labels apply primarily to church issues, not political or economic issues. Cardinal John O'Connor of New York, for example, is frequently called a conservative yet he is concerned about the poor, very pro-labor, and testified against the MX missile. But his strong views on abortion make him anathema to many political liberals. But there is some evidence that even the political orientation of the bishops has been affected by the recent appointments made by John Paul II. A survey of the bishops conducted by Richard J. Gelm found that the recently appointed bishops were split evenly between Democrats and Republicans (38 percent each) while those appointed under Paul VI were 59 percent Democrat and 17 percent Republican.[19]

Some observers of the American hierarchy focus on internal church issues when comparing bishops rather than on these political issues. As Msgr. John Tracy Ellis told the *National Catholic Reporter*: "I would characterize the Laghi bishops as theologically correct, meaning that they follow the line of the Holy See. They don't vary or wander away. . . . I don't think a man of very liberal sentiments and views would have a chance at all."[20]

Likewise Rev. Richard P. McBrien wrote in the *New York Times*: "These bishops tend to be uncritically loyal to the Pope and his curial associates, rigidly authoritarian and solitary in the exercise of pastoral leadership and reliably safe in their theological views. . . . Since 1980, with the exception of the Archdiocese of Chicago . . . , every major appointee has been more hard-line than his immediate predecessor."[21]

Also Peter Hebblethwaite writing in the *National Catholic Reporter* said: "certainly the episcopal appointments made under Pro-nuncio Archbishop Pio Laghi differ greatly from those made under his predecessor, Archbishop Jean Jadot. . . . It is unlikely we shall see another Kenneth E. Untener, bishop of Saginaw, in the National Conference of Catholic Bishops."[22]

Pio Laghi's promotion to cardinal in 1991, after returning to Rome, is a further indication that John Paul II preferred Archbishop Laghi's appointees to those of Archbishop Jadot who was never made a cardinal.

Archbishops Laghi and Jadot disagree with this analysis. "There is no difference between the appointments made by Laghi and myself," Archbishop Jadot told me in 1983. "Most of the candidates appointed I would have proposed as my number one choice. Some I would not have expected for the particular diocese they received. For example, I knew [Adam J.] Maida was a man to keep an eye on, but I had never thought of Green Bay for him. I knew that [Anthony J.] Bevilacqua would not remain an auxiliary in Brooklyn." It is noteworthy that Archbishop Jadot mentioned in 1983 men who eventually became archbishops of cardinalatial sees.

Neither do the U.S. bishops publicly agree with the media's categorizations although some agree privately. Archbishop Daniel Pilarczyk, made archbishop of Cincinnati under Archbishop Laghi and now president of the National Conference of Catholic Bishops, refused to generalize on the difference between the Laghi and Jadot appointments. "There is the folk wisdom that it has all gone conservative," he told me. "I mistrust those labels for one thing."

It is not clear, for example, that the Jadot bishops were really that "liberal." Archbishop Jadot told me that when he was in Washington, "If the priest has given a lecture or written an article against *Humanae Vitae* or for women's ordination, he would have a difficult time becoming a bishop. He is saying the opposite of the magisterium."

The liberal-conservative division should not be exaggerated. "By and large, this is a group of men who accept the teaching of the Catholic church and wish to teach it themselves," explains Russell Shaw, who from 1969-87 served as press secretary to the conference. Neither group is "unorthodox," he says.

> Yet the one group of bishops, the pre-1980s bishops, tends to be more tolerant with respect to divergences from the church's doctrine and discipline than the other people. They're willing to put up with more. It doesn't seem to bother them so much when among the

thousands and thousands of flowers that are blooming, there's a certain amount of poison ivy. They seem quite willing to go along with that situation and are not really disposed to do a great deal about it.

The other group of bishops, the bishops of the 1980s and post-1980s, seem somewhat more concerned about the integrity of the church's doctrine, and somewhat more disposed to try to insist on the integrity of the church's teaching. But again, the difference is not as the difference between night and day. It's a difference of emphasis.

Both groups certainly accept the church's doctrine and take it seriously, but the first group is more tolerant of dissent, and the second group is somewhat less tolerant of dissent.

It is too early to tell what kind of bishops will be selected under Archbishop Agostino Cacciavillan. During his first two years in office, he proved to be much slower in processing appointments than either Archbishops Jadot or Laghi.

Conclusion

The selection process for bishops in the United States ensures that those chosen will be loyal to the Holy See both in their dioceses and in the conference of bishops. This selection process more than anything else explains why the bishops' conference acts the way it does. The control of the appointment process by the Vatican explains why the conference is not confrontational with Rome and why it reflects in its documents the social and doctrinal teaching of the popes. The diocesan responsibilities of these bishops also make them sensitive to the pastoral needs of their people. When these pastoral needs conflict with Roman policies, the bishops can be between a rock and a hard place.

The involvement of the American bishops in the appointment process ensures that those appointed will fit comfortably into the episcopal club. They will reflect the episcopal norms of loyalty, team work, respect for colleagues, and a sense of tradition. Having embraced the same priestly vocation, having gone through the same seminary training, having been chosen from among their peers for episcopal office, all of this makes the bishops a group that shares most values and views in common. They have infinitely more that unites rather than divides them.

This common clerical culture and background will usually enable them to work together as a conference to find consensus or to compromise their differences.

What is most striking from an organizational perspective is how little influence the conference as an institution has in the recruitment of new members. Diocesan bishops are influential in choosing their auxiliaries, and some cardinals (Hickey, Law, and O'Connor) are influential through their contacts with the Vatican. But the conference as a whole has shown little ability to influence the selection process. The NCCB Committee on Selection of Bishops has proven ineffective, although the president can have some impact if his views are trusted by the pro-nuncio and Rome.

The role of the conference would be increased if the pro-nuncio shared his ternus with the NCCB president before sending it to Rome. The bishops of a region also might be given the right to present a ternus for a vacant see in their region. This ternus would be reviewed by the NCCB Committee on the Selection of Bishops which could send comments on it to the pro-nuncio. The NCCB committee might appropriately be responsible for drawing up the ternus for vacant archdioceses, with the bishops of the region allowed to comment on it.[23] This would provide a structured process for bishops to discuss episcopal appointments and would guarantee input from a wider range of bishops than now participate in the process. Such a reform would not be a novelty, but a return to the earlier tradition when the American bishops had a greater role in the selection process.[24] Rome is not interested in such reforms that would increase the role of the bishops in the appointment process. It prefers a more secretive and closed process involving fewer people. Such a process is more easily controlled by Rome.

What the NCCB/USCC does is not totally determined by its membership. Once appointed, the bishops must operate as a conference within an ecclesial environment that stretches far beyond the shores of the United States. It is an environment shaped by history, Catholic theology, and canon law. This ecclesial environment will be examined in the next chapter.

2. Corralling the Shepherds

A bishops' conference as such does not have a *mandatum docendi* [a mandate to teach].

————CARDINAL JOSEPH RATZINGER

The only purpose of the NCWC was to express the church's concern about the temporal affairs of the United States.

————BISHOP WILLIAM E. MCMANUS

The occasions when we act in ways that are canonically binding on all of us are rare.

————ARCHBISHOP DANIEL PILARCZYK

The NCCB/USCC operates within the theological and canonical framework of the Roman Catholic church. To many people brought up in the pre-Vatican II church, the National Conference of Catholic Bishops is an anomalous body in the Catholic church. It does not fit easily into the traditional hierarchical model of the church that places the pope at the top of the pyramid with bishops, priests, and laity at successively lower levels in the church. A few scholars, such as Cardinal Joseph Ratzinger, prefect of the Congregation for the Doctrine of the Faith, have questioned the teaching authority and canonical status of episcopal conferences. In 1983 when discussing a draft of the pastoral letter on peace with the American bishops, he said that "A bishops' conference as such does not have a *mandatum docendi* [a mandate to teach]. This belongs only to the individual bishop or to the college of bishops with the pope."[1]

In 1988 the Vatican issued a working paper (*instrumentum laboris*) on the theological and canonical status of episcopal conferences that took a similar tack. The draft document severely limited the authority of episcopal conferences.[2] The response to this draft from the scholarly community was very critical,[3] as was the response of the National Conference of Catholic Bishops.[4] The Vatican eventually dropped the draft in favor of starting over from scratch.[5]

What are episcopal conferences and how do they fit into the structure of the Catholic church? More particularly, what are the origins of the bishops' conference in the United States? And how has it been influenced by social and political events in the United States? To answer these questions, this chapter will first examine the history of regional and national groupings of bishops beginning in the early church. Next it will look at the experience of bishops working together in councils and conferences in the United States. Finally, a brief examination of church law governing episcopal conferences will be given. This background information is necessary because the American bishops must operate their conference within an ecclesial environment that cherishes history and tradition. This environment also has a very sophisticated internal legal system that must be respected by the bishops. The shepherds cannot roam where they will; they are corralled by history, theology, and church law.

Regional and National Groupings of Bishops

The episcopacy is an essential element in Catholic ecclesiology. The college of bishops, united with the bishop of Rome, is the supreme authority in the church. This college is most evident when it meets as a body in an ecumenical council to determine doctrine and discipline in the church. But the college exists even when not meeting in council. The Second Vatican Council did much to stress the collegial nature of the church, partially as a reaction to overcentralization of authority in the Vatican curia or bureaucracy. Collegiality became a byword in the post-conciliar church.[6]

Vatican II also stressed the importance of a bishop in his local diocese. Catholic theology refers to groupings of Christians around their bishops as local churches. Without a bishop, there is no local church. The bishop is the vicar of Christ for the people of his diocese, a successor to the Apostles. He is not simply the head of a branch office of the Roman Catholic church. As head of his local church, he is responsible for the spiritual welfare of his people, but he must exercise his leadership in the context of a universal church.[7]

Since the beginning of Christianity, individual bishops have wanted to exercise their authority in union with their neighboring bishops. In the early church this was often done through regional councils or synods that decided both doctrinal and disciplinary issues.[8] They met to deal cooperatively with all the problems that confronted them, whether it be lapsed Christians, heretics, or wayward clerics. Provincial councils elected bishops, consecrated them, and acted as courts of appeals for those excommunicated by their bishop. The Council of Nicaea (325) ordered bishops to meet on a province level twice a year. "Meetings were so frequent that the pagan historian Ammianus Marcellinus wryly observed that the public transportation system, during the reign of Constantius II (337-61), was paralyzed by Christian bishops traveling to and from their synods at the imperial expense."[9]

In the time of Leo the Great (440-461), the competencies of these councils were restricted not so much by subject matter as by their ability to reach consensus. If a provincial council could not reach consensus, the matter went to a metropolitan council. When consensus was lacking there, the matter could go all the way to Rome.

But by the 11th century, popes were successfully claiming the right to convoke local and national synods, to appoint legates to preside over them, and to review their actions. With the rise of papal power and the increasing role of ecumenical or worldwide councils, regional councils became less frequent and less important. The Council of Trent (1563) required local councils to send their decrees to Rome for revision and approval before they could be promulgated. Canon law continued to require the convening of particular councils every five years, but it restricted their authority and made their calling cumbersome. As a result, they were rarely convened.

The history of regional councils and synods is important because it shows that in the early church bishops joined in regional groups to deal with pastoral, doctrinal, and disciplinary issues. To reject this practice would be to reject centuries of church experience and tradition.

The rise of nation states and the separation of church and state in 19th-century Europe called for mechanisms by which local bishops could deal with their governments on a variety of issues. Bishops began meeting to develop plans and to form a united front in dealing with their government. By calling these gatherings *conferences* rather than *councils*, the bishops bypassed the restrictions imposed by canon law but also limited their authority. Unlike 19th-century councils, which met intermittently, these conferences were permanent entities that met on a regular basis.

One of the first conferences met in Belgium in 1830 to deal with issues posed by the revolution that took place earlier that year.[10] Other conferences were formed in many European countries, in Latin America, in Australia, and in missionary countries during the 19th century with the encouragement of Popes Pius IX and Leo XIII. "A very broad range of concerns marked the agendas of these regional and national meetings, as the bishops attempted to deal with the century's rapid social, economic, political, and cultural changes."[11] It was always made clear, however, that these conferences (unlike councils) were to deal with public policy issues and were to have no authority over church issues. The independence of the local bishop and the authority of Rome were not to be challenged.

The U.S. Experience

From its very origin, the conciliar and collegial tradition of the U.S. church has been very strong, "a tradition without parallel in the recent history of the western church," according to James Hennesey, S.J. "In the single century from 1783-1884 the entire American Church met in three general chapters of the clergy, a synod, a bishops' meeting, seven provincial councils that were also national councils, and three plenary councils. From 1890 on, the archbishops of the country, and later all the bishops, have met annually. No other nation, as far as I know, has such a record."[12]

When the American bishops met in council at Baltimore during the 19th century, they largely ignored American social and economic problems, according to Thomas McAvoy, a leading historian of the period.[13] They remained silent on political issues. The councils said nothing about slavery, and individual bishops supported opposite sides in the Civil War. A major purpose of the 1866 council was to show that the Catholic church, unlike other denominations, would not be divided by the Civil War.

The Baltimore councils dealt with many church issues such as a national catechism, the regulation of parish life, the administration of church funds, the pastoral care of freed slaves,[14] the training and supervision of the clergy, the establishment of parochial schools, the founding of the Catholic University of America, the discouragement of mixed marriages, the condemnation of secret societies, and the care of waves of immigrants. They also responded to periodic bouts of anti-Catholicism by defending the church and extolling the patriotism of American Catholics.[15] Rome's attempts to control the councils ultimately succeeded so that the decrees of the last Baltimore council in 1884 "were in essence dictated from Rome without deep consideration of American conditions."[16]

When the bishops met in 1889 to celebrate the 100th anniversary of the establishment of the American hierarchy, the archbishops agreed to meet annually. This was not difficult because they were going to meet annually anyway as members of the board of trustees of the Catholic University of America. Although they lacked the authority to make binding decisions as a council would, at their first meeting in 1890 the archbishops did make recommendations to the Holy See on episcopal appointments, sought a broadening of faculties for granting matrimonial dispensations, and suggested revisions in the faculties granted bishops by the Holy See. They also set up a committee to screen nominations of priests for military chaplaincies. They even decided to collect $100 each year from each archbishop to provide a secretary for the rector of the North American College.[17]

No plenary council has taken place since 1884. The calling of councils ended with the initiation of archiepiscopal meetings and with the appointment of an apostolic delegate, a papal representative, to the U.S. church in 1893.

The growing importance of the federal government at the beginning of the 20th century made some church leaders recognize the need for a national organization to look out for Catholic interests at the national level. John J. Burke, C.S.P., took the initiative in forming a National Catholic War Council during World War I.[18] Its purpose was to coordinate the Catholic war effort and to provide liaison with the federal government.

For the duration of the war, anti-Catholicism was put aside as "Members of the Catholic hierarchy found themselves courted by a steady stream of public officials who were openly anxious that the bishops should actively encourage their followers to participate as Americans in service of the Allied cause."[19] Catholic leaders "were also aware that anything less than full support of the war could lead to reprisals against American Catholics by zealous patriots." Thus both church and state found a useful instrument in Burke's War Council.

With the support of Cardinal James Gibbons of Baltimore, the archbishops at their annual meeting in 1917 agreed to the War Council and appointed an administrative committee of sympathetic bishops to oversee it. The bishops used the council to establish episcopal control over the Catholic war effort (including its finances), which had been in the hands of the Knights of Columbus, a Catholic lay organization.

The success of the War Council in dealing with the national government impressed the bishops and neutralized those who wanted the church to maintain a distance from American society. After the war, Father Burke argued strongly for a permanent organization to look out for the church's interests in Washington. "His experience with lobbyists, particularly those of the Federal Council of Churches and the Anti-Saloon League, convinced him that special interests could only be protected by organized effort."[20] In a memorandum, Father Burke argued that without a Catholic voice in Washington, the Federal Council of Churches—predecessor of the National Council of Churches—

would be "the ruling power in all legislation that affected religious and moral interests," and that Catholic absence from national politics would "practically leave the field clear to our opponents and the opponents of our Church."

His views prevailed and the bishops agreed to an annual meeting and a Washington-based staff with Father Burke as the first general secretary. The organization, renamed the National Catholic Welfare Council, had an administrative committee of seven bishops who could act for the hierarchy between meetings. The committee also oversaw the work of departments dealing with education, laws and legislation, social action, lay organizations, and the press.[21] Bishops were also appointed to work with the Catholic Hospital Association and to serve on committees for Polish relief and for decent literature and films. During World War II the War Relief Services, the precursor of the Catholic Relief Services, was established.[22]

"The daily activities of the Washington office resembled those of other interest groups. The NCWC acted as an information clearing house, issued pamphlets on social and educational issues, attended congressional hearings, maintained a news service for its constitutents, worked to increase the number of its lay affiliates, and formed associations with other national and international organizations."[23]

The National Catholic Welfare Council had opponents in the hierarchy. Cardinal William O'Connell of Boston thought an annual assembly of the hierarchy was sufficient and that an administrative committee and Washington office was unnecessary. The Rev. John Ryan, director of the council's new department of social action, further alienated conservative elements with his advocacy of liberal labor policies. Father Ryan's "Program of Social Reconstruction," issued by the four-member Administrative Committee of the War Council, became widely identified with the whole American hierarchy and known simply as "The Bishops' Program."[24] Although undoubtedly backed by most of the bishops, it was never voted on by all the bishops.

The enemies of the NCWC, who were a minority of the bishops but included the cardinals of Boston and Philadelphia, attempted an end run to Rome and persuaded the Consistorial

Congregation to issue a decree suppressing the council. The opponents had argued that the council was a threat to the autonomy of local bishops and to the authority of the Holy See. Even at this time Rome was concerned about the size and power of the American hierarchy.[25] Since Benedict XV died before the decree could be promulgated, the NCWC Administrative Committee petitioned the new pope, Pius XI, for a chance to present its case.[26] The petition was signed by more than two-thirds of the American hierarchy.[27]

The petitioners affirmed their loyalty to Rome and argued that the council was necessary to defend Catholic interests in the United States. The decree of suppression was quickly revoked, but Rome objected to describing the organization as a "council," which had canonical implications. It became the National Catholic Welfare Conference, a name it maintained until 1966. Rome and bishops nervous about their autonomy insisted that the conference be a voluntary body where attendance at meetings and financial contributions were optional. Thus, the conference lacked the juridical authority possessed by the Baltimore councils in the 19th century. "For many years," reports Cardinal John Dearden, "some bishops did not participate in the work of the NCWC."[28]

During much of its existence, the NCWC was controlled by Midwestern bishops led by Cardinal Edward Mooney of Detroit, Cardinal Samuel Stritch of Chicago, and Archbishop John McNicholas of Cincinnati. They worked to keep Cardinal Francis Spellman of New York, who had many high Vatican connections, from having power in the conference.

"There were always two factions," recalls Bishop William E. McManus, a member of the staff from 1945-57. "Mooney, Stritch, and McNicholas were the brain trust. They wrote the statements. They were the ones who had the inside track to the [federal] government." The other faction consisted of "Spellman and his cohorts with all the money." During their Washington meetings, the brain trust stayed at the Statler and the other group at the Mayflower. "The Detroit-Chicago axis kept Spelly at bay," recalls Archbishop Francis T. Hurley, another NCWC staff person from 1957-70.

"The Administrative Board issued all the statements in the name of the bishops," reports Bishop McManus. "The bishops never issued a statement, not in the 11 years" he worked for the conference. For their annual meeting, the bishops would arrive one day, have a full day's meeting, and then go home the next day. "There was hardly any discussion," reports Archbishop Hurley. "At that time the bishops' meeting was essentially the report of the chairman of each department, a report on Catholic University, a report on Catholic Relief Services, the annual statement of the bishops, and then go home in time for the Notre Dame-Army football game. Literally."

The conference and its Washington office issued numerous statements responding to the social, economic, and political issues of the day. It reacted to unemployment and economic crises with statements in 1919, 1930, 1931, 1933, 1938, and 1940.[29] These statements defended labor unions and called for tax reform, social insurance, proper housing for workers, government regulation of privately owned public services, and a living wage for workers. They also opposed child labor and monopolies. On domestic issues, they were very much in tune with the New Deal.

On the international scene, the conference denounced the persecution of the church in Russia in 1924, in Mexico in 1926 and 1934, and in Spain and Germany in 1937. Although the attitude of the U.S. government toward these countries might change for political or strategic reasons, the bishops were always attentive to the issue of religious liberty. Nor did the NCWC ignore traditional moral issues but condemned materialism, indecent literature, and divorce. The bishops also extolled good morals and the need for religious education and practices.

During the Second World War, the NCWC again joined the war effort, responding in 1942 "with a deep sense of revulsion" to the treatment of the Jews by the Nazis.[30] This time the bishops also began laying out the Catholic principles for a good peace in a series of statements. After the war, from 1950-57, an annual concern became the persecution of the church in Communist countries. The bishops also spoke out on secularism (1947), the Christian family (1949 and 1950), moral values (1951,

1952, 1960, and 1961), censorship (1957), traffic safety (1957), racial discrimination (1942, 1943, 1958, and 1960), birth control (1959), and refugees (1959).

In issuing statements on public policy, the NCWC responded to the political, social, and economic conditions of the times. It defended the economic interests of its people who, for most of this period, were in the working classes. As a result, its views were more "liberal" than American society as a whole. The NCWC also acted as the advocate of a religious minority whose patriotism was questioned by the majority. It supported the government during foreign wars, and it raised a voice defending the interests of the church whenever it was attacked either in the United States or abroad.

On most issues, the views of the bishops coincided with those in government. For the most part, the bishops supported Presidents Wilson and Roosevelt in wartime, and supported the New Deal's economic program.[31] The postwar anti-Communism of the Truman and Eisenhower administrations was supported by the bishops. As Catholics became more acceptable to American society, however, the bishops became braver in challenging American culture.

Often the bishops' statements found an inattentive audience. But widespread and favorable public attention was given to the 1951 pastoral letter, which was printed in its entirety in *The New York Times, The New York Herald Tribune, The Washington Star,* and *The St. Louis Globe Democrat.* Its section on "moral corruption in political life" was seen as an attack on the Truman Administration, while another section was seen as critical of the tactics of Senator Joseph R. McCarthy. The response to their 1955 letter calling for public aid to pupils in Catholic schools was vocal, and largely negative, from the non-Catholic community. The conference's 1958 letter against racial discrimination also stirred up editorial comment, mostly favorable in the North and unfavorable in the South.[32]

For the most part, the NCWC stayed away from church issues. "The only purpose of the NCWC was to express the church's concern about the temporal affairs of the United States," recalls Bishop McManus. "No one would have thought of taking up anything about seminary curriculum or about liturgy or priestly life and ministry. In those days, back in the 40s and 50s, I never would have dreamed of half of these committees that are now in the NCCB ever coming into existence." Bishop McManus recalls having proposed a study on a more equitable distribution of religious women among dioceses in the United States. Bishop Michael J. Ready reported back to him that "The bishops wanted you to be advised that the phrase 'interdiocesan' never occurs in their vocabulary." On the other hand, the NCWC was very active lobbying for federal aid to parochial schools.[33]

Second Vatican Council

The Second Vatican Council made episcopal conferences not only possible but absolutely necessary. The council called for reform, but the church, like any institution, had to find systems to manage change in a way that avoided chaos.

For example, the council called for vernacular liturgies. But how was this to be implemented? The pope and the Roman curia could not do translations for every language in the world. It was simply too much for them to handle and they lacked the expertise. On the other hand, if each bishop did a translation for his diocese, there could have been over 150 English translations of the Mass in the United States. Some mechanism between the pope and the individual bishops had to be found that could deal with church issues on a national scale.

Many council fathers had positive experiences with episcopal conferences and saw that they worked well in dealing with non-church issues. During the council the bishops met for discussions in national groups, and the conferences proposed candidates for various conciliar commissions. The bishops decided conferences could be a useful vehicle for implementing the council reforms and for dealing with other church issues. The theological status and teaching authority of episcopal conferences were debated, but their practical necessity was recognized by all.[34]

Without deciding the theological issues, the council gave the green light to episcopal conferences:

> Episcopal conferences, already established in many nations, have furnished outstanding proofs of a more fruitful apostolate. Therefore, this most sacred Synod considers it supremely opportune everywhere that bishops belonging to the same nation or region form an association and meet together at fixed times. Thus, when insights of prudence and experience have been shared and views exchanged, there will emerge a holy union of energies in the service of the common good of the churches.[35]

In discussing episcopal conferences, the council described them as "a kind of council in which the bishops of a given nation or territory jointly exercise their pastoral office by way of promoting the greater good which the Church offers mankind. . . ." It decreed all the bishops of a nation would be members, but only diocesan bishops and coadjutors have a deliberative vote unless the conference's statutes also give the vote to auxiliaries. Each conference should draw up its statutes providing for officers, committees, and a secretariat, and these statutes must be approved by the Holy See.

Using canonical language, the council allowed for limited juridical authority for episcopal conferences:

> Decisions of the episcopal conference, provided they have been made lawfully and by the choice of at least two-thirds of the prelates who have deliberative vote in the conference, and have been reviewed by the Apostolic See, are to have juridically binding force in those cases and in those only which are prescribed by common law or determined by special mandate of the Apostolic See, given spontaneously or in response to a petition from the conference itself.[36]

The council thus gave conferences authority over certain church issues. What specific responsibilities would be given to conferences by common law and special mandates would be determined by practice and by the revised code of canon law after the council. But the binding nature of these decisions was clearly expressed by the *Directory on the Pastoral Ministry of Bishops* issued by the Vatican in 1973:

> The bishop accepts with loyal submission the decisions legitimately taken by the conference and reviewed by the Apostolic See,

for they have the force of law through the Church's highest authority, and he puts them into practice in his diocese although he may
not previously have agreed with them or they may cause him some
inconvenience.[37]

Even nonbinding decisions should be respected by the bishops according to the directory:

> There are other decisions and regulations of the conference which
> do not have a juridical binding force; and as a rule the bishop makes
> them his own with a view to unity and charity with his brother bish-
> ops, unless serious reasons he has carefully considered in the Lord
> prevent it. . . .[38]

NCWC Becomes NCCB/USCC

When the American bishops returned home after the council,
one of the first things they did was reorganize their conference
to make it conform to the principles laid down by the Second
Vatican Council.[39] Meeting at the Catholic University of America
in November 1966, the bishops created the National Conference
of Catholic Bishops (NCCB) as the canonical body to deal with
church matters. It renamed and reorganized the NCWC as the
United States Catholic Conference to deal with public policy
questions. The USCC has no canonical authority. Some bishops
wanted the conference to be called the National Catholic Conference, but the initials NCC would have been confused with the
National Council of Churches.

Both the NCCB and the USCC kept the same basic structure
as the NCWC—a Washington-based staff, an assembly, subject-
matter committees, and an administrative committee for the
NCCB and an administrative board for the USCC. The bishops
added an elected president and vice president (the senior cardinal had presided at NCWC meetings while the NCWC Administrative Board elected its own chair). Several new committees
were also created for the NCCB: Liturgy, Canonical Affairs,
Doctrine, Priestly Life and Ministry, Priestly Formation, Pastoral
Research and Practices, etc. These new committees all deal with
church issues and have only episcopal members, whereas the

USCC committees also have lay, religious, and clerical members who enjoy an equal vote.

Those who worked with the NCWC and the NCCB/USCC saw marked differences between the two organizations. "There's just no comparison at all," reports Archbishop John Whealon of Hartford who became a bishop in 1961.

> The NCWC meetings were held at Catholic University and the senior cardinal would preside. He'd be up there alone and would run the show with an iron hand.
>
> The meeting consisted of a bishop who was in charge of a particular committee reading a report which obviously had been written for him by a staff member. He would begin with these words, "I know that all of you have already read the report (ha, ha, ha) and I wouldn't bother you with re-reading all of that material which you have already looked over." Then he'd laugh a little bit and then proceed to read the whole boring thing. Things got lively when someone would challenge the chair on some decision. That was all there was to it.

Bishop James Malone, who became a bishop in 1960, agrees that the conference changed dramatically.

> The big difference was that in the old structure, the appointed bishops in large sees were in charge of the meetings. The matters that were brought up were not researched or staffed to the extent that they are now, and really the scope of our interest was very limited compared to what it has become. The meetings were closed to the press, and therefore there were many statements made that had little or no basis, and largely they went unchallenged.
>
> Gradually we began to address issues, in my opinion, more substantively. I recall the careful way in which [Bishop] John Wright [of Pittsburgh] contributed to that 1968 statement "Human Life in Our Day." It was very carefully done, was reviewed with much more ownership by the membership than activities of an earlier time.

Archbishop John Quinn, who joined the conference a year after it was reorganized, agrees that it continued to change.

> It has changed a lot. It used to be that when I first entered the conference the cardinals all sat up at the front table with the president. If a cardinal suggested something in a meeting, then no doubt the bishops would vote for it. Or if an archbishop suggested something, it would probably be voted for. That changed, and that is not

the case now of course. Bishops vote on what they want, they don't vote on who says it. Really they did in those times.

1983 Code of Canon Law

The Catholic church has a very sophisticated internal legal system called the code of canon law. After the Second Vatican Council, the code of canon law was revised to adapt the church's legal system to the reforms of the council.[40] One of the new items dealt with in the code was episcopal conferences.

When discussing the code, it is important to note that bishops are not "given" authority or power by the code or by the pope. Bishops have their authority because they are bishops, just as priests have sacramental power because they are priests. The exercise of this authority, however, can be restricted by the Holy See in view of the unity and advantage of the universal church. Likewise, the conference's power is derived not from the pope but from the bishops themselves exercising episcopal authority in their particular churches. Again the Holy See can regulate this authority for the good of the universal church.[41] In fact, the authority of conferences is so restricted that it often looks like they receive what little authority they have from the Holy See.

The interrelationship between episcopal conferences, the Holy See, and the diocesan bishops was an area of tension during the code revision. As the code went through a series of drafts during the revision process, the authority of the conference was gradually reduced in each draft, "partly because of fears that the conference jeopardized church unity by exaggerating nationalism and impairing the legitimate autonomy of individual bishops."[42]

There was also disagreement over how to relate conferences and councils. The resulting 1983 code treated particular councils (which still are rarely called) as legislative entities, but viewed episcopal conferences primarily as instruments of pastoral communication and coordination among the bishops. Despite the primacy given to the communication and coordination functions of conferences, they also may exercise legislative authority in some areas. The confusing results reflected disagreements among the drafters.

What is clear is that some actions by a conference can be legally binding. The commentary on the new code published by the Canon Law Society of America (CLSA) distinguishes between two types of conference decrees that have the force of law: "General decrees are laws properly speaking, while general executory decrees are more precise determinations of how to observe laws."[43] General decrees require a two-thirds vote of the membership and must be reviewed by the Holy See before they take effect. The CLSA commentary argued that general executory decrees did not require such review, but simply notification of the Holy See.[44] Soon after the commentary's publication in 1985, however, the Vatican Commission for the Authentic Interpretation of the Code ruled that all decrees must be reviewed.[45]

This "review" in fact gives Rome an absolute veto over conference decrees. The "review" of decrees by Rome has delayed the promulgation of some decrees. It has caused tension between the Vatican and bishops of various parts of the world when Rome forces conferences to change decrees before they can pass review. The CLSA commentary complains:

> It [review] is designed as a safeguard to assure that decisions of particular councils [or conferences] are not contrary to general church law. It has also been used, however, for other purposes, including that of imposing on local churches a discipline which they themselves had not voted to assume, for in the "review" of the decrees changes have been made which were not the work of the council [or conference] in question but which must be promulgated with the authority of that council [or conference] since they appear in the final version of the decree.[46]

The Code of Canon Law contains about 84 canons that permit legislative action by episcopal conferences.[47] The cases mentioned are a combination of major and minor issues (see appendix D). Many canonists question the need for papal review for so many areas, but this is the system within which the NCCB must work.

Implementation of the code was begun when Bishop Anthony Bevilacqua was chair of the Committee on Canonical Affairs.

With the help of consultants from the Canon Law Society of America, Bishop Bevilacqua took the sections of the code calling for action by episcopal conferences "and put them in four categories," according to Msgr. Donald Heintschel, staff to the committee at the time. The first group needed immediate action, and the committee normally recommended a continuation of whatever was the current American practice. The second group could be delayed.

The third group needed interdisciplinary or intercommittee work before implementation. "The bishops, through the Canonical Affairs Committee, made the decision that some of the issues were not purely canonical," explains Monsignor Heintschel. "If they were to be handled in a pastoral fashion, then they had to be studied by a variety of committees" before a resolution was brought to the floor. For example, implementation of the canons on marriage and marriage preparation required input from the Liturgy Committee, the Committee on Pastoral Research and Practices, and the Committee on Ecumenical and Interreligious Affairs. Finally, the last group of canons the committee decided to "just forget about them." In many cases the conference has preferred to approve nonbinding "guidelines" rather than binding legislative norms. By 1991 the NCCB had taken legislative action on only 23 canons; most of these were noncontroversial, but some caused conflict, as will be seen in Chapter Six.[48]

Conclusion

The National Conference of Catholic Bishops is not an all-powerful institution operating independently of its environment. Rather it functions within the ecclesial environment of the Catholic church with its theology and canon law. To maintain their Catholic identity, the bishops must function within the context of the church's history and traditions. This ecclesial environment can radically change as it did during the Second Vatican Council with a resulting increase in the role and importance of episcopal conferences. In drawing up the NCCB/USCC statutes and bylaws, the bishops followed the direction of Vatican II and the 1983 Code of Canon Law. The post-conciliar period has seen and will continue to see attempts to increase and decrease the role of conferences, but clearly episcopal conferences are here to stay and are fulfilling an irreplaceable role in the church.

The U.S. conference of bishops is also affected by the political, economic, and social environment of the United States. War and peace, prosperity and depression, inflation and stability, social upheaval and retrenchment, the civil rights movement and feminism, the sexual revolution and fundamentalism, all have affected the conference and its agenda. The bishops have not and sometimes could not ignore these issues. How adequately they have dealt with them is always subject to debate.

Although the conference is made up of many bishops, there are some who play a more important role than others. The next chapter will look at the movers and shakers in the conference, how they are chosen and what they do.

3. Shepherding the Shepherds

The most difficult thing [about being president] was being on the spot with the press all the time.

——ARCHBISHOP JOHN QUINN

They want somebody who is not going to be excessively creative . . . because you don't want a Franklin Roosevelt in the conference.

——ARCHBISHOP DANIEL PILARCZYK

We historically have had able bishops who are not willing to invest the time in conference work.

——BISHOP JAMES MALONE

In the NCCB/USCC there have always been some bishops who have been more influential than others. This influence is based not on canonical distinctions but on the respect (or fear) these bishops are able to win from their peers. As will be seen in this chapter, leadership and authority in the conference come from democratic processes rather than hierarchical structures. With the backing of the other bishops, these leaders can have real impact on the direction of the conference. This chapter will especially look at the elections and roles of the NCCB/USCC presidents.

The NCCB/USCC is an assembly of equals, a flock of shepherds. In the conference, cardinals and archbishops have no special authority or privileges. They are legally equal to any other bishop. Nor do bishops from large dioceses have more authority than bishops from small dioceses. In theory, the bishop of Gallup, New Mexico, has equal rights with the cardinal archbishop of New York.

In ecumenical councils, precedence is given to higher ranking members of the hierarchy in ceremonies, seating, and speaking. Likewise in synods, precedence is given to rank. In the NCWC the cardinals used to sit at an elevated table looking down on the rest of the bishops. And the NCWC Administrative Board, mostly made up of cardinals and archbishops, effectively controlled the conference. But on most matters, the active bishops are treated with strict legal equality in the NCCB/USCC.

"The reality of the equality of vote, the equality of ordinaries and auxiliaries, large dioceses and small, and a respect for whatever contributions individual members may make," explains Cardinal Joseph Bernardin of Chicago, "supports the notion of *communio* and collegiality which is at the heart of the conference."[1]

Although all diocesan bishops are equal, auxiliary bishops and retired bishops have some legal limits on their role in the conference. According to canon law, only diocesan bishops (and coadjutors) can vote on conference statutes. According to the NCCB statutes, only diocesan bishops can vote on diocesan assessments or special collections. Nor, according to a 1989 ruling by the Vatican Commission for the Authentic Interpretation of the Code of Canon Law, can auxiliaries be elected president or vice president of the conference. Finally, retired bishops may attend meetings and speak, but they cannot vote as they can at ecumenical councils. Being over 75, most of the retired bishops stay home.

After experiencing the Second Vatican Council and the NCWC, the American bishops organized the NCCB/USCC to ensure the equality of the bishops. Except on money matters, they wanted to treat all bishops equally. They even had a protracted dispute with Roman officials because the NCCB wanted to allow retired bishops to vote, which had been the custom in the NCWC. Rome held firm and in 1978 the retired bishops were disenfranchised in the conference.

Despite the legal equality, it is unusual for an auxiliary to exercise significant power or influence in the conference. There was an unwritten rule that a bishop, especially an auxiliary, did not speak at his first meeting. When he entered the conference in 1971 as an auxiliary bishop, Archbishop John Roach of St. Paul recalls:

> The first couple of times that you got up [to speak], you got up with a good deal of trepidation. Whether it was a fact or not, you

kind of assumed that there was a pecking order, and [as an auxiliary bishop] you weren't very high on that order. I think that has changed.

Cardinal John Dearden, the first NCCB/USCC president, attempted to break down this hierarchical bias, but he was not totally successful. Archbishop Roach recalls that at his first meeting,

John Dearden took us up to his suite after the first day and said, "Now you're new, and I want to do some things. First of all I want to make you very welcome, and second I want to tell you that you're valuable, and third I want to tell you that if you've got something to say I want you to get up and say it."

That was remarkable. It just opened up the doors for me, at least, and I suspect for some others. It opened the door so that, while that first year I probably didn't say anything, I went home feeling I sure could in the future.

Elected Presidents

No large organization can function without leadership. Episcopal conferences have a democratic rather than a hierarchical system of choosing leaders. The NCCB/USCC membership elects its own leaders for three-year, nonrenewable terms: a president, vice president, treasurer, secretary, chairs of various committees, and other members of the Administrative Committee/Board. It also elects members of the boards of NCCB/USCC related organizations, such as Catholic Relief Services (CRS), the Catholic Telecommunications Network of America (CTNA), and the North American colleges in Rome and Louvain. The NCCB is also responsible for electing American representatives to the bishops' synod held periodically in Rome. These elections give an opportunity to see who are the movers and shakers in the conference.

The most visible leaders of the NCCB/USCC have been its presidents. When the conference needs a spokesperson, it is the president who must step forward. When the press wants a response, they will often address their questions to the NCCB/USCC president. When the president of the United

States or the pope wants to communicate with the U.S. bishops, it is usually done through the conference president.

The president chairs meetings of the NCCB/USCC assembly, the Administrative Committee/Board, the Executive Committee, the Committee on Priorities and Plans, the Bishops' Welfare Emergency Relief Committee, the Committee on Boundaries of Dioceses and Provinces, and the Committee on Selection of Bishops. He may, at his discretion, terminate debate in the assembly, subject to appeal which requires a two-thirds vote to sustain his decision. The president is an ex officio member of all conference committees, and he appoints the chair and members of ad hoc committees. The vice president chairs the Committee on Personnel and Administration. The treasurer chairs the Committee on Budget and Finance. The four officers (president, vice president, treasurer, and secretary), with one member elected by the Administrative Committee/Board, form the Executive Committee.

According to the NCCB/USCC bylaws, the president, vice president, treasurer, and secretary are elected for three years and cannot succeed themselves. For president and vice president, the election procedures call for each bishop to propose five names by mail (the election procedures for secretary and treasurer are the same as for NCCB/USCC committee chairs, which will be explained in the next chapter). The ten receiving the highest number of votes become candidates for president and vice president. If a bishop does not wish to run, the bishop with the next highest number of votes is placed on the ballot.

The bishops first vote for one of the ten bishops as president. If no candidate receives a majority on the first or second ballot, the third ballot is a runoff between the two candidates receiving the most votes in the second ballot. After the president is elected, the same procedure is used for selecting the vice president from the remaining nine candidates.

The presidents of the NCCB/USCC have been some of the most prominent and influential bishops in the United States. Each had his own style and responded in his own way to the challenges facing the church during his time in office.

John F. Dearden, 1966-71

John F. Dearden, archbishop of Detroit, was the first president of the conference (1966-71) at age 59.[2] It is not an exaggeration to call him the father or principal architect of the NCCB/USCC. He was on the committee that drafted the original NCCB/USCC statutes.[3] Bishop Ernest L. Unterkoefler of Charleston, S.C., another member of the committee, said, "Cardinal Dearden led the NCCB/USCC in carrying out the reforms of the Second Vatican Council. He set the pace for the future."[4] Archbishop John May of St. Louis called him "the key figure in helping the church in this country to implement the reforms of the Second Vatican Council and in guiding the bishops' conferences to the role they currently play in the life of the church."[5]

After receiving a S.T.D. from the Gregorian University in Rome, Father Dearden returned to serve his bishop, Edward F. Hoban of Cleveland, by first teaching at St. Mary's Seminary and then becoming its rector. At the age of 40, with the help of his bishop who was influential with the apostolic delegate, he was made coadjutor bishop of Pittsburgh in 1948. He succeeded to the see two years later. In 1958 he became archbishop of Detroit.

Before becoming president of the NCCB, he had been treasurer of its predecessor, the NCWC. He was also a member of the NCWC Administrative Board and chair of the Bishops' Committee on the Liturgical Apostolate when the liturgical changes began during the Second Vatican Council.

Known as "Iron John" before Vatican II, he was transformed by the experience of the council. At the council he played an important role as a member of the Commission on Faith and Morals. He became known as "the unobtrusive liberal" because his leadership style emphasized developing consensus. "Cardinal Dearden had that way of letting a discussion go and then being able to pull all of the pieces together," explains Archbishop John Quinn. Then he would "point the direction toward a resolution that would be generally accepted and everybody would get along, and most people would be reasonably happy with it in the end."

Cardinal Dearden also recruited people who would be influential in the conference, especially Bishop Joseph Bernardin who was general secretary under Cardinal Dearden. As general secretary, Bishop Bernardin became very close to Cardinal Dearden and perhaps can describe his presidency best:

> He was an extraordinary person. He had a very fine sense of the church and the direction in which the church should go, especially in light of the teaching of the Second Vatican Council. But he was never an aggressive type of person. He was always mild-mannered. But at the same time he was always very firm, knew exactly what he wanted, knew the direction in which the conference should move, the church should move, and he just kept going in that direction.
>
> He commanded a great deal of respect, so people were eager to work with him. In one sense he was a very easy man to work with, because you never had to second-guess him. He never had ups and downs in terms of his own psychological makeup. He was even-handed, even-tempered, so he was easy to figure out.

Msgr. George Higgins, who worked for the conference, agrees that Cardinal Dearden was "was a most gracious and patient man. He knew pretty well where he wanted to go, but he did not want to bruise people in the process. A man who was more abrasive would have failed. A man who was weaker would have failed. He had the right combination. He was not a sensational leader. He was not a great orator, he was low-key, but the bishops trusted him and he was very, very patient."

During Cardinal Dearden's presidency the conference made the transition from an organization run by the cardinals and archbishops to one that was more democratic and decentralized. A key policy in this transition was not allowing elected officials to succeed themselves. This insured that there would be a turnover in the Administrative Committee/Board and in the committee chairs.[6]

Archbishop Quinn expresses the view of most bishops in describing Cardinal Dearden's term as president:

> Cardinal Dearden was really a master. He had a wonderful grasp of the issues, a very balanced view, but he was also a master at running a meeting, and of bringing people together to a conclusion. He was really a very great president.

Cardinal Dearden was president during a rocky transition period in the American church when the conference had a heavy agenda. Archbishop Quinn recalls:

> He was president at an exceedingly difficult time. First, they had to implement all of the things from the council. Secondly, he had to reorganize the whole bishops' conference from scratch to put it into the terms of the council. That was very difficult. Then he was president when all these upheavals took place in the late 60s and early 70s and that was exceedingly difficult. Some of the dioceses were in conflagrations, and they were having demonstrations, and breaking into the [NCCB/USCC] meeting hall. It was an exceedingly trying time.

As president, he began the custom of making a major address at the conference meetings. Between meetings he also spoke out on issues like the Middle East (1967), the state of the church (1971), and the synod (1971).[7] In 1973 he spoke on the church's teaching on human rights before the Senate Foreign Relations Committee, establishing a precedent of presidents testifying before Congress.

During his term as president, the NCCB/USCC took on many controversial social and political topics.[8] Statements were issued on the Vietnam War (1966, 1967, 1968, and 1971), race relations (1966 and 1968), antipoverty legislation (1967), birth control and abortion (1966, 1968, 1969, and 1970), farm labor (1968), Biafra (1968), welfare reform (1970), the United Nations (1970), conscientious objection (1971), aid to Catholic schools (1971), and the environment (1971).

The conference also adopted statements on important church issues: penance (1966), clerical celibacy (1967 and 1969), Catholic schools (1967), the Dutch catechism (1967), ecumenism (1969), mixed marriages (1970), the Catholic press (1970), Catholic health facilities (1971), and the missions (1971). In 1967 it issued its first completely doctrinal pastoral letter, "The Church in Our Day." A year later the bishops approved "Human Life in Our Day," a major pastoral that responded to *Humanae Vitae*. During this period the conference also opened the National Office for Black Catholics (1970) and began the Campaign for Human Development (1970). It also adopted a due process procedure.

During Archbishop Dearden's term the bishops approved several liturgical reforms: English for the Eucharistic prayer, extraordinary ministers of communion, the cup for the laity, and Saturday evening masses. They also dropped meatless Fridays. A major historical, psychological, and sociological study of American priests was sponsored by the conference,[9] which also adopted a program on priestly formation (1970).

Archbishop Dearden became a cardinal in 1969 while serving as NCCB president, which placed the papal seal of approval on his work. While president he was also elected by the American bishops to two synods. The NCCB has continued the custom of electing its president to the bishops' synod ever since.

Cardinal Dearden continued to be influential in the conference after his term as president. He was chair of the NCCB Ad Hoc Committee for Observance of the Bicentennial that culminated in the Call to Action Conference held in Detroit in 1976. In 1973 and 1976 he was elected the third delegate to the bishops' synod after the NCCB had first chosen its president and vice president as delegates. He probably could have been elected to other offices if he had allowed his name to be put in nomination. In April of 1977 he suffered a heart attack, and he retired as archbishop of Detroit in 1980. His death in 1988 was universally mourned.

John J. Krol, 1971-74

John Krol, archbishop of Philadelphia, served as president from 1971-74. After receiving his J.C.D. from the Catholic University of America, Father Krol began teaching canon law at the same seminary where Father Dearden was teaching theology. Later he worked in the Cleveland chancery. As another Hoban protegé, at age 42 he was made auxiliary bishop of Cleveland in 1953 and then archbishop of Philadelphia in 1961. At the Second Vatican Council, Archbishop Krol was an undersecretary, but he did not go through the same conversion at the council that Archbishop Dearden did. He continued to have "a reputation as a conservative churchman who runs a tight ship."[10]

Archbishop Krol was on the Executive Committee and the Administrative Board of the NCWC. He chaired the NCWC committee in 1965 that reorganized the NCWC into the NCCB/USCC.

In 1966, Archbishop Krol came in second to Archbishop Dearden for president. "There was a spirited election between Dearden and Krol," according to a bishop who was there. There were three ballots before Archbishop Dearden emerged as the first president. Archbishop Krol was then elected vice president by a plurality of the bishops on the following ballot.[11]

While vice president, he was made a cardinal in 1967 along with Karol Wojtyla of Krakow. Thus as vice president he was a cardinal for two years while Dearden, the president, was only an archbishop. As vice president he was elected to two synods. While vice president, he also chaired the Committee on Pastoral Research and Practices when it coordinated and oversaw the committees on liturgy, ecumenism, canonical affairs, and doctrine. He was 61 when elected president in 1971.[12]

According to Cardinal Bernardin, who served both Cardinals Dearden and Krol as general secretary, "things went on pretty much the way they had gone on under Dearden, because he [Krol] had been part of all that while Dearden was president and had the most influence. Krol [as vice president] was part of it all. So things didn't change all that much." Monsignor Higgins agrees:

> Most people look back on his [Krol's] tour of duty as a good one. He was loyal to the conference. He would defend the conference; he would defend the staff. . . . Krol supported the conference, even if he didn't agree. He was the president, and he was going to support his people, you know. He was a team player. . . .
>
> He wasn't afraid of Rome. Krol, contrary to general impression, was not a Roman. He never was particularly happy in Rome. He would [rather] be out playing golf. But he was not afraid of Rome.

"He had a great sense of decisions correctly arrived at must be carried out," notes Russell Shaw, who was the conference press secretary. "Once a decision has been made, a decision has been made. And that settles it. And he very much was a team player. Before the fact he would fight fiercely for his point of view. He'd win sometimes, lose sometimes."

Cardinal Krol's style was very different from Cardinal Dearden's. He did not involve his vice president, Archbishop Leo Byrne of St. Paul, in a major way as he himself had been included by Cardinal Dearden. When he presided over conference meetings, he marched the bishops through the agenda and chided speakers to keep to the point. As the Rev. Hugh Nolan reports:

> Cardinal Dearden, not a canon lawyer, ran a rather free-wheeling meeting. Cardinal Krol, in contrast, is a highly respected canonist and a proficient parliamentarian. The conference organizers had been thinking of hiring a professional parliamentarian until they saw the Philadelphia cardinal in action. He did not hesitate to say from the chair, "To the motion, Your Eminence," when a prince of the church was sermonizing.
>
> Cardinal Krol conducted the meetings with much precision and order and so accomplished much, although some prelates did not care for the "lock step," as one bishop called it. The Philadelphia prelate had a knack for completing the agenda no matter how lengthy, and his presidency marked the dawn of a new historic period for the NCCB. Meetings were conducted more professionally with perfect parliamentary procedure. On one occasion he completed the agenda a full day ahead of time.[13]

Others who watched Cardinal Krol chairing the meetings do not remember "perfect parliamentary procedure." "It was chaotic when Krol chaired the meetings," recalls one bishop. "He once allowed three motions to roll around the floor at the same time. Bishop Malone regularly took to the floor to admonish the chair when Krol was in it. It was really in response to Krol's indifference to parliamentary procedure that we got Henry Robert."

As president, Cardinal Krol addressed each gathering of the bishops. He also addressed many issues between meetings such as good conscience procedures for divorced Catholics (1972), Poland (1972), negotiations for ending the Vietnam war (1972), abortion (1973), Soviet leader's U.S. visit (1973), Catholic schools (1973), modern warfare (1974), Nixon's resignation (1974), inactive Catholics (1974), and the laity (1974). In 1974, he testified in support of a pro-life amendment to the U.S. Constitution.

During Cardinal Krol's presidency the conference continued issuing statements on social and political issues: abortion (1972 and 1973), housing (1972), Vietnam (1972), prayer and religious instruction in public schools (1973), human rights (1973 and 1974), the Middle East (1973), prisons (1973), farm labor (1973 and 1974), the Farah strike (1973), capital punishment (1974), and the food crisis (1974).[14]

Important church issues were also addressed: Catholic education (1972 and 1973), religious education (1973), Catholic health care (1973), Mary (1973), the church life (1974), ecumenism (1974), and the charismatic renewal (1974). The bishops also approved a diaconate program (1972), an office of priestly life and ministry (1972), guidelines for conference statements (1973), and began work on a national catechetical directory.

During his presidency, the priesthood study was completed. From the beginning, Cardinal Krol had been the one supervising this study. As Bishop James Malone recalls,

> John was not conaturally sympathetic to studies on the psychology of the priesthood and the sociology of the priesthood, but he was able to be persuaded that this was needed. So he did not merely tolerate it, he promoted it. He was very helpful. If the president at that time had been someone who was more emotional, it would not have been as easy for some of our membership that didn't like the idea of these studies to be persuaded. But when John Krol said it was all right, then it certainly was all right.

Cardinal Krol's influence in the conference declined after his term as president, although he was still influential. He never again held elected office. After seeing him in action as president, most bishops did not want to place him in power again. Although nominated, he failed in 1976, 1979, 1981, and 1986 to be elected to the bishops' synod.

Cardinal Krol was respected for his decisiveness, financial acumen, and orthodox thinking. He chaired the committee investigating the finances of Catholic Relief Services when it came under attack in the press. Although he might disagree with some things done by the conference, he was committed to it as an institution and would not criticize it in public. He was recognized by the NCCB/USCC leaders and staff as a very effective witness on Capitol Hill. He testified in favor of the Panama Canal treaty and SALT II. His 1979 testimony in favor of SALT II was in some ways stronger than the position ultimately adopted by the bishops in their peace pastoral.[15]

After the election of John Paul II, Cardinal Krol's influence took on new life because of his friendship with the Polish pope. He was appointed to a Council of Cardinals examining Vatican finances, where he argued for professional accounting practices and annual public reports. He was one of the few American bishops allowed to continue in office much beyond his 75th birthday. When he did retire in 1988 at age 77, he was in poor health.

Joseph L. Bernardin, 1974-77[16]

Joseph Bernardin, then archbishop of Cincinnati, was the third president of the conference (1974-77).[17] Only 46 years of age when elected, he is the youngest president ever elected. After receiving a master's degree in education from the Catholic University of America, he worked in the chancery in Charleston, until at 38 years of age, he was made an auxiliary bishop in Atlanta in 1966. He was then the youngest bishop in the country. Two years later he was appointed general secretary of the NCCB/USCC, where he served until he was made archbishop of Cincinnati in 1972. As general secretary he served under Cardinals Dearden and Krol.

He is "a man of infinite patience," explains Russell Shaw. "Almost incapable of losing his temper. I say almost incapable; he would lose his temper occasionally. But very patient, very generous with people, enormously hard-working. He had and has a genius for bringing about consensus. That's his preferred style of operation, to go through that process of consensus-building. That's just Joe Bernardin; that's the way he is. But he's so good at it, and it has a lot of advantages."

Cardinal Bernardin is highly respected by the bishops and rarely loses an election when his name is put forward. In 1971, while he was general secretary and only an auxiliary bishop, he came in second to Archbishop Leo Byrne of St. Paul in the vice presidential election. As an archbishop in 1973, he was elected to the bishops' synod and continued to be selected by the NCCB to attend subsequent synods. The same year he was elected chair of the Communications Committee, which also gave him a seat on the Administrative Committee/Board where he has served almost continuously ever since.

Like his mentor Cardinal Dearden, Cardinal Bernardin's style is one of consensus-building. As general secretary (1968-72), he gained a reputation as a hard-working but cautious chief of staff who only moved when there was a consensus among the bishops. Cardinal Bernardin is "with no peer in his capacity for painstaking, bureaucratic work—a central requirement for both successful politicians and bishops," explains Eugene Kennedy.[18] As a former general secretary, he also paid more attention to the details of staff work than did other presidents. The bishops trusted him because he did his homework, respected their views, and never put forward proposals that would later embarrass them.

Archbishop Quinn describes him as "a great conciliator. He has a great gift for keeping peace and keeping people together, and of course he is a man who has a great sensitivity to issues and tried to keep a balanced approach, to weigh all sides. Certainly a very able man, no question about that."

As president he had a "genius for consensus" and he worked with patience and perseverance for consensus among the bishops, explains Father Nolan. "His style of leadership is collegial, marked by gentleness of manner and deep respect for the views and concerns of others."[19] As a result, he became adept at persuasion and compromise. "As the debate progressed," recalls Bishop Malone, Archbishop Bernardin "was always noting this thread of similarity and that thread of similarity. Then as things would move on he would present this mosaic and offer you the possibility of all these people united and he would call for a vote and do it very well."

This does not mean that everyone liked him. "Bernardin had his critics in the seventies, the same ones Dearden had before him," writes Professor Kennedy. "If he displeased conservatives, he disappointed the impatient progressives who wanted major changes rather than administrative readjustments in the church. Bernardin conceived of his task as making room for the church to develop without completely losing its shape in the process."[20] When Archbishop Bernardin was elected president in 1974, Cardinal Patrick "O'Boyle, gruff and unconverted, left the bishops' meeting immediately afterward, saying loudly, 'The only reason I came was to vote against him.'"[21]

Additional resolutions and statements on social and political issues were approved by the conference during the Bernardin presidency, including statements on the Panama Canal (1975 and 1976), the hungry (1975), family television (1975), handguns (1975), South Africa (1975), the economy (1975), housing (1975), farm labor (1975), New York City (1975), the aged (1976), immigrants and refugees (1976 and 1977), DNA research (1977), American Indians (1977), and religious liberty (1977).[22] The USCC Administrative Board also adopted a statement on political responsibility (1976), which was revised and reissued prior to subsequent presidential elections.

The bishops also approved a program for priestly training (1975), a pastoral plan for pro-life activities (1975), a national catechetical directory (1977), and statements on Catholic-Jewish relations (1975), Catholic schools (1976), religious education (1976), moral values (1976), the movie "Jesus of Nazareth" (1977), and the book *Human Sexuality* (1977). In 1977, they also responded to the bicentennial consultation, "Call to Action" meeting, and established a secretariat for the laity.

As president, Archbishop Bernardin spoke out frequently on a wide range of issues before the church and the nation. In 1975, he talked on the international year of women, Catholic universities, anti-abortion amendments, Israel, Vietnam, Indochina refugees, and civil religion. In 1976, he spoke out on Lebanon, Catholic schools, the charismatic renewal, the Supreme Court ruling on Missouri abortion law, the presidential election, the arrest of four U.S. bishops in Ecuador, the Detroit "Call to Action" conference, and general absolution in Memphis. In his last year in office, he expressed views on capital punishment, South Africa, human rights, and bishops and theologians. During his presidency, he passed on to the bishops and defended Vatican documents excluding women from the priesthood and limiting general absolution.

"Bishop, Archbishop, and now Cardinal Bernardin was quite diffident and kind of scared of interviews and press conferences at first," recalls Mr. Shaw. "But he became more and more accustomed to it over the years, and better and better at it until now I think he's exceptionally good. But it was a little painful at first, just trying to get him to do it at all. It was the sort of thing he knew he should do, it was part of the job, but it was like pulling teeth. It was a very painful experience for him to have to do it, initially."

"Joe was a cautious man," recalls Monsignor Higgins.

> What he tried to do was keep the Dearden heritage alive. But, he'd do it in a nice, quiet, cautious way. Joe doesn't take chances. . . . Joe has the sharpest antennae of anybody I've ever met. Nobody has to tell Joe that there is a problem looming. He senses things. He is particularly sensitive to people's feelings. Joe would never hurt anybody. Absolutely incapable of hurting anybody deliberately.

Despite his caution, Archbishop Bernardin became involved in controversy during the 1976 presidential election.[23] After meeting with each candidate, he said he was "disappointed" with Carter's position on abortion but "encouraged" by Ford's. This was understandably interpreted as an endorsement of President Ford, although the archbishop quickly denied that was the intent.

Five and a half years after laying down the presidency, Archbishop Bernardin was made archbishop of Chicago. Although some observers claimed he was more "liberal" than the Vatican wanted, he was also recognized as the only prelate who could bring peace to the Chicago archdiocese that was severely divided by the Cody regime. The Vatican also recognized his diplomatic skills exercised at the synods and used him during various crises, such as the Hunthausen affair.[24] He has also served on the Congregation for Bishops, the Pontifical Commission for Social Communications, the Pontifical Commission for the Revision of the Code of Canon Law, the Congregation for

Evangelization of Peoples, the Congregation for Sacraments and Divine Worship, and the Secretariat for Promoting Christian Unity.

He has continued to exercise more influence than any other past president. As chair of the ad hoc committee charged with writing the 1983 pastoral letter on peace, he became one of the most widely-known prelates in America. He originated the idea of the "consistent ethic of life" to provide an intelligible framework for the bishops' concern for all life issues: abortion, arms control, capital punishment, child care, welfare, peace, medical ethics, and euthanasia.[25]

He continued to be elected to conference posts: chair of the Canonical Affairs Committee in 1978, synod delegate in 1979, 1981, 1986, and 1989, chair of the Committee on Pro-Life Activities in 1986, and chair of the Committee for Marriage and Family Life in 1990. At the synods he was five times elected to the Council of the Secretariat of the Synod, serving on the council for 16 years. He is the only former president ever nominated for president again. He came in third on the first ballot to Archbishop Roach and Bishop Malone who were eventually elected president and vice president in 1980. The only other election he lost was in 1984 when he ran for membership on the board of Catholic Relief Services.

Although the cardinal is well liked in Chicago, in 1990 serious financial problems arose because of his inability to make tough decisions in cutting the archdiocesan budget. In 1991 the archdiocese was accused of being negligent by keeping in ministry a priest involved in pedophilia.

John R. Quinn, 1977-80

John R. Quinn, archbishop of San Francisco, became the fourth president of the conference (1977-80) at age 48.[26] As a seminarian he studied at the Gregorian University in Rome, and as a priest, he taught and was rector of the San Diego diocesan seminary. At the age of only 38, he was made auxiliary bishop of San Diego in 1967, one year after the creation of the NCCB. In 1971, he became bishop of Oklahoma City, which was made an archdiocese in 1972. Early in 1977 he returned to California as archbishop of San Francisco.

Before becoming president, Archbishop Quinn had been chair of the Committee on Pastoral Research and Practices (1971-74) and chair of the Liturgy Committee (1975-77). He was nominated but not elected as a synod delegate in 1973 and as vice president in 1974. In 1976 he was elected as an alternate delegate to the synod. He was a reluctant candidate for the presidency in 1977 because he had been archbishop of San Francisco for less than a year.

He is acknowledged as one of the brightest members of the hierarchy, but he has a low tolerance for small talk and social mixing. He was elected because of the bishops' respect for his intelligence and spirituality. He is more interested in the substantive issues that come before the conference than in the political process. Nor does he avoid tough issues. At the 1980 synod on the family, he volunteered to give the American presentations on contraception, divorce and remarriage, and the changing role of women. On other occasions he dealt with complex bioethical issues.

"He was interested in the big issues," recalls a member of the staff, "but let Kelly [the general secretary] take care of the rest, unless he got interested in something, and then he would dig in." He delegated more decisions to the general secretary than any other president. According to another member of the conference staff, he told the general secretary, "You do it, and if you need me, I'm there in California." Archbishop Quinn explains, "The amount of time I had to spend being president was not greatly different from the amount of time that I had to spend when I wasn't president but I was a member of two or three committees and a chairman of another one, and going to all those meetings."

Some observers said he got bored during assembly debates. During one particularly pedestrian debate, Archbishop Quinn passed the gavel to the vice president and went up to his room to play the piano. Bishop Malone remembers:

> Quinn allowed the expressions to go on, almost with a wan look, and say, "Well, is that about all that now?" and then call for a vote.

He seemed not to be engaged with the direction. But as with Roach, there was never any doubt about the way in which Quinn himself was positioned. But he was less eager to be the master weaver as Joe Bernardin was.

During Archbishop Quinn's presidency, the bishops continued issuing statements on domestic and international affairs, including war and peace (1978), refugees (1978 and 1980), justice (1978), the Middle East (1978), racism (1979), Cambodia (1979), Iran (1979 and 1980), conscription (1980), tubal ligation (1980), Marxism (1980), capital punishment (1980), El Salvador (1980), and cultural pluralism (1980).[27]

Important church issues were also dealt with: family ministry (1978), the handicapped (1978), black Catholics (1979), the papal visit (1979), Catholic higher education (1980), Catholic laity (1980), and ecumenism (1980). The bishops also voted to remove exclusive language from Eucharistic Prayer IV.

As president, Archbishop Quinn spoke out less than did Archbishop Bernardin. He addressed the issue of neutron warheads in 1978. He wrote President Carter on behalf of Southeast Asian refugees in 1978, and in 1979 he addressed the Catholic Health Association, and spoke out on Nicaragua, abortion, and Hans Küng. In 1980 he issued a statement on the assassination of Archbishop Oscar Romero and attended his funeral in San Salvador, where he and the others at the funeral were fired upon. But he avoided any involvement in the 1980 presidential election. He did not want a repeat of the 1976 disaster.

Besides prepared statements, the president also must respond to inquiries, something Archbishop Quinn felt uncomfortable doing. "The most difficult thing [about being president]," recalls Archbishop Quinn, "was being on the spot with the press all the time, for anything that happened anywhere. They were calling you and wanting to know, and sometimes you had to speak without much chance to consult. You knew that you were speaking as president of the conference—in a sense you are always linked with that—and it could be risky in the sense that you might not always represent everything that the bishops wanted to say."

Despite his reluctance as a spokesperson for the conference, he did fairly well. Archbishop Quinn was unusual as a spokesperson, according to Mr. Shaw, in that he "could take a complex, extremely convoluted question from a journalist and answer it in one word, such as 'Yes' or 'No,' and be fully comfortable with having given that kind of answer. I much admire that style. He carried it off with great aplomb and I take my hat off to him for having done it."

Archbishop Quinn has continued to be very influential in the conference whenever he has cared to speak out, as he did on the peace pastoral. In 1982 he was elected chair of the Committee on Doctrine where he quietly protected several theologians, including the Rev. Richard McBrien of Notre Dame, from being condemned by the Vatican.[28] In 1983, he successfully introduced several key amendments that strengthened the anti-nuclear stance of the bishops' peace pastoral. In 1986 he was elected chair of the Committee on Pastoral Research and Practices. Many were disappointed that he was not made a cardinal.

When asked by the Vatican to do an investigation of American religious, he skillfully turned a confrontational crisis into a pastoral dialogue between religious and bishops. His credibility and skills were again called upon by the Vatican in dealing with the Hunthausen crisis in 1987. These projects, on top of his administrative duties as archbishop of San Francisco, proved overwhelming for this scholarly and retiring ascetic. In 1987-88 he took a six-month sabbatical, but returned to serve the archdiocese of San Francisco.

John R. Roach, 1980-83

John Roach, archbishop of St. Paul, became the fifth president of the conference (1980-83) at age 59.[29] After receiving a master's degree from the University of Minnesota, he spent most of his priestly life in education as a teacher, headmaster, or rector of the seminary. At age 50, he was made an auxiliary bishop of St. Paul in 1971. Four years later, he was archbishop.

As an auxiliary bishop in 1974, Bishop Roach outpolled two diocesan bishops for the chair of the Committee on Vocations.

Six months later he was archbishop of St. Paul, and three years later he placed second in the presidential election after Archbishop Quinn. He was then elected vice president of the conference, the least senior candidate in the race.

Archbishop Roach was well suited to be president and many considered him the best president the conference had. "Roach had a great instinct for what was important," recalls Msgr. Daniel Hoye, his general secretary, "but he also knew how to delegate." He easily responded to the challenge of being president. He enjoyed interacting with people and getting things done. "I like the process of governing," explains the archbishop. "I like to work with people and to come to a judgment about the appropriateness of an action." Unlike Archbishop Quinn, he wanted to be involved in important decisions and did not delegate them to the staff. Unlike Cardinal Bernardin, he made decisions easily and quickly. Nor did he fear getting out in front of the troops and leading.

"He is a very bright and incisive man, and also decisive," explains Archbishop Quinn. "He was a very able president and represented the conference in the public forum very well because he is very articulate and also had a good grasp of the issues that he talked about."

"John is a genial gentleman," comments Bishop Malone.

> He is a pastoral bishop. He is not the theologian that John Quinn is, nor is he the strategist that Joe Bernardin is, but John Roach is a man whose goodness and concern flows out, and so in the chair his eye was on all the company. But it was very clear as we moved through any agenda where John Roach's heart was. . . . [He] was very sympathetic to the social gospel agenda, was not quite as sympathetic when niceties of canon law were being debated back and forth.
>
> In my opinion, Roach was a very good president of the conference. He was broad-gauged. He was able to sum up well what the issue was and help move it forward. He had a good sense of the house. He could tell you pretty well the way the vote was going to go. That was not an insignificant skill to have.

Archbishop Roach was also good at dealing with the press. "That air of candor and frankness that Roach had in speaking to media people was extremely good," recalls Mr. Shaw.

Under Archbishop Roach (and Bishop Malone), the NCCB/USCC adopted a mission statement and developed a process for approving goals and objectives. In June of 1982, the bishops met at Collegeville to reflect on their pastoral ministry.[30] The bishops also approved various liturgical texts (1982 and 1983) and a pastoral letter on Hispanics (1983). Issues of social concern continued to be dealt with in statements on the energy crisis (1981), Central America (1981 and 1983), abortion (1981), health care (1981), Social Security (1983), Namibia (1983), and the Ukrainian famine (1983).[31] The high point of his presidency was the approval of the pastoral letter on peace in 1983.

Central America was a continuing concern of Archbishop Roach's presidency. After being president only a month, Archbishop Roach responded to the murder of the U.S. churchwomen in El Salvador and called for an end to U.S. military aid to El Salvador. In 1981, he testified in favor of the Hatch amendment and he spoke on Jewish-Catholic relations, the neutron bomb, and public policy and the church. In 1982, he spoke on shared responsibility in the church, Lebanon, and defended the pope's meeting with Yasser Arafat. In 1983, he issued a statement on the peace pastoral and the Reagan administration.

Archbishop Roach continued to be influential in the conference after his presidency. In 1984 he was elected chair of the Committee on Priestly Formation. The following year he was convicted of drunk driving and subsequently became a member of Alcoholics Anonymous. When he spoke of this incident at a closed session of the bishops' conference, the response was a standing ovation from the bishops. In 1989 he chaired the committee drafting a statement on food and agriculture. The same year he ran for chair of the pro-life committee but lost to Cardinal John O'Connor. In 1990 he was elected chair of the Committee on International Policy where he furthered the conference's social justice agenda. As chair of that committee, he testified before the Senate Foreign Relations Committee in December 1990 on the Persian Gulf crisis, called for repeal of the UN resolution on Zionism, and asked that the most-favored-nation trade status of China be conditioned on its respect for human rights and religious freedom.

James W. Malone, 1983-86

At the age of 63, James Malone, bishop of Youngstown, was the sixth and oldest president of the conference (1983-86). He was a student at St. Mary's Seminary when Fathers Dearden and Krol were on the faculty. After ordination he was a curate in Youngstown but was later sent to the Catholic University of America to get a Ph.D. in education. He was the diocesan superintendent of schools and was ordained auxiliary bishop of Youngstown at age 40 in 1960. He became bishop of Youngstown in 1968.

In 1969 Bishop Malone was elected chair of the Liturgy Committee. As early as 1971, he was nominated as vice president of the conference. He was also nominated in 1973 for the synod but he lost to cardinals or archbishops. In 1975 he was elected chair of the Committee on Liaison with Priests, Religious and the Laity, beating out Edmund Szoka, the Bishop of Gaylord and later the cardinal archbishop of Detroit. In 1980 Bishop Malone was elected vice president and three years later was elected president.[32] He was the first and only non-archbishop to be elected either president or vice president. "I was on that slate from 1971 right through the decade," recalls Bishop Malone, "always the bridesmaid, but never the bride. So when I was nominated in 1980, I didn't really expect to be elected. It was really a surprise."

Bishop Malone presided over the conference with a relaxed and friendly style. He enjoyed being president, and his openness and humor were disarming. But underneath this bonhomie was a man with organizational skills who knew where he was going and kept inching the conference in that direction. Bishop Malone described how he kept briefed on what was going on in the conference, a pattern followed by many presidents:

> I would begin every day with a phone conversation with the general secretary that would run anywhere from 20 minutes to the

better part of an hour. The purpose of that is to stay up with the topics in the correspondence that come to the president and stay up with the issues that are arising in the work of the conference so that, day to day, the president has an immediate feel for what is going on and is briefed to the eyeballs.

Bishop Malone was willing to say controversial things, but he did so with a smile that was disarming. "He is a very methodical, orderly thinker, very articulate man," explains Archbishop Quinn. "He would also be very forthright, and very consistent in his views, and very able to defend them."

As a result, Bishop Malone was very good with the media. "I always thoroughly enjoyed having Bishop Malone in a press conference," recalls Mr. Shaw. "He's one of the few people whom I know who just naturally speaks in Ciceronian sentences. The kind of complex, highly structured sentences that would be a joy to diagram. So he was very good in the setting of a press conference."

During Malone's presidency, the bishops continued to make statements on political and social issues: religion and politics (1984), abortion (1984 and 1985), Nicaragua (1985 and 1986), Lebanon (1985 and 1986), Lithuania (1985 and 1986), Ukraine (1985), aid to education (1985), and economic justice (1986). Church issues addressed by the conference included: the permanent diaconate (1984), continuing formation of priests (1984), ecumenism (1984), campus ministry (1985), the missions (1986), and RCIA (1986).[33] In 1983, the conference also began making decisions on the implementation of the new code of canon law.

As president, Bishop Malone made statements on Central America, Ireland, South Africa, the MX missile, the U.S.-Soviet summit, ecumenism, and Jewish-Christian relations. He also reported on the state of the church and its future. During his presidency the Seattle crisis developed and was examined. And in 1985 he represented the NCCB at the synod of bishops in Rome.

Bishop Malone has continued to be influential in the conference after his presidency. That he has not been made an archbishop has been often commented upon. Some say he has not been promoted because of his health, but others believe that he made too many enemies in Rome while he was president. In a

1987 election, he lost to Archbishop Lipscomb the chair of the Committee on Doctrine, but in 1989 he was elected chair of the Committee on Domestic Policy.

John L. May, 1986-89

John L. May, archbishop of St. Louis, became the seventh president of the conference (1986-89) at age 64.[34] As a priest in Chicago, he served in parishes and worked in the tribunal and on priest personnel. He is the first NCCB president who was pastor of a parish. In 1959 he was appointed general secretary and vice president of the Catholic Church Extension Society, an organization raising money for the missionary areas in the United States. At the age of 45 in 1967, he was made an auxiliary bishop of Chicago under Cardinal John Cody. Two years later he became bishop of Mobile, where he gained respect for his quiet and organized style despite the handicap of being a Northerner and an integrationist. In 1980 he became archbishop of St. Louis.

In 1975, Bishop May, then of Mobile, was defeated by Archbishop Quinn for chair of the Liturgy Committee. In 1979 and 1982 he was elected a member of the board of Catholic Relief Services. In 1980 he came in third for vice president, and three years later he won the vice presidency.

His varied background helped him as president. "He had been a leader of the bishops for years," explains Archbishop Quinn. "As head of Extension in Chicago, he had a lot of contact with many places all over the United States, so he had very broad experience before he became bishop. Then he was auxiliary in Chicago, and then he went to Mobile, Alabama. So he has had a varied background, and that is reflected in his role as president. He has a good sense of the broader picture."

Archbishop May is a quiet, soft-spoken prelate who hates conflict and controversy. To some he appeared weak, but "May is stronger than some people think," reports Monsignor Hoye, his general secretary. "If it is a matter of principle, he will not move." Archbishop May earned trust and cooperation because of his tremendous capacity for listening to people without attempting to force his views upon them. "He is a good listener, and a careful thinker," reports Archbishop Quinn. "He sizes up the whole issue from the different points of view. I don't think he would jump into something blindly."

"I thought John would be too stodgy to be a leader," recalls Monsignor Higgins, a fellow Chicagoan.

> He's slow on his feet, he's a Luxemburger, he digs in, but he's been very good, much better than I thought he would be. His great quality is he's an honest guy. Not brilliant, but he tells you exactly what he is thinking. Bernardin, sometimes you have to guess what he is saying. John May has not an iota of the Roman in him.
>
> Malone was a politician; he loved Rome. He loved the maneuvering, something like [Cardinal Edward] Mooney [of Detroit]. Mooney loved that kind of maneuvering. John May would rather be out walking. Take a walk or maybe go out and play golf. He does it and does it as well as he can, but it is not something that he enjoys. Malone would rather go over there and fight with the curia than eat.

As archbishop of St. Louis, he gently nudged his priests toward liturgical renewal but he did it more through example than through fiats. At confirmations he always had women as lectors or ministers of communion. He encouraged singing and extended the cup to the congregation. This led one iconoclast to comment: "What does it take to keep the archbishop happy? Wine, women, and song."

As president he could not avoid the limelight or controversy. In his first press conference after Bishop Malone's farewell address, he spoke of the "perceived" disaffection of American Catholics from Rome. This qualification was jumped on by reporters as a repudiation of Bishop Malone's address that spoke of disaffection. Thus by trying to play down conflict, the archbishop found himself in the midst of it. His tendency to confuse things got him in trouble in 1988 at Collegeville when he gave contradictory interpretations of a vote on a contract between the conference and EWTN. And in the press conference at Collegeville after a closed door debate on AIDS, he indicated the bishops had voted in favor of the Administrative Board's statement when no vote had taken place.

The bishops under Archbishop May continued to address domestic and international issues: Kurt Waldheim (1987), Central America (1987), school-based clinics (1987), Korea (1987), AIDS (1987 and 1989), deterrence (1988), religious liberty in Eastern Europe (1988), immigration laws (1988), Vietnam (1989), abortion (1989), the Middle East (1989), farm policy (1989), and Third World debt (1989).[35]

The bishops also developed a pastoral plan for Hispanic ministry (1987) and responded to a pastoral plan for black Catholics (1989). They issued statements on priests' retreats (1989), retired priests (1987), and the relations between bishops and theologians (1989). They began a special collection for retired religious (1988). They developed an ecumenical marriage rite (1987) and a ceremony for Sunday worship without a priest (1989).

As president, Archbishop May issued statements on the Vatican procreation document (1987), the Waldheim controversy (1987), the role of the parishes, the 1988 summit, Lebanon, Panama, the Webster abortion case, and the burning of the Southern African Catholic Bishops' Conference office (1988). He welcomed the pope to the United States in 1987 and led the delegation of archbishops that met with the pope in 1989. He also had to deal with the controversy over the 1987 AIDS statement issued by the USCC Administrative Board. He addressed the Catholic Theological Society of America in 1989, calling for an end to right-wing attacks on American theologians. Also in 1989, he wrote President Bush pointing to the opportunity for peace and disarmament because of changes in Eastern Europe. The same year he also led the delegation of American archbishops, called to Rome to discuss the state of the church in the United States.

Daniel E. Pilarczyk, 1989-92

Daniel E. Pilarczyk, archbishop of Cincinnati, was elected president in 1989 after having been vice president since 1986.[36] He was 55 when elected.

Father Pilarczyk studied in Rome at the Urban University where he received a S.T.D. He returned to Cincinnati to be assistant chancellor and to earn a Ph.D. in classics at the University of Cincinnati. He is fluent in Italian and very competent in French, German, Spanish, Latin, and classical Greek. He was rector of the archdiocesan seminary until 1974 when, at 40 years of age, he was picked by Archbishop Bernardin to be his auxiliary. He was also Archbishop Bernardin's choice in 1982 for his successor in Cincinnati.

Archbishop Pilarczyk was naturally viewed in the conference as a Bernardin man. In 1975 he was nominated to be a member of the Education Committee (and therefore the Administrative Board) but lost to two other auxiliary bishops. Three years later while still an auxiliary, he was elected chair of the same committee, where he shepherded through a document on higher education. In 1981 he was nominated for the synod but received few votes. In 1982 he lost the chair of the Committee on Doctrine to Archbishop Quinn, and in 1983 he received a few votes for president and vice president. In 1984 he became chair of the Liturgy Committee, a position he had to relinquish two years later when elected vice president. In 1988 an aneurysm ruptured at the base of his brain, but he recovered fully after surgery. In 1990 he attended the synod of bishops as an elected representative of the NCCB.

Although a protegé of Cardinal Bernardin, Archbishop Pilarczyk is his own person with his own style. He is more informal and direct in his manner than the cardinal. He was always "Dan" to the Cincinnati priests while Archbishop Bernardin was never "Joe." Archbishop Pilarczyk makes decisions easily and is not terribly concerned if people disagree with him, although he can change his mind if the arguments are persuasive. He has written for *America* and other journals and is author of *Twelve Tough Issues: What the Church Teaches and Why*.[37] He refers to *Humanae Vitae* as "prophetic," saying that if people had followed its values, the crises caused by divorce and AIDS would have been avoided.

As president he is more direct in speaking than Archbishops Bernardin or May, but less interested in the politics of making things happen than Dearden, Bernardin, Roach, or Malone. He is a hard worker, but not as sophisticated in his theology as Archbishop Quinn. "I enjoy being a spokesman for the conference," says Archbishop Pilarczyk. He even confessed to enjoying chairing the general meetings.

Archbishop Pilarczyk's style is different from his predecessor. "Archbishop May's style was—you let the discussion go on until the discussion is over," explains Archbishop Pilarczyk. "That's a valid approach. My approach is—you let the discussion go on until you can't stand it any longer, and then you bring it to a close." In fact, presidents, including Archbishop Pilarczyk, have been very reluctant to cut off debate. The more common approach is to ask, "Haven't we discussed this enough?" At the conclusion of the first NCCB/USCC meeting Archbishop Pilarczyk chaired, Bishop Malone complimented him "for doing an effective and expert job as a benign but demanding taskmaster."

Within a week of taking office as president, Archbishop Pilarczyk was notified of the murders of six Jesuit priests in El Salvador by the Salvadoran army. He immediately wrote a letter to President Bush that was faxed directly to the National Security Office in the White House. Together with Cardinals Hickey and Law, he met with White House Chief of Staff John Sununu and National Security Adviser Brent Scowcroft to discuss El Salvador. This meeting was followed by another letter to the president expressing the concerns of the bishops over El Salvador.

His role as spokesperson for the conference went high profile before and during the Persian Gulf war. At their November 1990 meeting, the bishops asked him to write a letter to President Bush reflecting their discussions of the crisis in executive session. Archbishop Pilarczyk carefully avoided saying more than would be representative of the conference. "It was clear to me that it would not be appropriate or even possible for me to represent the conference and say the Persian Gulf war is unjust, or to say the Persian Gulf war is obviously a just war," explains Archbishop Pilarczyk.

> So the position that I took in those statements was, "Let's not rush into this. Are we going to be better off afterwards than before? This is a pretty serious thing we're in." Then when the war started, my statement was, "Let's be sure we wage war justly." I think that's about all the [NCCB/USCC] president could say. I didn't feel that I

was being muzzled or anything, but as spokesman for the conference, I've got to speak for the conference.

Following the war, he was called to Rome by the pope for a meeting of all the episcopal conference presidents whose nations fought in the Persian Gulf war. Later in 1991, he wrote President Bush about nuclear arms control and about the Middle East. He also condemned the Serbian attack on Croatia as a "pernicious, unjust war." At another meeting in Rome in 1991, he and members of the committee drafting the pastoral letter on women met with Vatican officials and representatives of other conferences concerned about the letter.

Despite his involvement in Central America and the Persian Gulf war as president of the conference, some believe his election marks a turning of the bishops away from social issues to internal church issues. Archbishop Pilarczyk himself admitted in his November 1991 address to the bishops that the conference had entered a time of introspection.

By temperament and training, Archbishop Pilarczyk is more interested in internal church issues than Archbishop Roach and Bishop Malone. As chair of a committee evaluating the conference staff, he recommended cutting the funding for the Social Development and World Peace office. As president he spoke out on internal church issues such as the priesthood, evangelization, and Catholics who run abortion clinics. As president he appointed an ad hoc committee chaired by Archbishop Oscar Lipscomb to respond to the Vatican draft of the *Catechism for the Universal Church*. The committee's response was very negative.[38]

Under Archbishop Pilarczyk, the conference approved guidelines for sex education, guidelines for catechetical materials, and statements on substance abuse, on Catholic schools, on the 100th anniversary of *Rerum Novarum*, and on the 500th anniversary of evangelization in the Americas. The bishops also voted to have a special collection for the church in Eastern Europe and to set guidelines for translating Scripture, including the use of inclusive language. In June 1991 the bishops discussed the future of the conference and decided to reduce conference expenses. Later in 1991 the conference approved statements on the environment, on children, on Native American concerns, presbyteral councils, and on the teaching ministry of bishops.

William H. Keeler, 1992-95?

William H. Keeler, at 58 years of age, was elected vice president in 1989, seven months after he had become archbishop of Baltimore.[39] If custom is followed, he will be elected president in 1992. After receiving a J.C.D. from the Gregorian University in Rome, Father Keeler returned to his diocese of Harrisburg where he served in the tribunal and as chancellor and head of the diocesan ecumenical commission. Like Archbishop May, he was a pastor, but only for two years. In 1979, at 48 years of age, he was made auxiliary bishop of Harrisburg; four years later he became its bishop.

As bishop of Harrisburg, the capital of Pennsylvania, he was elected head of the Pennsylvania Catholic Conference and was spokesperson for the bishops on state political issues. In this position he worked closely with Cardinal Krol of Philadelphia, who some say wanted him as his successor. After becoming a bishop, he continued to work in ecumenism where his specialty is dialogue with Jews. In 1984 he was elected chair of the Committee on Ecumenical and Interreligious Affairs in a race against then Bishop J. Francis Stafford. As chair he organized the meetings with ecumenical leaders during the 1987 papal visit.

"He was an excellent chair," reports Dr. Eugene Fisher, staff to the committee. "He's very efficient. He had the ability to move a meeting along expeditiously without hurrying it and without running over anybody's point of view. He did his homework before the meeting, knew what the agenda was, and before he went in, he pretty much knew where people stood on whatever the matter was, and so would make sure that the people who had strong views had their say. And if anything came up, he'd handle that too."

Before Pope John Paul II's 1987 visit to Miami, Bishop Keeler helped soothe Jewish feelings over Kurt Waldheim's meeting with the pope. As part of the agreement he negotiated, the pope met with Jewish leaders and wrote a letter to Archbishop May about the Holocaust and promised a papal statement on the topic.[40] In 1988, he was elected NCCB/USCC secretary over Archbishop Patrick Flores of San Antonio. As secretary, he was the only "bishop" attending the March 1989 meeting of the American archbishops with the pope and his curia.

"He's a very nice person," reports Msgr. Donald Heintschel, retired NCCB associate general secretary. "He's been really deeply interested in the whole field of ecumenics. He has done yeoman's work in some of the areas where he's worked there. I've always found him serious but having a good sense of humor. He is a good scholar and a person who has done his homework. He's prepared when he makes a statement. And in many ways he's courageous. When an issue that particularly appeals to him is at issue, he'll stand up and be counted. He's certainly by no means a liberal or anything like that, but he's just a very open, honest person."

Other observers, especially the press, would not give Archbishop Keeler high grades for courage or openness. One Baltimore reporter said interviewing him was like talking through a screen. "He will never rock the boat," was the way he summed him up.

Presidential Backgrounds

There are some similarities in the backgrounds of the presidents and vice presidents. Practically all were better educated than the average priest. Most as priests were teachers or rectors in seminaries.[41] Only two were pastors before becoming bishops. All had been singled out by their bishops for quick promotion. Most were made bishops at a very young age. The average American bishop was 49 when ordained a bishop, but five out of eight of the presidents were 40 or younger when made bishops: Bernardin, Dearden, Malone, Pilarczyk, and Quinn.

Geography

Midwestern prelates did very well in the first eight presidential and vice presidential elections (1966-89). No one was elected from the South or the mountain states. Cardinal Krol and Archbishops Quinn and Keeler were the only prelates from the East or West coasts to be elected president or vice president. Archbishop Quinn was elected following an impassioned speech by California Bishop William Johnson in the Administrative Committee/Board about how the western bishops felt left out of the conference leadership. "I am sure if he hadn't made that intervention," says Archbishop Quinn, "I probably never would have been elected president."

The rest of the presidents and vice presidents come from the north-central Midwest (all within 400 miles of Chicago): three (Bernardin, Malone, and Pilarczyk) from Ohio, two each from St. Paul (Byrne and Roach) and St. Louis (Carberry and May), and one (Dearden) from Detroit. When it is remembered that Cardinals Dearden and Krol originally came from Cleveland it becomes clear that Ohio has been a breeding ground for presidents.

The midwestern bishops "generally try to secure some kind of bloc," explains one archbishop. "They do act together." Since the votes are not recorded, verifying the accuracy of this assertion is impossible, but the success of the midwestern bishops would suggest either good candidates, good politics, or both. Also helpful to the midwestern bishops is a general distrust of the Northeast, which other bishops feel has always been too influential in the American church. This may lead bishops from the West and South to vote for midwestern candidates.

Vice Presidents Become Presidents

Another obvious pattern is that vice presidents are elected president if they run for the office. In five out of seven elections, the vice president (Krol, Roach, Malone, May, and Pilarczyk) succeeded the president in the next election (1971, 1980, 1983, 1986, and 1989). Of the two vice presidents who did not become president, Archbishop Leo Byrne withdrew his name and died before the election took place. Cardinal Carberry also withdrew because he was 73 at the end of his term as vice president. If he had been elected president at that age, he would have had to retire before his term as president expired.

Thus, no vice president who ran for president was ever defeated. They have always won on the first or second ballot. The bishops therefore recognize that in electing a vice president they are normally electing the man who will be president in three years. Serving as vice president gives him an introduction into the job, which is useful since the terms are so short. Those elected are also familiar with the conference and its operations through having served as members and chairs of committees in the conference.

Unless the incumbent vice president is not running, the election of the new vice president is usually more interesting than that of the president. Since the presidential election occurs first, some bishops use it as an opportunity to gain visibility for their vice-presidential candidates by voting for them even though they support the incumbent vice president for president. In every case, the bishop elected vice president was one of the three top runners-up in the presidential election.

Consensus Candidates?

In many elections the top runner-up in the presidential race is subsequently elected vice president (Archbishop Krol in 1966, Cardinal Carberry in 1974, Archbishop Roach in 1977, Bishop Malone in 1980, and Archbishop Keeler in 1989). These elections show a high degree of consensus among the bishops concerning candidates. In polarized elections, the winning faction would vote for its own candidates in both elections and reject the second highest presidential candidate for vice president.

In the elections of 1971, 1983, and 1986 the runner-up was not elected vice president, and there is evidence of polarization. In 1971, Bishop Bernardin came in second to Cardinal Krol for president but then lost to Archbishop Byrne for vice president. Being general secretary and only an auxiliary bishop undoubtedly hurt Bishop Bernardin in the election. In 1983, Archbishop James Hickey of Washington, D.C., came in second to Bishop Malone for president and then lost to Archbishop May for vice president. The most highly contested election was in 1986 when Cardinal Bernard Law of Boston came in second to Archbishop May for president and lost to Archbishop Pilarczyk for vice president. As will be seen later in examining the synod elections, 1986 was a very polarized year with Cardinal Law the point man for the minority faction.

Seniority and Rank

In a hierarchical and traditional organization like the Catholic church, it is logical to hypothesize that seniority (how long a person has been a bishop) and rank will affect election results. Seniority plays an insignificant role in presidential elections,[42] but rank is important. Every successful candidate for president or vice president, except Bishop Malone, has been an archbishop. No auxiliary bishop was ever elected NCCB president or vice president; in fact they were rarely nominated. Only Bishop Bernardin came close to being elected vice president as an auxiliary in 1971. In 1989 the Vatican Commission for the Authentic Interpretation of the Code of Canon Law ruled that auxiliary bishops were no longer eligible for president.

On the other hand, cardinals have not been especially successful in getting elected. John Krol was a cardinal when elected president in 1971, but he was only an archbishop three years earlier when elected vice president. The only other successful cardinal candidate was John Carberry who at the age of 70 was elected vice president in 1974. Other cardinals, such as William Baum, Terence Cooke, Timothy Manning, and Bernard Law, were nominated but not elected.[43] Cardinal O'Connor may have started a trend by withdrawing his name in 1986 after being one of the ten prelates nominated. In 1989, for the first time, there were no cardinals on the ballot, indicating they either received too few votes to be nominated or they withdrew their names.

There have been several explanations of the inability of cardinals to win presidential elections in the conference. As the job of the president became more time consuming, many bishops felt that cardinals were too busy with their large archdioceses and their work for the Vatican to devote sufficient energies to the conference. In the early days of the NCCB, the defeat of cardinal candidates may have represented a rejection of their predominance in the old NCWC. Even in the NCWC, great efforts were made to keep Cardinal Francis Spellman of New York from controlling the conference. In typical American fashion, the bishops may fear the concentration of power in the hands of a few men whose authority was hierarchically rather than democratically given.

All this suggests that to get elected president or vice president of the conference, one needs to be an archbishop (but not a cardinal) or a very respected senior diocesan bishop. Election chances also improve as one moves away from salt water. Most importantly, if the vice president runs for president, he gets it.

Synod Elections

A look at the elections for delegates to the synod of bishops in Rome will throw additional light on who are the leaders in the conference. The procedures for electing synod delegates have varied over time.[44] Since 1979, the bishops have nominated candidates during regional meetings (the conference is currently divided into 13 geographical regions). Additional candidates can be added to the ballot by any bishop with five "seconds." Each of the four delegates and two alternates is elected separately, with subsequent elections having the same slate of candidates minus the previous winners. If no candidate receives a majority on the first or second ballot, the third ballot is limited to the top two vote-getters.

Officers

The first delegate selected for every synod has been the NCCB president, who has always been elected on the first or second ballot. For three synods, the bishops chose as their second delegate the NCCB vice president—Cardinal Krol in 1967 and 1971 and Cardinal Carberry in 1976.[45] Since then, however, the vice president has not been elected to the synod.

Being the chair of the right NCCB committee at the right time helps one get elected to the synod. Bishop John J. Wright, who was chairing the ad hoc committee drafting the pastoral letter, "The Church in Our Day," was elected in 1967 because the synod was on doctrinal issues. In 1971 the bishops elected Cardinal Krol to the synod that discussed priesthood. Not only was he vice president, he also chaired the NCCB committee conducting a major study of the priesthood. Bishop J. Francis Stafford, a mere auxiliary, was elected in 1979 to the synod on the family since he was chairing the NCCB Committee on the Family. As chair of the Committee on the Laity, Bishop Stanley Ott was elected to the synod on the laity in 1986.

Sometimes acknowledged expertise can be more important than being a chair. In 1976, Bishop Raymond Lucker was elected to the synod on catechetics in a close race with Archbishop John F. Whealon. "Lucker was in the Education Department of USCC for several years [1968-71] and had earned the respect of the bishops while he was there," explained a bishop. "Also, he is a great favorite with the midwestern bishops, and they generally try to secure some kind of bloc, or whatever you want to call it, they do act together." Archbishop Whealon, chair of the committee drafting the "National Catechetical Directory," was elected as an alternate.

In 1989, Cardinal Hickey and Bishop John A. Marshall of Burlington, Vt., were elected delegates to the synod on priestly formation. The cardinal is chancellor of the Catholic University of America, chair of the bishops' Committee on the North American College, and former rector of the North American College. He is also a member of the Congregation for Seminaries and Educational Institutes. Bishop Marshall had chaired a major study of U.S. seminaries for the Vatican. The alternates chosen were Bishop James P. Keleher of Belleville, Ill., chair of the Committee on Priestly Formation, and Bishop Daniel Buechlein of Memphis, Tenn., who had been rector of St. Meinrad's Seminary in Indiana for 17 years and had worked on the national Program for Priestly Formation.

Geography and Rank

As with elections to president and vice president, midwestern bishops appear to do well in synod delegate elections. The South and the West have won two elections each from 1967 to 1989. The Northeast did a little better with nine victories, but the Midwest cleaned up with 19 synod delegates.[46] Two Hispanic archbishops have been elected to the synod, but no black bishop has ever been elected. Knowledge of Spanish and other languages at an international meeting is, of course, helpful.

Unlike the elections for president and vice president, being a cardinal helps one get elected to the synod: 41 percent of the delegates elected by the NCCB were cardinals,[47] 41 percent were archbishops, and 18 percent were bishops. The conference recognizes that cardinals carry more weight in Rome and therefore selects them as delegates.

Few prelates have been elected to more than one synod, another indication that power is dispersed within the conference. The exception is Cardinal Bernardin, who has been chosen by the NCCB to attend every synod since 1973.

As with the presidential/vice presidential elections, elections for synod delegates appear to produce consensus candidates. Often the candidate who comes in second in a race is chosen in the next election. Two interesting exceptions occurred in 1971 and 1986. In 1971, Bishop Malone came in second for the position of third delegate. He continued to come in second for the next three available positions. NC News noted that Bishop Malone was "considered a leader among the renewalist element in the hierarchy."[48] That element lacked the votes to send their leader to the synod. Even more dramatically, Cardinal Law came in second in every synod race in 1986, the same year he came in second for president and vice president.

Election Politics

Election politicking in the conference is low-keyed. Overt campaigning is considered counterproductive. Archbishop Quinn was a reluctant candidate for president. Bishop Malone was surprised to be elected since he had been passed over so many times before. No one admitted campaigning for office. "I don't think anybody campaigns," says Archbishop Roach.

> I know I didn't. I don't know anybody who did. I had been a chair of a committee, and I had been on two or three committees, and had been on my feet a little, not a lot, talking. I think you get to be known and visible. You end up on that list of ten people, and

then, depending on where the mood is swinging on that occasion, you end up winning the election or losing it.

As Archbishop Roach notes, to be elected, a bishop must be visible and active in the conference. Every president except Archbishop May had chaired one or more committees before being elected president. "I didn't campaign because if you go after something and get it, then you can't complain," joked Archbishop Pilarczyk. "If you just let it happen, then it's God's will and God has to take care of you." On the other hand, he admits "I became a candidate de facto during the summer of 1986 [when the NCCB met] at Collegeville. I gave a talk on ordained ministry that was very well received, and it was a good talk.[49] I think people realized that the big elections were coming up that fall, and I think that's what suggested my name to many people."

Bishops are reluctant to talk about election politics, but it is clear that Cardinal Dearden quietly pushed for Archbishop Bernardin's election as president, just as Cardinal Bernardin in turn supported his former auxiliary, Archbishop Pilarczyk.

The most serious politicking occurs when a group of bishops wants to block someone from getting elected. This appeared to happen in 1986 when Cardinal Law was repeatedly defeated, first for president and vice president and then for synod delegate and alternate.[50] Many bishops felt that Cardinal Law was not a team player and that he wanted to change the direction of the conference. He had hired Mr. Philip Lawler, an outspoken critic of the economic and peace pastorals, as the editor of his archdiocesan newspaper (he was later fired). Cardinal Law had also opposed the appointment of Michael Buckley, S.J., as staff to the Committee on Doctrine. Some "liberal" bishops who preferred Archbishop Rembert Weakland for vice president voted for Archbishop Pilarczyk because they thought he had a better chance of defeating Cardinal Law. In 1989 Cardinal Law was elected chair of the Committee on Migration where he has worked to prove himself as a team player.

"I think by definition, the president has to be a person of consensus," says Archbishop Pilarczyk.

He's not going to get elected president if he's off on some extreme. The bishops want a centrist, and they want somebody who has some skills, very often verbal skills. You know, Joe Bernardin, Jack Roach, Quinn, me. They want somebody who is not going to be excessively creative. That's fine; that's right on the money, because you don't want a Franklin Roosevelt in the conference. You want somebody that you can trust who's going to respect your opinions.

The American bishops choose prelates who will be followers more than leaders of the conference. When asked whether the bishops want a follower rather than a leader, Archbishop Pilarczyk responded, "they want, I would say, not a follower rather than a leader, but a representative rather than a creator." Outspoken prelates (Archbishops Anthony Bevilacqua, Raymond Hunthausen, Francis Hurley, Bernard Law, Roger Mahony, John O'Connor, J. Francis Stafford, Edmund Szoka, and Rembert Weakland) with strong views on issues are not elected president or vice president. The bishops are not looking for prophets who will shake the boat. Rather they look for team players who reflect the consensus of the body itself. But sometimes these strong personalities are elected to chair committees.

The NCCB/USCC presidents have come under fire from some members of the conference. At the November 1988 NCCB meeting, Auxiliary Bishop Austin Vaughan of New York criticized the former presidents who made up the ad hoc committee responding to the Vatican document on episcopal conferences. In an extraordinary speech to which the bishops responded with laughter and boo's, Bishop Vaughan attacked the former presidents of the conference as "not distinguished as ecclesiologists." "They are all strong leaders," he said, "they are not distinguished by their practice of collegiality."

I would have preferred on that kind of a committee, since it is for the defense of the rights of chickens, that a few of the turkeys might have been represented on the committee. It looks a little bit like a committee of foxes [boo's]. No, it was friendly foxes [laughter]. But friendly foxes can be like friendly human beings to turkeys around Thanksgiving Day [laughter, boo's].

The NCCB does not reelect its presidents as do some other conferences. For example, the Conference of England and Wales has continually reelected Cardinal Basil Hume as its president. In other conferences, the primate is often ex officio the president of the conference. The U.S. conference abhors a concentration of power and prefers a turnover in leadership. With only a three-year term, a president can get some of his agenda started, but it would have to be completed by later presidents.

The presidents have not run on platforms or had agendas to push through the conference. Even if they did, it would be difficult to do. Bishop Malone points out:

> Looking at the structure of the conference, one recognizes that the president who arrives at the president's chair has an entire agenda that is already in motion. The life of the conference carries forward on the shoulders of the various committees, so the committees were at various stages of involvement in problems proper to canon law, liturgy, theology, or social action. So it is not a matter of the president setting an agenda, it is a matter really of the president presiding over the activities that are ongoing.
>
> I just had a real sense that we had a good conference, we had great freedom within the committees to move an agenda, and I didn't see myself as being directive of them.

The bishops exercise leadership in the conference especially through their service as elected officers or chairs. Election to such positions is as much a burden as an honor since the bishops already have full-time jobs in their dioceses. Because of their local commitments and because of the vast agenda of the conference, these leaders need help if they are going to perform well. The principal source of assistance to the president and chairs is the Washington-based staff of the NCCB/USCC, which will be examined in the next chapter.

4. The Shepherds' Staff

I don't believe for a minute that the bishops wrote those two pastorals. I think it was the staff.

——JUSTICE ANTONIN SCALIA.

Isn't that curious, Mr. Justice, I hear many people saying that about Supreme Court decisions.

——MSGR. ROBERT LYNCH

The conference's clout comes from the bishops. The conference's agenda has to come from the bishops. Staff who don't understand that shouldn't work here.

——JOHN CARR

The NCCB/USCC and its leaders deal with a wide agenda of business: pastoral letters and statements, conference budgets and finances, canon law and liturgy, pastoral workshops and refugee resettlement, lobbying and litigation, etc. This agenda comes from many sources. Canon law, for example, authorizes conferences to act in many areas (see Chapter 2). The Holy See often asks the conferences for reports on various topics or for comments on documents drafted in Rome. Suggestions also can come from any bishops who would like the conference to do something. Ideas are also generated by the bishops' staff. Often these suggestions are in response to problems or opportunities facing the church or the world.

However the suggestions arise, the conference and its committees will be helped by the conference staff that is called the general secretariat. Conservative Catholics attack the staff claiming that the "liberal" staff controls the bishops, something that both the bishops and the staff deny. The *Catholic Eye* refers to the staff as a bureaucratic apparat whose "reigning tradition" is "Dissent as Usual."[1] In this chapter we will examine the role of the NCCB secretariat in helping the bishops make the conference work.

General Secretary

The NCCB/USCC staff is headed by the general secretary who is responsible for hiring, firing, and directing the bishops' staff. He attends meetings of the Administrative Committee/Board, and he is a member of the Committee on Budget and Finance and the Committee on Priorities and Plans. During conference meetings, he sits next to and advises the president. Most importantly, the general secretary must see that the bishops' will is served.

Everyone I interviewed acknowledged the importance of the general secretary in the smooth functioning of the conference. The presidents affirmed that their assistance was absolutely necessary, and every president expressed high satisfaction with the work of his general secretary.

The general secretary is nominated by the president, with the concurrence of the Administrative Committee/Board, and elected by a majority vote of the entire body of bishops for a five-year term. He can be reelected for additional one-year terms. Before 1988, the general secretary was nominated by the president and approved by a two-thirds vote of the Administrative Committee/Board. Those supporting the change denied that it was an attack on the incumbent general secretary, Msgr. Daniel Hoye.[2] But the procedure was changed after Monsignor Hoye was criticized by some bishops for hiring Michael Buckley, S.J., as staff to the Committee on Doctrine. Father Buckley had signed a letter stating that the theological arguments in the 1976 Vatican declaration against the ordination of women were not persuasive.[3] Monsignor Hoye notes that he changed 80 percent of the staff during his tenure, and this was the only appointment causing controversy.

NCWC Staff

When the NCCB was formed in 1966, it retained and reorganized the staff of the NCWC. By current standards, the NCWC staff was small and underfunded. It was a collection of uncoordinated offices staffed by talented individualists who often had to raise their own money. "They had very small staffs in those days," recalls Msgr. George Higgins, who went to work for the NCWC in 1944. "Much depended upon the initiative, the imagination, the ability of particular people in a particular department to see how far they could go, how far they could stretch their money, how much they could say publicly that they could get by with."

The supervision by the bishops was often benign but distant. The bishop directors or chairs of the offices were usually supportive. "There was an episcopal chairman for each department," reports Monsignor Higgins. "You saw very little of him. About the only time that I can recall that he got involved was, if they [the staff] wanted to issue a public statement, they'd run it by him." Most statements were simply approved by the general secretary. Monsignor Higgins reports that he saw his chair rarely. Some, like Archbishops Francis Keough and William Cousins, he only saw once a year when he had dinner with them and gave them a copy of the department's annual report.

Bishop William McManus, who as a priest worked for the NCWC education office from 1945-56, agrees. "The bishops did not take much interest in their departments," he says. "It was a nominal thing. It was very disheartening. We'd have some bishop appointed our director, and he wouldn't even come over to the office. You might get a letter once in a while from him, when he wanted a favor. But they didn't take it seriously." A major project of the education staff during the 1950s and 1960s was lobbying for federal aid to parochial schools.

The NCWC staff also worked on preparing the statements that would be issued by the conference. "There was a lot of monkey business in that," confessed Bishop McManus.

> Tom McCarthy [the NCWC press officer] and I could not stand [Senator] Joe McCarthy—just loathed him. We wanted the bishops to condemn him without knowing they were doing it. We were working on this draft of the statement [1951 pastoral letter] and got in an oblique phrase condemning character assassination. And it worked. The papers had headlines: "Bishops Condemn McCarthy For Character Assassination." Tom, who was in charge of the information office, might have helped them [the press] read that.

I can remember the two of us sitting out in the staff house with a thesaurus trying to pick the word that would get it, yet the bishops wouldn't recognize it. Terribly crooked. To get anything done, to have any kind of influence, you had to work through those statements.

With the reorganization and expansion of the conference after Vatican II, the bishops began to take a more active interest in the conference and to exert more direct control over the staff.

The general secretaries played an important role in the NCWC. John J. Burke, C.S.P., the first general secretary (1917-36), is rightly considered the founder of the NCWC.[4] He had been editor of the *Catholic World* and a founder of the Catholic Press Association. He served through World War I, the anti-Catholic campaigns of the 1920s, the depression, and the early Roosevelt years. His reports to the Administrative Committee touched on numerous issues over the years: "Russian relief work, the Church and the American Occupation administration in the Caribbean, the Volstead Act, the peace movement, the rise of the Nazis, Philippine independence."[5]

Father Burke played politics at the highest levels, often meeting with the president of the United States. He "seems to have been on friendly terms with Harding, Coolidge and Franklin D. Roosevelt. There was a cool formality about his relations with Herbert Hoover and Woodrow Wilson. . . ."[6] He opposed federal involvement in education and was worried about the expanding federal bureaucracy. He met with President Harding and argued successfully for a Catholic to succeed Justice Pitney on the Supreme Court in 1922. The same year Father Burke even got President Harding to send word to the Vatican that he would be displeased by the suppression of the NCWC.[7] Under Father Burke's direction, the NCWC intervened in *Pierce v. the Society of Sisters*, which ruled unconstitutional an Oregon law outlawing nonpublic schools. Father Burke also represented the Vatican in negotiations with Mexico during the persecution of the church there. He died after almost 20 years in office, shortly after he had been made a monsignor.

Another important member of the staff during this period was Msgr. John A. Ryan, author of the bishops' "Program of Social Reconstruction" in 1919 and a drafter of the bishops' statement "Church and Social Order."

Monsignor Burke's successor, the Rev. Michael J. Ready (1936-44), had worked with Monsignor Burke as assistant general secretary since 1931. "Mike Ready was kind of a showman," recalls Monsignor Higgins. "He was out front. A handsome fellow, active. He was generally socially minded; he was a [Cardinal] Mooney type." He came into office during the depression and when the Ku Klux Klan was at its height. In 1941, he gave the benediction at Roosevelt's inauguration. During the war, he worked closely with the USO, the War Relief Services, and the National Refugee Service. During the war the NCWC press department also provided information on Vatican views and activities. During Ready's tenure, the conference built an office building for its Washington staff. He left the staff in 1944 to become bishop of Columbus, Ohio.

Monsignor Ready was followed by the Rev. Howard J. Carroll (1944-58) who also had been assistant general secretary. He was general secretary at the end of the war and the beginning of the postwar period. "Howard was a timid administrator, a very careful administrator," recalls Monsignor Higgins. "Everything was in memos. You wouldn't get a phone call, you'd get a memo. Everything was for the record. He was preoccupied largely, in my time there, with the USO and that whole business of setting up care for the soldiers all over the world." He represented the U.S. bishops to the Vatican on immigration issues and served on committees set up by the federal government. In 1957 he was made bishop of Altoona-Johnstown, Pennsylvania.

Bishop Paul F. Tanner was the last general secretary of the NCWC and the first of the NCCB/USCC (1958-68). He was also in 1965 the first to be a bishop while general secretary. He had been with the NCWC staff since 1940 and assistant general secretary since 1945. He was especially involved in NCWC youth programs and Catholic Action. His years as secretary included the Kennedy-Johnson years, when controversy surrounded aid to Catholic schools and church involvement in poverty programs.

"We are as different as day and night," recalls Archbishop Francis Hurley, who as a priest was Bishop Tanner's assistant general secretary. "His general approach is noninvolvement, mine is put my nose into everything." "Paul's desk was cleared by 10 in the morning," reports Monsignor Higgins. "That's an exaggeration, but, he was kind of a 'hands off' administrator" who would pass things on to others. "He kept things going, and he was easy enough to work with—but no great leader."

Bishop Tanner was general secretary during the Second Vatican Council, but there was little involvement of the conference in the council. "We did not do much from the conference," reports Archbishop Hurley. "Tanner took the attitude that this nice suggestion will result in a meeting of some kind and that will be the end of that. The involvement of the conference was mechanical; we made arrangements to go to Rome, made arrangements in Rome for various things."

Bishop Tanner conveyed to the American bishops the instructions from the Vatican that they were not to meet as a national group during the council. "As a result, during the first session of the council, there were no American meetings," recalls Monsignor Higgins who attended the council as a peritus over Bishop Tanner's objections. "The Germans and the French and the Belgians were meeting around the clock. But our bishops were going their own way. It changed after they finally saw that this was ridiculous. Then they used to meet regularly." Toward the end of the council, a NCWC staffer went through all the council documents and itemized those areas that the bishops' conference should give attention to.

After the council, a major study of the conference and its staff was conducted by the consulting firm, Booz, Allen, and Hamilton. "They went through the standard interview of everybody," recalls Archbishop Hurley.

> Then we started a process of aligning all of the parts. Nobody was going to get fired. We were talking about refining and reorganizing and realigning what we had in place. It was a traumatic thing

because of the stresses and strains developed as we put different agencies under certain departments and began to formulate some descriptions of what each was doing. It was threatening to many of the staff. We spent hours on who belongs where, and that is where a lot of the personality factors surfaced. The objection was "I don't want to be working with so and so."

After the reorganization there were two organizations, the NCCB to deal with church matters and the USCC to deal with public policy. Under the new statutes and bylaws, Archbishop John Dearden of Detroit was elected president for the NCCB/USCC. He immediately began looking for a new general secretary to implement the Booz, Allen, Hamilton study. In 1968 Bishop Tanner became the diocesan bishop of St. Augustine, Florida.

Joseph Bernardin, 1968-72

Joseph Bernardin's rise in the hierarchy began when Paul Hallinan became bishop of Charleston, S.C., where Father Bernardin was the chancellor and secretary to his predecessor. Bishop Hallinan liked the young priest and not only kept him in those positions, but brought him to Atlanta as his auxiliary in 1966. Archbishop Hallinan was a close friend of Archbishop Dearden, since both prelates were originally from Cleveland.

"Dearden used to hear Hallinan talk about me sometimes," reports Cardinal Bernardin. "During the one or two meetings [of the NCCB] I attended while I was still auxiliary, I was looked over, I found out later, by Dearden."

Archbishop Dearden had Archbishop Hallinan tell Bishop Bernardin that he wanted him as general secretary of the conference. Bishop Bernardin said no. "I really didn't want to come to a bureaucratic job in Washington," recalls Cardinal Bernardin. "I was very, very happy in Atlanta" and probably would have been named archbishop of Atlanta since Archbishop Hallinan was dying. Later, during a meeting in Santiago, Chile, Archbishop Dearden spoke to Bishop Bernardin directly.

We were having cocktails. "Oh incidentally," he said, "I am not sure when Paul Tanner [the general secretary] will be leaving, but as soon as he leaves, then you will come."

"But Archbishop," I said, "didn't Archbishop Hallinan talk to you, didn't he tell you my decision?"

"Oh, yes," he said, "he told me how you felt, but that really doesn't count." I remember being very disturbed, and going into his [Bishop Medeiros's] room, and I was really beside myself. I said, "Bert, he's not giving me any choice!"

This beginning did not bode well for a good working relationship between the president and the 40-year-old general secretary. "I must admit that at first I found it hard to warm up to him," recalls Cardinal Bernardin. "I guess that was because I was very young and had always seen him as kind of a father figure. He had been called 'Iron John' in Pittsburgh. But toward the end of the first year he began to take me into his confidence, and whenever he would come to Washington we would have meals together, and little by little we became very close friends." Even so, he did not call Cardinal Dearden by his first name until he himself was a cardinal.

Looking back, Cardinal Bernardin could see that the appointment "was the best thing that could have ever happened to me, and I am not speaking of appointments that I have received since then, but in terms of getting to know the church in this country and the universal church."

Bishop Bernardin is the only general secretary (other than the first one) who was not working on the conference staff immediately before his appointment. All the others were promoted from within. As general secretary, Bishop Bernardin supervised the reorganization of the staff that had been recommended by Booz, Allen, and Hamilton, the management consulting firm brought in by the bishops to study the workings of the conference. When this study was being discussed by the bishops, "I never paid any attention to it, because it just was not my cup of tea," confesses Cardinal Bernardin. "So, when I was told to come here, I was given these two big volumes, and I was told, 'It is your responsibility now to implement this.'"

The Booz, Allen, Hamilton study set the basic structure that is still in place today—the USCC, the NCCB, their committees, and staff. Bishop Bernardin went around the country talking to chairs of the various committees about their committees and the staff that they would need. Some of the staff from the old NCWC was already in place, but many new staff people had to be hired. "All of the central offices had to be restructured, like the finance office, the office of government liaison," explains Cardinal Bernardin. "Those would be the central service offices."

This restructuring occurred in a turbulent environment. Bishop Bernardin began working part time in the middle of April 1968 and full time on July 18. On July 25, *Humanae Vitae* was issued, and soon many theologians and priests were criticizing its opposition to birth control. Cardinal Bernardin explains how the conference responded in a unique process that was never used again.

> The theologians came out with their statement, and we had to come out with a statement. Dearden and I, and I guess maybe the members of the executive committee, we developed a little statement. Then we had to call every metropolitan, dictate the statement to him, and then he in turn had to call each suffragan and get his OK. So within a matter of some hours we could say, "Here is a statement of the bishops' conference." It was a mild statement, but good, and the vast majority agreed with it, so that we could speak as a conference.

During this time, Bishop Bernardin was secretly asked by Paul VI to try to resolve the conflict over *Humanae Vitae* between Archbishop Patrick O'Boyle of Washington and some of his priests. Bishop Bernardin's involvement in this conflict was questioned by bishops who asked by what authority the NCCB/USCC general secretary was getting involved in an internal diocesan dispute. The Washington priests were suspicious of him because they thought he had been appointed by Archbishop O'Boyle, while the archbishop was unhappy with his involvement. As a result, Bishop Bernardin was unable to settle the conflict, which ultimately was resolved by Cardinal John Wright at the Vatican Congregation for the Clergy.

As general secretary, Bishop Bernardin served Cardinal Dearden well. "Bernardin and Dearden worked like a team," reports Monsignor Higgins. "Bernardin was extremely efficient. He's not a daring man, but he was extremely efficient." He was careful in supervising the staff to make sure that they served the bishops. Cardinal Bernardin explains:

I always made sure that anything that needed approval beyond staff always got that approval. We never assumed anything. Staff had responsibility, under my supervision, to work within the framework of accepted policy. For example, if a policy had been determined by the bishops in this particular area, then the day's business is done within that framework.

My responsibility was twofold, to make sure that what we did as staff was always within the framework of policy, and also to make sure that in the development of policy the bishops had the final say, and the bishops participated in a way that they could make that final decision. In all of the time that I was general secretary and even later as the president, there was never any evidence that staff was trying to take over.

Obviously, if you have intelligent people working full-time, they have ideas, they are creative, and they are paid for it. Now, if you just take a back seat as a bishop, then the staff is going to do it. But I really don't know of people at the staff level who said, "By God, we are the ones who are going to do it, and they have to toe the line for us." That really did not exist, and the critics of the conference who say that don't really know what they are talking about. I think that those critics, basically, are in disagreement with what the bishops are doing, and it is easier to blame staff.

Bishop Bernardin was admired by those who worked for him. "He was a master at chairing a meeting," recalls one staff person. "I've been in meetings where I just knew this thing is going to blow up and there's no way that anything can get resolved and people are going to leave here pissed. And he did it then, and I would say, son of a gun, this thing is going to come off. He was a master."

Bishop Bernardin "was very different" from his successor, the Rev. James Rausch, according to James Jennings, who served them both. "Jim admired him, he just idolized him because of that stuff he could do," reports Mr. Jennings. "But he'd also get impatient with him, because Joe did not front an agenda. He did not show an agenda, which of course is part of the wisdom and skill of doing what he does. He has an agenda, and that is, 'Keep this thing together.' Jim tended to say, 'Hell with it, don't keep it together, that's the problem. It's together, we've got to break it up to see what's going on.'"

As general secretary Bishop Bernardin usually kept in the background, but he spoke in 1972 on Vietnam, busing, and tax exemption of churches.[8] He testified before Congress about UN sanctions against Rhodesia (1973). He defended the Campaign for Human Development when it was attacked by conservatives (1972).

Bishop Bernardin continued to serve Cardinal John Krol when he succeeded Cardinal Dearden as president. In 1972, Bernardin was appointed archbishop of Cincinnati. After becoming an archbishop, Bernardin continued to be very active in the conference as president and the chair of a number of committees, including the one that drafted the peace pastoral.

James Rausch, 1973-77

Succeeding Bishop Bernardin was the Rev. James Rausch, by all reports a uniquely active general secretary. "He was bright, enthusiastic, ambitious, and dedicated to the church," reports Mr. Jennings, who worked for him both in the conference and in Phoenix. "Jim felt that the role of the general secretary was to lead the conference of bishops." John Carr agrees: "Rausch wasn't as much a manager as he was a leader." Father Rausch had been USCC associate general secretary under Bishop Bernardin since 1970 and was 45 years of age when appointed in 1973. He was made an auxiliary bishop the same year. He had studied in Rome where he received a doctorate in pastoral psychology from the Gregorian University.

"Rausch loved the job because it gave him a big platform," recalls Archbishop John Roach, a fellow Minnesotan. "He could barely wait for Bernardin to get out of town, so he could make a statement. He loved it. That was definitely not the role of general secretary, but that was Jim Rausch's idea of the general secretary. Kelly and Hoye are not like that, they wouldn't do that."

During his first year in office Bishop Rausch spoke on "Aid, Trade, and Population Policy," agricultural aid to the Third World, human rights, the energy crisis, the Supreme Court school aid decisions, and on the relations between bishops and theologians. He also withdrew from the Interreligious Committee of General Secretaries after the National Council of Churches testified against tuition tax credits without giving him prior notice. He later rejoined.

In 1974 he issued statements on amnesty for draft evaders, the impeachment of President Nixon, trade with the Soviet Union, and food programs. In 1975 he spoke out on ethnic neighborhoods, church fund raising, U.S. policy toward Africa, South Africa's membership in the UN, and the Supreme Court school aid ruling. In 1976 he opposed contraceptive ads on television and radio, supported the Public Works Act, preached at Orlando Letelier's funeral, and spoke on hunger in the Third World. In 1977 he addressed the United Farm Workers convention.[9]

"Jim was certainly—in my experience—the most activist of the general secretaries," recalls Russell Shaw who worked for the conference from 1969-87. "His commitment to social justice was very sincere, and it came out of his personal background, growing up as a poor boy in rural Minnesota."

Bishop Rausch expanded the USCC staff dealing with justice and international issues and hired the Rev. Bryan Hehir to head that office. As general secretary, he testified at congressional hearings on trade, foreign investment, foreign aid, and agricultural policy. He "spoke out on such issues as housing, full employment, health care, the aged and human rights situations in Chile, Brazil, South Africa and Panama."[10] He also cared about the needs of migrant workers and undocumented workers. He criticized the television program "Maude," and objected to advertising contraceptives on television.

The conservative Catholic press saw Bishop Rausch as an enemy. In 1976, the *Wanderer* accused him of "outrageous conduct" by "his unholy alliance with the Marxist enemies of the

Chilean government," and questioned "his suitability for conducting the affairs of the United States Catholic Conference."[11]

Bishop Rausch attempted to improve relations between the bishops and Jimmy Carter during the 1976 presidential election, but these efforts proved counterproductive. He encouraged the meeting between the candidate and Archbishop Bernardin that concluded with Archbishop Bernardin being quoted in the press as disappointed with Mr. Carter's position on abortion.

Monsignor Higgins, who agreed with Bishop Rausch in substance, considered him "almost recklessly over-confident. Rausch was a daredevil." Surprisingly, Bishop Rausch got away with this even while Cardinal Krol was president. But Bishop James Malone notes, "if Rausch was making any statements, it was with the full knowledge and approval of John Krol." The two got along very well even to playing cards together. Cardinal Krol "fortunately had a very good relationship with Jim Rausch," reports Monsignor Higgins. "Rausch swore by him. He could get almost anything out of him." And Cardinal Krol defended the staff against criticism.

As general secretary, Bishop Rausch also had to take orders. One that he strenuously objected to was the hiring of Msgr. Richard Malone as staff to the Committee on Doctrine. "It was Bernardin who foisted Dick Malone on the conference," reports Monsignor Higgins, "over Jim's violent objection. Finally Bernardin said, 'Jim, this is an order. I'm the president.' Jim never got over that. His turf had been trespassed on." Monsignor Malone used his position to report to Rome on bishops, theologians, and NCCB/USCC staffers who he felt did not follow Vatican policy. The replacement of Monsignor Malone with Michael Buckley, S.J., by Monsignor Hoye was a bitter disappointment to right-wing Catholics. As the *Catholic Eye* noted, "the real power Buckley will wield is the ability to shield fellow-Dissenters from Rome."[12]

Bishop Rausch was also interested in church reform, and what ultimately did him in was the Detroit Call to Action. Monsignor Higgins recalls:

That was his baby. He's the one who suggested it; he's the one who pushed it hard. He got a lot of money for it, and nothing was going to stand in the way of it. He had a daring about him. Bernardin never would have done that. Rausch had great self confidence, and was willing to take chances.

After the Call to Action conference, Bishop Rausch was made bishop of Phoenix. "I suspect, to a greater extent than anybody suspected at the time, that they got rid of him," says Monsignor Higgins. "Sent him to Phoenix." Russell Shaw believes he was also hurt by his involvement in the 1976 presidential election.[13] "He was tending to try to smooth the relationships, to pour oil on the troubled waters of the relationship between the bishops and the Carter campaign in 1976," explains Mr. Shaw. "I think, to mix my metaphors, he got burned doing it, as a lot of us did."

Bishop Rausch believed he was destined for higher things. When one staff person suggested he would make a good archbishop of San Antonio, Bishop Rausch responded in all seriousness, "Well, it is very nice of you to say that, but you know, it is not a cardinalatial see." After becoming a bishop, he failed to win any leadership positions in the conference. In 1979 he was defeated by an auxiliary bishop for a seat on the Committee on Social Development and World Peace.

When he died in 1981, the *New York Times* labeled him "a leading liberal in the hierarchy." A friend and fellow Minnesotan, former Vice President Walter F. Mondale, called the bishop "an eloquent and influential voice for social justice and religious values in American life."[14] Later general secretaries did not imitate Bishop Rausch's high-profile style. John Carr, who worked under Bishop Rausch and later returned to work for Monsignors Hoye and Lynch, noted the later secretaries' "principal concern was that the role of the bishops be clear and that we carry it out. They're not ideological people. They're men of principle and integrity, but they don't have a personal agenda."

Thomas Kelly, 1977-81

Thomas Kelly, O.P., like the first general secretary John Burke, C.S.P., is a religious. He took vows as a Dominican in 1952 at the age of 21. After receiving his doctorate in canon law (J.C.D.) from the Angelicum in Rome, he became secretary to the Dominican provincial in New York and worked in the New York archdiocesan tribunal.

Before coming to the NCCB/USCC secretariat, Father Kelly worked six years for the pope's representative in Washington. "That brings you into constant contact with the working of the conference," he explains. He would make "a very close perusal of the decisions that are made in the conference. I read all the minutes for those years. So it is not like I was just coming in out of no place in 1971."

Father Kelly was hired by Bishop Bernardin as associate general secretary in 1971 to handle the NCCB side of the conference. With a degree in canon law and knowledge of the internal operations of the Vatican, Father Kelly was an asset for the conference. He became general secretary in 1977 at the age of 45. "It is not a very easy job," he confessed. "I did not like it very well. There is so much that is going on at one time, and there are so many interests that have to be dealt with, and there are a lot of human differences that have to be taken into account."

Those he served while they were president had a high regard for his work. "I had one of the most outstanding general secretaries in Bishop Kelly," reports Archbishop Quinn, "a man of good judgment, a man who knew he was not the president of the conference, and never tried to think that he was, and a very efficient, competent, able man. He prepared the way of everything for me and focused it, and it was all very clear. We talked on the phone every day."

Bishop Malone agreed:

Kelly tended to be unobtrusive, but a very gifted man intellectually, very able in the way he could write. He would go from one to another to be sure as he touched bases that all things were in order. He came also with the confidence of having been over at the [Vatican] delegation, so that was not a question mark to him, he knew that area. He was a very good person to work with. He was always right up to date on everything.

A staff person described Bishop Kelly as the "obedient servant to the bishops, but he knew whom to talk to, and when to have somebody intervene in the course of a discussion. There would be votes that would occur on the floor of the conference, things would happen around the conference, and you knew they happened because he made them happen. But his name was never associated with any of them."

According to those who worked for him, Bishop Kelly hated budgets and finances. It was his successor, Msgr. Daniel Hoye, who did much to organize these areas and to bring more professional management and planning techniques to the conference offices. "Kelly wasn't into management by objectives or any of that kind of stuff," explains a staff person. "He didn't really favor staff meetings. His idea was 'I've got an open door. Any time you want to come in, just come in and we'll talk that way.'"

Temperamentally, Bishop Kelly also found it difficult to fire people who needed firing. "When you went in to see Kelly, you were always aware that he was a priest and he was a pastor," remembers a staff member. "He had pastoral sensibilities and he related to his staff not only as their boss, but he was somebody that you could talk to." Despite his reluctance to fire people, a number were laid off at the end of his term for budgetary reasons.

As general secretary he spoke out on public issues less frequently than Bishop Rausch. He did make statements on grain reserves (1977), full employment (1977), immigration (1977), abortion (1978 and 1980), Soviet trials of dissidents (1978), test-tube babies (1978), federal spending (1978, 1979 and 1981), military aid to El Salvador (1979), youth employment (1979), fair housing (1979), land reclamation (1979), television deregulation (1979), capital punishment (1979), extension of Voting Rights Act (1981), and tuition tax credits (1982). He also spoke on Paul VI's contribution to peace (1977), the election and death of John Paul I, and the election of John Paul II (1978).[15]

In 1981 he was made archbishop of Louisville. As archbishop he continues to play an important role in the conference and has been elected secretary, chair of the Committee on Religious Life and Ministry, and chair of the Committee on Nomination of Conference Officers. He also oversaw the 1987 visit of John Paul II to the United States.

Daniel Hoye, 1982-89

When Bishop Kelly was looking for an associate general secretary to replace himself on the NCCB side of the conference, the Rev. Daniel Hoye was recommended by the Rev. Frederick R. McManus, professor of canon law at the Catholic University of America. Bishop Kelly was looking for someone trained in the new Code of Canon Law, and Father McManus recommended his former student because he thought he "would fit in and would not take it all that seriously."

"My bishop asked me to go down to be interviewed for the job," recalls Monsignor Hoye. "That was the first I heard of it. I had to look it [the NCCB/USCC] up in the Kenedy directory to see what it was." Father Hoye was the third man offered the post. One could not take it because his bishop would not let him; the other turned the job down. As associate general secretary, Father Hoye was involved in implementing the new code of canon law.

In 1982, he was asked by the president, Archbishop Roach, to be general secretary. The outgoing general secretary, Archbishop Kelly, says that Monsignor Hoye was Archbishop Roach's choice. But Archbishop Roach recalls, "I relied very heavily on Tom Kelly's recommendations. I didn't know Dan all that well; he was associate secretary. I had looked at him and had watched him, and I liked him. I did a lot of things with him. But in Kelly's mind there just wasn't anyone else who was even close. And I agreed with him. His judgment was perfect." Bishop Malone, then vice president, agrees that Father Hoye was an ideal choice because of "his obvious intelligence, quickness, and his ability to work with people, his demonstrated ability to express himself."

There was some uneasiness about Father Hoye's young age. At 35 he was the youngest general secretary ever appointed. "I never thought Dan Hoye would make it," recalls Monsignor Higgins. "He was so young, you know. Very, very young when he got the job. But as far as I can see from talking to the bishops, he was held in high respect. For a young man, much more independent than I ever thought he would be."

At the time of Father Hoye's appointment there was debate about whether the general secretary had to be a bishop or not. The four preceding general secretaries (Kelly, Rausch, Bernardin, and Tanner) were bishops while they were in office. Some argued that the job would be impossible for a priest, because "bishops would only listen to bishops." At the time, Bishop Kelly argued that the general secretary need not be a bishop and Archbishop Roach agreed. In response to Bishop Rausch's high profile, some bishops wanted a general secretary who was clearly staff and not a spokesperson for the conference. Father Hoye, too young to be a bishop, fit this bill perfectly. "If you look at my statements and compare them with my predecessors, like Rausch, you would find I have spoken less," reports Monsignor Hoye. "There was the desire that the president be the spokesman."

Monsignor Hoye did speak on political issues for the conference. He supported immigration reform (1982), tuition tax credits (1983), refugee aid (1984), tax reform (1985), sanctions against South Africa (1986), the church's tax exemption (1987 and 1988), civil rights (1988), the Panamanian bishops' letter on Panama (1988), and the return of Bishop Julijonas Steponavicius to his Lithuanian diocese (1989). He opposed cuts in Medicaid (1984), restoration of capital punishment (1984), partisan use of the bishops' peace pastoral (1983), President Reagan's visit to Bitburg Cemetery (1985), abortion (1985), television advertising of condoms (1987), and federal funding of abortion (1988).[16]

He also spoke on internal church issues such as the Vatican call for religious to retract their signatures to a *New York Times* abortion ad (1984), catechesis (1986), the pope's meeting with Kurt Waldheim (1987), and church finances (1988).

Many observers of the conference agree with Msgr. Robert Lynch that "Dan Hoye was probably the best general secretary the place has ever known, and I've known a lot of them. I've told Cardinal Bernardin and Archbishop Kelly that I believe this, and they agree." Monsignor Hoye had the low-keyed, self-effacing approach of a classic civil servant. He was "extraordinarily gifted," explains Bishop Malone, "in his ability to get things done, to organize, to move. He was, he is among the best. He organizes well, he writes well, he respects people, he has convictions, he expresses them, he works within the organization responsibly, but he is not a rubber stamp. He understands the balance. He is not the one to get his own way. He is to carry out policy, but at the same time, in the councils that are making the policy, he has a say."

The staff interviewed agreed with this positive evaluation of Monsignor Hoye. "He was an excellent manager," recalls Sharon Euart, R.S.M., who was then in charge of planning, "very direct, very well organized, and had a gift for retaining all the information he needed about any topic in order to give it some direction. A good man besides being a good manager. He had wonderful instincts and intuition about people and also about how to work within the system, to the best of the conference." "Hoye had a different style than Kelly," reports another staff person. "Suddenly we had more staff meetings, we're all sitting around the table and an agenda."

Many remarked that Monsignor Hoye was not ambitious and therefore did not fear crossing the powerful when his job required it. "He wasn't afraid of the pro-nuncio or the cardinals or anybody else," remarked Monsignor Higgins. Many interviewed felt that by standing up for the conference against the Vatican, he lost his chance to become a bishop. Every general secretary except John Burke, who died in office, was eventually made a bishop.[17] After leaving the conference, Monsignor Hoye returned to his diocese as a pastor.

Monsignor Hoye hired Francis X. Doyle as the first lay associate general secretary to deal with finances and administration. Under Monsignor Hoye the conference adopted a much more sophisticated budgeting and planning process. Although it was not very successful in closing offices, it did impose a coordination between offices that was needed as the conference staff grew. On the USCC side, an important force in this effort toward coordination was the Rev. Robert Lynch whom Monsignor Hoye hired as associate general secretary. Having been responsible for the NCCB side of the conference while associate general secretary, Monsignor Hoye had to learn the USCC side as general secretary. For his successor, it was exactly the opposite.

Robert N. Lynch, 1989-

The Rev. Robert Lynch had the most unusual path to the general secretary's job. He started his career in 1965 as a layman teaching at an Ohio Catholic high school for $4,000 a year plus lunch. Within two years he had organized the first lay teachers' union and negotiated an increase in salaries and equal pay for women teachers. Recognizing that his talents would be better employed for them rather than against them, the Ohio bishops hired him in 1969 as government programs coordinator for the Ohio Catholic Conference. In this job he successfully lobbied for increased funds for Catholic schools and supervised their use.

In the fall of 1971, Bishop Bernardin asked Archbishop Paul Leibold of Cincinnati if the USCC could borrow Mr. Lynch for six to nine months to set up a national effort for tuition tax credits. He stayed almost four years, first founding and running Citizens Relief for Education by Income Tax (CREDIT), and later the National Committee for a Human Life Amendment (NCHLA), both grass-roots lobbying efforts.[18]

The first organization faded away after U.S. Supreme Court decisions in 1973 made it unlikely that a tax credit for Catholic school pupils would be upheld as constitutional. NCHLA, on the other hand, was created in response to the Supreme Court decision of 1973 in *Roe v. Wade*. Monsignor Lynch recalls:

> We had been considered successful in our grass-roots organizing for tuition tax credits—building in a very short time a pretty considerable constituent base in the private schools. When that failed and it

was felt that a similar strategy should be used to secure a human life amendment, I suddenly became, not an educator anymore, but a pro-lifer.

In 1975 he left the conference to complete his studies for the priesthood at Pope John XXIII Seminary in Weston, Mass., and was ordained for the archdiocese of Miami in 1978. In June of 1979 he received a telephone call from the general secretary, Bishop Kelly. As Monsignor Lynch recalls the conversation, Bishop Kelly said,

> "The pope's coming." And I said, "You have my condolences." He said, "I want more than your condolences. I want you to come here and organize the trip. I've asked around and everybody thinks you're the person to do that." So I came from Miami having only been ordained 13 months, left a great parish and organized the papal visit of 1979.

After organizing the pope's visit, he returned to Miami to become rector of the college seminary. When Monsignor Hoye became general secretary, he asked Father Lynch to come back. He begged off. "I told him that I had not been in Miami long enough," explains Monsignor Lynch, "and that I owed it to the seminary." Monsignor Hoye asked him again in 1984 and he became associate general secretary for the USCC part of the conference.

As associate general secretary, Father Lynch again coordinated the pope's visit in 1987. He also coordinated the public policy and lobbying side of the bishops' conference. Before his arrival, there had been many turf battles between various offices. He made the staff meet and work out coordinated policies and positions. "I'd bring them together and let them fight it out," explains Monsignor Lynch. "Then after they had clawed each other's eyes out, I would try, as best I could, to suggest a middle ground or a compromise that would work."

Monsignor Lynch is viewed as a good manager by the staff. "He's good at process, and he runs a good meeting," explains Mark Chopko, general counsel to the NCCB/USCC. "He knows what questions have to be asked. He's not afraid to raise the hard questions, he's not afraid to tell people that they're out of bounds. He has a very free and open style about how he runs his conference. But you know, when he makes a decision, he makes a decision, and he doesn't pussyfoot around."

In 1988, a 47-year-old Lynch was nominated by the NCCB/USCC president, Archbishop May, to succeed Monsignor Hoye as general secretary. "Hoye, I, Malone, and others talked about the best man for the job," reports Archbishop May.

> It was pretty much a consensus of those who worked with him that Lynch, by reason of his background and his service, was the man for the job. I wrote to all of the bishops in the country and asked for their suggestions. I got very few back. I wanted to know if they had any objections [to Lynch]. There were two or three objections.
>
> There were some complaints voiced at Administrative Committee that I did not go through a search committee, that I probably should have done it more openly. I just said that the president had that prerogative to make a nomination. It was up to me to find somebody that in my judgment would be able to do the work and would be able to work with me.

Under the new procedures, Father Lynch's appointment had to be approved by the full assembly. Although he was clearly a protege of Monsignor Hoye, conservative bishops were undoubtedly pleased by his past work as organizer of NCHLA. His appointment was easily approved (243-20).

To replace himself as USCC associate general secretary, Father Lynch hired the Rev. Dennis Schnurr who, like Father Kelly before him, was working in the Vatican nunciature. Although he had no experience in public policy questions, he proved to be a quick learner. His insights into Vatican operations will undoubtedly be useful to the conference. As associate general secretary for the NCCB side of the conference, Monsignor Lynch appointed Sharon Euart, R.S.M., a "brilliant canonist," according to Archbishop Kelly. She is also a pastoral planner and the first female associate general secretary. "She is a whiz," says Archbishop May.

Since his election in 1989, Monsignor Lynch has spent much time traveling for the conference. The reluctance of the bishops to pay for conference activities has forced him to cut back in the staff. He has not been high profile as a spokesperson for the conference. In a 1990 speech to the Knights of Columbus, he defended the hiring of Hill & Knowlton and the Wirthlin Group to help the conference in a pro-life public relations campaign. The same year he opposed limiting the charitable tax deduction as a means of reducing the federal deficit and supported government funds for private schools. In 1991 he wrote a public letter to U.S. Trade Representative Carla Hills on negotiating with Mexico on a free trade accord.[19]

Office

The general secretary has under him three associate general secretaries. One (Francis X. Doyle) deals with finances and administration. Another (Sharon Euart, R.S.M.) supervises the NCCB staff while the third (Rev. Dennis M. Schnurr) supervises the USCC staff. These are appointed by the general secretary with the approval of the Executive Committee. Also reporting directly to the general secretary are the secretary for communications (Richard Daw) and the secretary for planning (also Sister Euart).

The NCCB associate general secretary has under her the offices dealing with planning (this had been her responsibility before becoming an associate general secretary), ecumenism, evangelization, liturgy, doctrine, permanent diaconate, priestly formation, priestly life and ministry, laity and family life, women, and pastoral practices, and black Catholics.[20] The NCCB offices are small, normally no more than one or two professional staff people. The USCC associate general secretary has under him the offices for general counsel, government liaison, Hispanic affairs, education, pro-life activities, migration, and social development and world peace. The largest office, Migration and Refugee Services, helps resettle refugees and is primarily funded through government grants. No other office has more than a dozen professionals, while some have as few as one or two.

The division of the staff does not perfectly follow the division of responsibilities between the USCC and the NCCB. For example, the pro-life office that serves an NCCB committee is under the USCC associate general secretary because of the office's concern about public policy on abortion. Some offices under the USCC associate general secretary deal with church issues as well as public policy. For example, the office of Hispanic Affairs is very much concerned about the pastoral needs of its constituents. Likewise, the education office is interested not only in legislation affecting schools but also in religious education programs.

The associate general secretary for finances and administration has under him the offices for dealing with various collections (American Board of Catholic Missions, Campaign for Human Development, Latin American), finances, accounting, personnel, general services, library, and the archives. He also supervised the construction of the new NCCB/USCC office building into which the staff moved in the spring of 1989. More will be said about finances in Chapter 9.

Since the divisions between the USCC and the NCCB are not strict and clear, the general secretary and his associates have to work as a team in coordinating the staff. For example, if the USCC education office is working on sex education guidelines, at a minimum this would have to be coordinated with the staffs of the pro-life office, the doctrine office, and the office of pastoral research and practices. The last two are currently staffed by the same priest.

Monsignor Lynch describes the problem and his way of dealing with it while associate general secretary.

> Probably the saddest thing about bureaucracies is the isolation of different units of people, and that they never are able to iron out their difficulties. I bring them together every other month for what I call "senior staff." They had not been doing that. We even went away once for an overnight to talk about issues of prioritizing the legislative agenda and other things about life in the conference and how we can make it work better. Now, they'll have strong, vehement arguments with each other about how to approach an issue.

Serving the Chairs

The staff is directly responsible to the general secretary, but they also serve the conference committees. This dual responsibility can cause problems, but the problems are infrequent according to Monsignor Lynch.

The handbook is fairly clear, and it limits the role of chairmen to basically convening and presiding over the meetings of the committee, which give the staff its work for the given year. Some of our employees find it frustrating to work for a committee, take directions from a committee, and then perhaps be criticized by the executive office for not performing the way the executive office wants when they think they're serving the committee well.

I have had one of my eight units several times make that claim about the difficulty. Some staff members would cultivate the favor of the committee chairman and not worry too much about the general secretary. That's foolhardy. Because it's my name at the bottom of the check. The chairmen come and go every three years, the general secretary stays for five. But I'm a little sympathetic if they're occasionally caught in a bind, but that seldom ever happens. It's really not a very real problem. Most bishops are busy at home, and they don't want to run the staff, they don't want to run the organization.

"The general secretary hires and fires the secretaries, and is indeed your boss," agrees a former member of the staff. "On the other hand, you have this committee sitting out here, and if you want to initiate a new activity, the first thing you need to do is get the committee behind you. So you really have two different people to whom you report."

"The challenge for anybody in one of these roles is to win the confidence of the general secretary and of your committee chair," explains John Carr. "You don't have to agree on everything, but they have to be convinced that you have the interests of the church at heart and that you do good work. And then you can agree and disagree. But if you don't have their confidence, these could be awful jobs."

Conclusion

The general secretary and the president are in almost daily contact to discuss issues before the conference. "We talk about the trips to Rome," explains Archbishop Pilarczyk who traveled to Rome five times in 1991. "Frequently, the staff will be drafting letters for me, and they will fax the texts to me, and I will revise the texts. Then I'll be in touch with Bob Lynch and say, 'No, you've got to change this and you've got to change that.'" The president would also be informed about staff changes. "I tell the general secretary I need such and such, and he gets it for me," says Archbishop Pilarczyk.

Except Bishop Bernardin, all the general secretaries were groomed for the job by their immediate predecessors. All had been associate general secretaries to their predecessors. "They always selected somebody from within the conference," explains a staff person. "The political complexity of that organization and having to know where the bodies are buried and everything else, just demands that." Bishop Rausch and Monsignor Lynch came from the USCC side of the conference, Bishop Kelly and Monsignor Hoye from the NCCB side. When they became general secretaries, they already knew one side of the conference well and they quickly learned the other side.

The staff has come under criticism from conservative Catholics. "That the bishops have addressed mainly liberal issues can be explained largely by the political bias of the staff of the Department of Social Development and World Peace," wrote J. Brian Benestad for the Ethics and Public Policy Center.[21] The staff was also attacked in the conservative Catholic press.

"The staff was criticized bitterly by some persons, and one who was criticized a lot was Bryan Hehir," reports Archbishop Quinn. "I always defended him, and I would continue to defend him. In my opinion, Bryan is one of the most gifted priests, and one of the most exemplary priests that we could possibly have, and I would defend him to anybody, and I did. There were other staff people from time to time criticized, but we had a splendid staff, a very gifted one, and I thought they were very fine." Others criticized by the right included Msgr. John Ryan, Msgr. George Higgins, Michael Buckley, S.J., Mr.

Thomas Quigley,[22] and Msgr. Daniel Hoye. But when they were attacked, many bishops, including the leadership, came to their defense.

Despite Bishop McManus's confession about the staff plot to condemn Senator McCarthy, the staff has been subservient to the bishops. The system for controlling staff and making sure that they reflect the bishops' views in their testimony and statements has been strengthened over time, as will be seen in Chapter 7. "The conference's clout comes from the bishops," explains John Carr. "The conference's agenda has to come from the bishops. Staff who don't understand that shouldn't work here."

Making the staff work for the bishops is the job of the general secretary. "God has been so good to us in giving us general secretaries," Archbishop Roach believes. "You consider the high quality of those guys: Bernardin, and in spite of what I said of Jim Rausch, he was a superb general secretary, and Kelly and Hoye, you just can't get any better. They are just amazing, and Bob Lynch will be the same way."

"Our conference has been greatly blessed in the caliber of its general secretaries, going back to Bernardin," agreed Archbishop Pilarczyk. "There has not been a loser in the lot. When you consider the amount of detail and the amount of personnel work, and the general crap that they have to deal with day by day and month by month, anybody who can run the conference well as general secretary can run anything well."

What these men had in common (except perhaps Bishop Rausch) was a willingness to put aside their own agendas in order to serve the bishops. These were not ideologically driven men. Rather they were in the mold of the classic civil servant or staff person who serves the institution. When they got in trouble with either individual bishops or the Vatican it was because they were defending conference policy or the conference itself. After becoming archbishops, both Bernardin and Kelly continued to play important roles in the conference as committee chairs, members of the Administrative Committee/Board, and in the case of Archbishop Bernardin, as president. Bishop Rausch, on the other hand, failed to get elected to anything.

Other members of the staff who have become bishops and been influential in the conference include Cardinal William Baum (ecumenical office), Cardinal Bernard Law (ecumenical office), Archbishop Francis Hurley (associate general secretary), Bishop Raymond Lucker (education office), Bishop William McManus (education office), Bishop James McHugh (pro-life office), and Bishop Lawrence McNamara (Campaign for Human Development).

Because of their work before joining the conference staff, many of the staff are used to working for the church and the hierarchy. "The majority of our staff have served local bishops and have a sense of what their needs and problems and irritations are," explains Mr. Carr. This diocesan experience is very helpful when the staff works with NCCB/USCC committees in developing programs, statements, and policies.

The bishops themselves are split over the influence of the staff. Most bishops have a knee-jerk reaction against the idea of bureaucracy in the church, but when they look closely at individual offices and staff persons, they tend to like them. As will be seen in Chapter 9, the bishops want to cut bureaucracy, cut the budget, but when specific offices are mentioned, their episcopal defenders arise. A 1991 NCCB/USCC survey of the bishops found that 39 percent believed "that the staff of the Conference exercises too much influence upon the actions and agenda of the Conference."[23] But most bishops (55 percent) disagreed.

Some offices of the conference clearly have more support among the bishops than others. When given a list of 30 NCCB/USCC offices and asked "how important is each office to the work of the Conference," the bishops ranked the offices in order of importance: general secretary, general counsel, liturgy, pro-life, priestly life and ministry, Catholic News Service, education, vocations and priestly formation, doctrine and pastoral practices, government liaison, American Board of Catholic Missions (collection), social development and world peace, Hispanic affairs, ecumenism, laity and family life, Campaign for Human Development (collection), Migration and Refugee Services, black Catholics, evangelization, publishing and promotion services, Latin American secretariat (collection), missions, communications, media relations, communications campaign (collection), research, permanent diaconate, science and human values, communications policy, and film and broadcasting.[24]

Offices dealing with communications (film and broadcasting, communications policy, communications campaign, media relations, communications, publishing and promotion) did poorly. High ranking are offices that directly serve institutional, diocesan, or clerical needs: general counsel, liturgy, education, priestly life and ministry, Catholic News Service, vocations and priestly formation, and American Board of Catholic Missions. The politically active offices (pro-life, government liaison, and social development and world peace) also did well.

Although the staff may do much of the work of the conference, it is the bishops who set the direction of the conference and decide policy. The development of direction and consensus is begun in the NCCB/USCC committees. These committees are essential to the operation of the conference, which meets as a body only a few days each year. In the next chapter we will look at these committees and how they operate within the conference.

5. Shepherds in Committees

> The life of the conference carries forward on the shoulders of the various committees.
> ———BISHOP JAMES MALONE

> Activists tend to get elected chairpersons of committees.
> ———ARCHBISHOP JOHN ROACH

> Unless we fight it out in the committee, unless we reach some consensus there, we will never get the consensus.
> ———CARDINAL JOSEPH BERNARDIN

Because of its size and the extent of its agenda, much of the work of the bishops' conference must be done in committees. This chapter will examine the variety of committees in the conference, the selection of committee chairs, the role of the committees in developing consensus, and the role of the Administrative Committee/Board.

There are 62 committees listed in the conference directory, 49 for the NCCB and 13 for the USCC.[1] USCC committees can have lay, religious, and clerical members, while the NCCB committees are made up entirely of bishops. The directory divides the NCCB/USCC committees into two categories: executive level and general membership level. The executive level committees deal mostly with administrative issues (budget and finance, personnel, priorities and plans) of the conference, while the membership committees deal with substantive policy.

The membership level committees are further divided into standing and ad hoc committees. The number of standing or permanent committees has grown over time.[2] The chair of a standing committee is usually elected by the assembly, and then he picks the other members of the committee. The chair and members of an ad hoc committee are usually appointed by the president to serve until the committee concludes its business. Ad hoc committees cease to exist after three years unless they are reauthorized upon recommendation of the Administrative Committee/Board and by a majority vote of the conference. When this rule was first implemented in June 1991, nine ad hoc committees were reauthorized. Only the ad hoc Committee on Farm Labor was dropped when its chair, Cardinal Mahony, admitted it had not met in 15 years.

Any categorization of the conference committees is somewhat artificial, but some distinctions are useful to show that committees serve many purposes and do many different things. The NCCB/USCC committees fulfill a variety of functions in the conference: administrative, grant-making, oversight, dialogue, and policy-making. Some committees are constituency-oriented, some are policy-oriented. Although some committees fulfill more than one function, usually one function predominates.

The administrative committees deal with internal conference administration: planning, preparing budgets, supervising finances, establishing personnel policies, nominating committee chairs, determining diocesan boundaries, and setting the agenda for assembly meetings. Ad hoc administrative committees have been involved in assessing the conference and the national collections, and in preparing special assemblies. The Administrative Committee/Board will be discussed in detail later.

Some committees distribute money from national collections to various church organizations and other agencies, including some conference offices. Committees whose function is primarily grant-making include the Bishops' Welfare Emergency Relief Committee,[3] the American Board of Catholic Missions, the Church in Latin America Committee, the Campaign for Human Development Committee, and the Ad Hoc Committee on Aid to the Church in Central and Eastern Europe and the U.S.S.R. National collections will be discussed in Chapter 9. The Communications Committee distributes money from the Communication Collection and also oversees CNS[4] and the NCCB/USCC Communications Department (Media Relations,

Communications Policy, Film and Broadcasting, Publishing and Promotion, and Printing).

Committees whose function is primarily oversight would include committees overseeing the American College at the University of Louvain and the North American College in Rome. These committees also act as the board of governors for these colleges under civil law. The Committee on Migration oversees the $10-million USCC Migration and Refugee Services, but it also discusses conference policy on immigration law. The USCC also elects independent boards to oversee the separately incorporated Catholic Relief Services (CRS) and the Catholic Television Network of America (CTNA).

Committees whose primary function is dialogue would include the Bishops' Committee on Ecumenical and Interreligious Affairs (BCEIA) and the Committee on Science and Human Values. BCEIA is one of the busiest committees since its members participate in numerous ecumenical dialogues with non-Catholic church leaders and theologians. This committee involves many Catholic theologians as collaborators in its work. The Committee on Science and Human Values dialogues with scientists on the relationship between science and religion.

Some NCCB/USCC committees are constituency-oriented. They dialogue with specific organized groups within the church, work to see that the church is sensitive to the concerns of these groups, make recommendations about church policy toward them, and sometimes run programs (workshops, publications, etc.) to serve them. Thus there are committees whose primary focus is on Black Catholics, Native Americans, Hispanics, Catholic Charismatics, Catholic college presidents, laity, women, priests, deacons, and religious. These are usually "friendly" committees with members who are sensitive and sympathetic to the concerns of these groups.

Finally some committees are issue- or policy-oriented. They are frequently occupied with drafting or approving pastoral letters, statements, guidelines, reports, pastoral programs, liturgical texts, or other documents. Some standing committees deal primarily with internal church questions: liturgy, canon law, pastoral practices, missions, evangelization, doctrine, priestly formation, and vocations. There are also ad hoc committees to deal with the economic concerns of the Holy See, stewardship, and a pastoral response to proselytism. Other committees are oriented to public policy questions: domestic social development and international policy. And some committees have an agenda that covers both internal church issues and public policy questions: marriage and family life, pro-life activities, women in society and the church, education, and communications.

Constituency- or policy-oriented committees are more likely to be involved in studying issues and making recommendations to the assembly than are administrative, grant-making, dialogue, or oversight committees. On less important matters they might issue statements in their own name as long as these are consistent with past statements of the conference. Normally committee reports or statements have to be approved by the Administrative Committee/Board before publication by a committee.

Some committees sponsor research on specific questions. The Committee on Priestly Life and Ministry published several studies on the ministry, spirituality, and sexuality of priests.[5] The Committee on Education gathered together studies done on religious education. And the Committee on Pastoral Research and Practices did a study of the use of the new forms of the sacrament of reconciliation.

Sometimes committees also respond to inquiries from the Vatican, other bishops' conferences, the government, or individual bishops. For example, the Committee on Doctrine did a study of Renew, the parish renewal program, at the request of a number of bishops. Another report by the committee was on the book *Human Sexuality*. Likewise, in response to requests from bishops, the Committee on Priestly Life and Ministry discussed what bishops should do with alcoholic priests and priests who test HIV-positive. Such reports would not be binding on the bishops, but they would provide suggestions and recommendations.

Some committees, through their staffs, develop programs, publications, workshops, teleconferences, or other educational materials for use in dioceses and parishes. The Communications Committee, for example, sponsored a conference on religion and politics prior to the 1988 election. The Committee on the Laity has been very active in putting on conferences and workshops, for which it normally finds outside funding.

Finally, committees also maintain liaison with other national groups concerned about the same issues. The committees through their staffs keep contact with other organizations interested in education, communications, abortion, social justice, and world peace. In short, without the committees the conference could not function.

The busiest committees would include "the committee on liturgy, the committee on doctrine, the committee on pastoral research, the committee on education, and the justice and peace committee," reports Archbishop John Quinn who has served on many of them. "There is always something percolating in those committees." Some committees are very busy for a time and then less busy. For example, before revision of the code of canon law in 1983, the Committee on Canonical Affairs was very busy responding to drafts of the code with the help of the Canon Law Society of America. After the revision, it dealt with the sections that had to be implemented by the conference. Now it is less active.

Selection of Chairs

The chair of a committee can have a tremendous impact on what is accomplished through appointing members to his committee, directing its staff, and running committee meetings. A chair who has the confidence of the body of bishops has an easier time getting his committee documents and resolutions passed by the assembly. It is obviously important who is chosen to chair these committees.

The chairs of most standing committees are elected by the entire conference membership. A few committee chairs (for the Nominations Committee, the American College at Louvain, the

North American College in Rome) are elected by and from the committee members who themselves are elected by and from each of the 13 NCCB/USCC geographical regions. The boards of CTNA and CRS also elect their own chairs.

Nominations Committee

To nominate the NCCB/USCC secretary, treasurer, and chairs of standing committees, the conference has a Committee on Nomination of Conference Officers consisting of elected representatives from the conference's 13 regions. Surprisingly, despite the importance of this committee, the members are not normally the movers and shakers in the conference. For example, in 1991, there were no archbishops on the committee and only two of the members had ever been elected committee chairs.

"The way someone tends to find himself on the Nominating Committee is if he's not on any other committee," explains a retired staff person. When meeting in regions, the bishops "look around and they see some poor guy who's not serving on anything else. That means the person de facto is not active in the conference, because they're not on any other committee. Their knowledge of who is good at what, and who has expertise is limited, since they haven't served on conference committees. You tend to get people who really don't bring a lot of expertise to the function they have to serve." On the other hand, such a system puts the nominations into the hands of the "silent majority" in the conference, rather than the activists.

The 13 committee members elect their own chair. The nomination process begins with each member of the conference filling out a preference form indicating which committees he is willing to serve on, either as a member or a chair. After reviewing these forms (which are returned by fewer than 15 percent of the bishops)[6] and requesting suggestions from the bishops, the Nominations Committee selects two candidates for each vacancy. Ineligible for nomination as chair is any bishop who is currently a chair or who has stepped down from a chair within the past year. Those elected serve for three years. These rules were adopted to encourage turnover in the leadership of the conference.

"Some bishops who are on the Nominating Committee definitely represent and only speak for their own regions," reports Msgr. Donald Heintschel who staffed the committee. "They'll argue for people from their own region. Others are a little more universal or catholic in their [perspective]. These are generally people who know the conference of bishops a little bit better and know the varieties of people who are in the conference." Not surprisingly, many nominees for committee chairs come from states with large episcopal delegations: New York, California, Pennsylvania, Ohio, and Texas.

The Nominations Committee looks for people who are qualified to be chairs of particular committees. For example, former seminary rectors would normally be nominated for the Committee on Priestly Formation, former educators (e.g., former superintendents of schools) for the Committee on Education, canon lawyers for the Committee on Canonical Affairs, Hispanics for the Committee on Hispanic Affairs, blacks for the Committee on Black Catholics, and Spanish speakers for the Committee on Latin America. Previous work in the area of ecumenism would be needed for the chair of the Committee on Ecumenical and Interreligious Affairs. Previous service on a committee also helps a member get nominated to chair that committee. There is also an unwritten rule that the chair of the Committee on Pro-Life Activities should be a cardinal.

Candid discussions in the Nominations Committee are very important. "When I was chairing," explains Archbishop Thomas Kelly, "I was very careful to make everybody speak the truth and to promise never to talk about it afterward. So we had this big discussion about how we felt about this one or that one. That openness and candor managed to break down some defenses. And whenever I sensed that there was any kind of difficulty, I always had a written ballot."

The chair of the Nominations Committee asks the nominees if they are willing to run, without telling them whom they will be running against. If a bishop is unwilling to be a candidate, the committee must find another. "This [1989] has been a particularly difficult year," reports Bishop Anthony Bosco, chair of the Nominations Committee when 11 chairs had to be filled. Those who say no "might not feel competent," explains Archbishop Quinn. "Or they don't have time, or it is too expensive to travel back and forth to Washington." Some bishops, especially of large dioceses, do not want to take time away from their dioceses. Western bishops are also reluctant to devote time to traveling to and from meetings that usually take place in Washington, D.C. Bishops of smaller dioceses had also complained of the travel expenses, so in 1991 the conference agreed to pay for travel to committee meetings beginning in 1993.

A brief curriculum vitae on each nominee is distributed to the bishops before their meeting. Sometimes the candidates proposed by the Nominations Committee do not receive universal approval. "They say, 'Why didn't the nominating committee ask so and so, the obvious candidate for this?'" reports Archbishop Kelly. "And then you are not allowed to say, 'Well, we did ask him, and he said no.'" Others complain when the Nominations Committee proposes candidates who represent the same views. "I have tried to get nominees who represent different points of view," explains Bishop Bosco. But the ballot might become unbalanced because "somebody has not accepted the nomination and the alternate may be of the same political stamp as the other guy that was nominated," explains Archbishop Kelly. The Nominations Committee tries "to balance the ticket so that the bishops have a choice, not only just about the issue, but whether in your judgment the fellow has experience."

As a check on the Nominations Committee, any member of the conference can nominate a candidate if he gets five "seconds." This happens rarely. "It is only if they put up two people that would be regarded as very liberal for a post," reports a former Nominations Committee chair. "Then generally somebody will put up a conservative candidate." The opposite can also happen, as in 1991 when two conservatives were nominated to chair the Committee on Priestly Life and Ministry and a liberal was nominated from the floor.

The committee's nominees usually come in first and second. In over 20 years, only three candidates not nominated by the Nominations Committee have ever been elected: Bishop Ernest Unterkoefler of Charleston as chair of the Committee on the Permanent Diaconate in 1968, Bishop John O'Connor of Scranton as chair of the Committee on Social Development and World Peace in 1983, and Bishop Stanley Ott of Baton Rouge as chair of the Committee on the Laity in 1984. In some peoples' minds, the 1983 and 1984 floor nominees were more conservative than the committee nominees.

Bishop Unterkoefler's election came as no surprise. As chair of the ad hoc committee on the diaconate, he had prepared the guidelines for the diaconate that had been approved in April 1968. More than any other bishop, he was the father of the U.S. diaconate program.

In 1983, Bishop O'Connor of Scranton was recognized as a comer. He had just completed work as a member of the ad hoc committee that drafted the peace pastoral. Despite his opposition to parts of the pastoral, he voted for it and publicly supported it. The other two candidates were Bishop James Lyke, the black auxiliary bishop of Cleveland (later to become the archbishop of Atlanta), and Bishop Lawrence McNamara of Grand Island, Nebraska, who had been the executive director of the Campaign for Human Development. On the third ballot, Bishop O'Connor defeated Bishop Lyke 134-120. Two months later he was made archbishop of New York.

In 1984, the two candidates for chair of the Laity Committee were Bishops Kenneth Untener of Saginaw, Mich., and Raymond Lucker of New Ulm, Minn. According to one staff person, the southern bishops, meeting at an episcopal ordination, decided to nominate Bishop Ott because they felt left out of the conference leadership.[7] Bishop Untener withdrew after the first ballot when he came in third. Bishop Ott then defeated Bishop Lucker 154-111.

Who Wins?

In the election of chairs, rank carries weight with the electorate but seniority does not. Whenever a lower-ranking bishop is pitted against a higher-ranking bishop, the higher ranking bishop wins almost 70 percent of the time.[8] Cardinals do better than archbishops and bishops, archbishops usually do better than bishops, and diocesan bishops usually do better than auxiliaries.

The exceptions are often remarked on, as in 1986 when Auxiliary Bishop Joseph Sullivan of Brooklyn defeated Archbishop Roger Mahony of Los Angeles for chair of Social Development and World Peace. No one was more surprised than Bishop Sullivan who thought he had been put up as a sacrificial lamb. Bishop Sullivan is widely respected among Catholic Charities directors who may well have spoken to their bishops for him. In addition, Archbishop Mahony was out of favor that year for opposing the appointment of Michael J. Buckley, S.J., as staff to the Committee on Doctrine.

Often such upsets are indications of rising stars in the episcopacy. Of the 19 auxiliary bishops who defeated higher-ranking bishops between 1968 and 1985, six became archbishops: Hickey (1968), Quinn (1971), Roach (1974), Mahony (1976), Marino (1977 and 1985), and Pilarczyk (1978).[9] Three of these were elected president.

Lower-ranking bishops who have defeated higher-ranking bishops in recent elections (1986-90) are: Auxiliary Bishop J. Terry Steib of St. Louis, Auxiliary Bishop John Vlazny of Chicago (now bishop of Winona), Auxiliary Bishop Joseph Sullivan of Brooklyn, Bishop James Keleher of Belleville, Auxiliary Bishop Edward O'Donnell of St. Louis, Auxiliary Bishop Wilton Gregory of Chicago, Auxiliary Bishop Anthony Pilla of Cleveland (now bishop of Cleveland), Auxiliary Bishop Alfred Hughes of Boston, and Auxiliary Bishop Robert Morneau of Green Bay. The odds suggest that there are a couple of future archbishops and a president in this group.

Nomination and election of auxiliary bishops to chairs is, however, uncommon. Auxiliaries are rarely elected chairs of major committees, but rather less important committees like the Committee on Vocations and the Committee on Communications. Although vocations is a critical problem in the church, no one knows what to do about it. Perhaps also the bishops choose a younger bishop for this chair just as they often choose a young and personable priest to head their vocation office. And since the Communications Committee chair presides over press conferences at NCCB/USCC meetings, the auxiliary may simply be a sacrificial lamb thrown to the wolves.

Besides the chairs, the conference also elects one additional member to each USCC committee.[10] Often the defeated candidate for chair is elected to the committee. These elected members are automatically members of the Administrative Committee/Board. Frequently those nominated to the Education Committee, the Communications Committee, and the Committee on Social Development and World Peace have been auxiliary bishops. Perhaps the Nominations Committee sees this as a way of allowing greater participation for auxiliary bishops who make up about one third of the conference. Many of those auxiliaries elected members of USCC committees have later gone on to become chairs or officers in the conference.[11]

Election politicking for committee chairs is low-key. As one bishop described the process: "If somebody, like a popular former president of the conference, thinks that somebody ought to be elected, and campaigns in some quiet fashion for him, it is wonderful to see how that works. It really does work." Between 1985 and 1989, two auxiliaries (O'Donnell and Steib) of Archbishop John May and two (Gregory and Vlazny) of Cardinal Joseph Bernardin were elected chairs in the conference. Auxiliaries of Cardinals Bernard Law and James Hickey have also been elected chairs.

But in most elections, the higher-ranking prelate wins the chair. In fact, any time a cardinal runs for a chair, he wins.[12] "You put a cardinal down and it is almost inevitable that he is going to get elected," explains Archbishop Kelly. "That is why they generally don't stand for committee chairs. Bernardin is one of the few who is willing to do that because if they put their name in, they are almost inevitably going to get it. It is very difficult for them, with all their other responsibilities, to run a committee well."

Auxiliary Bishop Edward J. O'Donnell of St. Louis in 1986 was nominated for chair of the Pro-Life Committee in what he jokingly called a "titanic clash" with Cardinal Bernardin. "When I received the request to allow my name to be entered, I inquired what good bishops do in a situation like that and was informed that you accept the nomination and pay your dues," he recalls. "I myself voted for Cardinal Bernardin, not out of any sense of propriety but in the sense that he was obviously the better choice, and I really cannot understand the motivation of anyone who voted for me." Bishop O'Donnell was swamped by a better than three-to-one vote.

The Committee on Pro-Life Activities has always had a cardinal in the chair "because we needed visible leadership," explains Archbishop Kelly. Cardinal Terence Cooke chaired an ad hoc pro-life committee for many years until his death, when Cardinal Bernardin was appointed. In 1986 it became a standing committee, and Cardinal Bernardin was its first elected chair. He was followed by Cardinal O'Connor in 1989.

Interestingly, the Nominations Committee has never had two cardinals run for the same chair. The committee does not generally nominate cardinals because the members feel "it is not fair to ask them to take on heavy committee work," reports Archbishop Kelly. "Heavy committee assignments are roles given to bishops who have relatively small dioceses and have a little time to deal with. You can be away from the diocese, and it doesn't hurt anything. But the people who have those mega-places, that really is difficult." The size of one's diocese does not always deter a man from being nominated and elected. In 1987 Roger Mahony, archbishop of the largest diocese in the United States, was elected chair of the Committee on International Policy, one of the busiest committees in the conference.

The election procedures for committee chairs encourage the dispersal of power among many bishops. The term of office is only three years, and the incumbent may neither succeed himself nor be elected to another chair until he has been out of office for a year. "That was Dearden's insistence," recalls Archbishop Kelly. "I remember that he was adamant about that." These rules make it difficult for a prelate to be reelected chair of the same committee[13] or to be elected chair of another committee. This was done consciously in reaction to the practice in NCWC. "The way the NCWC was set up," explains Archbishop Kelly, "the Administrative Board did almost everything. The bishops could just send the same ones back again and again, and some of the cardinals just stayed forever."

Despite the odds, some prelates who have the confidence of the bishops have been elected chairs of three or more different committees: Cardinal Joseph Bernardin for Communications, Canonical Affairs, Pro-Life Activities, and Marriage and Family Life; Archbishop Patrick Flores for Montezuma Seminary, Church in Latin America, and Permanent Diaconate; Cardinal James Hickey for Priestly Formation, Pastoral Research and Practices, Doctrine, Human Values, and North American College; Cardinal Bernard Law for Ecumenical and Interreligious Affairs, Pastoral Research and Practices, and Migration; Bishop James Malone for Liturgy, Liaison with Priests, Religious and Laity, and Social Development and World Peace (Domestic Policy); Archbishop John Quinn for Pastoral Research and Practices (twice), Liturgy, and Doctrine; Archbishop John Roach for Vocations, Priestly Formation, and Social Development and World Peace (International Policy); Archbishop John Whealon for Doctrine, Ecumenical and Interreligious Affairs, and Pastoral Research and Practices.[14] Four of these men (Cardinal Bernardin, Bishop Malone, Archbishop Quinn, and Archbishop Roach) were also presidents, indicating the high level of respect they hold among the bishops.

Ad Hoc Committees

Besides standing committees, the NCCB/USCC also has ad hoc committees whose chairs and members are usually appointed by the president to deal with particular issues. Sometimes the members are invited to serve by the chair after consulting with the general secretary. Creating ad hoc committees is one of the president's most important powers since he can use it to bypass a standing committee and influence the direction of the conference.

Some ad hoc committees lasted no longer than a few days while the assembly was in session. Others have continued for years although the conference has a sunset provision requiring their reauthorization by the assembly or the Administrative Committee/Board after three years. Some committees started as ad hoc committees and eventually became standing committees.[15] Ad hoc committees have been appointed to deal with a wide variety issues. They have been used to draft major documents like the "National Catechetical Directory," the peace pastoral, the economic pastoral, the 1989 statement on the Middle East, and the 1989 statement on HIV/AIDS.

Sometimes an ad hoc committee is appointed because the standing committee is too busy to deal with a topic. The Committee for Social Development and World Peace, for example, has a large agenda, so large that the committee was split in two in 1989 into domestic and international sections. "You can't overload a committee that way," explains the Rev. Bryan Hehir who staffed the Committee on Social Development and World Peace and the ad hoc committee writing the peace pastoral. "You can staff two committees, but you can't funnel all new business through the business of the same committee." Likewise, the Committee on Doctrine told the president it did not have time to respond to the Vatican document on episcopal conferences.

Ad hoc committees are also appointed to deal with issues that could come under several jurisdictions and that need special expertise. Thus the 1989 statement on the Middle East was drafted by an ad hoc committee chaired by Archbishop Mahony, who was also chair of the Committee on International Policy. He was helped by Archbishop William Keeler, an expert on Jewish-Catholic relations, and Cardinal O'Connor, head of the Catholic Near East Welfare Association.

Staffing such a mixed committee can be difficult since it involves many offices. On the Middle East statement, "the primary staff work was done by this office," explains Robert P.

Hennemeyer, director of the Office of International Justice and Peace. "Secondary roles were played by ecumenical affairs and the Near East foundation. It was confusing for a while, but after a while, as we got comfortable with each other, it worked all right." The ad hoc committee on HIV/AIDS was also staffed by several offices.

Some people believe ad hoc committees are sometimes appointed to take an issue away from a chair or committee who the president does not think is up to the task. Thus some believe that the catechetical directory was taken away from Bishop William McManus, chair of the Education Committee from 1975-78, and the peace pastoral was taken away from Bishop Mark Hurley, chair of the Committee on Social Development and World Peace from 1980-83. On the other hand, these projects were so time consuming it is difficult to see how their committees could have dealt with anything else while working on these documents.

Committees as Consensus Builders

As will be seen in the next chapter, the NCCB/USCC assembly prefers to operate by consensus. In the development of consensus, the committees perform an essential role. A common strategy for developing consensus is to appoint a committee whose members are respected by the other bishops. The president appoints all the members of an ad hoc committee, while the members of a standing committee are normally appointed by its chair. Thus when faced with developing a response to the controversial Vatican draft document on episcopal conferences in 1988, NCCB/USCC President John May appointed an ad hoc committee composed of all the former presidents of the conference. These prelates had both the respect of their peers and the expertise to respond. Any other bishops would have had a difficult time getting the bishops to approve a response so highly critical of a Vatican document. The presence of Cardinal Krol on this committee also made it difficult to categorize it as liberal.

In order to develop consensus, the members of a committee need to represent the various views in the conference. "If the committee is balanced, then they will listen to all sides before they make a recommendation," explains Monsignor Hoye. "If it is not balanced, then they may go off on their own." If a balanced committee reaches an agreement, it is likely the conference will follow. It is noteworthy that the first thing both Cardinal Bernardin and Cardinal O'Connor did after being elected chair of the Pro-Life Committee was to appoint the other to the committee.

Likewise, for the peace pastoral, Cardinal Bernardin realized that "unless we fight it out in the committee, unless we reach some consensus there, we will never get the consensus" in the assembly. Thus the drafting committee included Auxiliary Bishop Thomas Gumbleton of Detroit, a member of Pax Christi, and Auxiliary Bishop John O'Connor of the military ordinariate, a former Navy chaplain. "I needed people like Cardinal O'Connor, who represented a certain point of view," explained Cardinal Bernardin. "Without him I would never have been able to do it. I also needed Tom Gumbleton, so that worked out fine." "I wanted articulate people at the extremes," said Archbishop Roach, the president who appointed the ad hoc committee, "and I don't mean that pejoratively."[16] Likewise, Archbishop Rembert Weakland, chair of the committee that drafted the economic pastoral, felt that Archbishop Thomas Donnellan of Atlanta, a fiscal and theological conservative, was a key player in the committee.

Each year members of the conference are asked to fill out a preference form indicating which committees they are willing to serve on as members. Listed on the forum are only those committees that will have new chairs because the first job of a new chair will be to appoint members to his committee who serve as long as he is chair. The committees have five to seven members. Additional bishops can be appointed nonvoting consultants or advisors to popular committees such as Black Catholics, Doctrine, Ecumenical and Interreligious Affairs, Evangelization, Liturgy, Migration, Priestly Life and Ministry, Pro-Life Activities, and Religious Life and Ministry.

Since I was denied access to the preference forms, it is uncertain which committees are most popular, which bishops are turned down for membership, and which bishops do not volunteer to serve. What is clear is that in 1991, 96 bishops, or almost one-third of the membership, were not members or consultants of any standing or ad hoc NCCB/USCC committees.[17] Another 57 were members of only one committee. On the other hand, 42 bishops were on five or more committees. Most of these latter bishops were members of the Administrative Committee/Board.

At the June 1991 NCCB/USCC meeting, Archbishop Pilarczyk admitted that there was a "melodic motif" that sounds throughout the conference periodically that suggests that chairs pick their friends. He noted, however, that only 15 percent of the bishops return the preference forms on committee membership. Some bishops from poor dioceses said they cannot afford the travel expenses to attend committee meetings. As a result, beginning in 1993 the conference will reimburse the travel expenses of committee members who request it. But most observers believe that bishops who are not on committees are simply not interested in serving.

The NCCB committees have only bishops as members, but they often use consultants who participate actively at committee meetings. The USCC committees (Education, Communications, Social Development, and International Policy) have both bishops and nonepiscopal members. The Social Development and International Policy Committees, for example, have had international bankers, labor union officials, and former governors and ambassadors as members. A geographical spread is also desired on the committee. Normally the staff draws up a list of potential lay members and the chair selects whom he wants. "The chairs I worked under were very interested in who the bishops were," explains a staff person. "The non-bishops I could recommend, and they would rubber stamp, so the non-bishops were in 99 percent of the cases, my own choice." The nonepiscopal members are invited to serve by the chair after consultation with the general secretary and the president. They cannot serve more than two consecutive terms.

Although the bishops always have a majority on the USCC committees, absenteeism is higher among the bishops so that the working committee often may have a majority of laity. Because of their experience and expertise, the lay people are helpful within the committee, but in selling the results to the Administrative Committee/Board or to the assembly, it is the bishops who make the difference. "If you don't have a strong corps of bishops, you can't have an effective committee," reports John Carr, secretary for Social Development and World Peace. "When push comes to shove, when the Administrative Board is making a decision, when it's before the body, the fact that Jerry Apodaca [former governor of New Mexico] was involved doesn't cut much. Or Tom Trebat [of Ford Foundation] or Jean Wilkowski [former ambassador]. [Archbishops] Mahony or Roach or Lipscomb or whoever cuts."

The committee members are dependent on staff work, but they are not rubber stamps to staff ideas. "Generally speaking, the staff, who were energetic, imaginative, and creative, were never able to get past the committee what the committee didn't want," explains Bishop Malone. "There is a sense of ownership which the bishop has about the work of the conference that allows the least talented among us to get on his hind legs if he feels he is being pushed around."

Importance of Chairs

The chair of a committee contributes a great deal to its success. All of the bishops have experience working with committees in their dioceses, but some are better at it than others. "If a strong personality among the bishops headed the committee, the committee took on new verve and vision," explains Bishop Malone. "For example, when Jim Hickey—who is a very energetic and forceful person in an organization way—when he took on the Committee for Human Values, a committee that had been languishing for a purpose suddenly saw its purpose and saw as well many facets of its activity that had been untouched."

Some chairs are knowledgeable in the topics of their committees before taking charge. Archbishop Weakland brought to the Liturgy Committee "a tremendous background in liturgy and music," according to the Rev. John Gurrieri who staffed the committee. "He was always on top of the material." Likewise, Archbishop Daniel Pilarczyk with a doctorate in classics "was able to deal with a lot of translation issues and questions, grasp them, and present them to the bishops convincingly." On the other hand, Archbishop Bernardin did not have a degree in canon law and yet was elected chair of the Committee on Canonical Affairs in 1978. As chair, he was greatly helped by the canonists from the conference staff and from the Canon Law Society of America.

Being well organized, especially on the busier committees, is important. Archbishop Pilarczyk "is able to organize the agenda very well, and get everybody to speak, and know the proportion of time you spend on one item over against another," says Father Gurrieri.

But different chairs have different styles. None more exemplify this difference than Cardinals Bernardin and O'Connor. Cardinal Bernardin is "the kind of chairman who opens up a question and gets everybody else talking about what they want to do first," explains Richard Doerflinger, who staffs the Pro-Life Office.

> He talks last and says, "Well what I hear everyone saying here is . . . ." He draws it all into a consensus statement. We have very few votes in that committee. Most things are done by consensus, and done by a consensus crystallized through his restatement of what people are saying. He really is an incredible chairman, an incredible man for building agreement in a group.

Cardinal O'Connor, on the other hand, has "a very different style," says Mr. Doerflinger.

> Cardinal O'Connor stated his own preference for what he'd like to do first. But then he went around and said, "Now how do you react to that?" And got comments from everybody and took it all in.
>
> He likes to really thrash out an issue and he'll mix it up with you, and it's a much more polarized kind of discussion. But it blows over very quickly, and at the end of the meeting, he's slapping you on the

back and saying, "Great discussion." He likes to get all the disagreements out there and even sharpen them so that you know what the disagreement is and resolve the disagreement. Or, if necessary, just say "Well, we can't agree on this and maybe we'll have to move on to something else" or realize that this is going to need further discussion.

The participation of the staff in the committee discussions varies with chairs. Most, like Cardinals Bernardin and O'Connor, encourage staff participation. Some, like Archbishop Adam Maida and Bishop John Keating, have had committee meetings without the staff. If the chair has mastered the material on the committee's agenda, meeting without the staff can make the less prepared committee members dependent on him for expert advice.

The chair plays a critical role in developing consensus within the committee. In a standing committee, the chair appoints the other members of his committee, which, as indicated above, can be very important. He also works with the committee staff and runs committee meetings. Who is chair can also have a strong impact on how a committee proposal is met by the assembly. A chair who has the confidence of the body of bishops has an easier time getting his committee documents and resolutions passed by the assembly. "That's absolutely crucial," explains the Rev. Bryan Hehir, the bishops' international expert. "There are certain people the conference is not going to repudiate."

Persistence and courage also make a difference. "Bishop [Bernard] Flanagan, from Worcester, was a courageous old man," recalls Monsignor Heintschel, "a man who fought for the American procedural norms [for annulments] on the floor of the conference and eventually won it." Likewise, the persistence of Bishop Ernest Unterkoefler, chair of the Diaconate Committee, helped create the diaconate program in the United States.

Committee Procedures

Once a committee and its chair are in place, they cannot simply do anything they want. The conference has procedures and policies for guiding committees in their work. The conference as a whole develops policies and plans that guide the committees, as will be explained in Chapter 9. The conference's 1971 regulations also require that joint pastorals and formal statements "be formally initiated only by the general membership or the Administrative Committee in consultation with the appropriate committees." In 1981, this was made more explicit so that a committee had to get the assembly's approval before drafting a major statement. This regulation was aimed at keeping committees from drafting pastorals that no one was interested in. The regulations indicate that time constraints may not always permit this ideal, but the assembly must be given the opportunity to say whether it wishes to consider a particular issue before a draft is formally presented.

Before an item is dealt with by the assembly, the committee and its staff may hold hearings, consult widely, and prepare a series of drafts for discussion. A final draft must be circulated to all the bishops, with requests for suggestions at least one month before it is considered at a conference meeting. For major documents, a committee will distribute preliminary drafts for comment.

A series of questions and answers, presented by Cardinal Krol and adopted by the assembly in 1973, describes the process employed in preparing a conference document:

> A statement can be drafted in many different ways. It can be written by one author. It can be divided into sections and each section can be written by a different person. It can be written from the start by a bishop or bishops. It can be drafted by a consultant or consultants and submitted for review to a committee of bishops.
>
> It can be prepared through a process of extremely wide consultation at the national and local levels; consultation can be restricted to a small number of specialists in the field being treated; or there can be no consultation at all. Circumstances will dictate the process—including the time available, the purpose or purposes of the document, the preexistence (or non-existence) of widespread consensus in

the Catholic community regarding the subject matter, etc. In so far as possible, a process should be devised and implemented which is suited to the exigencies of this particular document.

Also, in the future it may prove increasingly desirable to provide interested individuals and organizations outside the bishops' conference with drafts of major documents and invite them to submit their criticisms and suggestions for revision—without, of course, guaranteeing that their views will prevail. Among other things, such a procedure is likely to increase the acceptance of bishops' statements among concerned parties.[18]

Wide consultation during the drafting of important documents has been a hallmark of the U.S. bishops' conference. "To Teach as Jesus Did" was the first pastoral letter to be approved after public consultation on a first draft. It was sent in January 1972 to all the bishops with the suggestion that they consult widely with their educational staff and nonprofessionals. "Within two months the USCC Washington office had received over 500 pages of comments, suggestions, and proposed changes, all reflecting each bishops' extensive consultation with his staff and with other persons whose counsel he had sought and received."[19] "It was Ray Lucker [then director of the education office] who conceived the process that has now become standard of drafting a document, and getting it out in the field," recalls Bishop William E. McManus who chaired the drafting committee. "So we had wide, wide consultation. It went through that whole procedure and established a very important precedent."

The public consultation on the 1977 "National Catechetical Directory" was even more extensive than for the 1972 pastoral on education.[20] It took six years to complete and involved three drafts. "There were national, regional, and diocesan consultations," recalls Bishop Lucker, "that generated hundreds of thousands of written interventions."[21] There were consultations on all three drafts. Archbishop John Whealon of Hartford, who chaired the drafting committee, recalls the extensive consultation:

> The text was printed by *Our Sunday Visitor*, printed in tabloid form, and thousands of copies circulated through the country. We

asked for responses from dioceses, from bishops, Catholic groups. We welcomed all the responses and as a result of that, issued a second draft and did the same thing. And then [we did] the third draft, [and a] third consultation.

The first draft was given rather rough treatment by many people, which seems to be rather standard. The second was looked at much more favorably. And the third was well-received, so we improved the whole time.

Now the results of it, I do believe that it generally terminated the polarization that was so bitter at that time. It didn't solve all of our problems and we still have them, but it did a great, great deal.

The "National Catechetical Directory" has proven highly successful. After more than a dozen years, it continues to be a practical guide for religious educators and textbook writers. Likewise, after going through extensive consultation and a number of drafts, the economic and peace pastorals had wide impact.[22] Often these consultations took place in diocesan pastoral councils and the diocesan bishop would forward the results to the drafting committee.[23] Some drafting committees also held hearings modeled on congressional hearings where experts would testify on specific topics. Thus experts on military and foreign affairs made presentations to the committee drafting the peace pastoral, and economists and business persons testified before the committee drafting the economic pastoral.

Whether a proposal is going to pass easily or have trouble on the floor depends on several factors, according to a staff person: "the nature of the issue, who is the chair, what is the track record of the committee on this issue, where does the pope stand, are there other bishops' conferences involved, is there going to be much pressure from outside?" Some of these factors will be considered in the next chapter.

Administrative Committee/Board

When a committee wishes to submit an item to the full assembly, it must first go through the NCCB Administrative Committee or the USCC Administrative Board, which set the agenda for their respective bodies and act in the name of the conference between meetings of the assembly. The 53 members of the Administrative Committee and the Administrative Board are identical: the president, vice president, treasurer, secretary, the chair of the board of directors of Catholic Relief Services (CRS), the chair of the board of the Catholic Telecommunications Network of America (CTNA), the chairs of NCCB/USCC standing committees, one elected member of the USCC committees, and for one year, the immediate past president of the conference. Representatives are also elected by the 13 NCCB regions.[24] The committee/board meetings are open only to bishops and a few staff.

Since the Administrative Committee/Board controls the agenda, it can keep a committee item from going to the floor, but tradition limits this power. "It's pretty hard to say no," explains Archbishop William Keeler, "because the chair comes in and has got the enthusiasm and commitment of a committee behind him." From an earlier day there was a strong resistance on the part of individual bishops—that the Administrative Committee should not be a gatekeeper to the floor of the conference," reports Bishop Malone. "As the years went on and as the agenda became bigger and more complex, there was a recognition that there had to be some sorting out of this."

"There is a gatekeeping function," reports Archbishop Pilarczyk, "but there is also a certain sentiment that the Administrative Committee does not have the right to keep a chairman from the floor with his thing." Rarely does it come to a showdown. "Often enough, it will happen that the chairman comes along with something," explains Archbishop Pilarczyk, "and the Administrative Committee says, 'This is awful. We hope you won't do this because of this, this, this. And what about that, that, that?' And the chairman will say, 'Thank you very much, I withdraw.' And he comes back half a year later with something else."

After listening to the Administrative Committee/Board criticize his proposal, a smart chair "realizes that it is not going to go any place unless there is more work done on it," explains Bishop Malone. "So then he takes that back to his committee and it will reappear maybe the next time."

The group can be brutal about saying to a committee chair, "You're not ready, that's not ready," if the proposal is immature or premature or just "dumb," according to Archbishop Roach. "Now you [as chair] have a chance there to try to persuade them that they're wrong and that you want to go to the full body, but they've got a chance to say, that is not going on the agenda. And that is a very healthy thing, very healthy."

Technically, the Administrative Committee/Board only approves the item for presentation to the assembly, but it sometimes recommends changes that a wise committee chair takes seriously. "Often the chairman will change a statement in response to what he hears from the Administrative Committee," explains Monsignor Hoye. "The Administrative Committee gives him an idea of what the bishops think."

The Administrative Committee/Board, which meets privately four times a year, is a key player in the development of consensus. When a chair brings an item to the 53 member Administrative Committee/Board, he quickly gets a taste for how the rest of the conference will respond. Many of the "movers and shakers" in the conference are present on the Administrative Committee/Board, notes Bishop Malone. "So a bit of consensus-building is really done on the Administrative Committee because they have the first cut at any of the proposals that are needing approval." Because of the various interests represented in the committee/board, he notes, "There is an opportunity to hear how deeply felt that group expresses its opinion on an issue" and "to hear not only what is said, but who says it."

Besides setting the agenda of conference assemblies, the Administrative Committee/Board can allow committees to issue documents, except those on priesthood, in their own names. Although committee documents have less authority than documents from the Administrative Committee/Board or from the assembly, they are frequently seen as "conference" documents by the public and media. Allowing committees on occasion to issue statements is opposed by only 17 percent of the bishops, while 83 percent believe that the committees can and should be authorized to issue statements in their own name.[25]

The bishops are willing to allow committees to issue statements because the Administrative Committee/Board provides a check on NCCB/USCC committees to make sure that they do not act independently of the conference and publish statements that would be objectionable to the rest of the conference.

But any document focusing on the ministry or life of priests must be reviewed by the whole NCCB assembly. A number of bishops were unhappy with the publications of the Committee on Priestly Life and Ministry which the Administrative Committee/Board had approved for distribution. *Reflections on Priestly Morale,* published in 1988, especially came under criticism for being too negative and for reflecting the views of a limited number of experts and priests.[26] In June 1989 the conference in executive session voted that any publication about priests had to be reviewed by the assembly. Issues touching priests have always been sensitive for the bishops, as will be seen in the next chapter.

Sometimes the Administrative Committee/Board likes a committee document so much that it adopts it as its own. The Education Committee "went to the Administrative Board with a request to do a statement on values and public education," reports the Rev. Thomas Gallagher, secretary of the education department. "In the course of their deliberations on that, they made that their own. That was not a bad thing for us because it gave the statement more weight. In fact, we had hoped that they would do that, and that's why we went in the other way. If we had asked for that, they might not have done it."

The Administrative Committee/Board has frequently issued statements in the name of the conference.[27] In the international field, the committee/board has been especially concerned about civil wars (Nigeria in 1968, El Salvador in 1981, Namibia in 1983, Nicaragua in 1985 and 1986, and Yugoslavia and the Soviet Union in 1991) and refugees and migrants (East Pakistanis in 1971, South East Asians in 1978, and the world in 1982). Other statements on international topics include: human rights in Chile and Brazil (1974), the Panama Canal (1975), peace (1978), South Africa (1985 and 1986), Third World debt (1989), and Eastern and Central Europe (1990).

The Administrative Committee/Board has also spoken on ethical and social issues in the United States: abortion (1973), religion in public schools (1973), clemency for war resisters (1974), hunger (1974 and 1975), New York City's financial crisis (1975), gun control (1975), TV family viewing period (1975), Youngstown steel mill closing (1977), the draft (1980), Social Security (1983), tuition tax credits (1983), communications (1985), federal budget (1986), Ku Klux Klan (1987), moral education in the public school (1987), AIDS (1987), school-based clinics (1988), homelessness and housing (1988), immigration policy (1988), and euthanasia (1991). Beginning in 1976, the Administrative Board has also issued a statement every four years on political responsibility and voting. When speaking on these questions, the Administrative Committee/Board would take positions on public policy questions and also discuss the role of the church in responding to these issues.

The Administrative Committee/Board also dealt with internal church issues such as the Catholic charismatic renewal (1974), Catholic teachers' unions (1977), sterilization in Catholic hospitals (1977), an affirmative action plan for NCCB/USCC (1979), lay ministry (1980), the pastoral care of immigrants (1986), and priests and child abuse (1989).

What statements can be approved by the Administrative Committee/Board and what should go to the entire conference is a disputed issue. "If it is a short statement and in accord with established policy, it is fine for the Administrative Committee to do that," explains Archbishop Kelly. "If it is something relatively new that we haven't looked at before, and that might impact on everybody, then they would take it to the body of bishops, especially if it is a longer document."

Time constraints can mean that if the Administrative Committee/Board does not speak, the opportunity will be gone before the assembly can meet and act. This is often the case with an international crisis, a refugee situation, or an issue that is being considered by Congress. Also, if the agenda of the assembly is packed, the Administrative Committee/Board might deal with an item of less importance that cannot wait.

Sometimes the Administrative Committee/Board will initiate consideration of a complex and controversial topic that is later taken up by the full assembly. In these cases, the Administrative Committee/Board statement establishes a precedent or framework for what the conference might do. Dealing with peace and disarmament followed such a step-by-step process. In 1978, the Administrative Committee/Board issued a three-page statement on peace and disarmament. "It's high on poetry and low on analytical stuff," comments one staff person, but it put the bishops on record. Then the board debated what position to take on SALT II and decided to support it. Later, Cardinal Krol testified for the conference in favor of the treaty. "So we went from the 1978 statement to the Krol testimony, which was 18 months later," recalls Father Hehir. "The next step beyond that was the decision in 1980 to write the Peace Pastoral" which was completed in 1983.

Likewise, the Administrative Committee/Board spoke on the Panama Canal 20 months before the assembly did. The board also spoke on El Salvador nine months before the assembly passed a statement on Central America in 1981.

The committee also issued a statement on school-based clinics in 1988 before the assembly did. Originally the issue was going to be dealt with on the local level, "but the interest among bishops around the country was so intense and so many of them were being hit with that problem and having to issue statements of their own," recalls Mr. Doerflinger. "Ultimately we felt this statement should be looked at by all the bishops to make sure that they agree that this is the right approach to take."

Whether to have a document issued by a committee, the Administrative Committee/Board, or the assembly is sometimes a debated point. Going to the full assembly increases the authority and visibility of the statement, but it also increases the time and effort involved in processing it. Sometimes a committee will want to issue a statement on its own because it is easier and will not involve amendments from other bishops.

In 1989 the Administrative Committee debated which body should issue a statement on vocations drafted by the Vocations

Committee. Many wanted vocations to be treated by the full body or by the Administrative Committee, since it is such a serious issue. On the other hand, the bishops felt the Vocations Committee statement was inadequate and would need extensive work before it would be ready for higher approval. The Administrative Committee decided to allow the Vocations Committee to issue the statement rather than have it delayed indefinitely.

Other considerations come into play. "It depends on how technical the statement is sometimes," explains Mr. Doerflinger.

> The guidelines for technical legislation on life-sustaining treatment, those were just a Pro-Life Committee statement. It was approved for issuance in our name by the Administrative Committee and that was because it really was a set of guidelines, a kind of advisory document. We didn't want to give it the kind of authority it might take on from going to the general body.
>
> Something like the pastoral plan for pro-life activities, on the other hand—which was sent to the body of bishops first in '75 and was reaffirmed with revisions in '85—that actually called on the church and church agencies and institutions throughout the country to take certain action in light of the seriousness of the abortion issue. You can't call on dioceses to do something unless all the bishops have signed off on it. That had to be given much higher authority.
>
> So sometimes it's a matter of the level of authority you want to give to something, the level of clout. Sometimes it depends on how many bishops have been having to deal with this already in their own dioceses.

Frequently several reasons will argue for issuing a statement by the Administrative Committee/Board rather than the entire assembly, as happened with the statement on the Third World debt. "The agenda for the general meeting was so crowded," explains Robert P. Hennemeyer. "The circuits were overloaded. To have added another major statement to that agenda would have just been impossible. Also, the precise week the Administrative Board was meeting was the week that the World Bank and the IMF were holding their annual meetings, and Third World debt was on everybody's mind. So we thought it was timely, and it relieved the general meeting. And some of us think for subjects that are somewhat specialized, or somewhat arcane, maybe the Administrative Board is the body to issue it."

In general, the bishops approve of the work of the Administrative Committee/Board, although 31 percent of the bishops think it is too powerful.[28] The conference appears to swing back and forth in its view of how active the Administrative Committee/Board, should be in issuing statements. Sometimes the bishops say, "We don't want all this stuff [in the assembly], and why isn't Administrative [Board/Committee] doing it?" explains Archbishop Kelly, "until the Administrative [Board/Committee] does something that they don't like, and then they immediately get angry about, 'Why isn't this coming to us?'"

"There is a built-in tension between what the Administrative Committee should do and what the full body should do," admits Archbishop Pilarczyk.

> At any given moment, on the Administrative Committee, you'll have somebody saying, "This should not be decided here, this should be decided by the full body," and you'll have somebody else saying, "No, we have the responsibility when the full body is not in session, and we cannot abdicate our responsibility."
>
> So it's not a cut-and-dried thing. The Administrative Committee has to make a judgment call. And, as with all judgment calls, you can differ. It's a prudential judgment, and part of the essence of prudential judgment is that another prudent man could make a different judgment.

The AIDS statement issued by the Administrative Board in 1987 proved to be very controversial. Archbishop May, president at the time, recalls:

> We had been importuned to do something because of the pressure at that time to say something about this new epidemic of AIDS. We were given to understand that the bishops wanted something done. So when we got the statement finished, we decided to issue it even though very shortly thereafter, all the bishops were coming together—in fact, in a couple of days.

"By hindsight," he admits, "it certainly would have been more prudent to wait until the entire conference was in session" and then present it as a draft document. But since under the rules the conference could not vote on it at that meeting, "We would have had to push it back then until the next general session" in another six months, he says.

The most controversial paragraph of the AIDS document dealt with condoms, and many bishops preferred that the Administrative Board deal with it because they did not want the bishops debating condoms in front of the press. Rather than settling the condom issue, the board's statement caused an embarrassing public debate among the bishops.

The Administrative Committee/Board, with 53 elected members, accounts for about 17 percent of the conference membership. "Our critics don't like to admit that our governing board is incredibly large by comparison with governing boards of other similar-sized membership organizations," notes Monsignor Lynch. It has a geographical spread because 13 members are elected from the 13 NCCB/USCC regions. "The Administrative Committee is a pretty good reflection of the total body," says Archbishop Roach. "Maybe a few more activists, because activists tend to get elected chairpersons of committees, but other than that it is pretty much representative."

Many participants argue that the discussions in the Administrative Committee/Board are better than in the assembly because the committee/board is smaller and the meetings are closed.[29] "I've always felt the best discussions in the conference are in the Administrative Board," reports Father Hehir. "The trouble is, they're not public, but that also is what contributes to the discussion. You can define an issue very nicely within the board and then get a really good debate on it. You never get the same analytical clarity in the body's debate as you do at the board."

The discussions, because they are private, tend to be more open and frank. When discussing a proposed statement on the Middle East in 1989, the Administrative Committee talked about the reactions to the draft from Arab and Jewish groups in the United States and abroad, and as a result the draft that went to the assembly was refined considerably to reflect their concerns. The Administrative Committee/Board members are also more frank in privately discussing their legislative agenda and strategy, their relations with Rome, and financial and personnel issues.

National Advisory Council

Before an issue even reaches the Administrative Committee/Board, it is considered by the U.S. Catholic Bishops' National Advisory Council (NAC). This 63 member advisory group to the Administrative Committee/Board is composed of bishops, diocesan priests, religious, and lay members.[30] The bishops come from the Administrative Committee/Board so that they can feed the reflections of the council into the committee/board deliberations. The religious are selected by the Conference of Major Superiors of Men and the Leadership Conference of Women Religious. The laity and priests are selected on a regional basis in different ways in different regions. The at-large members are appointed by the NCCB/USCC president, who often looks for people to represent groups not elected to the council: for example, young people and ethnic groups. The council's members come from a variety of occupations: judges, doctors, housewives, teachers, legislators, sociologists, and laborers. The council is staffed by Francis Doyle, associate general secretary.

"I have never seen an organization with such deep love and concern about the church and such a sense of bonding that occurs among the group," says Msgr. Donald Heintschel, who worked with them for 17 years, either as a member or as staff support. "It comes out of their prayer experience, their liturgical experience, their concern about their being credible, their concern about doing an honest task with the material that they have been given, and to honestly give their opinions to the bishops about what they've heard and what they believe."

The National Advisory Council meets to discuss the agenda of the Administrative Committee/Board before the Administrative Committee/Board meets. NAC members receive the same agenda material that the Administrative Committee/Board members get. The NAC Executive Committee picks out six or seven issues for the NAC to concentrate on, rather than trying to superficially cover everything on the agenda of the Administrative Committee/Board. "They'll shape the agenda for their meeting," explains Ms. Leckey, executive director of the NCCB Secretariat for Family Life, Laity, Women, and Youth. "They go through all the documentation and say what it is that they should really be giving their attention to."

When the NAC meets, it gets briefed by the NCCB/USCC staff, discusses the issues selected by the Executive Committee, and makes recommendations to the Administrative Committee/Board. Normally it would make recommendations on all the major issues before the Administrative Committee/Board. NAC has made recommendations on many issues, especially marriage and family life, catechetics, youth, vocations, women, lay ministry, priestly life, resigned priests, and shared responsibility (especially in parishes, priests' councils, and diocesan pastoral councils). After the Administrative Committee/Board adjourns, these recommendations are referred to the appropriate offices and committees of the conference. The officers of the NAC also meet with the conference staff to convey the NAC's recommendations to them.

The NAC is advisory to the Administrative Committee/Board, not to the entire NCCB/USCC. At the beginning of the Administrative Committee/Board meeting, the NAC chair presents a 10-15 minute oral report and a 20-page written report on the NAC discussions, but no report is given to the full body of bishops. After giving the report, the NAC chair leaves and the episcopal members of the NAC act as "designated hitters" during the Administrative Committee/Board meeting, noting the position taken by the NAC on various agenda items.

The NAC observers attend the NCCB/USCC assembly meetings, and the NAC chair used to make a presentation at the close of the bishops' meeting giving the consensus of the NAC observers as to how the bishops' meeting went. "That went about three or four times," explains a former NAC member. "The bishops didn't like to hear what they were hearing. So they decided they would appoint a bishop editor to edit what they heard, and that stopped that."

Because the NAC recommendations are confidential, "Their effect has been hidden, which is too bad," comments Msgr. Daniel Hoye, former general secretary of the conference. "There have been documents that have been killed or changed or put off because of advice from them to the Administrative Committee." For example, an early draft of the pastoral letter on campus ministry was sent back to committee on recommendation of NAC. Also, in 1989 the NAC voted 21-4 against having the Administrative Committee approve a statement on vocations. Instead the document was published as a statement of the Vocations Committee.

On the other hand, the same year, by 31-2 the NAC recommended the Vocations Committee "research the wider extension of a married, ordained priesthood." Later the council also opposed the statement on lay preaching. These recommendations were ignored by the bishops. In 1991, the NAC recommended the publication of a secret document on the morality of terminating nutrition and hydration for dying patients, which was later discussed in executive session at the November bishops' meeting. The document was not made public until six months later.

The work of the NAC has not been purely reactive. "They also have proactive agenda that they've been developing over the years," explains Ms. Leckey. Among the items on this agenda have been women, lay ministry, and resigned priests. It was the NAC that asked the Laity Office to study diocesan pastoral councils, which resulted in a major study and many workshops.[31] "That got passed on to the Administrative Committee, then to our office, and then I brought it to the Laity Committee and they said 'Let's do it,'" recalls Ms. Leckey. "We did a study with Gene Hemrick and had workshops. Jim Provost was involved in this. George Wilson facilitated the whole thing. That was a very good project. It really began with one woman [in the NAC] who said, 'What in the world are these councils doing all over this country?'"

The meetings of the NAC are closed and its recommendations are secret, so it is difficult to analyze its operations and judge its effectiveness. Those interviewed believe that it has been an effective if weak instrument for lay input into the NCCB/USCC. That the council's recommendations have not always been followed might be considered a weakness, but this is also a clear indication that the council is willing to make recommendations that are controversial and challenging to episcopal views.

Support for the council among the bishops is weak. A 1991 survey found 41 percent of the bishops wanting to reduce its small budget of $77,000.[32] This was a higher percentage than for any other item in the NCCB/USCC budget. Giving its recommendations only to the Administrative Committee/Board may limit its support among the other bishops who have no experience with it. Some believe that the council would be more effective if its recommendations were public.[33] On the other hand, open sessions might make it more difficult for free and blunt discussion. In addition, publicity to critical views of the NAC might make it lose support among the bishops and make it subject to criticism from the Vatican. Because of the current climate in the church, attempts to strengthen the NAC at this time might kill it.

Someday the NAC might evolve into a national pastoral council, which would be the logical way for facilitating dialogue between bishops and the laity on the national level. There was a spurt of interest in the idea of a national pastoral council in 1970, but experiences in the Netherlands made the Vatican very negative toward such councils.[34] The U.S. experience with the Detroit Call to Action also soured many U.S. bishops on the idea of a national pastoral council. They did not want to provide a forum for views at odds with the hierarchy. In addition, there were unresolved questions about how such a council would be structured.

Some people think that the NAC was Cardinal John Dearden's backdoor attempt to have a national pastoral council.[35] The NAC was less threatening than a national pastoral council since its role was limited to reviewing the agenda of the Administrative Committee/Board and making recommendations to it.

Conclusion

An examination of NCCB/USCC election procedures and election results shows that power is dispersed in the conference. The conference has constructed a system that makes it difficult, but not impossible, for someone to retain power over a long period. Short, nonrenewable terms for officers and committee chairs mean that there is a rapid and constant turnover of the elected leadership of the conference. As can be seen in table 5.1, only 22 bishops have served ten or more years on the Administrative Committee or Board in the 26 years from 1967-92. Over half these bishops are retired or deceased, which means that they can no longer be elected to the committee/board.

The election rules guarantee that a small episcopal clique cannot control the conference. On the other hand, the rapid turnover of leadership also reduces the ability of the leadership to develop the expertise and contacts that are useful in furthering the goals and interests of the conference. Often officers and chairs find they must finish the work begun by others and have little time to initiate new projects.

Despite the rapid turnover in offices, there are movers and shakers in the conference to whom the membership regularly turns for leadership. One way of identifying these leaders is to see which bishops have the longest tenures on the Administrative Committee or Board. Table 5.1 lists the bishops who have served ten or more years on the committee or board from 1967 to 1992. Many NCCB/USCC officers are clustered at the top of this list. Also on the list are men who had been elected committee chairs or who have regional rather than national support.

The conference leadership is to some extent self-selected because a bishop has to be willing to do the work required of a leadership position. How many bishops turn down the chance for leadership positions is uncertain. Since only 15 percent of the bishops return the annual committee preference form, bishops are clearly not beating down the doors trying to become chairs. Anecdotal evidence indicates that some prelates approached by the nominations committee do decline to run. Others are not asked because it is known they do not want the work. Being an officer or a committee chair is an honor but it also takes time and work. Bishop Malone notes, "We historically have had able bishops who are not willing to invest the time in conference work."

Table 5.1: Bishops With Ten or More Years on the NCCB Administrative Committee/Board (1967-92)[36]

Name	Number of Years
James Malone	20
Joseph Bernardin	19
John Quinn	16
+ John Krol	15
John May	15
+ Terence Cooke	14
John Roach	14
+ Thomas Donnellan	13
Daniel Pilarczyk	13
James Hickey	12
+ William Connare	11
+ John Carberry	11
Thomas Kelly	11
+ Timothy Manning	11
John McGann	11
+ Ernest Unterkoefler	11
Patrick Flores	10
+ Andrew Grutka	10
+ George Guilfoyle	10
+ Philip Hannan	10
+ Mark Hurley	10
+ John Whealon	10

+ Retired or Deceased

The NCCB/USCC leaders must work through conference committees and structures which further encourage teamwork and consensus-building. As will be explained in the next chapter, sometimes the committees are successful in developing consensus and sometimes they are not. But making decisions by consensus is a clear goal of the conference. Consensus in committee increases the chances of having consensus in the assembly.

6. A United or Divided Flock

It is commonly seen as unwise in the NCCB to raise three issues: holy days of obligation, age of confirmation, and new special collections.
————ARCHBISHOP JOHN MAY

Ambiguity is a legitimate and treasured part of our moral tradition. Perhaps the consensus will be on ambiguity.
————ARCHBISHOP JOHN ROACH

Can [the NCCB/USCC] speak to our age in a prophetic voice, or does the necessity of consensus mute its voice?[1]
————CARDINAL JOHN DEARDEN

The meetings are too large, the agenda too heavy, the time is too short.
————BISHOP AUSTIN B. VAUGHAN

I know of few comparable groups who would accomplish so much with such a high degree of unanimity in only a few days.
————ARCHBISHOP JOHN MAY

The ultimate authority for the NCCB/USCC is all the bishops gathered in assembly. These assembly meetings occur, for the most part, in public and disclose conflict and consensus among the bishops. The NCCB/USCC has developed procedures for reducing conflict and fostering consensus, including the use of *Robert's Rules of Order*. This chapter will examine the workings of the NCCB/USCC assembly and the areas of conflict and consensus among the bishops.

In the 25 years since the close of the Second Vatican Council, the Catholic church has gone through more change than it did in the last 300 years. This has been a time of much controversy and conflict. It would be a miracle if the NCCB/USCC were free of the conflict that afflicted the church during this period. At the same time, it would be false to see the bishops' conference as the site of constant turmoil and division.

Just how split are the American bishops, and what specific issues divide them? For this analysis, I will separate the conference agenda into three parts: pastoral letters and statements, internal church administration (especially liturgical and canonical issues), and internal conference questions, especially finances which will be dealt with in Chapter 9.

Consensus, or Majority Rule?[2]

Much of the theological and canonical writing on episcopal conferences urges bishops to make decisions by consensus rather than by simple majority vote. It is felt that consensus decision-making more accurately models the church as a faith community united in charity. Imposing a decision opposed by 49 percent of the bishops could be harmful to unity.

The *instrumentum laboris* on the theological and juridical status of episcopal conferences, for example, urged episcopal conferences to have "in possible cases, the indication of the goal of pursuing a morally unanimous consensus, without making this a juridical norm, which would seem too paralyzing."[3]

Canon law does not normally require unanimous consensus before a juridic body can act. Although the Code of Canon Law, quoting Justinian, states that "what touches all as individuals must be approved by all,"[4] the code rarely indicates where this rule applies. And the meaning of the terms "touches" and "approved" is much debated by canonists.[5]

Normally, what is required of juridic bodies is less demanding than consensus: "that action will have the force of law which, when a majority of those who must be convoked are present, receives the approval of an absolute majority of those who are present. . . ."[6] In other words, as long as a majority of the body is present, a majority of those present may make legally binding decisions.

For episcopal conferences, however, more than a simple majority is required for legally binding decisions. According to canon law, decisions that are binding on the bishops must be approved by at least a two-thirds majority of the conference membership and must be reviewed (*recognita*) by the Holy

See.[7] Strictly speaking, this canonical requirement applies only to general "decrees,"[8] not to pastoral plans, nonbinding guidelines, or pastoral statements or letters. For example, the 1987 pastoral plan for Hispanic ministry required only a majority of those present and voting. Likewise, reaffirming the pastoral plans for pro-life activities (1985) and for marriage and family life (1990) required only a majority. In fact, all three items were overwhelmingly approved.

In 1968, however, the American bishops decided to require a two-thirds majority vote of their membership for approval of "joint pastorals" and "statements" by the NCCB or the USCC.[9] This self-imposed restriction is not required by the Code of Canon Law. In its regulations, the bishops' conference distinguishes among "joint pastorals," "formal statements," "special messages," and "resolutions and other brief statements."[10] In the minds of some, these categories reflect a hierarchy of authority, although the levels of authority attached to the various types of documents have never been clearly explained.

The difference between a joint pastoral and a formal statement is procedural, not substantive. "They seemed to be almost interchangeable," admitted Archbishop John Roach, then NCCB president, except that a joint pastoral may only be issued by the NCCB assembly, while a formal statement may be approved by either the NCCB or the USCC assembly.[11]

The bishops have tended to use joint pastorals for more important pronouncements. But formal statements also carry great weight. "A formal statement is one with an official character which commits the conference to a particular position."[12] Formal statements by the NCCB require a two-thirds vote of the membership, but formal statements by the USCC can be approved by two-thirds of those present and voting at a meeting.

Special messages, resolutions, and other brief statements can be approved by two-thirds of the bishops "present and attending the general meeting."[13] More importantly, less notice to the membership and less review by committees is required of these latter documents before their consideration by the assembly. They often respond to concerns that arise at the last minute before or during a meeting. In 1991 the conference approved two documents called "reflections," one on priests' councils and the other on the teaching role of bishops. "Reflections" are not covered by the two-thirds rule and therefore the documents only required a majority vote.[14] These documents were called "reflections" because the bishops did not want to give them the authority of a statement or guidelines.

The rules governing statements were proposed, according to the Rev. Walter J. Woods, "in order to deal more effectively with problems related to the number of statements being considered, the priority among them, the need to assure sufficient consideration of a text before voting on it, and the very process of amendment and approval."[15] The "rules facilitate the formation of a consensus among the bishops and insure that they will have control over the actual text to be adopted or rejected."[16]

These regulations apply to both the NCCB and the USCC. Cardinal Lawrence Shehan of Baltimore, who drafted the 1968 regulations, attempted to distinguish the kinds of statements that would be issued by each:

> The body of U.S. Bishops may speak collectively through either of its two agencies, the NCCB and the USCC. Which agency is used depends upon the determination of the Bishops and the subject matter involved. No hard and fast rule can be set for the choice of one agency as opposed to another. As a practical matter, however, the language of the Booz, Allen & Hamilton report provides a general guideline.
>
> NCCB shall address itself to "matters pertaining to the canonical rights and responsibilities and pastoral role of the United States hierarchy functioning as a national episcopal conference."
>
> USCC shall address itself to "matters in which the Bishops collaborate with others in social, economic, civic and educational affairs."[17]

The problem with this distinction is that the bishops, when dealing with "social, economic, civic and educational affairs," have often wanted to issue pastoral letters and not simply "formal statements." Since the USCC cannot issue pastoral letters, these matters had to be dealt with by the NCCB. For example, in 1972 when the conference wanted to issue the pastoral letter "To Teach as Jesus Did," the initial drafting was done by the USCC Education Committee and staff. The document was then debated in the USCC assembly. After amending the document, the USCC voted (187-30) to recommend that the NCCB issue it as a pastoral letter. The bishops then adjourned as the USCC and immediately reconvened as the NCCB and passed the pastoral (197-29).[18]

More recently, the conference has skipped such procedural gymnastics and simply had the debate take place in the NCCB assembly, even if the initial work was done by a USCC committee and staff. The result has been a gradual diminishment of the distinction between the two assemblies that have the same membership.

What has been the record of consensus and conflict within the NCCB/USCC on pastoral letters and statements? Have decisions been made by consensus or have a small majority imposed their will on the rest of the bishops? What have been the issues that divided the bishops and on what issues has there been consensus?[19]

Pastoral Letters and Statements

If the only evidence examined is the final vote on pastoral letters and statements, the NCCB/USCC appears to be an organization with a high degree of consensus. Of the 121 NCCB/USCC assembly statements printed in *Pastoral Letters of the United States Bishops* for 1966-1988,[20] the minutes[21] indicate that at least 50 (41 percent) passed unanimously (see appendix C).

These include resolutions on political-ethical issues such as birth control (1966), race relations and poverty (1966), welfare (1967), aid to parents of Catholic school students (1971 and 1985), the environment (1971), population programs (1972 and 1973), pro-life constitutional amendments (1973), the Middle East (1973, 1986 and 1987), farm labor (1973, 1974, and 1975), pro-life activities (1975 and 1985), the economy (1975), housing (1975), Human Life Foundation (1975), migrants (1976), Cuban and Haitian refugees (1980), hostages in Iran (1980), health care (1981), the Ukraine (1985), immigration reform (1985 and 1988), food and agriculture policy (1985 and 1988), Korea (1987), school-based health clinics (1987), treatment of the handicapped (1987), and religious freedom in Eastern Europe (1987).

Total consensus was also shown on statements covering church issues like the *Dutch Catechism* (1967), "Christians in Our Time" (1970), the Campaign for Human Development (1970), the missions (1971), Eucharist and hunger (1975), the movie *Jesus of Nazareth* (1977), church arbitration procedures (1978), the papal visit (1979), the laity (1980), the mission of the conference (1981), Hispanics in the church (1983 and 1987), liturgy (1983), evangelization (1985), world mission (1986), and retired priests (1987).

Twenty other statements received nearly unanimous approval with ten or fewer negative votes: three statements on Vietnam (1966, 1971, and 1972), "Human Life in Our Day" (1968), abortion (1970), directives for health facilities (1971), housing (1972), Catholic-Jewish relations (1975), society and the aged (1976), political responsibility (1976), American Indians (1977), religious liberty in Eastern Europe (1977), the bicentennial consultations (1977), justice (1978), the handicapped (1978), the Middle East (1978), Central America (1981), "The Challenge of Peace" (1983), campus ministry (1985), and "Economic Justice for All" (1986).

Another 31 statements passed on voice votes with no one concerned enough to ask for a written ballot (only six bishops are needed to require a written ballot): peace (1967 and 1968), clerical celibacy (1967 and April 1969), Catholic schools (1967), the race crisis (1968), due process in church (1968), farm labor (1968), abortion (1969), poverty (1969), prisoners of war (1969), ecumenism (1970 and 1974), welfare reform (1970), the Catholic press (1970), the United Nations (1970), birth control laws (1970), the declaration of human rights (1973), prisons (1973), the world food crisis (1974), ecclesiastical archives (1974), guidelines for fund raising (1977), family ministry (1978), Cambodia (1979), Iran (1979 and 1980), Central America (1983 and 1987), Lebanon (1986), and Lithuania (1986).

Thus of the 121 NCCB/USCC statements published in *Pastoral Letters*, all but 19 passed on voice votes or with ten or fewer bishops in opposition. On five of the 19 statements the vote results are unknown although they received at least a two-thirds vote.[22] The remaining 102 statements cover issues that divided American society and the church, but the bishops achieved consensus on them. Before examining the statements that had some opposition, it is important to emphasize how extraordinary is this level of consensus. It is empirical evidence supporting the view that consensus formation is a highly-prized operational norm of the NCCB/USCC.[23]

Conflict: Capital Punishment 1974 and 1980

No statement of the NCCB/USCC was ever adopted by a small majority. Only one statement was approved by less than two-thirds of those voting: the 1974, one-sentence USCC "Resolution Against Capital Punishment" passed 108-63.[24] The bishops broke their own regulations in approving this resolution with less than a two-thirds vote.[25] But no one made a point of order when Cardinal John Krol, the NCCB/USCC president, declared the resolution passed on a majority vote.

Bishop John L. May, then of Mobile, offered the one-sentence resolution after a seven-page statement on capital punishment, written by the Committee on Social Development and World Peace, was defeated in the assembly on a close vote (103-119). This committee statement has the distinction of being the only statement ever formally defeated by the assembly, although other statements have been tabled.[26] After the statement's defeat, Bishop May immediately offered his one-sentence resolution. As Archbishop May recalls:

> There was a lot of fussing going on and people were modifying statements and throwing in amendments and all this kind of stuff on capital punishment. I just thought it'd be much simpler to put what we really believed, just that.

If I'm not mistaken, Cardinal Law—of course he was bishop of Springfield then—he leaned over to me and said, "Why don't we just say. . . ." And I said, "Yeah, it's a good idea." So I did it. I do remember how all the quibblers fell aside. They all just kind of quit.

The debate on the resolution was postponed for two days. After the resolution was debated, Cardinal Krol ended discussion and called for a vote, commenting that "this matter had been debated more than any other four or five topics."[27]

Six years later, the 1980 "Statement on Capital Punishment" passed 145 to 31 with 41 abstentions, the highest number of abstentions ever recorded in the conference.[28] The bishops again broke conference regulations in adopting this statement. Before 1981, "formal statements" required a two-thirds approval of the entire membership, not a two-thirds of those casting votes.[29] Since no bishop made a point of order, the statement became conference policy.

The closeness of the votes indicates that the two capital punishment statements were the most controversial statements ever issued by the conference. Many bishops were concerned that a rejection of capital punishment might appear to be a rejection of church tradition that for centuries had acknowledged a state's right to execute criminals. On the other hand, many other bishops wanted to show that the hierarchy held a fully consistent ethic of life and was opposed not only to abortion but also to capital punishment. In addition, bishops disagreed on whether to condemn capital punishment in principle (it is intrinsically wrong) or on contingent grounds (not an effective deterrent, inequitably applied, undercuts value of life in society, etc.). Approving such controversial statements required breaking or bending their self-imposed regulations requiring a two-thirds vote on statements.

More Conflict

Five other statements approved by the NCCB/USCC had more than 30 negative votes on final passage: the 1966 "Pastoral Statement on Penance and Abstinence" (156-32), the November 1969 "Statement on Celibacy" (145-68), the April 1970

"Statement on Abortion" (114-52), the 1976 statement "U.S.-Panama Relations" (170-61), and the "conclusion" of the 1970 "Statement on the Implementation of the Apostolic Letter on Mixed Marriages" (172-49).

Penance 1966

The 1966 minutes give little information on the conflict over the "Pastoral Statement on Penance and Abstinence" at the first meeting of the NCCB. Archbishop John Cody of Chicago introduced the revised text that had taken into consideration "insofar as possible" the *modi* (amendments) submitted by 30 bishops. The statement, which Bishop John J. Wright helped to write, announced the reduction in the number of days of fast and abstinence to Ash Wednesday and Good Friday. At the same time, the bishops wanted to avoid the impression that they were downgrading penance or that all laws could change.

After approving the statement, the bishops added an additional paragraph saying that Catholics should understand "that fast and abstinence regulations admit change, unlike the commandments and precepts of that unchanging divine moral law which the church must today and always defend as immutable."[30] This final addition was probably an attempt to placate those who originally voted no.

Celibacy 1969

The handling of the November 1969 "Statement on Celibacy" is interesting if ambiguous. At one point 68 bishops voted against issuing the paper, which strongly defended clerical celibacy, as a conference document. Can it be inferred from the vote that 68 bishops favored optional celibacy? Probably not.[31]

Actually, there were three votes on the celibacy statement. First, the document's content was approved in substance, subject to amendments, with only one negative vote. Second, the bishops voted 145-68 to issue the document as a conference statement, rather than merely to make it available to the bishops. Third, a series of amendments were unanimously accepted.

The different results for the first and second votes are interesting. Although only one bishop voted against the document in substance, moments later 68 voted against issuing it as a conference statement. Why did these 67 additional bishops suddenly turn against the document?

Some bishops felt the statement was too defensive and apologetic in tone. They observed it did not relate celibacy to ministry, and they feared that priests would believe the bishops were unaware of the problems confronting their clergy. But these points had been made during the debate before the first vote. Those who changed their votes probably felt that the document was good enough for private distribution to the bishops but not good enough for publication. In dealing with issues touching priests (seminaries, vocations, priests' retreats, lay preaching), the bishops are always concerned about how their decisions will be perceived by their priests.

Another influence may have been the manner of voting. The first vote was public (by voice or a show of hands) but the second was secret (by ballot). Some have argued that public votes coerce the minority into going along with the majority. Others argue that public votes discourage bishops from voting against Vatican policy. Both factors could have been at work here if some of the 67 favored optional celibacy but were afraid to say so publicly. The *periti*, nonepiscopal experts who had helped prepare the statement, were less reticent: they indicated before the meeting that they did not want to be associated with the statement as it was drafted.

Abortion 1970

Issuing the April 1970 "Statement on Abortion" was opposed by 52 bishops. Does this mean that 52 bishops favored abortion? Not likely. The bishops appear to have been objecting to procedure, not substance.

The conference had already issued "Human Life in Our Day" (1968), a pastoral letter that included four paragraphs on abortion. As more states liberalized their laws, the NCCB Administrative Committee decided that more needed to be said. The NCCB approved on a voice vote a short statement on abortion in 1969.

The 1970 statement was presented by the Rev. James T. McHugh, then director of the USCC Family Life Division, and later bishop of Camden, N.J. A revised version was prepared by an ad hoc committee headed by Bishop Raymond J. Gallagher in light of the *modi* (amendments) they received during the meeting. More *modi* were suggested when the revised version was presented. The president, Cardinal John Dearden, asked that the committee again revise the draft and bring it back to the assembly.

Some, however, felt that this procedure would delay the document. Archbishop Philip Hannan moved that the ad hoc committee be authorized to revise the document in light of the observations made on the floor and then proceed immediately to the release of the document in the name of the conference. Most of those who voted in the negative probably agreed with Cardinal Dearden that the committee should come back to the assembly for final approval of the revised text. Seven months later, in November 1970, a "Declaration on Abortion" passed with only eight negative votes. This was the last statement of the bishops before the Supreme Court decision in *Roe v. Wade* (January 22, 1973). All subsequent statements on abortion have been overwhelmingly approved.

U.S.-Panama Relations 1976

In 1976 the NCCB issued a statement supporting the Panama Canal Treaty. Considering how divided American society was over returning the Canal Zone to Panama, it is surprising that the American bishops were not more divided than the final vote of 170-61 implies. The lobbying efforts of the Panamanian hierarchy, led by Archbishop Marcos McGrath of Panama City, played a pivotal role in overcoming the bishops' reluctance to touch this political controversy. Despite the "heated debate"[32] and the 61 negative votes, the statement had a profound political impact. The Carter Administration identified the conference as its most important supporter in the Senate ratification of the Panama Canal Treaty.

Mixed Marriages 1970

Finally, there is the 1970 "Statement on the Implementation of the Apostolic Letter on Mixed Marriages." This was the third draft of the statement; the second draft failed to receive a two-thirds vote in a mail ballot. Each section of the third draft was discussed and amended on the floor in accordance with the discussions. Each section was voted on separately. The "conclusion" received the most negative votes (172-49), and there was no vote on the whole document.

The minutes give no details about the debate or amendments, and the USCC press releases give very little information. A reading of the text does not reveal anything very controversial in the "conclusion." Perhaps some bishops objected to instructing the USCC Family Life Division to "develop basic pre-marriage and marriage education programs incorporating the norms and spirit of this document." The NCCB committee on ecumenism was also asked "to explore the possibility of an ecumenical form for mixed marriage." Or perhaps some bishops voted in the negative because they wanted something in the conclusion that was not there.[33]

Mostly Consensus

Another six statements received 20-30 negative votes: the 1969 "Statement in Protest of U.S. Government Programs against the Right to Life" (143-20), the 1972 pastoral "To Teach as Jesus Did" (197-29), the 1976 statement "Teach Them" (153-30), the 1976 statement "Let the Little Children Come to Me" (201-23), the 1976 pastoral "To Live in Christ Jesus" (172-25), and the 1979 pastoral letter "Brothers and Sisters to Us" (215-30).

Thus from 1966 through 1983, only 13 of the 121 NCCB/USCC statements published in *Pastoral Letters of the*

United States Bishops had more than 19 negative votes. The rest were approved by voice vote or received fewer than 20 negative votes. As a result, 89 percent[34] of the NCCB/USCC statements were supported by at least 90 percent of the bishops voting. This presumes that on voice votes fewer than 11 percent of the bishops voted in the negative, a fairly safe presumption since it only takes six bishops to require a written ballot.

Judging from the final votes on documents in *Pastoral Letters*, the NCCB/USCC is clearly an assembly that operates by consensus. Although this is a fair judgment, it is an incomplete picture. Judging the NCCB/USCC only by the final votes on documents in *Pastoral Letters* would be like judging a restaurant by the food brought to your table. It would be an accurate judgment, but it would miss all the excitement that goes on in the kitchen. Thus although the 1983 peace pastoral and the 1986 economic pastoral both passed with only nine negative votes, hundreds of amendments were offered and voted on before the final ballots.

Conciliar Procedures

An examination of the legislative histories of the 121 statements published in *Pastoral Letters* shows that some statements achieved consensus almost immediately, but others achieved it only after much debate and many revisions.[35] Despite what their critics may say, the statements of the American bishops are not approved with little or no consideration. This may have been true in a few instances when sessions were closed to the public, but since the press has been admitted in 1972, the bishops have given statements due consideration before approval.

How statements were discussed and revised changed over time in the conference. The procedures followed in the assembly in its early years were modeled on those of the Second Vatican Council.[36] The move from conciliar rules to *Robert's Rules of Order* began during Cardinal Krol's presidency (1971-74) and was formalized under NCCB President Joseph

Bernardin (1974-77). Although either set of rules can be used to develop consensus, conciliar rules give more influence to conference leadership and the drafting committees, while parliamentary procedures strengthen the assembly vis-à-vis the drafting committees and the conference leadership.

When operating under conciliar rules in the past, the assembled bishops would discuss a draft and suggest modi (amendments), but the amendments were rarely voted on. The drafting committee would use its own judgment in determining which modi to accept or refuse. The committee was supposed to accept those that would increase consensus, but without a vote to show the mood of the assembly, the decision was subjective.

For example, 30 bishops offered *modi* to the 1966 "Statement on Penance and Abstinence," but these were not voted on. Instead the drafting committee, chaired by Archbishop Cody, would either accept the *modi*, in which case they were included, or reject them, in which case they were forgotten. Likewise, a draft of "The Church in Our Day" was mailed to the bishops a month before their November 1967 meeting. The bishops discussed a revised version that was circulated at the meeting. *Modi* on both versions were submitted to the drafting committee headed by Bishop John J. Wright, but it appears that no amendments were voted on. Bishop Wright also made changes, "generally stylistic in nature," after the document was approved.[37]

If the leadership of the conference was unhappy with a draft or its revision, it could also expand the number of bishops working on the document. Expanding the committee was usually a strategy for developing consensus. For example, in 1967, the "Statement on Celibacy" was first drafted by the Committee on Doctrine chaired by Bishop Alexander Zaleski. A second draft was presented by Cardinal Krol, the NCCB/USCC vice president. The final draft, revised after the floor discussions, was presented by Bishop Wright who was helped by a drafting committee including Cardinal Krol, Archbishop John Carberry, Archbishop Paul Hallinan, Bishop Loras Lane, and Bishop Zaleski.

A less complicated procedure was used on the 1967 "Statement on Peace." Cardinal James F. McIntyre of Los Angeles simply moved that the statement be accepted with any changes or additions the drafting committee might wish to make in view of the comments given on the floor. This motion passed, indicating a high degree of confidence in, or deference to, the committee.

The process of approving the 1968 pastoral "Human Life in Our Day" proved to be much more complicated. It is the first statement on which there were a number of amendments and votes. Before the November meeting, Bishop Wright surveyed the membership to see what kind of pastoral they wanted. The responses showed that most bishops wanted to do more than simply quote from Vatican II and *Humanae Vitae*. They wanted to discuss abortion and birth control (194-19), to give pastoral guidance to the faithful (161-17), and to deal with the morality of war (153-44), including the Vietnam War (121-67). But just over a third of the bishops opposed applying the principles of Vatican II to the Vietnam War.

The issues of "guiltless" contraception and dissent were considered so delicate that the bishops voted to have the results of their ballots on these issues kept confidential even from themselves, even though the votes took place in a closed meeting. A third vote occurred on whether the bishops wished to say that those who are subjectively guiltless in practicing contraception have nonetheless done something that is objectively evil. Also, regarding the morality of contraception, several terms were suggested: "sin," "objective disorder," "objective evil," "disorder." A written ballot determined that "objective evil" would be used. It appears that the vote counts in these instances were never revealed to the bishops who probably feared they would be leaked to the press or the Vatican. As a result, it is impossible to measure the degree of conflict and consensus on the motions, but the final document had the support of all but eight bishops.

Likewise at the same meeting, the bishops voted 145 to 65 to omit any reference to the grape boycott in their 1968 "Statement on Farm Labor," apparently because they feared upsetting small farmers in the Midwest.[38] Within five years, in a 1973 statement that passed unanimously, the bishops supported the boycott until the workers were allowed to choose a union through a secret ballot.

In 1970, the conference tried a new procedure and had separate votes on each of the eight sections of the "Statement on the Implementation of the Apostolic Letter on Mixed Marriages." Each section received more than a two-thirds vote, with the "conclusion" receiving the most negative votes, as described above.

In 1971, the push toward consensus is seen when the bishops worked on their "Resolution on Southeast Asia." After Cardinal McIntyre had failed to have the resolution tabled, it passed 158-36. But the bishops appeared to be upset that so many voted in the negative. One sentence of the text was changed, and the resolution repassed with just two no's. The original sentence read: "It is our firm conviction, therefore, that further prosecution of the war cannot be justified by traditional moral norms." This was changed to read: "It is our firm conviction, therefore, that the speedy ending of this war is a moral imperative of the highest priority." By making the statement more ambiguous, the bishops increased consensus.

Open Sessions: More Amendments

With the opening of NCCB/USCC meetings to the press in 1972, the actions of the conference became more public and the offering of amendments became more frequent. That year the pastoral letter on education, "To Teach as Jesus Did," received only a few minor amendments.[39] The major challenges to the document were beaten back, in one case by the smallest of margins. Bishop Romeo Blanchette, who prided himself as a defender of orthodoxy, offered an amendment adding the words "which cannot essentially change" to a section on church teaching. Archbishop John Whealon, chair of the Committee on Doctrine, and Bishop John Quinn argued that Bishop Blanchette's concerns were dealt with elsewhere in the document. A voice vote was inconclusive, and when the ballots were counted, the amendment lost 102-103. Another motion by Bishop George Lynch "that any teachings contrary to the Catholic faith should not be permitted under the guise of academic freedom or for other alleged reasons . . ." lost on a voice vote when it was opposed by the Committee on Education.

During the same meeting, the 1972 "Resolution on the Imperative of Peace" was amended by Archbishop Patrick O'Boyle, over the objections of the drafters, to include a reassertion of the right of self-defense (138-60). This is one of the first instances of a document being amended in a way that was opposed by the committee that drafted the statement.

Robert's Rules of Order

With the election of Archbishop Joseph Bernardin as NCCB/USCC president, the conference completed the move to *Robert's Rules of Order* and in 1975 even hired as parliamentarian Mr. Henry Robert, the grandson of the author.[40] For the most part, amendments were few and noncontroversial until November 1976, when the bishops offered 55 amendments to the pastoral letter on moral values, "To Live in Christ Jesus." Another 61 amendments were offered in 1977 to "The Bicentennial Consultation: A Response to the Call to Action." Clearly by 1976, individual bishops felt free to challenge and change documents prepared by conference committees.

"To Live in Christ Jesus" was drafted by an ad hoc committee chaired by Bishop John McDowell. Before any amendments were even offered, Bishop Francis Mugavero tried to send the letter back to committee because he felt it was too harsh in tone. He lost 65-162. As far as can be determined by the minutes and press releases, the bishops supported the committee's preferences most of the time in accepting or rejecting amendments.[41] Of the 55 amendments offered, 43 were approved. One was close enough to require a standing vote, the rest were decided by voice votes.

Often the amendments reflected a tension in the conference between those bishops who wanted to insist on the obligation to follow church teaching and those who wanted to show pas-

toral concern for people. The assembly has tended both to accept amendments that strengthen the presentation of church
teaching, and to reject amendments that tone down the pastoral concern. Thus an amendment changing "ask them" to
"urge them" in the section dealing with birth control and the
faithful passed, but another amendment to drop "understanding" as a modifier to "pastoral" was defeated. The assembly
refuses to choose between being sensitive pastors and
emphatic teachers. The bishops want to be both.

The 1977 response to the bicentennial consultation gave the
bishops' reply to the Detroit Call to Action conference, which
had representatives from dioceses from all over the United
States. Here again, the assembly almost always followed the
recommendations of the drafting committee in dealing with
amendments.[42] A little over half the amendments were approved. Again the conflict was often between those who
wanted to articulate clearly the hierarchy's positions on issues
and those who wanted to show sensitivity to the people who
participated in the Detroit meeting. Rather than being confrontational, the bishops tended to treat the Detroit participants
with respect, accepting what they could, while reaffirming the
bishops' and Vatican's position on controversial issues like
women priests, celibacy, and birth control.

Sometimes the bishops used parliamentary procedure to dis-
pose discreetly of controversial issues. For example, several
recommendations from the Detroit conference were referred to
NCCB or USCC committees with little comment and were
never heard of again. A similar procedure was used on an
amendment from 27 bishops calling for more dialogue with
the pope after his 1979 visit. Although many bishops felt there
should have been more opportunities for dialogue between the
pope and various groups, including themselves, few wanted to
make a public issue of it in the resolution they passed following the pope's visit. The amendment was referred to the ad
hoc committee on the papal visit. Although the amendment
never reappeared, structured dialogues as well as papal
speeches were scheduled in his 1987 visit. In March 1989, the
dialogue continued with the American archbishops meeting

with the pope and curial officials in Rome for 12 hours of discussions.[43]

Group Amendments

At their November 1977 meeting, the NCCB became clogged with amendments as it considered the "National Catechetical Directory."[44] Over 300 amendments were proposed, although about half were withdrawn by their authors before a vote. The assembly usually followed the recommendations of the drafting committee, but in 15 cases it changed the text against the wishes of the committee. In a few instances, the assembly approved as many as 12 amendments to the directory at once, but most amendments were voted on individually. This experience convinced the bishops that another way had to be devised for handling minor amendments.

After the "National Catechetical Directory," the assembly frequently considered nonsubstantive and stylistic amendments in groups. Thus when considering the 1978 "Statement on the Middle East," the assembly voted at one time on 13 amendments that were acceptable to the drafting committee. A similar procedure dealt with 32 amendments to the 1978 "Pastoral Statement on the Handicapped."[45] The bishops approved both motions unanimously. Likewise, 64 amendments were accepted in one vote to the 1979 pastoral letter on racism, "Brothers and Sisters to Us."

This grouping of noncontroversial amendments speeded up the assembly process. Often by accepting these amendments the committee also expanded the support for its document among the bishops. One committee instructed its staff to accept any amendment sent in by a bishop that did not contradict the text. Eventually the conference developed a system of listing amendments in three groups: minor or noncontroversial amendments acceptable to the drafting committee, minor or noncontroversial amendments rejected by the committee, and substantive amendments. Amendments in group one and two would be voted on as a group unless someone requested a separate vote. Amendments in group three are voted on individually.

The committees continued to turn down amendments that they thought were detrimental to their work. In 1980, the Committee on Social Development and World Peace opposed an amendment exempting terrorists from the ban on capital punishment in its document, and the assembly followed the committee. Likewise, when amendments infringing on academic freedom were offered to the 1980 document on higher education, the Committee on Education succeeded in getting the assembly to reject them.

In 1981, on the other hand, when the Committee on Social Development and World Peace accepted an amendment to delete a reference critical of U.S. arms shipments to El Salvador from their "Statement on Central America," Archbishop James Hickey objected. He feared that the deletion would look like a retreat from the conference's earlier opposition to U.S. military aid to El Salvador. The assembly agreed and preserved the committee's original text. Likewise when the same committee agreed to strike a section dealing with drugs and smoking from "Health and Health Care," the assembly balked. In both cases, the assembly felt the committee had gone too far in accommodating individual bishops and their amendments. In attempting to satisfy a minority, the committee had lost the majority.

"The Challenge of Peace" (1983) was debated and amended during a two-day meeting in Chicago. A straw vote on an earlier draft in November 1982 showed that the bishops approved of the socio-political analysis (234-44), the use of Scripture and tradition (202-64), the theological principles and moral conclusions (141-114), the practical strategies for peace (191-68), but they were unhappy with the tone, style, length, and intended audience (110-139). The draft as a whole was supported (195-71).

At the May 1983 meeting, the bishops for the most part supported the drafting committee's position on amendments.[46] There were so many amendments to consider that the conference for the first time voted to limit debate on amendments.[47]

About 140 votes were taken, and only in about 13 cases did the assembly go against the drafting committee. One hundred fifteen amendments (Group IV), approved by the committee, were accepted in one vote. And, for the first time, another vote rejected 111 amendments (Group III) at once.

The votes going against the committee show that the assembly was often more "liberal" than the committee, which had tried to maintain consensus by pleasing "conservatives." In three amendments by Archbishop John Quinn, the assembly strengthened the document's position against first use of nuclear weapons. The assembly also supported the idea of a global body that would have authority to settle international disputes and impose peace. The assembly, with the approval of the drafting committee, also went back to an earlier draft calling for a "halt" to nuclear weapons rather than simply a "curb."

The most interesting vote placed the assembly on record against *any* use of nuclear weapons, a position Cardinal Bernardin, chair of the drafting committee, later got the assembly to reverse. "I was really upset," confessed Cardinal Bernardin. "I said, 'My God, if this stands, then we have gutted some of the main arguments for deterrence.' That was a very critical matter, because I had the committee behind me saying, 'We can't go along with this.' The whole argumentation for deterrence would have gone down the drain."

Cardinal Bernardin explained to the assembly that it was difficult to defend the possession of nuclear weapons for deterrence if any use of them was immoral. Since the bishops were going to accept deterrence conditionally, they had to leave the question of use open, Cardinal Bernardin argued. Otherwise there was the danger of falling into consequentialism—claiming that the end (peace) justified the means (threatening to do something immoral). Less out of conviction than out of trust in Cardinal Bernardin, the bishops reversed themselves.

The bishops also wanted to add to the letter the strong words against nuclear deterrence from the 1976 "To Live in Christ Jesus" and from the congressional testimony of Cardinal

Krol on SALT II.[48] Those statements said that "Not only is it wrong to attack civilian populations, but it is also wrong to threaten to attack them as part of a strategy of deterrence."[49] Again Cardinal Bernardin was able to stop the bishops from going beyond what the drafting committee and the Vatican felt was defensible.

In 1985, the bishops unanimously adopted a pastoral program on pro-life activities. Two amendments were controversial. An amendment by Bishop Michael F. McAuliffe was passed 117-116, reconsidered, and then defeated overwhelmingly. The amendment would have given the NCCB Committee on Pro-Life Activities the authority to coordinate diocesan pro-life activities. The amendment was ultimately defeated because the bishops did not want the conference to infringe on the autonomy of the local bishop in his diocese. Another amendment by Bishop Stanley Ott added to the document language dealing with other life issues besides abortion. Initially the voice vote was inconclusive. On repetition, it was declared passed.

The 1985 pastoral letter on campus ministry had a rough going through the conference, although only four bishops voted against the final document. The critics wanted the Catholic identity of the ministry stressed more strongly.

The 1986 pastoral on the economy was debated at length, but only one minor amendment was approved over the objections of the committee. Like the earlier peace pastoral, the economic pastoral went through two drafts and an extensive and wide consultation process. A chapter on agriculture was added to placate bishops from rural dioceses. After 47 separate voice votes on amendments, for the first time in their history the bishops voted 210-40 to close the floor to amendments. They then passed the letter with only nine negative votes.

Internal Church Issues

The bishops do not spend all their time debating and writing pastoral letters and statements. A good bit of their time as a conference is devoted to internal church issues like liturgy, priestly formation, and canonical issues. These were often more controversial than political issues.

Liturgy

Reform of the liturgy was one of the great initiatives of the Second Vatican Council. Liturgical changes affected every parish and every Catholic, and they were divisive at every level of the church. Since liturgy impacts directly on Catholic life, bishops are very concerned about how any proposed change will affect their local churches. Although most liturgical matters did easily pass the assembly, it is not surprising that the bishops were sometimes divided over liturgical issues.[50]

Every liturgical text and ceremony has to be approved by a two-thirds vote of the bishops before it can be used in the United States. As a result, the bishops have voted on about 212 recommendations from the Liturgy Committee from 1966 through 1991. Matters ranged from the momentous to the trivial, from putting the Mass into English to approving the text of prayers for the feast of Junipero Serra.

An examination of floor votes shows that liturgical matters are much more conflictual than pastoral letters or statements. The Liturgy Committee suffered more defeats than any other conference committee. "Every bishop feels he knows everything there is to know about liturgy," explains Archbishop Quinn, "and consequently has an opinion about everything." Since the bishops hold strong personal opinions on liturgy and since liturgical changes directly affect parish life, the conference does not automatically defer to liturgy experts or to the Liturgy Committee.

At least 30 (14 percent) recommendations of the Liturgy Committee were defeated when they failed to get a two-thirds vote from the assembly. Some defeats were not final. For example, the following committee defeats were temporary since the assembly eventually approved the proposals a year or more later: women lectors (1967: 95-107), Communion more than once a day under certain circumstances (1968: 126-74), Communion under both kinds under certain circumstances (1968: 131-63; 1970: 142-80), confirmation by priests of those baptized at the Easter Vigil (1970: 131-90), dropping "men" from "for all men" in the Eucharistic consecration (1979: 157-98), optional Communion in the hand (1970: 117-107; 1973: 113-121).

Other committee proposals were never approved: special rules for small group Masses (1967: 100-106; 1968: 116-87; 1969: 104-107) or special groups (1970: 140-83; 1971: 105-120); a special liturgy for children (1968: 98-107; 1969: 97-101); allowing priests to say Mass in a stole without a chasuble (1969: 25-169) or in a chasuble without a stole (1969: 31-173); the option of using the ICEL translation of the "Our Father" (1969: 94-86); the option of using the ICEL Apostles' Creed (1969: 124-73) or the old translation of the Apostles' Creed in place of the Nicene Creed (1978: 96-124); allowing relatives of the deceased to give a greeting at the funeral (1970: 138-81); a Mothers' and Fathers' Day liturgy (1971: 136-80); transferring the Solemnity of Mary (January 1) to Sunday (1973: 120-113); a book of prayers (1982: 125-115); the inclusive language Grail Psalter (1984: 117-154); Eucharistic Prayer A (1986: 112-123); allowing bishops to permit laypersons to conduct funeral services (1990: 113-136).

"There's always been a suspicion about liturgy in the U.S. bishops' conference," reports a staff person, "unlike other English-speaking conferences, where whatever the episcopal commission on liturgy recommends is approved, since they trust the committee. But I don't think they've trusted the committee since it was first started, with Paul Hallinan as chairman."

Even when the Liturgy Committee wins, a sizable bloc of bishops sometimes votes against it. Besides the 30 recommendations that went down to defeat, there were 86 recommendations that had 20 or more bishops voting no. Thus 55 percent of the liturgical matters voted on by the bishops had twenty or more negative votes as opposed to only about 10 percent of the pastoral letters that had the same number of negative votes.

Bishop James Malone, chair of the Liturgy Committee at the time, remembers presenting the special liturgy for children:

The rite that we had sketched was, we thought, quite appropriate. We planned carefully, that I would make a presentation, that others on the committee would rise to affirm it.

Archbishop Thomas A. Connolly of Seattle led the charge against it. He stood with gripping sarcasm, talked about little kiddies with their balloons bouncing off the choir stalls, rising above and all. Well he systematically went through the rite and left it in ribbons.

Liturgical matters would undoubtedly be even more conflictual if the conference were not a member of ICEL (the International Committee on English in the Liturgy).[51] This international committee, whose episcopal members are elected by the English-speaking bishops' conferences, was formed during Vatican II to develop common English liturgical texts that could be used throughout the world. The conferences are consulted as texts are being translated, but the bishops can only accept or reject the final text as it stands. If they change the text, it would no longer be an ICEL or common text. As a result, the NCCB considers liturgical texts under what amounts to a closed rule—no amendments can be offered. Without this procedure, the bishops would offer scores of amendments.

Although the conference does not change texts, it does sometimes change liturgical rules proposed by the Liturgy Committee. For example, in 1985 it reversed the committee and voted to allow the American flag to remain on a coffin as it is brought into church for a funeral liturgy. The committee, following Vatican norms, had recommended removing the flag at the church door and placing a white pall over the casket.[52]

Ultimately, the conference accepted most liturgical changes allowed by Rome, although the conference moved slower than its committee would have liked. Often the NCCB acted only after other conferences had led the way. For example, Communion in the hand was approved in Canada long before it was approved in the United States. And the Liturgy Committee sometimes wanted to ask for additional changes beyond those permitted, but often the other bishops balked. For example, the special liturgies for children and small groups were developed by a subcommittee of the Liturgy Committee, but these were not approved by the bishops who did not want such liturgies in their parishes.

The Rev. Frederick McManus, staff to the committee at the time, remarks, "It is ironic that guidelines for liturgies with children, which were not accepted [in 1968 and 1969], were less radical than the directory on the subject issued in Rome in 1973."[53] On the other hand, when the committee could get conference support for additional requests, often these were turned down by Rome, as will be seen in Chapter 8.

Holy Days

One of the most controversial and long-running issues of the conference has been holy days of obligation. "I think there's an authentic difference of pastoral opinion," explains Archbishop Daniel Pilarczyk.

> Some bishops are saying, "Look, people don't come anyway, and why should we have this obligation that they don't pay any attention to?" Others are saying, "People don't come anyway, so we should keep the obligation and work on it so that they do come."

Proposals to resolve the issue have been offered by the Committee on Pastoral Research and Practices, an ad hoc Committee on Holy Days, the Committee on Liturgy, and the Committee on Canonical Affairs. All have failed, which has meant a continuation of the status quo.

As early as 1967 the issue of holy days was brought to the bishops, only to be tabled. A 1969 survey of the bishops, conducted by the Committee on Pastoral Research and Practices, found the bishops divided over what to do with the holy days celebrating the Assumption, the Ascension, All Saints, the Immaculate Conception, and the January 1st holy day. Some have favored eliminating the obligation, others favored transferring the feasts to Sunday. In 1969 the bishops voted to retain the obligation for January 1 (148-47) and voted down a recommendation of an ad hoc committee to eliminate the obligation for the Immaculate Conception (58-150). In 1973 the Liturgy Committee's recommendation to transfer the Solemnity of Mary (January 1) to Sunday failed to receive a two-thirds vote

(120-113). In 1983 the conference failed to muster a two-thirds vote to remove the precept for January 1 (152-146) and the Assumption (132-173), despite the recommendation of the Canonical Affairs Committee. Nor did the conference agree to transfer the Ascension (156-131).

The arguments for and against each recommendation varied, but some bishops appeared uncomfortable with the idea of imposing moral obligations that many people are ignoring. The inconvenience of the feasts was also noted: January 1 is a week after Christmas; Ascension Thursday is not a civil holiday; August 15 comes when people are on vacation. Those favoring the feasts argued their spiritual benefits.

Although not mentioned in the debates, one bishop admitted that many bishops did not want to give up the collections on these feast days. Archbishop Pilarczyk disagreed.

> Some years ago when Cardinal Bernardin was still in Cincinnati, we discussed this Holy Day thing in our priests' council, and we talked about it for about an hour, and I think there was some consensus that there are too many and we probably should do away with some. Nobody mentioned the collection, nobody.
>
> Bernardin was astounded and I was astounded. That doesn't seem to be the issue, possibly because the collections are so small that they're not worth worrying about. However, I live at a downtown church, we are packed full for just about every Mass on a holy day with business people, the downtown people. Now, I suspect that the pastor of that church would not want to see many changes in holy days, because that collection is important for him. But I don't think it's that important to most priests.

In September 1989, the NCCB/USCC National Advisory Council voted to reduce the number of holy days to Christmas and one feast of Mary. The issue came before the bishops again in November 1991. A majority, but not two-thirds, wanted to move Ascension Thursday, the Assumption, and All Saints Day to Sunday. Barely two-thirds voted to eliminate the obligation for January 1, August 15, and November 1 when they fell on Saturday or Monday.

Canonical Affairs

The Canonical Affairs Committee has not done quite as badly as the Liturgy Committee. Canonical Affairs avoided many conflicts in implementing the 1983 Code of Canon Law by recommending that, at least temporarily, the national norm on many issues be whatever the local bishop decides in his diocese.[54]

Of the 79 recommendations submitted to the NCCB by the Canonical Affairs Committee from 1967 through 1991, eight were defeated or tabled. These included a recommendation on *imprimaturs* which was referred to the Vatican Commission for the Revision of the Code of Canon Law (1967), two recommendations allowing bishops to dissolve nonconsummated marriages (1970), a proposal to allow bishops to deal with laicizations (1970), continuation of a series of procedural norms for speeding up annulments (1972), and three recommendations on holy days (1983). Another eight recommendations had 20 or more bishops voting against the committee. Four of these dealt with annulment procedures (1969), two dealt with holy days (1983), one with allowing limited terms for pastors (1983), and one allowing general absolution only if individual confession was unavailable for at least 30 days (1988). In only four of these did the negative votes exceed 40. The recommendations on annulments required Vatican approval and will be discussed in Chapter 8.[55]

Doctrinal and Catechetical Issues

Preserving and teaching the faith has always been a concern of bishops. Much of this teaching is done through pastoral letters and statements that have already been discussed. The conference also has a Committee on Doctrine and a Committee on Education. The Committee on Doctrine has brought few matters to the floor. Its 1989 document on theologians and bishops began with much controversy but ended up being approved with only nine negative votes. The document had been six years in development since it had been recommended by the professional societies of canon lawyers and theologians.[56] In

1987, an earlier draft had been almost tabled on a vote of 80-92, at which point the absence of a quorum was noted and the conference was forced to adjourn. Ultimately the document was approved in 1989 with only nine negative votes. In 1991 the conference passed on a voice vote a document on the teaching ministry of bishops that had also gone through numerous drafts.

With the Liturgy Committee, the Committee on Doctrine also developed in 1990 criteria for using inclusive language in the lectionary and for translating Scripture for the lectionary. Both were hotly debated, but after defeating attempts to amend them, the conference approved both. The document dealing with inclusive language received 35 negative votes and the other document passed on a voice vote.

Dealing with catechetical issues has often been difficult and controversial in the conference. As mentioned above, the NCCB took days to deal with the amendments to the "National Catechetical Directory" in 1977. In 1990 the conference discussed guidelines for catechetical texts and for teaching about human sexuality. Both guidelines, proposed by the Committee on Education, were hotly debated, but the first passed unanimously and the second passed on a voice vote.

Conference Procedures

The conference has also been divided at times over its internal operations. Many bishops opposed allowing the press into their meetings until the bishops voted to admit the press in 1971 (144-106). Those like Russell Shaw and Bishop Malone, who led the fight to open the conference, believe that it made an enormous difference in the way the bishops collectively do business, both in style and substance.

The bishops have also debated at length whether to have one or two meetings a year and where to have them. Thus in 1979 the conference voted against having two meetings a year (95-155), and in 1983 it voted for two meetings (142-101). Raising assessments or taxes on dioceses to support the conference has often been controversial (more will be said about conference finances in Chapter 9).

Another touchy issue is the power of the conference over the bishops in their dioceses. Practically anything that mandates or requires action by a bishop will be controversial, even in areas where the conference is allowed or even required to act by canon law. The conference is an assembly of barons very jealous of their autonomy. When describing a proposal to the bishops, a chair will often emphasize that it is merely a "guideline" that the local bishop can ignore. Outside of the liturgical texts, it is difficult to find many conference actions that are actually binding on the bishops.[57]

A striking example of the reticence of the bishops to give authority to the conference was the Pastoral Plan for Pro-Life Activities adopted in 1985. An amendment passed giving the Committee on Pro-Life Activities authority to "coordinate" diocesan pro-life activities, but it was later reconsidered and defeated when the bishops realized they had given authority over themselves to a conference committee. Likewise, although the conference passed nonbinding "guidelines" for lay preaching in 1988 (195-42), it failed to pass binding "norms" in 1991 (107-141) (see Chapter 8).

In 1988 the bishops passed a controversial response to the Vatican draft document (*instrumentum laboris*) on episcopal conferences (205-59).[58] The conference response was highly critical of the draft. Although few bishops were willing to defend the Vatican draft, many bishops did not want to appear critical of the Vatican. For example, Cardinal Edmund Szoka felt that the suggestions to the Vatican on how to proceed with the document were improper. His motion to strike this section lost on a tie vote (147-147). The section was subsequently toned down through amendments.

Areas of Consensus and Conflict

In this analysis I have concentrated on assembly floor votes as a means of measuring conflict and consensus in the NCCB/USCC. I have purposely avoided basing the study on quotations from the floor debate because an impassioned speaker may be speaking only for himself or a few bishops. For example, although the spirited attacks on the peace pastoral by Archbishop Philip Hannan provided colorful quotations to the press, he had practically no support in the assembly.

An examination of the votes in the NCCB/USCC assembly indicates that the body normally acts by consensus or near-consensus. The bishops' conference appears to find it much easier to obtain agreement on pastoral letters than on liturgy and canon law. Wide consensus exists among the bishops on the economic and political issues, although a vocal minority can sometimes oppose the consensus. But even in liturgy, the conference approved 85 percent of the Liturgy Committee's recommendations.

Disagreements have occurred over general absolution, holy days of obligation, the age of confirmation (see Chapter 8), Communion in the hand, and the pastoral sensitivity with which moral teaching is presented.

In an address to a closed meeting of the NCCB/USCC in June of 1990, Cardinal Bernardin discussed the issue of conflict and disagreement among the American bishops.

> People inside and outside the church make money by attempting to portray a divided church, a divided hierarchy, one which finds it difficult to witness effectively to our common faith because of deep differences in theology and pastoral approach. The spirited and open way in which we conduct our yearly business can unwittingly support such a notion because some think that we always walk or should walk in lock step with each other. Episcopal statements and action, as well as other church events which take place in our own dioceses, are often used as springboards for promoting the notion of episcopal disunity.
>
> There are surely significant differences among us. . . . Even when there is general agreement on the principles which shape certain issues, we differ in the way we think those principles should be applied in concrete situations. I have in mind such things as our response to the AIDS crisis; the abortion debate, especially as it relates to the political situation; the use of capital punishment; the provision of child care; our response to the tragedy playing itself out in El Salvador, etc. It is only human and therefore to be expected

that such differences in approach will exist among us. In aggregate, they provide a certain richness to Catholic life in our country.

To say, however, that differences in approach necessarily constitute deep divisions among us is to ignore . . . that the church's leadership has always been gifted with different approaches. Nonetheless, from the time of the apostles, who reflected the Lord's mandate, there has always been a strong insistence on unity in essentials, in those things that touch the faith; a burning desire to build up the community of faith so that it can give an effective, credible witness to Christ and his Gospel—in every place and era. Over the years, our conference, I believe, has maintained a good balance between the unity which is so essential to the church's well-being and the natural, constructive diversity which flows from the many gifts and charisms of its members.[59]

Executive Sessions

Although most meetings of the assembly have been open to the press since 1972, the bishops meet in executive session without the press at least once every time they gather. Often these sessions take place in the afternoon on the third day of the gathering. By making these executive sessions a regular event, the bishops can meet to discuss issues and problems privately without signaling a major crisis. The Administrative Committee/Board decides which topics should be scheduled for executive session and which for public sessions. Since by definition executive sessions are secret, information on them is limited.[60]

Before discussing what is done in executive session, it is important to emphasize that most of the work of the conference is done in the open. Beginning in 1972, all pastoral letters and statements have been amended and approved in public sessions.[61] Liturgical texts, pastoral plans, and directories have also been acted on in public. In their early stages of development, some of these may have been discussed in executive session, but the actual amending and approval was done in the open.

"There is a little different tonality in the executive sessions, but not much," reports Archbishop Pilarczyk. "We follow the same procedures. It's a little more free and easy, but I don't perceive that it is the case that the real business gets done in the executive sessions, because there just isn't time." The executive session normally lasts only two to four hours.

Topics that tend to be treated in executive session are sensitive or controversial. Some reasons that might lead the Administrative Committee/Board to send an issue to executive session would include: if some bishops disagree with Rome on the issue, if the issue might "scandalize the faithful," if the issue might create negative publicity, if a person's or an organization's reputation might be at stake, or if the bishops feel they cannot discuss the topic honestly in public. Likewise the bishops decided in 1991 to discuss a secret paper on the morality of terminating nutrition and hydration for dying patients. Many bishops did not want to admit that there were open questions here and that the bishops were uncertain.

"Sex and money," was one archbishop's joking description of what the bishops talk about in executive session. A financial issue discussed by the bishops in June 1989 was the question of appropriate compensation for religious working for church organizations. Because of declining numbers and high retirement costs, religious women were asking for increased compensation. Various dioceses were responding in different ways, causing confusion and inequality. Although no national policy was decided, after the meeting the bishops had a better understanding of the issues and what other bishops were doing.

In June 1991, the entire meeting was closed for discussions of finances of the conference. The Administrative Committee/Board wanted "every bishop to be able to say, 'I had every opportunity to say what I wanted to say,'" explains Archbishop Pilarczyk. Executive sessions also allowed bishops to say they could not contribute more to the conference because they faced financial crises at home, something they may not want to admit publicly. In addition, the leadership wanted bishops to be free to say whatever they wanted about conference offices. Since some comments might reflect negatively on conference personnel, it was felt this would better be done in private.

The bishops have also discussed and approved motions to seek money from diocesan bishops to pay legal fees for court cases and to finance grass-roots lobbying for tuition tax credits or against abortion. Other financial issues discussed by the bishops have included guidelines for diocesan finances and fund raising, retirement benefits for bishops, accusations of mismanagement against Catholic Relief Services, and papal finances. Some of these issues, such as CRS and papal finances, were also discussed in public sessions, but bishops would not ask embarrassing questions during public sessions. The guidelines for diocesan finances were also sensitive since they directly affected every bishop. On the one hand, bishops did not want the conference telling them how to run their shops; on the other hand, they realized that financial scandals or mismanagement in one diocese could have a negative impact on the reputations of all dioceses.

Some sexual issues have also been treated in executive session. Sterilization and tubal ligations in Catholic hospitals were discussed, and committee statements were ultimately released.[62] The book, *Human Sexuality*,[63] was discussed in executive session in 1977, as was a LCWR (Leadership Conference of Women Religious) publication, *Choose Life*. Some critics felt *Human Sexuality* abandoned traditional Catholic teaching, while the conference Pro-Life Office criticized *Choose Life* for not clearly giving the church's teaching on abortion. Although many bishops disliked these publications, they did not want to get into a public debate over them. Rather, they had the conference president and general secretary bring their concerns to the attention of the authors.

Another sexual problem that bishops did not want to discuss in public was pedophile priests. "People have said the bishops have never dealt with that," comments Archbishop Pilarczyk. "Well, that's not true." They discussed it in executive session in 1985, 1987, and briefly in 1991.[64] "This pedophilia thing just blew the minds of a lot of bishops," reports Archbishop May. The legal, financial, and morale impact on a diocese was described, as well as the effect on the children and their families. "A lot of bishops felt they had nothing like that in their dioceses," says Archbishop May. "Then they began to realize that this can happen to any bishop around the country, and it's probably going to. That took a lot of real honest talk, and obviously that's not the kind of thing that you would be doing [in open session]."

A few bishops in executive session have called for consideration of optional celibacy. They are reluctant to bring this up in public because of papal opposition to its discussion. Laicization of priests was also discussed in 1979 when the Vatican made it more difficult for resigned priests to be laicized.

Relations with Rome were a frequent topic of executive session, "especially during those years when the scuttlebutt was that Rome was very unhappy with us," reports Archbishop May. The bishops do not want to discuss in public topics where some of them might disagree with Rome. Such topics have included: First Communion before first confession, women lectors and acolytes, annulment procedures, pastoral care of divorced and remarried Catholics, Catholic membership in Masonic societies, Communion under both kinds on Sunday, process for selection of bishops, papal finances, an ecclesiastical mandate for theology teachers (canon 812), revoking the imprimatur of *Christ Among Us*, Tridentine Mass, the use of grape juice at Mass by alcoholic priests, and the Vatican treatment of Archbishop Raymond Hunthausen. More will be said on these topics in Chapter 8.

Other issues have been treated in executive session because of their potential impact on local dioceses. Guidelines for the ministries of catechist and minister of sacred music were discussed and postponed. The bishops had difficulty determining what the guidelines should be and they feared creating official ministries that might be interpreted as positions of status rather than service. Likewise the bishops also had extensive discussions to draw up guidelines for accepting converted married ministers, especially Episcopal priests. They also discussed the possibility of sabbaticals for bishops.

Politically controversial topics have also been discussed in executive session, especially the bishops' strategy for passing a pro-life amendment and obtaining federal funding (or tuition tax credits) for Catholic schools. Thus in 1989 the bishops discussed pro-life strategies after the Webster decision, and in 1990 they received a report on Hill & Knowlton's work for the Pro-Life Committee. Abortion and funding for Catholic schools have also been discussed frequently in public sessions. In November 1990, the bishops voted to discuss the Persian Gulf in executive session where they authorized Archbishop Pilarczyk to write President Bush to express their concerns.[65] The motion to hold the discussion in executive session was made by Cardinal Bernard Law, the American prelate closest to President George Bush. "That vote deprived the whole church and the world of their reasonable right to know how the bishops arrived at the moral conclusions openly reported after the closed session," complained Bishop McManus.[66]

After the executive sessions have concluded, bishops have sometimes expressed regret that the meeting was closed. After public disagreement among the bishops over the USCC Administrative Board's AIDS statement, the bishops met in executive session in the spring of 1988. While leaving the statement in place, the bishops decided to have an additional statement by the entire assembly. By all accounts, the discussion helped heal the division among the bishops. At the press conference following the session, the bishops regretted that the press had missed the discussions.

"Strangely, the bishops of late have been hidden behind closed doors when they were at their best, debating and deciding controversial questions," writes Bishop William McManus, "but have exposed themselves to the media when they were at their worst, tediously discussing trivial topics."[67]

Factors Encouraging Consensus and Conflict

There are several factors that encourage consensus building and compromise in the conference. Catholic theology encourages the image of the hierarchy acting as a united magisterium. Open sessions discourage bishops from being too divided lest they "scandalize the faithful" and give headlines to the press. Episcopal norms of mutual respect and brotherhood also temper the debate. The reluctance of bishops to pass binding decisions means that bishops disagreeing with nonbinding guidelines can simply ignore them rather than fight them. And conference rules requiring a two-thirds vote for approval of most decisions encourage consensus-building and compromise before the vote takes place.

Other factors, however, work to make compromise difficult. Some liturgical and canonical questions require definite decisions that cannot be compromised. Sometimes the bishops deal with issues of principle or theology that they believe cannot be compromised without betraying the faith. If the bishops are divided over such issues, they tend to sidestep them (as they did in the discussion of condoms in AIDS education programs) or they use ambiguous language that covers over the conflict. "Ambiguity is a legitimate and treasured part of our moral tradition," explained Archbishop Roach when the bishops were working on the peace pastoral. "Perhaps the consensus will be on ambiguity."[68]

In the debate over the "National Catechetical Directory," Archbishop Whealon, who chaired the drafting committee, admitted, "There were ideological difficulties never solved, so the text has a certain neutrality and a certain compromise, a balance in it, that speaks to the professional religious educators."

What makes the conference very nervous is anything that might be interpreted as a retreat from traditional church teaching. The relaxing of the fast and abstinence laws in 1966 caused concern. The 1972 Blanchette amendment wanted to emphasize the unchanging nature of church doctrine. Also the 1972 O'Boyle amendment, reasserting the traditional right of self-defense, was inserted in the "Resolution on the Imperative of Peace." Objections to capital punishment encountered similar concerns in 1974 and 1980.

This same impulse made the bishops supportive of *Humanae Vitae* in their pastoral letter of 1976, and nervous about some recommendations of the Detroit Call to Action conference. The assembly also had difficulty understanding how any use of nuclear weapons could be justified under the traditional just war theory. At the same time, they did not want to be branded as consequentialists because of their arguments in conditionally approving deterrence. The controversies over the Administrative Board's 1987 AIDS statement and over the statement on doctrinal responsibility are other examples. Amendments that emphasize orthodox teaching are usually supported by the conference. For example, in 1989 the bishops objected to a liturgical document that spoke of the Eucharist as bread. The bishops adopted three amendments adding "eucharistic" or "sacred" as modifiers to bread or substituting "hosts" for bread.

The bishops are also very reluctant to appear in conflict with Rome. If a bishop wants to amend a document by adding a quotation from the pope, it usually passes, even if the drafting committee objects. In the debate over the 1990 guidelines on teaching human sexuality, Bishop Raymond Lessard wanted to add a controversial quote from the Vatican Congregation for the Doctrine of the Faith stating that although not a sin, homosexual inclination "is a more or less strong tendency ordered toward an intrinsic moral evil; and thus the inclination itself must be seen as an objective disorder." Archbishops William Borders, John Quinn, and others feared the quotation would be misunderstood as saying homosexual persons are evil. In a classic compromise, Cardinal Bernardin proposed stating that a homosexual "orientation in itself, because not freely chosen, is not sinful" while putting the quotation from the congregation in a footnote.

The bishops over the years have developed processes and procedures for building consensus. For example, before a committee can initiate work on a pastoral letter it must now get approval from the conference. On major letters, the committee then holds hearings and consults with the various experts and constituencies interested in the topic. A series of drafts can be circulated and discussed. The more controversial a document, the more drafts it goes through. Suggestions and amendments are solicited from the bishops. When the bishops finally debate a document, amendments can be offered and voted on.

The assembly usually follows the drafting committee's recommendations. This could indicate: a) a high degree of congruence in thought between the members of committees and the members of the assembly; b) a high level of trust in the committees by the assembly membership; c) a conflict avoidance strategy by which the committees anticipate the desires of the assembly when drafting documents or accepting amendments (this raises the question of who is following whom); and/or d) a willingness of most bishops to compromise rather than fight in public.

"Whether a thing passes or not has to do with the level of trust that the chairman establishes and the level of competence that the chairman establishes by whatever means at his disposal," explains a staff person. "If a chairman doesn't seem to be able to deal with the issues, often the bishops are going to vote against him."

The assembly is not a rubber stamp for the drafting committees. *Robert's Rules of Order* allows any bishop to offer an amendment. If he has support in the assembly, the drafting committee is overruled. Interviews indicate that drafting committees often modify their documents so as to expand consensus before they bring them to the assembly. Committees that suffer the most defeats, Canonical Affairs and Liturgy, often must present action items that cannot be modified but demand a yes or no decision.

Increasing Conflict?

Many bishops and conference observers expressed the view that conflict is increasing in the conference. Often they describe this as a conflict between the more "liberal" bishops appointed under Archbishop Jadot and Paul VI and the more "conservative" bishops appointed under Archbishop Laghi and John Paul II.[69] Several people who have occupied key positions in the conference expressed this belief, but did not want to say so on the record. "There was a small group of progressives who grew in number and were controlling in the conference," explains one person. "Now, with appointment of new bishops, the conference is more conservative."

"There's substantial truth to conventional wisdom on the subject, namely that you have at least two distinct groups of bishops within the episcopal conference in the United States," reports Russell Shaw, who worked for the conference for many years as press secretary and ghost writer. "You have the Jadot bishops and the post-Jadot bishops, John Paul II bishops. Everybody recognizes that. While it's much too simplified a way of describing the reality, nevertheless there's a substantial element of truth to that. The difference, the distinction, and the division have expressed themselves very publicly and very dramatically on a couple of occasions recently, especially with respect to that first statement on AIDS."

Some people have also argued that as more conservative bishops have filled the conference, it has backed away from its social justice agenda. They claim the conference has been less active since the passage of the peace and economic pastorals. But other factors are also at play. "The bishops liked the peace letter, they liked the economics letter, they liked the other statements on social concerns," explains Ron Krietemeyer.

> At the same time, there was a desire that it not be quite as time-consuming. They had spent a lot of energy engaging in that. And there was a little burnout on major statements just because of all the attention that it took from them. They were just barely done with the peace pastoral letter, and the first draft of the economic pastoral hit the desk. After they got through the final vote on that, it was like, "Okay, we'll take a little break here."

Even after the economic and peace pastorals, the bishops approved major statements in 1989 on Vietnam and the Middle East, and a 1988 report on the moral evaluation of nuclear deterrence. The bishops still appear to agree on economic and peace issues, although other issues have divided them. "In some areas, at least, it is more difficult to obtain a consensus than it was in the earlier days," said Cardinal Bernardin. Difficulties arise over doctrinal matters, he notes. "I think the AIDS statement is certainly an example of what I mean. Everybody entered into that in good faith. Nonetheless, there were some real differences as to what we should say or the differences as regard to what was actually said in the document."

"While we are all orthodox," he continued, "I think there is greater concern or anxiety that we express these things in a way that will not be misunderstood. That was evident, for example, in the document on the relationship between theologians and bishops. There was a lot of anxiety expressed about that."

"I don't see us backing up at all on social issues," reports Archbishop Roach. "But on church issues, I think that the ecclesiology voiced frequently today on the floor is a little more conservative than was true of the past. Again, I don't want to belabor that too much, because I am not sure that is as bad as some people think it is, but I think it is there."

Archbishop John Whealon disagreed that there is more conflict today. He recalled that the good old days were not as peaceful as they are remembered.

> We had some magnificent disagreements back in the old days. I can remember the day when Cardinal McIntyre walked out and said he would have nothing more to do with this NCCB/USCC business. Nobody knew quite what to do about it; nobody had ever quit the NCCB before. But there were people in those days who would express themselves much more eloquently. They'd make impassioned speeches on the floor. We have none of that now. I think the bishops themselves are much more calm about what they do and what they say.

Some conference structures and procedures have reduced conflict. For example, more documentation is sent out before meetings than in earlier days. Interested bishops have a chance to study it and give written suggestions to the committees. Some earlier fights occurred when bishops were given insufficient time to reflect and have a say on the issues.

But conflict will always be present in the conference. Bishop Malone recalls meeting with his Liturgy Committee after one of its many defeats in the early 1970s.

> We would as a committee sit down and take stock of where we were and what we could try to do next. We would often make the statement that ten years from now the Liturgy Committee will have

an easy time because these old-timers will die off and a new and enlightened species will come along and take their place. I have since come to realize that every generation produces its own spectrum of differences.

Desire for Unity and Consensus

Talk of division within the American hierarchy has to be balanced by "the fact that all of the bishops, virtually without exception, want to hang together," explains Mr. Shaw.

> You can put it in cynical terms: "If we don't hang together, we'll hang separately," and there's some of that spirit in the organization.
>
> But they also have a highly developed sense of responsibility to the church as a whole, and they perceive quite correctly that divisions in the ranks of the hierarchy are not going to serve the interests of the people of God, and the bishops really should, in everyone's best interests, try not only to give the image of working together, but to make working together a reality.
>
> Now, given that these differences of approach and style and policy and emphasis and conviction and so forth do exist among them, I suspect that the very sincerely motivated attempt to continue to hang together and work together has tended to slow things down and perhaps to create a situation of, if not precisely stalemate, an inability to get things done, or to get things done quickly, or perhaps to tackle some questions and issues that they realize are simply beyond their capacity at the present time.

Most of the bishops would agree that it is better for them to appear to agree. "I don't want to say image in any phony sense," says Archbishops Pilarczyk, "but it is probably better for the church in the long run if the bishops are perceived as being of one mind. Now, in the short run, maybe it's just as well if some bishop says I disagree with that occasionally, because not everything we do is equally important. But by and large, I think it is better for the church if the bishops are perceived as being of one mind."

The desire for consensus encourages compromise. But some bishops feel that compromise weakens the episcopal voice. "Can [the NCCB/USCC] speak to our age in a prophetic voice, or does the necessity of consensus mute its voice?" asked Cardinal John Dearden.[70] "It is nice to advocate consensus as the final goal of something," Bishop Austin Vaughan told the conference in 1988, "but if consensus is to be a rule, every step of the way, then we are not going to wind up getting anywhere because the things that everybody can agree on, apart from procedurally, are not a whole lot."

The bishops prefer to operate on a consensus model of decision-making, but that is simply not always possible. When they are not "of one mind," then they want to be seen as people who can work out differences and arrive at a working consensus with which most of them can live. Through trial and error, the bishops attempt to deal with disagreements and expand agreement through discussion and compromise. But "no matter what you do, there are some people who aren't going to be satisfied," says Archbishop Pilarczyk, "not because they are difficult people, but because every time you make a decision, there's another side to it. And if somebody thinks the other side was more important than the side that you backed, well, they're going to disagree with you. However, my experience has been that the bishops disagree in a very humane and respectful way. I have never been attacked; I have never been demeaned."

Part of the consensus comes from the knowledge that bishops can often ignore conference decisions in their dioceses. "It may also be that the bishops who don't like stuff just go home and forget it," says Archbishop Pilarczyk. "That's fine, but they would not go to the press and say, 'This was outrageous.' There's a kind of understanding that you've got your vote. You vote it up or you vote it down. If you've lost, you've lost, and you can do whatever you want to do about that at home." This especially applies to pastoral letters and statements. "I know of no situation, ever, in which a local bishop changed his position as the result of a mandated teaching document from the conference," reports Archbishop Francis Hurley. Thus the price of consensus can sometimes be ineffectiveness.

But it would be a mistake to see compromise and silence as the primary roots of consensus. In the spring of 1991, a confidential NCCB/USCC survey found that 94 percent of the bishops agreed "that the actions taken by the full body in plenary assembly do represent my views as a local bishop."[71] Only 13 percent agreed "that the Parliamentary Procedures utilized at general meetings work to the detriment of episcopal collegiality." Clearly the vast majority of the bishops are pleased with the procedures and actions of the assembly.

Although it is difficult (and beyond the scope of this book) to measure the implementation and effectiveness of conference decisions and recommendations on the local level, the conference's role in national politics is more easily examined. The next chapter will examine the impact of the NCCB/USCC on national politics, especially on national elections and congressional legislation.

7. Shepherds Among the Wolves

To condemn kings, not serve among their servants, is my open office!
——THOMAS A'BECKET[1]

The U.S. Catholic Church is the most effective political force advocating the liberal agenda.
——STEPHEN D. JOHNSON AND JOSEPH B. TAMNEY[2]

Until the bishops decide an issue, we don't move.
——JOHN CARR

From their very beginning in the 19th century, a primary purpose of episcopal conferences was to provide a mechanism for dealing with government officials. This was certainly the primary purpose of the NCWC when it was founded during the First World War. Msgr. John J. Burke, the first general secretary, believed that the church needed the NCWC to look out for Catholic interests, just as other interest groups had Washington-based organizations to look out for theirs.

The issues of concern to the NCCB/USCC include a much broader agenda than would be covered by most other interest groups. Part of the agenda includes issues that impact on the financial and legal well-being of the institutional church and church organizations: aid to Catholic schools, funding of Catholic social services, tax exemption of church entities, tax deductions for charitable giving, and the impact of government laws and regulations on church organizations.

Other issues that do not directly impact on the church are also of concern to the bishops. The conference has taken positions on abortion, civil rights, communications policy, criminal law, family policy, welfare reform, farm policy, labor legislation, and military and foreign policy. The motivation for these positions is the bishops' concern for social justice and morality. On the other hand, the conference has a policy against endorsing candidates for electoral or appointed offices. Nor does it make financial contributions to electoral campaigns.

The active involvement of the conference in public policy issues has been challenged. Especially vocal have been the critics of the bishops' positions on peace, economic issues, abortion, and aid to Catholic schools. Just before the November 1982 meeting of the bishops to discuss a second draft of the peace pastoral, the Reagan White House launched a preemptive strike by releasing to the press a letter highly critical of the draft from National Security Adviser William Clark.[3] The attack was counterproductive and simply generated more publicity for the bishops' letter.

"They played right into the bishops' hands on that one," recalls Russell Shaw, NCCB/USCC press secretary at the time. "If there had been a better way of calling attention to what the bishops were doing and getting publicity for what the bishops were going to say, you'd have to tell me what it was. It was as if some perverse spirits had taken charge of the White House and were causing them to do things to call further attention to this episcopal document which apparently they didn't like at all."

Sometimes the White House is more friendly. The day of his election as president of the conference, Archbishop John Quinn was invited to the White House. "I was elected in the morning," he recalls, "and within an hour or so I received an invitation from Vice President Mondale to come to lunch at the White House. I was scheduled to have lunch with Archbishop Jadot, the apostolic delegate, that day. So I called him and he said, 'You must go to the White House.' So I went, and during the lunch President and Mrs. Carter came in to say hello."

Early in his administration, President Reagan also invited a group of bishops to visit him in the White House. "He had an open agenda," reports Archbishop John May, NCCB/USCC vice president at the time. "He invited us to say whatever we liked. [Cardinal] Szoka brought up the whole question of race relations in this country, and he spoke of course, of the situation in Detroit. And he told the president, very honestly, that black people don't look for much from him, that that's their feeling and that's his image with them. And we would like to help in any way we can."

Some critics have accused the bishops of breaching the wall separating church and state when they push for legislation that would enshrine their moral views. This is a simplistic view of the First Amendment. Bishops do not lose any of their constitutional rights as citizens when they are consecrated. They still have the right of free speech, assembly, press, and petition. They even have the legal right to run for political office, although church rules prohibit it. Clergy in other churches have not held back from being candidates. For example, Senator John Danforth (an Episcopal priest), the Rev. Pat Robertson, the Rev. Jesse Jackson, and numerous other black ministers have run for office. In fact the bishops have been more restrained in exercising their constitutional rights than have some clergymen, such as the Rev. Jerry Falwell, the Rev. Martin Luther King, the Rev. Pat Robertson, the Rev. Jimmy Swaggart, and the Rev. Jesse Jackson. Ordination does not eliminate constitutional rights, nor does it instill in the bishops a political wisdom superior to that of their fellow citizens.

A grayer legal area involves the use of the church's tax-exempt funds.[4] Congress, in granting certain groups a tax-exempt status, forbids them to devote a substantial portion of their resources to lobbying. The meaning of a "substantial portion" is vague. Does it mean a dollar amount, that is, $1 million is substantial, but $100 is not? Or does it mean a percentage of the budget or assets, 75 percent is substantial, but 1 percent is not?[5] A percentage figure applied to the Catholic church could be very large if the definition included the financial resources of all the dioceses, parishes, schools, hospitals, and other institutions in the United States.

Attempts to litigate these issues have been unsuccessful. One tax-exempt organization argued that any restriction on lobbying was unconstitutional because the government cannot require the giving up of a constitutional right (to petition) in order to obtain a benefit (tax exemption). The courts refused to accept the case, saying that the organization did not have standing to sue.[6]

Similarly, the tax laws forbid tax exempt organizations from participating in or intervening in any political campaign for or against any candidate for public office. The Abortion Rights Mobilization (ARM) argued that the tax exemption of the bishops' conference should be withdrawn because the Catholic church had violated the tax code by helping pro-life political candidates and fighting pro-choice candidates. After nine years of litigation, the courts decided that ARM did not have standing to sue.[7] In settling a case with Jimmy Swaggart Ministries, the IRS indicated that although ministers can be involved in political campaigns, an endorsement of a candidate by a minister at an official function of the organization would be considered an endorsement of the candidate by the organization.

The Catholic church has usually been careful to avoid compromising its tax exemption. Every four years, the USCC general counsel distributes a memorandum advising church officials what is permissible and prohibited activity during an election year.[8] For example, the conference tells editors of Catholic newspapers not to endorse candidates and, if they accept political advertising from one person, they should accept it from all candidates. But editorials about legislation before Congress are not discouraged. "You don't attack persons, you go after ideas," explains John Gouldrick, C.M., former director of the Pro-Life Office. That is "basic charity. Plus the IRS is a major factor. We got in a little bit of trouble probably earlier, going after Ferraro." No matter what the law, the Internal Revenue Service is reluctant to litigate a complex case involving the tax exemption of the Catholic church, freedom of the press, freedom of petition, and freedom of religion.

Elections

The involvement of U.S. bishops in politics has been controversial both within and outside the conference. In 1975, the conference adopted the "Pastoral Plan for Pro-Life Activities," which called for the "development in each congressional district of an identifiable, tightly-knit, and well-organized pro-life unit."[9] Out of this pastoral plan came the National Committee for a Human Life Amendment, which works through grass-roots lobbying and political action for the passage of a human life amendment to the U.S. Constitution. The committee does not endorse candidates, but it does distribute literature showing how members of Congress voted on pro-life issues.

The emphasis on abortion has led many to accuse the bishops of being concerned about a single issue. Partly as a response to this criticism, beginning in 1976, the USCC Administrative Board has issued a statement on "Political Responsibility" every four years, prior to the presidential election. The statements urge Catholics to vote, but do not tell them whom to vote for. The statements also list issues of concern to the bishops. Normally the statements do not break new ground but reflect in summary form positions taken by the bishops previously. The statements also apply previously established policy to new circumstances. Although these statements are primarily aimed at voters, they also provide a mandate for staff activity on a variety of issues.

The statements have been fairly noncontroversial and widely supported by the bishops, but sometimes controversy arose over which issues should be emphasized and given priority. "It used to be real *Sturm und Drang* getting out those statements on political responsibility every few years," explains Mr. Shaw. "'In what order will we list these issues?'" The bishops decided to list the issues in alphabetical order, which greatly reduced conflict over priorities. "We pro-lifers came out on top," explains Mr. Shaw, "because our issue began with an 'A'." One member of the staff felt that Mr. Shaw fought a lonely battle against some issues in the political responsibility statement, and that when he left the USCC staff the statement became noncontroversial.

In any case, listing the issues in alphabetical order avoided the appearance of saying that abortion was more important than anything else, while still listing it first. In 1976 the eight issues were abortion, the economy, education, food policy, housing, human rights and U.S. foreign policy, mass media, and military expenditures.[10] By 1980 those interested in peace issues learned the rules of the game and changed the title of their issue from "military expenditures" to "arms control and disarmament," which moved it from last to second place after abortion.[11] Agricultural issues were always listed under "Food" lest they outrank arms control.

The length of the document has grown over time, as has the number of issues covered. In 1976 the statement covered eight issues in 3,400 words; by 1992 there were 17 issues and 8,700 words.[12] Besides abortion and arms control, the 1980 statement covered ten other issues: capital punishment, the economy, education, family life, food and agricultural policy, health care, housing, human rights, mass media, and regional conflict in the world.[13] In 1984, the same issues were listed, and civil rights and energy were added for a total of 14.[14] And in 1988, the issues were the same as in 1984, except that energy was dropped and immigration and refugee policy were added.[15] For the 1992 election the Administrative Board added euthanasia and substance abuse. In addition, civil rights was reclassified as "Discrimination and Racism."[16]

Since the 1970s, the conference has also sent a bishop or staff person to make presentations to the Democratic and Republican party platform committees.[17] These presentations repeat the issues raised in the political responsibility statements and in other statements of the conference. The conference also sends a questionnaire to the presidential candidates asking their positions on various issues listed in the political responsibility statement. USCC lawyers judge that distribution of the responses to the questionnaire meet IRS criteria for nonpartisan voter education.[18]

Conference officials are cautious about being co-opted by politicians of whatever stripe.[19] During the 1976 presidential campaign, the conference was asked to send someone to Plains, Georgia, to brief Jimmy Carter on the bishops' concerns. Although he had only been with the conference for a short time and was a low-level staff person, John Carr was picked to go by Bishop James Rausch, the general secretary.

Bishop Rausch did not want to send someone with a Roman collar who could easily be identified and photographed.

Mr. Carr recalls being telephoned by Bishop Rausch at 10 P.M. and being told, "We've been invited to be a part of the briefing for the Democratic nominee, and we don't want it to be too high-level, but we don't want to be embarrassed, so you're going. I want you to talk about the housing and economic stuff you've been working on. I want you to talk about pro-life, and I want you to talk about tuition tax credits. And stay out of the media." Mr. Carr had not worked on the last two issues and argued someone else could make the case better, but to no avail.

At 7 A.M. the next day, he was on his way to Georgia with several people who ended up in the Carter cabinet, including Ray Marshall, Michael Blumenthal, and Stuart Eisenstadt. After a four-hour briefing session, Mr. Carr was taken "to the Plains train station where there are more cameras than I have ever seen in my life." Mr. Carter was planning to introduce everyone and have them talk about the briefing. Mr. Carr recalls:

> I went up to Eisenstadt and I said, "I can't do this." He says, "What do you mean, you can't do this? Tell them what you told him. Do that stuff about abortion and tuition." I said, "If you put me up at that microphone, I'm going to have to say we're looking forward to our meeting with President Ford. You don't want that."

Mr. Eisenstadt explained this to Mr. Carter and Mr. Carr was not introduced.

Later in the 1976 campaign, matters got worse.[20] Mr. Carter asked to meet with the bishops in the hope of emphasizing areas of agreement while downplaying disagreements over abortion. Bishop Rausch, the general secretary, encouraged the meeting although Archbishop Joseph Bernardin, then NCCB/USCC president, was reluctant.[21] In any case, Archbishop Bernardin and the other members of the NCCB/USCC Executive Committee met with Mr. Carter. Comments made by Archbishop Bernardin after the meetings were interpreted as an endorsement of President Ford. Russell Shaw, press secretary to the conference, remembers it vividly.[22]

God knows why Carter chose to meet with the delegation of bishops in a room off the lobby of the Mayflower Hotel, but he did. So Carter's holed up in a room off the lobby of the Mayflower with Bernardin and some others. And then Carter comes out and vanishes, he and his entourage.

And we're left with a maddened press corps demanding to know what happened, what went on. [In response to a question] poor Bernardin said, "Yes we talked about abortion with Mr. Carter and we were disappointed with his position."

I mean, if you think we got into things like that with malice aforethought, we didn't. Things just happen. Archbishop Bernardin used that famous word "disappointed" and all hell broke loose. A firestorm in the media and all sorts of pressures and conflicts within the bishops' conference and so forth. It was a very difficult and trying few weeks.

After a few weeks, the Ford Administration caught on to the fact that maybe they had a good thing going for them with the Catholic bishops, so they invited a delegation of bishops over to the White House. I was hauled along as the press secretary for the bishops' conference. The delegation of bishops went into the president's office by themselves, and they left me sitting in the Cabinet room. They were in there for half an hour or so talking with President Ford, and then they came out and they knew they had to go out into the press room and talk to the press. They sat down with me and discussed among themselves, "What are we going to say to the press?"

You may think I'm making this up, but I'm not. I recall one of them saying—I honestly don't remember which one—I recall one of them saying, "Let's tell the press that we were encouraged by President Ford's position on the abortion issue." I really recall thinking to myself, "I don't believe that's going to be a good idea." But for whatever reason, timidity or ennui or something, I didn't say anything. So that's what they did. They went out and told the White House press corps that they were encouraged by President Ford's position on the abortion issue, just as a few weeks earlier they'd been discouraged or disappointed by Governor Carter's position. Once again, all hell broke loose.

I can assure you, I don't want to tell horror stories or go into too much of this, but I can assure you that the staff of the bishops' conference were just ripping one another up one side and down the other all this time. Fierce internal fighting about the wisdom and prudence of what the bishops had been doing out there in the political arena.

It all came to a head for the bishops' conference during the Administrative Committee meeting of September of that year, when the Administrative Committee, after having agonized at considerable length, finally adopted a statement in which they more or less tried to back away from the whole issue, successfully or unsuccessfully I don't know. But things died down after that. It was a tough few weeks.

[It's] a great example of how things just happen and people just respond without a lot of forethought to situations.

The statement approved by the Administrative Committee noted "some public misperceptions concerning the nature and purpose of the meetings with the candidates. . . . We reject any interpretation of the meetings with the candidates as indicating a preference for either candidate or party. There are elements of agreement and disagreement on many issues between our positions and those of the major parties, their platforms and their candidates."[23] On abortion the committee stated:

Abortion and the need for a constitutional amendment to protect the unborn are among our concerns. So are the issues of unemployment, adequate educational opportunity for all, an equitable food policy, both domestic and worldwide, the right to a decent home and health care, human rights across the globe, intelligent arms limitation and many social justice issues.

When Archbishop John Quinn became president, he told the general secretary he did not want a repeat of the 1976 fiasco during the 1980 election. He kept a very low profile during the election and the media gave more attention to the "new right" and the "Moral Majority."[24]

In 1984 and 1988, the NCCB/USCC presidents continued to avoid controversy during the elections, but other prelates, such as Cardinal John O'Connor of New York and Bernard Law of Boston, were not so hesitant. Cardinal O'Connor's attacks on the 1984 Democratic vice presidential candidate captured headlines across the country. Geraldine Ferraro, a Catholic, supported public funding of abortion, a position opposed by the bishops. The NCCB/USCC leadership neither joined the attack nor came to her defense, although they kept quoting the statement on political responsibility, indicating the bishops' concern for other issues besides abortion. This did little to take the spotlight away from Cardinal O'Connor's disagreements with Ms. Ferraro.[25]

Meanwhile, the ad hoc committee drafting the economic pastoral delayed releasing a new draft until after the 1984 election lest the bishops be accused of trying to influence the election. On the day of the election, the new draft was Federal Expressed to all the bishops so they would have it before their meeting, which was held six days after the election.

In 1988 when President Bush asked to see the NCCB/USCC president during the campaign, Archbishop May consented. The archbishop gave him a copy of the USCC Statement on Political Responsibility. "I'm sure he never saw it before, and I just put that before him," explains Archbishop May. "It had such things as capital punishment and so on. He thought, I suppose, the usual thing would be on abortion, but there were a lot of things there, a lot of life issues, the questions of budget and debt and so on." But in 1988, the candidates and the media were less interested in the bishops, perhaps because both candidates were less comfortable with religious rhetoric, and the Republicans felt they could do better with crime (Willie Horton) than abortion as an issue.[26]

Church Lobbyists

From its very beginning, the conference has had an office dealing with laws and legislation.[27] Soon after its founding, the NCWC had to deal with proposed federal regulations for obtaining altar wine during Prohibition. "Almost immediately telegrams poured in from bishops and priests from all over the country with different and sometimes contradictory suggestions, causing much confusion among government officials."[28] On the authority of the NCWC Administrative Board, the staff met with government officials to work out a suitable procedure.

For many years the conference's primary concern was laws that directly affected the church or church-related organizations, for example, tax exemption and aid to schools. The lawyers working for the conference saw their role as defending the institutional interests of the church and not working for social justice. This began to change in the mid-1970s as the conference began to take a more activist role in social justice issues on Capitol Hill. One staff person from that period recalls describing to a Government Liaison lawyer the work he was doing on a statement on economic issues. "This guy looked across the table at me and said, 'Over my dead body. That's going to confuse a lot of people.'" The passage of the peace and the economic pastorals, together with changes in staff, have resulted in more openness to lobbying for social justice.

The USCC secretariat now has a Government Liaison Office with four lobbyists and a director.[29] This office has primary responsibility for representing the bishops to the U.S. Congress and executive branch. Each lobbyist covers an interest area reflecting the legislative agenda of the conference and the division of committee jurisdiction on Capitol Hill. This allows the lobbyists to develop expertise in their area of responsibility and to develop contacts on the Hill.

One lobbyist deals with taxes, welfare, Supplemental Security Income, and Medicaid, which are under the jurisdiction of the House Ways and Means Committee and the Senate Finance Committee. Another covers immigration, civil rights, and criminal justice (gun control and the death penalty), which are under the jurisdiction of the House and Senate Judiciary Committees. A third lobbyist originally dealt with education, but his responsibilities were expanded to cover labor issues, which are the responsibility of the same congressional committees that deal with education. He also picked up school lunch programs sponsored by the agricultural committees and then other nutrition and agricultural issues, including food stamps. A final lobbyist deals with pro-life issues, which are dealt with by several congressional committees including Labor, Health, and Appropriations. He also covers health issues because health legislation often has abortion-related issues. He also handles communications issues.

Interestingly, these lobbyists all concentrate on domestic issues. None specializes in military or international issues, despite the bishops' pastoral letter on peace. "International justice and peace is kind of kicked around," admits Frank Monahan, director of Government Liaison. "I've handled it," and others have backed him up.

In the mid 1970s, any lobbying on military issues was out of bounds. "We could advocate increases in domestic spending for housing and health care and hunger and for welfare relief, but we were not to suggest in any way, shape, or form that the defense budget might be too large," recalls one staff person. "That was grounds for firing." The peace pastoral opened the door for some lobbying, for example, against the MX missile. The end of the Cold War has opened the door wider.

The Government Liaison Office works closely with six other USCC offices concerned about public policy issues: the Communications Department, the Domestic Social Development Office, the Education Department, the International Justice and Peace Office, the Migration and Refugee Services, and the Pro-Life Office.

"Government Liaison is our Federal Express, it's our courier service," explains Msgr. Robert Lynch, the general secretary.

> They don't make policy, but they carry the policy from the conference to the Hill. We do not allow the program units to do their own lobbying, for a variety of reasons, control being one of the more important ones. We encourage the Government Liaison Office to make use of the talent in the program office to accompany them and to help make the case, but we don't allow them to initiate contacts and to design the plan for lobbying for their own issue. Government Liaison devises a lobbying plan and implements that lobbying plan to achieve a desired end or goal.

Mr. Monahan explains how his office works with others in the conference.

> The actual lobbying is supposed to reside in our office, but obviously when you've got an agenda that big, we can't be the experts in every issue. So we work in a team relationship with John Carr's [So-

cial Development and World Peace] department and Nick DiMarzio's [Migration and Refugee Services] office and bring them into play when we need that expertise.

They do all the policy analysis, they do the testimony writing, and that sort of stuff. They decide who they want to represent their views up on the Hill, whether it's a staff person or a bishop. They monitor the issues in much more depth. We do a much more superficial monitoring of a much wider range of issues. Then we team together and decide how we want to carry an issue forward in the lobbying program.

In the actual lobbying, the lobbyists would bring to the Hill the appropriate experts from the other USCC offices. These experts can explain to congressional members and staff the arguments supporting the conference's position. As these experts become known to people on the Hill, they are consulted directly as issues develop and progress through the legislative process. Coordination here is important so that the conference staff are all speaking with the same voice to the Hill.

Working together is especially important when an issue touches the concerns of several offices. For example, the Civil Rights Restoration Act of 1988 was a major concern of the Domestic Social Development Office which wants to improve the treatment of minorities in the United States. On the other hand, the Education Department and the General Counsel's Office were concerned about how the law might apply to Catholic institutions. Also, the Pro-Life Office worried about the bill's impact on abortion. All these concerns had to be considered before the conference could support a particular bill. As long as the proposed bill listed abortion as a civil right, the conference opposed the bill. Once that was eliminated, the conference helped line up votes to override the president's veto.

Because the perspectives of the various USCC offices differ, they also vary in their willingness to compromise on the issues involved in a complex piece of legislation. For example, on child care, the Catholic social service agencies were more willing to compromise on church-state language than were the schools. Catholic Charities have an easier time passing the "secular test" than do schools. Differences among the staff sometimes have to be resolved at a higher level. "When you can't agree, you go to the associate, and he may take it to the general secretary or you may ask to have it taken there," explains John Carr, secretary for Social Development and World Peace. "If he's in doubt, it goes to the Executive Committee; if they're in doubt, it goes to the Administrative Board." If these staff differences reflect differences among bishops or conference committees, the matter would go to the Administrative Board.

Conference Positions

The positions taken by the USCC are determined by the bishops and not by the lobbyists or the other USCC staff, although the staff obviously plays a major role in developing these positions for the bishops. Most positions taken by the USCC have a long history rooted in the pastoral letters and statements issued by the conference and its committees over the years. In some cases the conference and its committees have taken very specific stances, while in others they have articulated general principles. In either case, the staff could not lobby for a position that contradicted conference policy without inviting criticism from their opponents and getting in trouble with the bishops. Adopting a new policy would require extensive internal review by the staff and approval by the appropriate conference committee. If the issue is controversial, the committee would take the matter to the Administrative Board.

"The mythology that you have a Machiavellian staff or runaway staff is just so out of line with my experience, where everything of significance has to be authorized," reports Mr. Carr. "I've never been in a more accountable position. I think that's the way it ought to be. The conference's clout comes from the bishops. And the conference's agenda has to come from the bishops. Staff who don't understand that shouldn't work here."

The process for reviewing testimony or letters to government officials is extensive and detailed. The review makes sure that the staff is saying what the bishops want and that different offices are not contradicting each other. Consideration of who would sign the letter or give the testimony would be part of the review.

Normally the process begins with a staff person drafting a letter (or testimony). After review and approval by his departmental secretary, it would be sent for review to the appropriate committee chairs, to Government Liaison, Media Relations, General Counsel, and other interested offices. The conference has a "Consultation Form" (see page 202) attached to the presentation when it is circulated. On the form must be noted the specific source of conference policy that supports the position taken in the presentation. The source might be a pastoral letter or a position taken by a conference committee or the Administrative Committee/Board. The staff must always show that what they say is backed up by episcopal authority.

The "Consultation Form" also asks if the issue being addressed has a financial or regulatory impact on Catholic institutions. If the answer is "yes," then an assessment of the impact must be attached. For example, when Congress considered legislation on requiring public buildings to be accessible to the handicapped, the conference supported the idea but worried about how it would affect the church institutions. On the one hand, the conference had approved a statement in 1978 calling on churches to make themselves accessible. On the other, it feared government interference in religious affairs. The administration and the National Council of Churches called for a total exemption for churches. After much internal debate, the conference decided it could live with a requirement of ramps and accessible rest rooms. But it opposed government interference in the design of worship space or in the selection of ministers. The cost of installing elevators to make Catholic schools accessible was also a concern. Ultimately, Congress granted a total exemption to churches.

On the "Consultation Form," the offices consulted are asked to indicate if they have "no objections," "suggested revisions," or "objections" to the text. They would look at it, give their advice, and sign off on it if they have no objections. Serious

---

Consultation Form for Presentations and Letters to Congress

Initiating Office _____ Date circulated: _____
Presentor/Signer _____ Date responses requested: _____
Press release desired: Date letter to be mailed: _____
    [ ] yes [ ] no   Date testimony to be delivered: ____

Type: Letter _____ Testimony _____ Other _____
Subject matter: _____
Specific source of conference policy: _____
_____

Does this issue being addressed have a financial or regulatory
impact on Catholic institutions?   Yes _____
                                          No _____

Has this been assessed?   Yes _____
(If yes, documentation is attached)   No _____

Congressional body to which
presentation is to be made: _____
Comments on content: (Attach copy)
_____

The following opinions have been expressed by the offices indicated concerning the TEXT which is attached.

Department/Office	No Objections	Suggested Revisions	Objections
Committee Chairmen			
Department Secretary/			
Office Director*	_____	_____	_____
General Counsel	_____	_____	_____
Government Liaison	_____	_____	_____
Media Relations	_____	_____	_____
Other: _____	_____	_____	_____
_____	_____	_____	_____
_____	_____	_____	_____

Text Approval: _____ Date: _____
                General Secretary

Copies of approved text in final form are to be provided *in advance
of public release* to: General Secretary; Office of General Counsel; Office of Government Liaison; Office of Media Relations; any other
office formally consulted.

* This does not refer to offices within a department.

objections and major revisions would require extensive negotiations among the staff. Finally, the text must be approved by the general secretary.

If a committee chair is the one to testify, the draft may be done by a member of the staff, but the bishop decides what he is going to say. A chair's testimony would have to be cleared by the NCCB/USCC president. The presidents themselves are very careful on their own testimony. Cardinal Krol "worked hard" on his SALT II testimony, according to the Rev. Bryan Hehir, the USCC staff person on international issues. "We had two or three drafting sessions on that testimony. He knew that testimony was very sensitive. And he took it and sent it out to other people, and then he'd ask us questions."

These procedures make it difficult for the conference to react quickly to changing political events. "We are not a terribly responsive entity in the sense we do not move quickly," explains Mr. Carr.

> Some people consider that a weakness. But my sense is that that's the price you pay for being a strong entity—an entity that really reflects what the bishops want. When we go to the Hill or to other bodies, people know that the USCC represents the bishops. Some other church bodies have a problem in that "Who do you speak for?" is a confusing question, and the answer is even more confusing. In our case, nobody ought to be very confused, because until the bishops decide an issue, we don't move.

When absolutely necessary, the conference can move quickly. When six Jesuits were murdered in El Salvador, a letter from the NCCB/USCC president was processed quickly and faxed directly to the National Security Office in the White House. The director of the international office was already scheduled to testify on El Salvador before a Senate subcommittee. Changes in the testimony were "walked through" the various USCC offices within a couple of hours. Since the testimony was still being written, approval was based on verbal descriptions of the testimony.

In the review process, any legislation that touches abortion is especially sensitive. As Richard Doerflinger of the Pro-Life Office confesses, "Unfortunately, a significant part of our job in Congress is to take social legislation that is of great interest to the conference and to say, 'Gee I'm sorry, but there is an abortion problem here.'" Abortion can touch many issues: foreign aid, medical insurance, Medicaid, civil rights, school-based clinics, the Equal Rights Amendment, etc. Even the participation of pro-choice members of Congress at conference events on other topics has been vetoed by the Pro-Life Office.

Although all the offices agree with the conference's position against abortion, there can be disagreements over tactics. For example, Senator Edward Kennedy introduced a bill requiring employers to provide health care to their employees. The bill did not exclude abortion. "That's something we've flagged in that bill, which of course is also a bill of very great interest to the conference because of our support for broader health insurance," reports Mr. Doerflinger. "So we end up having to throw some complications into the social justice agenda here. Then we have to talk to Senator Kennedy about correcting this little problem in this bill, which Senator Kennedy is not all that interested in doing."

"The policy of the conference, at least where abortion is concerned, is to not say you are for a bill until it's fixed," explains Sharon Daly, former director of the Social Development Office and now with the Children's Defense Fund. This office wanted to support the health care bill on the condition that it was made abortion-neutral. The Catholic Health Association had done this, but the conference would not support the bill until it was fixed.

Making sure that legislation is abortion-neutral can be technically and politically complex. During consideration of the family and medical leave bill, the Pro-Life Office wanted to make sure that employers were not forced to give paid leave to someone having an abortion, although if complications occurred after the abortion they could be covered. "We didn't want to put in the bill that it didn't cover abortion, because the feminist groups would have gone berserk, and they were the major supporters of the bill," explains Ms. Daly. "We didn't want to create a problem that would kill the bill. After elaborate discussions with the Pro-Life Office and Government

Liaison and General Counsel, and the counsel of the House committee and the Senate, we came up with language that will do the trick, but you don't know it's there unless you're looking for it. The feminist groups felt that they could live with it, because they didn't want an abortion problem, and of course they know we can win on these things."

Sometimes the offices can be very helpful to one another. For example, once the family and medical leave bill was abortion-neutral, "Father Gouldrick [of the Pro-Life Office] wrote a letter to Congress urging that they adopt that pro-life measure and got their legislative people working on it around the country," reports Ms. Daly. "And when they help, it makes a difference." Mr. Doerflinger explains that the Social Development Office "suggested that a letter from the Pro-Life Office to the more conservative congressmen—to highlight the way this bill offers alternatives to abortion for a woman who is pregnant and is afraid of losing her job because she has to take maternity leave—would be an argument that would hit home with congressmen who want to be supportive of the pro-life agenda."

Likewise, many liberal groups were attempting to get more poor women covered for prenatal care under Medicaid, but it was the conference pro-life lobbyist who got Republican Henry Hyde to cosponsor the legislation with Democrat Henry A. Waxman. It was also the pro-life lobbyist who urged Republicans to include drug treatment for pregnant mothers in the drug bill. "A lot of drug treatment programs right now apparently won't take pregnant women," explains Mr. Doerflinger.

> If the child gets born and has some disability due to the drugs or allegedly due to the treatment, they're afraid of lawsuits, liability. They, in effect, if not explicitly, say "Well, go off and get an abortion and we'll take you." That's of great concern to the Social Development Office and also to us. So we want to get some federal funds targeted specifically for drug treatment programs for pregnant women, encourage some of these programs to take up that cause.

"The other advocates in town of children and poor people don't have access to the kinds of Republicans and conservative

Democrats that we have access to because of the pro-life agenda," explains Ms. Daly of the Social Development Office.

The positions taken by the conference must consider not only the views of the bishops and staff, but also the interests of Catholic agencies providing social services with public funds. For example, on an issue like child care, the bishops are committed in their economic pastoral to increased government spending, but they also have other concerns as well. "We want better child care for poor kids, for families where both parents have to work," says Mr. Carr. "But we also provide some of the best child care in the country. That gives us insights that we bring to the debate. It also requires us to stand up for our rights in this. There are folks who want to read us out of the provision of public services."

Legislative Priorities

So many issues are of potential concern to the bishops' conference that it would be easy for its staff to be overwhelmed. "Everybody's pet project had claim to their total time and talents," explains Monsignor Lynch, the general secretary. The conference also could find its own legislative agenda being lost as it responds to current events and crises. In addition, the various conference offices have competing priorities.

Before the opening of a new Congress, the conference attempts to set its legislative priorities. A March 1989 memorandum from the Office of Government Liaison explains the purpose of the process:

1) To identify issues of concern to the Bishops that are likely to be addressed by the new Congress, as well as identify which of their legislative interests ought to be on the congressional agenda.

2) To determine which of these issues are the most important in order to prioritize NCCB/USCC agenda.

3) To assess the level and intensity of activity which the Conference staff has to commit to influence congressional action on these issues.[30]

"I'm trying to do two things with this process," explains Frank Monahan, chief lobbyist for the conference. "I'm trying to help the management make the tough decisions when they need to prioritize. I'm also trying to make everybody a little bit more honest about how we really are dealing with issues."

The process begins with the various conference committees reviewing policy issues with their staffs and deciding what should go forward. Involved in the process are six USCC offices and their committees concerned about public policy issues: the Communications Department, the Domestic Social Development Office, the Education Department, the International Justice and Peace Office, the Migration and Refugee Services, and the Pro-Life Office. The program is then reviewed and approved with changes by the Administrative Board.

A new development in the USCC legislative program for the 101st Congress (1989-90) was an attempt to define four levels of priorities in lobbying issues. In all cases the issue must be "substantively important."[31] But its ranking as a USCC priority is highly dependent on political judgments about what will take place on Capitol Hill. In order to be a "Priority One" item, the issue must be "addressed in legislation *which is likely to be enacted by Congress.*" For a "Priority One" issue, "*The USCC expects to commit all appropriate lobbying efforts to amend, pass, or defeat specific legislation.*" Priority One also includes issues for which "the USCC intends to commit the necessary resources at the 'grass roots' to insure that Congress take action," even if congressional action is uncertain.

How well the system will work remains to be seen. Problems are evident since the number of Priority One, Two, and Three items increased in 1991, the same year the bishops decided to cut the budget.[32]

For the 102nd Congress (1991-92), NCCB/USCC departments have the following items listed as Priority One concerns (see appendix C):[33]

> Communications Department: the "fairness doctrine" in broadcasting; consumer protection and greater public access to cable television;
>
> Domestic Social Development Office: legislation dealing with employment discrimination; unpaid leave for workers with illness,

newborn or ill dependents; increased funding for low-income housing by community-based organizations; funding for substance abuse treatment for pregnant women and their children;

Education Department: full funding of Chapter 1 programs aiding low-income and educationally disadvantaged Catholic school students in compensatory education programs; funding of $200 million under Asbestos School Hazard Abatement Act; funding for new child care legislation;

International Justice and Peace Office: diplomatic solutions to conflicts in El Salvador and conditioning further aid on progress in human rights and in the prosecution of those who murdered church people; aid to Panama and Nicaragua, and support for human rights in Guatemala and Haiti; a just and stable peace in the Persian Gulf and the Middle East;

Migration and Refugee Services: funding for refugee admissions and for refugee assistance overseas; reauthorization of the Refugee Act of 1980 with expansion of refugee definition;

Pro-Life Office: the Hyde amendment (prohibiting funding of abortions); the Doran amendment (preventing use of public funds for abortion in the District of Columbia); the denial of foreign aid funds for organizations promoting abortion.

To be a "Priority Two" item, the issue must be "addressed in legislation *which is likely to be seriously considered* by Congress on which *the USCC expects to take a formal position and may or may not commit additional efforts to influence its disposition by Congress.*" The conference staff track these issues during the congressional sessions and propose additional action when appropriate.

To be a "Priority Three" item, the issue must be "addressed in legislation *that is likely to be seriously considered* by Congress on which the USCC *expects to take a formal position but does not intend to commit additional efforts to influence* its disposition by Congress." This strategy is called "witnessing." This category allows the conference to take a symbolic stand on an issue through a letter or testimony without devoting lobbying resources to the issue. "We engage in the debate, but we don't actually do a lot of hands-on lobbying, trying to influence decisions or how legislation is actually written," explains Mr. Monahan. Members of Congress "are looking for good ideas, they're looking for direction from the church community," he says. This is done through letters, "good testimony and high profile witnesses. Oftentimes, it doesn't go much beyond that, in terms of actual lobbying."

Gun control was a Priority Three issue for the conference in 1989. Originally it was not listed as a priority, even though the bishops had taken a position in favor of gun control. The American Jewish Congress, for whom gun control is a high priority, lobbied the USCC for support. "And we were told by the people in Congress that a letter from the bishops would be helpful in terms of moving that legislation," explains Mr. Monahan. "We decided to write a letter up there. It's one of those things where we're doing one letter." A similar set of events led the conference to send a letter supporting the reporting of "hate crime" statistics, a bill that passed in 1990. By 1991 gun control moved up to Priority Two.

It is in the area of witnessing that Mr. Monahan sees the process forcing the conference to be honest about its efforts. "Let's not say 'Yeah, we worked on this issue,' when what it entailed was five minutes to write a letter and we didn't do another damn thing."

The fourth category is not even called a priority, but simply listed as "important." This applies to issues "addressed in legislation *which may or may not be taken up by Congress and which the USCC intends to closely monitor and track to determine what the USCC's commitment might be.*" In this category tend to be issues that the USCC considers important but are less likely to be considered in the current Congress. This is the "holding bin category" according to Frank Monahan. This prioritizing of issues helps the lobbyists. "If you're getting too much coming at you in the same time," says Mr. Monahan, "and somebody is trying to bring a new issue up from the holding posture, you've got the basis, based on this planning process, to say, 'Wait a minute, we can only do so much.'"

After the priorities are set, the conference still maintains some flexibility to respond to political events. "Educational vouchers are not the top priority now [February 1989], for the same reason that budgetary constraints seem to make it impossible to think of other things," explained Monsignor Lynch. "But if in the second session of the 101st Congress, they get hot, does that mean we can't help? Of course not. Does that mean we need approval from the Administrative Board and Committee? I'll inform them, but we're not going to stand idly by waiting for a March or September meeting. I'll get my authority from the Executive Committee and then move forward to try to have a plan to make the most of that moment."

A month later when the priorities were presented to the Administrative Board in March 1989, the bishops accepted the priorities that were developed by the conference committees and staff. But the board insisted that "the education agenda include a commitment to a pro-active program of seeking public assistance for Catholic school parents and students. . . . Any and all opportunities to secure increased or new financial assistance will be seriously pursued during the current Congress."[34] The board showed its willingness to impose its priorities on the staff. Shortly after this decision, there was a shakeup in the staff of the education department. In 1991, support for President Bush's education initiatives became a Priority Two item.

Making the Case

In making its case on the Hill, the conference's strengths are in its moral authority and in the quality of its presentations. Members of Congress like having the bishops' conference on their side. Bishops and staff have testified before Congress many times for the conference.[35] During the 101st Congress (1989-90), the USCC had 212 formal communications with Congress, of which 23 were testimonies and the rest were mostly letters. The conference usually does not have to ask to testify, rather it is the congressional committee that asks the conference to send someone to testify. Because of this demand for testimony, the conference can dictate conditions for appearing. For example, if a bishop is to testify, he does so by himself and not as part of a panel. If the congressional committee insists on a panel, the conference will send a staff person to testify.

"Whenever possible, we take a bishop," explains Sharon Daly, director of the Domestic Policy Office. "It just has much more impact. I used to be of the opinion that in the absence of a bishop, we should pick somebody else who wears a Roman collar. I still think in certain committees that that's the best thing to do."

Msgr. Daniel Hoye, the general secretary, "would always give me a hard time when I wanted a collar to be at a press conference," recalls Ms. Daly. "He said, 'Here you are, Sharon, you keep saying that we are supposed to give more responsibility to laypeople and women, and then you always come in here and, you feminist, you want me to have a collar at this press conference.' And he was right."

For maximum visibility, the president of the conference will testify but his appearances on the Hill are rare. Some presidents enjoyed testifying more than others. Cardinal John Dearden as NCCB/USCC president testified on human rights. While president, Cardinal John Krol, with other cardinals, testified in favor of a pro-life constitutional amendment in 1974. Cardinal Krol also testified for the SALT II and Panama Canal treaties. Archbishop John Quinn never testified, but Archbishop John Roach (with Cardinal Terence Cooke) testified in favor of the Hatch amendment.

More frequently the chair of a conference committee will testify rather than the president. In December 1990 Archbishop Roach, chair of the USCC Committee on International Policy, testified before the Senate Foreign Relations Committee on the Persian Gulf crisis. Likewise Archbishop Roger Mahony was very active as chair of this committee. When Congress invited the bishops to testify on housing, Bishop Joseph Sullivan, chair of the Committee on Social Development, appeared with Bishop James Malone, a past president. They brought along people from Catholic agencies with practical experience working with the homeless. They had "somebody who eight blocks from the Capitol serves homeless women in a shelter run by the archdiocese," recalls Mr. Carr. "At the table was somebody who built 2,500 units of housing, who said HUD is the problem, not the solution. It is that combination of moral vision and practical experience that gives this institution more ability to make a difference."

The conference followed a similar strategy in bringing in Catholic child care providers—from Catholic Charities, schools, and parishes—to meet with government officials to discuss the child care proposals. Mr. Carr recalls:

> The Bush people came in and said that "a tax credit would help you; it's wonderful." And they [the providers] said, "Well, it wouldn't help many of our poor families." The Democrats came in and said, "We have this proposal," and they said, "but your church-state stuff would cut us out." They [the providers] helped us develop criteria, which the bishops then modified and accepted, that allowed us to work for a good set of priorities.

Not all the government relations work is aimed at the Hill, some is also directed at the executive branch. Secretary Jack Kemp of HUD met with bishops and staff concerned about housing. "When we met with Kemp," reports Mr. Carr, "we had our regular committee, but we brought in six or eight people from around the country who we had heard were doing the best housing stuff. Very few people know as much about homelessness as we do. And we said, 'We're doing it; we were doing it before it was trendy. Now that it is trendy, we don't want to stop doing it.'"

When the committee chair is the archbishop of New York, he can be very effective in lobbying the executive branch. Sharon Daly explains how Cardinal O'Connor lobbied Margaret Heckler, secretary for Health and Human Services, for homeless people who were being denied SSI benefits because they had no address.

> In my other jobs [before working for the conference], I'd used all kinds of pressure from coalitions and the state agencies who wanted these people on SSI so they wouldn't have to pay the bill, and nobody was getting anywhere. I briefed him [O'Connor] for about half an hour. People really underestimate him. He really is so good, and he really does care about poor people, and he knows how to pay attention to the important things.

I got an appointment [with the secretary] the day I called, because I'm calling to make an appointment for Cardinal O'Connor. That's very different from any place I'd ever worked. The head of the SSI program and Social Security Administration would be there. So we go in, and Cardinal O'Connor explains, makes the pitch. Everything we asked for were things under the secretary's control.

Well, she said yes to everything. I couldn't believe it. It was so wonderful. It was so different from taking a group of advocates, because first, she said yes. Secondly, she followed up. All the stuff actually got done.

In a later SSI case, another HHS secretary attempted to reduce benefits to reflect any groceries recipients were receiving from churches or other groups. Ms. Daly was quoted on the front page of the *New York Times*, criticizing this action. After reading the story, Cardinal Bernard Law telephoned Vice President Bush on Air Force 2 and by the afternoon, the decision was reversed.

Sometimes the lobbying goes all the way to the top. When John Quinn was NCCB/USCC president, he went to see President Carter. "I went to see the president in the name of the bishops' conference to ask him to authorize the boat people to come into the United States," explains Archbishop Quinn. He told Carter "that we would guarantee housing and employment for them, that our entities would stand behind this and see to it. And in a few days he gave that authorizing order."

Coalitions

In discussing the conference's legislative agenda, it is important to distinguish those areas where it is a major player and sometimes the only player, from those areas where it works in coalitions with other groups. The USCC participates in the Conference on Civil Rights, the Low-Income Housing Coalition, the Full Employment Action Committee, and in a coalition supporting national health insurance. The conference would also work with other church organizations, but "We were of the position that we were always better off going to those central coalitions and then sharing notes on our own about the religious contribution, but not trying to set up a separate religious advocacy network," reports Ronald Krietemeyer of the USCC staff on justice and peace.

The conference works in coalitions with a variety of groups. "We're with the Moral Majority on abortion; we're with the ACLU on capital punishment," explains Mr. Carr. Because of the division of staff responsibilities by topic area, different members of the USCC staff usually work with different coalitions. Mr. Carr, who usually works with the "liberal" coalitions, remarks, "I kiddingly say I do more advocacy for the pro-life agenda in the conference than the pro-life folks because I work with many people who oppose that agenda. I can't go to a cocktail party without getting into a fight on abortion."

Sometimes there is tension within the conference about being in coalition with groups that have positions the conference opposes. "When can you sit down with NEA and the AFL-CIO and the American Civil Liberties Union and when can't you?" was a question, according to Mr. Krietemeyer. "In general, we are of the mind that if the goal was consistent with our goal, then we can be specific to that point. The fact that we might disagree on other questions of public policy, whether it was capital punishment, Central America, or abortion, shouldn't stop us from working on low-income housing when that's the best group to do it."

On a complex piece of legislation, the bishops' conference might be with different coalitions depending on the issue. For example, the USCC has been part of the Leadership Conference on Civil Rights for many years, but broke ranks with the "pro-choice" members of the coalition over abortion. As originally drafted, the Civil Rights Restoration Act would have required institutions to provide abortion funding as part of their health insurance plans. The USCC argued that the bill should be abortion-neutral and found itself aligned with many people who opposed the entire bill.

"We came under immense pressure from all sides to back down," recalls Mr. Monahan. The dispute kept the bill bottled up in committee for four years. When it finally came to a vote in the House committee, the USCC position won handily, much to the surprise of its new chair, Representative Augustus Hawkins. The conference also easily had the votes it needed in the Senate. "Once we got what we wanted," explains Mr. Monahan, "we jumped on the bandwagon. We were in alliance with all the people we'd been fighting with for four years to get the bill passed, and to override the veto." Without the abortion issue, the bill became veto-proof.

By being part of the civil rights coalition, the conference could push for protection of families from discrimination in housing. "We strongly opposed racial discrimination and handicapped discrimination," recalls John Carr. "But we also opposed discrimination against families with children. We became the people in the coalition who said, 'that has really got to be part of this.'"

Some efforts of the conference meet with organized opposition. When the USCC opposed deregulation of the radio and television industry that would lessen local control, "The NAB, the National Association of Broadcasters, asked all the Catholics working in radio stations among its members to write to their bishop," recalls Richard Hirsch. They were to tell the bishops "that this local crap coming out of the USCC was absolutely fallacious and if deregulation came along, we were going to take care of you, bishop.' So I had a major battle both from our own bishops and then from the industry." After deregulation, most free time for religious programs disappeared.

Litigation

Besides lobbying Congress and the executive branch, the conference does litigation in the courts. Like any major corporation, the conference has problems that require legal advice and sometimes litigation: zoning laws, taxes, copyright, liability questions, disgruntled employees, and contracts. In addition, the conference gets involved in litigation that threatens or advances the institutional interests of the church. The first significant court case involving the conference was *Pierce v. Society of Sisters* (1925), also known as the Oregon Schools Case, which dealt with the right of parents to send their children to nonpublic schools.

"We were involved in either litigating or filing *amicus* briefs, writing about, commenting on, speaking on all the key religious clause decisions from that point forward," explains Mark E. Chopko, general counsel to the conference. Recently the conference has been in court cases dealing with abortion, nonpublic school aid, NLRB jurisdiction in Catholic schools, tax exemption of religious organizations, dial-a-porn, capital punishment, religious clubs in public schools, and the right to die.[36]

"We will try to get into more of the civil rights cases, social justice cases," explains Mr. Chopko who heads up a team of six lawyers. At the same time, with the changing makeup of the Supreme Court, litigation on aid to Catholic schools and on abortion will continue and probably be more successful in the future.

"I don't think the bishops are served by a strategy that just says, 'Well, let's file something to show the flag,'" explains Mr. Chopko. "We want to win, we want to make a difference. If you want the bishops' conference to have influence on the decision makers, you should give the decision makers what they need to decide a case—that is, a brief that is written on the issues."

Because he wants to have an effect, Mr. Chopko directs his brief at the legal issues in the case. For example, although the church may see right-to-die cases as involving medical ethics, the courts may see it differently. The judges are "going to decide a privacy case," explains Mr. Chopko. "They're not going to decide a medical ethics case. Now in a year, when they decide a medical ethics case, you can come back and say, 'What do you think?' But for now, it seems to me that they're going to decide a constitutional case and that's what I want to write on in an *amicus* brief. I don't want to write on medical ethics or Catholic moral teaching, although those are other things that the conference has an interest in."

In deciding litigation strategy, much is left to the judgment of the general counsel. "I share that judgment with the key staff and with the key committee, and with the general secretary," explains Mr. Chopko. "So far, no one's told me that I can't do it, and so I'll move ahead. That's pretty much the process for all these other briefs as well."

Many groups would like to have the USCC on their side in litigation. "We get solicited in all sorts of cases: Native American rights cases, immigration cases, asylum cases, civil rights cases, some that we can contribute to, and others that we can't," reports Mr. Chopko. "There is a lot of pressure for the conference to sue the United States over employer sanctions" against those employing undocumented workers. He was reluctant to take on the last case because he did not think the courts would grant the conference standing to sue unless the government attempted to enforce the law against a Catholic organization.

Effectiveness

How successful is the conference in its efforts in dealing with government officials? After the 101st Congress (1989-90), the USCC Office of Government Liaison issued an 81-page report describing congressional action on legislative issues of interest to the conference.[37] Lobbying on bills frequently got into highly technical details. In general, the conference did well, except that programs for the poor were often not funded to the extent needed.

Legislation that passed with USCC *lobbying* support (more than just a letter and testimony) included: limiting advertising aimed at children; regulating dial-a-porn; the Child Nutrition and WIC Reauthorization Act; eliminating the death penalty provisions from the crime bill and forbidding the death penalty where racially discriminatory; expansion of Medicaid to poor women and infants; funding of the Ryan White AIDS Resource Act; raising the minimum wage; technical amendments concerning SSI benefits to children; the Asbestos School Hazard Abatement Act; ensuring equitable participation of private school students and teachers in math and science programs; repeal of Section 89 of Internal Revenue Code; allowing legal aliens to own and operate fishing vessels; safe haven for Salvadorans and Nicaraguans; appropriations for refugee and migrant assistance; special status for Soviet and Indochinese refugees; the child care bill; the Doran amendment; defeat of amendments allowing abortions in military hospitals; the Hyde amendment; the Americans with Disabilities Act. Obviously the USCC lobbyists were not the only people working for the passage of these bills. And not every word in all these bills was supported by the USCC, but for the most part they enacted positions supported by the conference.

Losses for USCC lobbyists in the 101st Congress included three vetoed bills: the civil rights bill, the medical and family leave bill, and the bill limiting covert aid to Angola in 1990. Limited funding of programs was also a disappointment since the "USCC supports increased funding for domestic programs serving low-income people; supports developmental assistance to Third World countries and legislation to provide debt relief of Third World countries; urges U.S. to meet its obligation to the U.N., and requests increased funding for refugee programs."[38] Obviously, there were other USCC-supported issues, like aid to Catholic schools, that never came to a vote.[39]

After having worked as an anti-poverty advocate for many years, Sharon Daly found the bishops' conference a good place to work. "I've spent my whole life doing things for poor people and trying to move bureaucracies, trying to move institutions," explains Ms. Daly. "And this is a great fulcrum to move institutions. It may be one of the best you can work from in Washington if you're trying to move the administration or the Congress or get other folks, other organizations mobilized. Once the Catholic conference is moving on something, it really does make a difference."

There are several reasons given for the conference's effectiveness. First, it is clear whom the staff represents—the bishops. Some church lobbies in Washington work without clear direction or an identifiable constituency.[40] Second, although deciding policy in the conference can sometimes be slow, decisions are not made lightly and when they are made they tend to stick. The conference does not respond to every change in the political winds or the morning headlines.

Although those inside the conference believe that their positions are internally consistent, many political observers are surprised that the bishops can be with "conservatives" on abortion and "liberals" on social welfare. The seemingly "conservative" position of the bishops on some issues also helps them play a key role when they go against expectations. "It gives a lot of people political cover to do the right thing," explains Ms. Daly.

> For example, when the bishops opposed discrimination against persons with AIDS in employment and housing and services and so forth, that really undercut efforts on the Hill supporting discrimination. That would have been a much bigger issue if the Catholic bishops' position had not been clear. That's an important thing for people with AIDS, ultimately making sure that they get health care and all the other kinds of services. I think the bishops will make a big difference in that.

Those who have looked at the conference lobbying efforts from the outside have also been impressed. "The U.S. Catholic Church is the most effective political force advocating the liberal agenda," reports Stephen D. Johnson and Joseph B. Tamney. "It is the Catholic church that is the leading religious actor, with other liberal religious groups in support."[41] In *Representing God in Washington*, Allen D. Hertzke investigated the role of religious lobbies in Washington.[42] He found that the U.S. Catholic Conference was particularly adept at getting access to congressional offices because of the quality of the information provided by its staff.

> This fact, combined with the focused agenda of the Conference, has earned it the envy of both liberal and conservative church groups. One conservative congressional aide, who said he wanted the fundamentalists to be more effective, observed that: "They should take a lesson from the Catholic Conference. For example, on fetal experimentation their staff assistant got in touch with moral theologians and medical scientists to put out a position. They had been thinking about it." On the liberal side, while the Bishops joined a number of Protestant lobbies in opposing the MX missile, they were able to argue that their opposition flowed out of their "care-

fully delineated" position in the Peace Pastoral on nuclear arms. Moreover, none of the liberal church groups has produced a document of comparable length and complexity to the bishops' draft letter on the U.S. economy, and it is widely used by liberal Protestants.[43]

Another reason for the effectiveness of the conference is that the Catholic church is a major provider of services. The *Non-Profit Times* reports that Catholic Charities USA, at $1.5 billion is the largest U.S. charity.[44] "We are significant because of whom we represent," says Mr. Carr, "and the fact that we have experience, and that part of our contribution to the social welfare of this country is not just the pastorals we adopt, but the schools we run and the shelters we run." The USCC can testify to the effect various proposals will have on these services. This is especially effective when the conference describes how changes would affect the congressional member's district or state. Having Catholics and church institutions in every congressional district does not hurt.

Grass Roots

The conference has had mixed results activating lobbying efforts from the grass roots. "Politically the Church is largely a paper tiger in this day and age," admits one staff person. "The bishops' bark doesn't necessarily result in a concomitant bite, in a political bite. We're not radically different from labor unions who cannot deliver their members. People are making up their own minds on what they will support and what they won't."

Few efforts have been made to organize people on the local or parish level. An effort to organize a tuition tax credit lobby (CREDIT) died when Supreme Court decisions made it irrelevant. The National Committee for Human Life Amendment was also organized as a grass-roots group to work against abortion.[45] But usually, the conference depends on state Catholic conferences and dioceses to mediate its contacts with the grass roots.

"When states didn't have conferences we contacted the local bishops and said, 'Can we come in and organize a grass-roots mechanism?'" explains Msgr. Robert Lynch, who organized the NCHLA.

We set up congressional district action committees, particularly in the states without conferences. We had coordinators in the parishes in every congressional district. People signed up, at Mass or after Mass, that they would be willing to write a congressman or send a letter or make a telephone call, when the right people push the buttons on behalf of the human life amendment. So we had quite a network established, particularly in the states without conferences.

In the states with conferences it was a different story. They didn't want us to come in and do political action and political work because they felt they already had the structure. What was particularly painful was that in a state like Rhode Island, which was 66 percent Roman Catholic in those days, they had one member of the House and two senators and they were all three anti-human life amendment and pro-abortion. So we had less success in the Catholic states and, even in those days, more success in the states where Catholics were fewer in number. Massachusetts would be another good example of a state with a high concentration of Catholics, and yet we had Teddy Kennedy and Ed Brooke in the Senate in those days, and Bob Drinan in the House.

In 1990, the NCHLA initiated "Project Life," a national letter-writing campaign to persuade Congress to support pro-life legislation. Each parish or church organization was asked to send a minimum of 50 letters or phone calls to its representative. "NCHLA received 197 reports, representing 32 dioceses in 21 states. These reports verify that approximately 100,000 letters and post cards were sent and nearly 200 phone calls were made to more than 100 members of Congress. . . . Almost 200,000 Project Life flyers were distributed nationally."[46] Despite news reports indicating that pro-choice advocates were gaining strength, the 101st Congress ended with all federal pro-life policies intact.[47] However, the committee believes that the 1990 election caused a net loss of approximately eight pro-life votes in the House.[48]

Except on abortion and the tuition tax credit, the conference has not attempted to organize grass-roots lobbying for its program. "Grass roots is, for all practical purposes, a misnomer, because we are really talking with intermediate folk," admits Mr. Monahan. The conference does not have a direct line to the parishes. Usually, the conference depends on state Catholic conferences and local dioceses to get the word out and drum up support. As Mr. Monahan explains:

> We put it out through the church structure, which is basically the diocese. In 30 states, a key factor is the [state] Catholic conference folk. Where it goes from there depends on how important that issue is to those people at that time and the other priorities they're working on and how hard we push them to say, this is really important, that the message gets through to Senator X or Congressman X, because we're out there making a difference, in terms of this legislation.

The Social Development and World Peace department has an outreach coordinator who sends material to dioceses, diocesan social action offices, state Catholic conference directors, and Washington-based religious and public interest groups. Another 400 subscribe to the service. "We ask people to write their congressperson," explains Nancy Wisdo, who coordinated the program and is now director of the Social Development Office. Sometimes they are asked to write foreign governments on behalf of religious liberty.

Ms. Wisdo admits the limits of mailings. "We get a very mixed message, because on one hand they [the recipients] say it's a great mailing and they really like it and they like getting all the information," she reports. "On the other hand, they say, 'but we don't read it because it's too big and could you please cut it down?' I worked at the local level, and I know that mailing comes and you tend to put it on a pile with the other stuff that you haven't read yet." Another problem is that often, because of the way Congress works, the alerts come in rapid succession and overwhelm the ability of the local people to respond. Despite these limits, she felt that in 1989 the conference was successful in stimulating letters on the minimum wage, Eastern Europe, and El Salvador.

Often requests come for information and guidance from those outside Washington. A social action office, bishop, or state Catholic conference might want to say or do something on an issue, but they want to make sure that it is consistent with positions taken on the national level. "State Catholic conferences and dioceses call in," reports Ms. Daly, "and say this is what's happening, have you got any advice on what we could try to do, who could be our allies on this, and so forth." They ask for information and guidance from the conference.

A former member of the staff believes that the lack of grassroots support hampers the USCC lobbying effort:

> Anybody who's worth their salt in this field always wages a two-pronged attack. One is you have a strong Washington contingent that goes and hammers up on the Hill. Then you have your grass roots and you get people from their state to bother the hell out of them, because they're the ones who are going to reelect the bozos.
>
> Now the conference by and large is good with its Washington operation. The problem is, a lot of the dioceses don't give a hoot about legislative priorities of the conference, and it's that second thing that delivers the bacon ultimately. So if you don't have the support of the dioceses, you don't have your grass-roots support.

Conclusion

The bishops have attempted to use the American political process to advance their goals and values, sometimes succeeding and sometimes failing. Whether they succeed greatly depends on the political environment, other political actors, and the issues of the day. Once they enter the political arena they are subject to manipulation by politicians with their own goals. "Party leaders and presidential candidates have, at different times on different issues, tried to use the bishops to expand their electoral bases and morally ground their policy platforms," explains Professor Timothy A. Byrnes.[49] Who manipulates whom is often the question.

Through their lobbying efforts, the bishops have advanced a broad range of issues under the umbrella of the consistent ethic of life and their pastoral letters. But in electoral politics, the bishops have effectively put abortion first. And for no other issue, except the tuition tax credit, have the bishops developed and implemented a detailed blueprint for grass-roots education and action.

In the halls of Congress, the consistent ethic is alive and well. On the campaign trail, it is overwhelmed by concerns about abortion. The confrontations between bishops and candidates during elections have been mostly about abortion. As Professor Byrnes writes:

> To say in the heat of a campaign [1976] that you are "disappointed" in the views of one candidate and "encouraged" by the views of another is at least to imply support for the latter candidate. In the same way, to call abortion the "critical" issue of a campaign in which the Republican candidate pointedly opposes abortion and the Democratic candidate just as pointedly supports it, is to suggest, albeit indirectly, a preference for the Republican candidate.[50]

The bishops play in an arena wider than boundaries of the United States. As part of an international church, they are sensitive to and influenced by factors outside the United States. As part of the Catholic church, the conference needs support in Rome if it is going to function. Dealing with Rome has often been more difficult for the bishops than dealing with the federal government. Certainly the bishops have been more divided in the face of Rome than of Washington, as will be seen in the next chapter.

8. The Shepherds and the Chief Shepherd

They [the Holy See] are always talking about the autonomy of the single bishop. It's a smokescreen. What they mean is that it is easier to deal with one bishop than with a hierarchy.[1]
——REV. JAMES H. RYAN

I do not perceive that we go there [Rome] to be called on the carpet, nor do we go there to bang on the table.
——ARCHBISHOP DANIEL PILARCZYK

Many of the prefects and other curial officials had minimal knowledge about the church in the United States. Some officials knew very little factually, or had a very distorted picture of the church in our country.
——CARDINAL ROGER MAHONY

As members of the college of bishops, the American bishops are united with Catholic bishops around the world under the leadership of the bishop of Rome. Because of this relationship, the American bishops must interact with other bishops and with the pope's staff in the Vatican curia. This interaction often, but not always, takes place through the National Conference of Catholic Bishops.

That the Vatican gives special attention to the U.S. church is not surprising. "The Church in the United States, because of its size, wealth, and access to the media, has an exceptional influence—a ripple effect—on the Church in other countries," explained Archbishop John Roach. "If the Holy Father has singled us out for special attention, that is a recognition of the influence we exercise as a very large, active, and visible conference of bishops—influence of which we may not always be fully aware ourselves because of our preoccupation with circumstances here at home."[2]

"You have to remember, you are a super power," Pope John Paul II told the officers of the conference in 1988. "We are not just talking about politics and economics, your role in the free world. You have to remember that the church in the United States has tremendous influence. The people of the world watch what is said there in the church of the U.S., what you are doing."[3] Sometimes the Vatican considers this a positive role, as in 1991 when Archbishop Agostino Cacciavillan said that the NCCB document on the teaching mission of bishops could be used as a model and point of reference for bishops in other countries.

The relationship between the American bishops and the Vatican has often been described in terms of conflict and confrontation. Before examining areas of conflict, it is important to emphasize the high level of harmony existing between the American bishops and Rome. Much of this harmony is based on consensus between the bishops and Rome, but equally important is an episcopal deference to Roman authority when disagreements do occur.

Many factors have encouraged this harmonious relationship. Because of the separation of church and state in the United States, American political officials have not competed with Rome for influence over the internal affairs of the church. As a result, American political officials never fostered an anti-Roman faction within the church, as did some of their European counterparts. In the early years of the church in the United States, Rome gave little attention to this far-away and small Catholic community. Rome was busy dealing with the French Revolution, Napoleon, and revolution within the Papal States.

With the growth of the American church through immigration and the rise of the United States as a world power in the second half of the 19th century, the Vatican began paying more attention to the U.S. church. Simultaneously, the First Vatican Council was stressing the power and importance of the bishop of Rome. This perspective was reinforced by the hostile Protestant environment that was found by the immigrants.

Attempts by a few theologians and bishops to give an American flavor to Catholicism led to the papal condemnation of Americanism in 1899. This condemnation, plus the later condemnation of Modernism encouraged bishops and seminary professors to reject any suspicion of heterodoxy. Because of the First Vatican Council, loyalty to the pope became a convenient measure of one's orthodoxy. Seminary training after the condemnation of Americanism and Modernism reinforced these views among the clergy from which the bishops came.

Improvements in communications, divisions among the American bishops, and the appointment of an apostolic delegate in 1893 allowed the Vatican to increase its influence over the American church at the turn of the century.[4] Episcopal appointments were made by the pope with the help of Vatican officials who looked for loyal churchmen (see Chapter 1). To get promoted to a higher office, a bishop needs Roman support. Bishops are unlikely to be very critical of those who placed them in power and can promote them.

Thus, through training, personal preference, recruitment procedures, or political expediency, most American bishops agree with most Roman policies. This episcopal attitude toward Rome cannot fail to have an impact on actions by the NCCB/USCC. Normally the American bishops and their conference are very deferential toward Rome. When differences do occur, the bishops try to downplay them, keep them out of the press, and resolve them through quiet dialogue with the Vatican.

Episcopal deference by the NCCB is reinforced by law. As an episcopal conference, the NCCB is required by canon law to seek Roman review of many of its actions (see Chapter 2). When approval is not necessary, the bishops are still very sensitive to Rome's reaction to their work. The media's inclination to focus on conflict encourages bishops to tone down any differences with the Vatican.

The conference also works to help the pope in his service to the universal church. For example, the Vatican has asked the conference for its reactions to reports by the commission involved in ecumenical dialogues. The conference also publishes and distributes papal statements and encyclicals. The conference has a Committee on the Economic Concerns of the Holy See, which is trying to increase the Peter's Pence collection in the United States.

The conference also devoted extensive staff time and funds to making the pope's 1979 and 1987 visits to the United States a success. Before his visits, the conference produced a television documentary that was broadcast widely throughout the country. The actual logistics of the visits were organized by the Rev. Robert Lynch who worked for the conference, and the USCC Public Affairs Office coordinated press relations. When the television networks said they would give the 1987 visit only limited coverage, the USCC Communications Department arranged pooled coverage that was linked by satellite to local television stations and to 200 cable systems serving 20 million customers. The NCCB/USCC was also instrumental in setting up the pope's 1987 meetings with other religious leaders in Miami, South Carolina, and Los Angeles.

A Channel of Communications with Rome

The relationship between the American bishops and the rest of the Catholic church is an important concern of the National Conference of Catholic Bishops in two ways. First, the NCCB acts as a channel of communications between the American bishops and other bishops, especially the bishop of Rome. Second, the NCCB must be sure its actions are consistent with its collegial relationship with Rome and the rest of the college of bishops.

The NCCB keeps in contact with episcopal conferences around the world, especially through regional conferences such as CELAM (Consejo Episcopal Latino-Americano), SECAM (Symposium of Episcopal Conferences of Africa and Madagascar), FABC (Federation of Asian Bishops' Conferences), and the Council of European Bishops' Conferences. The officers visit these and individual conferences, and most bishops visiting the United States stop by the conference's Washington office. The general secretary also attends an annual meeting of the general secretaries of the European conferences, which provides a forum for exchanging information.

"Frankly, I don't think Rome is in favor of us being in communication with all these conferences," confessed one archbishop. "But all these conferences ask us, because we have the resources and we have the size. They want to be in touch with the United States because of its role in the world, and so they ask to talk to us. We're always the one conference that all these others are dealing with. If I were in one of those offices in Rome, I would wonder after a while, is this a second curia?"

As a channel of communication, the NCCB facilitates the exchange of information between the American bishops and the Holy See. Individual bishops write to and receive letters from Rome directly. The U.S. bishops also visit the Vatican every five years for *ad limina* visits.[5] But issues of concern to many dioceses are brought to the conference by the bishops for communication to Rome. For example, the bishops used the conference to express to Rome their concerns about the treatment of theologians,[6] the slowness in processing laicizations of priests, the revision of the Code of Canon Law, and the bypassing of local bishops in allowing priests to celebrate the Tridentine Mass.

On issues of general interest to all the bishops, the Vatican normally deals with the conference if for no other reason than to avoid the expense of communicating with all the bishops individually. Frequently, the Vatican contacts the conference through the pro-nuncio in Washington. Thus the conference has been one channel through which the Vatican has communicated to the American bishops its concerns about Archbishop Hunthausen, altar girls, religious women, seminaries, theologians, liturgical abuses, preaching by lay persons and religious, attacks on the Vatican in Catholic papers, the use of general absolution, the increasing number of annulments, the laicization of priests,[7] tubal ligation in Catholic hospitals,[8] etc.

In none of these areas could the conference as an institution be said to be the cause of the problem. These are diocesan problems that would have existed whether there was a conference or not. In most cases the NCCB lacked the authority to intervene in local dioceses to deal with the problems. But the NCCB is a convenient channel of communications between Rome and the bishops, with the NCCB leadership often acting as spokespersons for the American bishops.

"The president's job is in large measure to deal with the Holy See," explains one archbishop. "It looms very significantly. There are many, many things that never come to the light of the press or of the bishops in this connection, really very difficult problems, things that other people would call interference. This is one of the tensions that goes with the postconciliar church."

The NCCB and Rome

The conference is more than a channel of communication, it is an actor in the church. The National Conference of Catholic Bishops in its own actions must operate within the international communion of the Roman Catholic Church. It is not a totally autonomous and independent agent. Theology, canon law, and custom demand that it be respectful of Rome and of other episcopal conferences. Thus the actions and agenda of the conference are topics of discussion between the NCCB and Rome. As a result, the Vatican asked the American bishops to discuss issues of international importance with representatives from other conferences: the peace pastoral with German and French bishops; the Third World debt question with Latin American bishops; and the women's pastoral with several conferences.

Communications between Rome and the NCCB/USCC take place through visits, correspondence, and the pro-nuncio. The NCCB/USCC presidents deny that the visits have been as confrontational as portrayed in the press. "I find those visits very cordial, very open and friendly," reports Archbishop Pilarczyk. "We have always been treated with courtesy and friendliness. . . . I do not perceive that we go there to be called on the carpet, nor do we go there to bang on the table."

According to some bishops, the difficulties between Rome and the conference have often resulted from bad communications. "To the extent that there are tensions in the relationship," said Archbishop Roach in his final address as president of the conference, "they arise in not a few instances from misperceptions and misinformation on both sides. . . . we must seek and find ways of overcoming these failures in communication."

After attending a theological consultation in Rome in September of 1983 with 90 other American bishops, Roger Mahony, then bishop of Stockton, wrote to Archbishop Roach:

> It did become obvious to us, however, that many of the Prefects and other Curial officials had minimal knowledge about the Church in the United States. Some officials knew very little factually, or had a very distorted picture of the Church in our country.

He suggested bringing Vatican officials to the United States to learn about the American church first-hand.

Since the late 1970s, the conference president and the general secretary have visited the Roman congregations at least once a year. To improve communications with Rome, Bishop Malone increased the visits to twice a year and included the NCCB/USCC vice president. As Bishop James Malone recalls:

> I discovered that when I got over there they really didn't know us very well. So I began the practice of twice a year and then added the vice president to that group so that there would be more continuity from us. That has been helpful.

Archbishop Daniel Pilarczyk agrees that the personal contact at these meetings has been helpful. "The reason we go twice a year is precisely to keep the lines of communication open," he explains, "so that if there's some difference of opinion, it's not those faceless bureaucrats over there facing the faceless rebels over here. It's Pilarczyk and Keeler and Lynch and so and so."

Before regular visits were initiated, the conference would hear rumors and "insinuations," explains Archbishop John May. "Some cardinal or archbishop heard from his friend in Rome this and that." The idea was to "clear the smoke away," and "lay everything on the table." The results of these meetings are often relayed to the Administrative Committee or to all of the bishops in meetings from which the press is barred.

When visiting Rome, the NCCB/USCC officials would sometimes bring the appropriate NCCB/USCC committee chair and staff to meet with appropriate Vatican officials. Whom they would meet with would vary, although there were certain offices they would usually visit. "We would always see the secretary of state, the Congregation for Bishops," explains Archbishop John Quinn, "and then it would depend on what agenda items we had." Archbishop Pilarczyk listed some congregations he would visit:

> We generally see the Congregation for the Doctrine of the Faith, Divine Worship, Clergy, Education, Bishops. Depending on what else is on the agenda, we might go to Religious, we might go to Migration and Tourism, Archbishop Cheli's shop. Almost always we go to Cardinal Etchegaray at Justice and Peace.

The NCCB/USCC leaders visited the Congregation for Education to discuss American seminaries, a Vatican document on higher education, and other educational issues. They visit the Congregation for Divine Worship to discuss liturgical and sacramental matters. With the Congregation for Clergy they discussed catechetics, celibacy, and pedophilia. "Pedophilia just blew their minds," reports one participant. "They couldn't understand the legal ramifications. Cardinal Innocenti would very often say, 'Why don't you do this or that?' It was a rather simplistic solution, not knowing American law."

The officers would also visit the Congregation for Doctrine of the Faith, headed by Cardinal Joseph Ratzinger. "We spent more time perhaps there than we did anywhere," reports Archbishop May. Cardinal Ratzinger "would be talking about various doctrinal trends in this country, certain books, certain writers and what was happening. He was very concerned about different things."

The NCCB/USCC leaders and chairs of committees drafting statements would visit the Congregation on Doctrine of the Faith and other appropriate offices. For example, Archbishop Oscar Lipscomb as chair of the NCCB Committee on Doctrine visited with the Congregation on Doctrine of the Faith in 1989 to discuss the NCCB document on the relationship between theologians and bishops. Likewise Cardinal Joseph Bernardin and Archbishop Rembert Weakland, when working on the peace and economic pastorals, met with Cardinal Ratzinger and with the head of the Pontifical Council for Justice and Peace. The Congregation for Doctrine of the Faith was also consulted about a document on nutrition and hydration being prepared by the Pro-Life Committee.

"Basically, these are informative sessions, informative for them," explains Archbishop Pilarczyk. "I call it 'show and tell.' 'This is what we've got and this is what we're doing.' They may have questions, or they may say, 'Look, this other thing has come up now and we think you ought to look into this.'"

With visits to Rome six months apart, communications between the conference and Rome can move at a snail's pace. As Archbishop Pilarczyk describes it:

> The dialogue goes in six-month exchanges, because that's when the officers go over there. So the officers go over and say, "Look, six months ago you said this, this, this. Now we think that, that, that." They said, "Okay, let us think about that." So we go home and come back six months later, or maybe they'd write over in the meantime. Then you'd have to say, "Okay, that's fine, but this isn't." It just takes a long time.

Many NCCB/USCC officials know Italian, having studied in Rome, but occasionally there are linguistic problems. More critical are differences in perspective because of the different responsibilities, as Archbishop Pilarczyk explains:[9]

> You've got the problem that they see things from a perspective that we don't. That's not to say that ours is valid and theirs isn't, or vice versa. They have responsibilities that we don't have. Sometimes they're trying to make this great big point, which we think is not very significant, but it's significant to them, and vice versa.

Often the NCCB/USCC officers would get insights into what was going on in Rome from the Americans working in Rome. Archbishop Paul Marcinkus "was very helpful from time to time," according to Archbishop May, a fellow Chicagoan. "Every time we went over there, we'd probably have one meal with him. So we'd get a lot of background." Also helpful were Cardinal William Baum and Archbishop John Foley. As budget director for the Vatican, Cardinal Edmund Szoka will also be a well-informed source. In addition, there are American priests working as staff in Vatican congregations.

Because of these visits, "By the 1980s, the conference committee staff had become more sophisticated than earlier," reports Bishop Malone. "They, by their dealing with the congregations in Rome came to know the mind of the Holy See. So they became more considerate as they drafted things."

The interaction of Rome and the NCCB/USCC has varied depending on the issues and the principal actors involved. Although there has been hardly any disagreement on social, economic, and political issues, there has been some conflict over "church" issues like liturgy, annulments, and canon law.

Social-Economic Agenda

Despite the controversy that the social, economic, and political agenda of the bishops has stirred up in the United States, there have been few conflicts between Rome and the American bishops on these issues. Just 100 years ago, the papacy led the way in emphasizing the social agenda of the church in the encyclical *Rerum Novarum* by Leo XIII. The strong support of the papacy for labor unions, a just wage, and social programs to help families has been echoed by the American bishops acting through their conference. This was reinforced by the Second Vatican Council and Popes John XXIII, Paul VI, and John Paul II.

During the papacy of John Paul II, some Catholic conservatives have tried to portray him as a supporter of laissez-faire capitalism. In fact, he is probably to the left of the American bishops on economic issues. These conservatives want to use the papacy as a club to beat the American bishops into line. Some of them simply have no knowledge of papal teaching on social and economic justice. Others are more cynical in their manipulation of public opinion. For example, when John Paul II issued his encyclical *Sollicitudo Rei Socialis* in 1987 and *Cen-*

tesimus Annus in 1991, they were welcomed by some conservatives who selectively quoted his attacks on government controls that were aimed primarily at Eastern Europe. Attempts were made to talk William F. Buckley into muting his criticism of *Sollicitudo Rei Socialis*, lest his attacks sabotage conservative attempts to co-opt the encyclical. Mr. Buckley was too independent to be silenced although he was less sarcastic than when he greeted John XXIII's encyclical with "Mater si, Magistra no."

An examination of the Vatican response to the economic and peace pastorals of the American bishops is instructive. The economic and peace pastorals were severely criticized by American conservative Catholics. Michael Novak, George Weigel, William F. Buckley, William Simon, Alexander Haig, William Clark, Phyllis Schlafly, Philip Lawler, John P. Lehman, Clare Boothe Luce, J. Peter Grace, and others criticized one or both letters.[10] But the Vatican had few problems with the substance of these letters.

The 1983 peace pastoral received the most attention from the Vatican.[11] The Vatican had three major concerns.[12] First, Rome did not want the American, French, and German bishops saying different things about the morality of NATO's nuclear weapons.[13] The image of a united magisterium would be compromised if different episcopal conferences were teaching different positions on such an important moral issue. The January 1983 exchange in Rome between the American drafting committee and some European bishops did much to alleviate this fear.

Second, the Vatican wanted the American bishops clearly to distinguish between moral principles and their prudential applications. The principles could be backed by the authority of the church, but their application to specific policy recommendations could not. Pope John Paul II made this point with Cardinal Bernardin during lunch on the day after he received his red hat. As Cardinal Bernardin recalls:

> Hè wanted to talk to me about the pastoral, and his concern that we not attach magisterial authority to prudential judgments. I explained to him that I agreed totally, that I thought we had covered

it, that we would go back to the committee and go through it again and make it even clearer than it was before. We had a good discussion about the pastoral, but that was his main concern. He was afraid it would cause division in the church if every prudential judgment we made was perceived as being defined doctrine.

The third concern of the Vatican dealt with the moral argument supporting deterrence. Some moralists argue that if the use of nuclear weapons is immoral, then threatening to use them is also immoral because the threat expresses a conditional intention to do what is threatened.[14] Defending deterrence as a means of avoiding nuclear war would be to argue that the end (peace) justified the means (threatening to do something immoral). Permitting evil means because of a good end is consequentialism, a theory criticized by the church. Thus for deterrence to be moral, some use of nuclear weapons had to be moral.

To avoid the taint of consequentialism, the drafting committee listed many uses of nuclear weapons that it considered immoral, but it never said that *all* uses of nuclear weapons were immoral. This loophole permitted deterrence without falling into consequentialism. When the NCCB assembly adopted an amendment stating that all uses of nuclear weapons were immoral, the committee got the conference to reconsider and then defeat the amendment.[15]

A close reading of the pastoral letter will find that its acceptance of deterrence is primarily based on a 1982 quote from John Paul II at the United Nations. He said, "In current conditions deterrence based on balance, certainly not as an end in itself but as a step on the way toward a progressive disarmament, may still be judged morally acceptable." No one in the Vatican could argue with that without accusing the pope of consequentialism. The only bishop who openly disagreed with the pope was Cardinal John Krol who preferred "morally tolerable" to "morally acceptable."

Vatican interest in the 1986 economic pastoral was even more limited. U.S. internal economic policy is of little interest to the Vatican unless it affects other nations. The Vatican had heard from many Third World bishops about the troubles caused by their nations' foreign debts. As a result, the pope asked the U.S. bishops to meet with Latin American bishops to discuss the Third World debt crisis. The drafting committee met with bishops from Latin America, and what the pastoral letter said was generally acceptable to the Third World bishops.

In 1987 the Pontifical Justice and Peace Commission issued a statement on the debt crisis in response to requests from Third World bishops.[16] These same bishops pressured the Americans for more support, which resulted in a 1989 statement on debt by the USCC Administrative Board.[17]

What led to ambiguity concerning the Vatican attitude toward the American pastoral letters was the slowness of the pope to praise them. Major pastoral letters normally would be publicly affirmed by the pope in speeches to American bishops. Silence by Rome is interpreted as disfavor. Thus during his 1979 visit to Chicago, John Paul II extensively quoted and praised the bishops' 1976 letter "To Live in Christ Jesus." But in 1987 he did not mention the peace or economic pastorals when speaking to the bishops in Los Angeles. During the entire visit, he never referred to the peace pastoral and mentioned the economic pastoral only twice in passing.

Some observers felt that Vatican anxiety about the pastorals focused on the public consultative process by which the letters had been developed rather than on their substance. According to this theory, the Vatican objected because the process was too "democratic" and gave the appearance that church teaching was uncertain and debatable. "There may have been some concerns about the process that was used, but that was never stated explicitly," reports Ronald Krietemeyer, who worked on the economic pastoral. Visiting bishops from other countries would also tell the staff, "We don't understand why the bishops' conference would issue a draft," according to Mr. Krietemeyer.

At a 1991 meeting in Rome to discuss the draft of the NCCB pastoral letter on women, Vatican officials and bishops from other countries expressed fear that wide public consultation before issuing a pastoral letter would weaken church authority.[18] "The American conference of bishops had begun to practice the principles that we are used to in a democratic society," explains Archbishop Rembert Weakland. "But the Church is not a democratic institution, and the Pope wanted to restore control to the Vatican."[19] Many non-American bishops have the impression that with public consultation "church teaching is up for grabs to whoever shouts the loudest," Archbishop Pilarczyk said.[20]

At the same time, there is much curiosity about the process. There is "a fascination with the openness of it," reports Mr. Krietemeyer. He received "a lot of calls from bishops' conferences and staff as they would be coming through Washington, just wanting to ask about the process." They would ask "How did you do that? How did it work?"

Other observers felt that the Vatican was simply jealous that the American pastorals were getting more attention and publicity than papal pronouncements. Finally, papal silence also could have been out of deference to the Reagan and Bush administrations, which through their ambassadors to the Holy See lobbied against the letters.

During their ad limina visits in 1988, the pope finally spoke favorably of the American bishops' peace and economic pastorals. He praised the bishops for their support of solidarity and development in the face of world interdependence. Some bishops felt this was the result of a change in speech writers and the pope's positive experience of the U.S. church during his 1987 visit. The pope even said some positive things about the first draft of the NCCB pastoral on women. Finally, when the American archbishops met with the pope in 1989, social and economic issues were not even on the agenda, which suggests that they were not a major point of contention between the archbishops and the Vatican.[21]

International Affairs

The NCCB/USCC and its predecessor, the NCWC often spoke out on international issues, especially when the church was under attack in a country. This was done with the active, if sometimes secret, encouragement of the Vatican. Rather than an opponent, the Vatican usually sees the NCCB/USCC as an ally in the area of international politics, especially in defending the rights of the church. Through their statements, letters, and visits, the American bishops have drawn attention to the condition of the church in revolutionary Mexico, in Spain during its civil war, in Germany before the Second World War, in Communist countries, and more recently in the Middle East and Latin America.

Sometimes a visit can be a very effective way of bringing international attention on the condition of the church. For example, when some U.S. bishops visited Cuba, Fidel Castro asked to see them. "We said we will come on condition that the Cuban bishops are with us," reports Archbishop May. "He received them then, for the first time. The same thing was true in Mexico," which has an anticlerical history. Carlos Salinas, the new president of Mexico, "was friendly, but he never received the officers [of the Mexican bishops' conference]. When we went down there as the officers of the American conference, he invited us, and we said we'll come with our counterparts, the Mexicans." The president agreed. When Cardinal John O'Connor, chair of the USCC Committee on Social Development and World Peace, visited Nicaragua he was able to get Cardinal Obando y Bravo, the papal nuncio, and President Ortega in the same room talking, "which was not thought possible in those days," according to William M. Lewers, C.S.C., staff to the committee.

The conference's statements on international issues extend beyond questions of religious liberty to many other issues of international justice and peace. The conference believes that it has good sources of information on what is happening around the world. "In foreign policy, we have in some cases as good or better sources of information as the State Department," claims John Carr. "Being a national institution in a universal church gives you opportunities and information and insights that you just couldn't have anywhere else." Through contacts with foreign bishops, religious orders, American missionaries, Catholic Relief Services, Migration and Refugee Services, and the Vatican, the conference has sources who have direct contact with people in every corner of the world.

The American bishops working on a foreign policy issue also have access to American and foreign officials at the highest levels. Members of the bishops' ad hoc committee on the Middle East met with heads of state or foreign ministers in Israel, Egypt, Syria, Lebanon, and Jordan while visiting that region. These officials wanted to be heard by the bishops before they wrote their statement on the Middle East. Likewise World Bank and U.S. Treasury officials wanted the bishops to understand their proposals for dealing with the Third World debt before the bishops issued a statement on the debt crisis. Finally, the bishops find representatives of nongovernment organizations and academic experts very willing to give their views and advice. For example, those presenting testimony to the committee drafting the peace pastoral included Harold Brown, Lawrence Engleberger, Eugene Rostow, Edward Rowney, James Schlesinger, Gerard Smith, Casper Weinberger, and others.

Often the conference can bring together a variety of parties to discuss an important international issue. For example, in 1991 a group of American and Mexican bishops heard presentations from U.S. and Mexican trade officials, businesspersons, ethicists, and American labor representatives on the question of a free trade agreement between Mexico and the United States.

Often what the conference does in the international field is in response to requests from other episcopal conferences. For example, the NCCB/USCC leadership is often invited to visit other episcopal conferences in their countries. These conferences benefit locally if their governments know that bishops in the United States are paying attention to what happens to the church there. Delegations of American bishops have visited China, Vietnam, Central and South America, Africa, the Middle East, Eastern Europe, the Philippines, and Asia. Sometimes these national conferences are simply looking for moral support, other times they also want financial assistance from the U.S. bishops. Often they hope the American bishops can influence American foreign policy toward their countries.

Positions taken by the USCC on international issues are influenced by the views of other conferences. The American bishops supported the Panama Canal Treaty because of lobbying by Archbishop Marcos McGrath of Panama. Similarly, the bishops got involved in the Third World debt, "not because the Treasury Department is interested in it," explains Mr. Carr, "but because every Third World bishop we talked to in the last three years says, 'What are you people going to do about the debt?'"

Likewise the Philippine bishops invited a group of U.S. bishops to the Philippines "because they think U.S. policy has a lot to say about what goes on in the Philippines," reports Mr. Carr. Discussion topics included "human rights concerns, the U.S. bases, support for the Aquino government, and U.S. involvement with Marcos."

Similarly, the initiative for the 1989 USCC statement on Vietnam came from outside the conference. Neither the bishops nor the USCC staff wanted to reopen the wounds of the Vietnam War. But the Vietnamese bishops felt that diplomatic recognition of Vietnam would benefit the church as Hanoi became less isolated from the world community. With encouragement from the Vatican, the American bishops called for more religious freedom, but also for diplomatic recognition of Vietnam by the United States. Recognizing Hanoi was not a popular position in the United States. The American bishops would have sidestepped this issue if it had not been requested by the Vatican and the Vietnamese bishops.

The American bishops have an unwritten rule that they will not issue a statement about a foreign country without consultation with the local bishops' conference. "We can't do anything on South Africa without a clear reading that it's in support of the South African bishops' position," explains Mr. Carr. The same is true on "Central America or the Philippines." For example, in 1989 before the USCC staff testified before Congress following the killings of the six Jesuits in El Salvador, their testimony was cleared with the archbishop of San Salvador.[22]

Also on Nicaragua, the American bishops echoed the Nicaraguan bishops in condemning human rights violations by the Sandinistas while simultaneously opposing military aid to the Contras. Cardinal "Obando y Bravo came I don't know how many times just pleading for the cut-off of all this military aid that goes down there," reports Archbishop May. "He said all this is just continuing the war and the conflict, and people are being killed by the thousands, and I guess he thought we could do something to influence American foreign policy."

When the local hierarchy changes its position, the American bishops quickly follow suit. A good example of this occurred when the South African Catholic bishops dropped their support for economic sanctions against South Africa in August 1991. As late as July 1991, the USCC was issuing statements supporting sanctions. By September the American bishops had reversed themselves to be in line with the South African Bishops Conference.

If the local bishops do not want the Americans to speak, they normally remain silent. During the period when thousands were "disappearing" in Argentina, the American bishops said little because the Argentine bishops said there was no problem and opposed any involvement by the American bishops. When the Rev. Bryan Hehir mentioned human rights difficulties in Argentina in congressional testimony, the Argentine bishops complained. After a liberal bishop was mysteriously killed in an automobile accident, the Americans queried the Argentine conference. It responded that the bishop was a bad driver, so nothing was said. Most observers believe he was murdered because of his support for human rights.

Likewise the Irish bishops have not encouraged the U.S. bishops' conference to say much about Northern Ireland. When an international controversy arose over the building of a Carmelite Convent at Auschwitz, the U.S. bishops' conference issued a "no comment" because it was an internal Polish issue. Interestingly, this did not stop Cardinal Law, Cardinal O'Connor, and Archbishop Mahony, whose archdioceses contain large concentrations of American Jews, from speaking as individuals and calling for moving the convent to another location.

This rule of NCCB/USCC deference to the local hierarchy strictly applies only to the internal affairs of the foreign country. The American bishops' positions on American foreign policy or programs aimed at another country cannot be totally determined by the bishops of that country. Since they are American programs, the American bishops have a right to speak out on them. But the American bishops are reluctant to take positions opposing the local bishops. Sometimes there are disagreements among the local bishops. Thus in El Salvador, some in the bishops' conference are at odds with the archbishop who wanted to condition and reduce American military aid. Here the American bishops have gone with the archbishop. The U.S. conference has tended to nuance its position. Thus it opposed military aid *until democracy was restored*, or it opposed *increased* aid, or it supported *cutting* aid rather than eliminating it.

Similarly in 1978 there were disagreements within the Philippine Bishops' Conference over U.S. policy toward the Philippines. After visiting the Philippines, the Rev. Bryan Hehir of the USCC staff drew up a report that was reviewed by the Philippine Bishops' Conference. The Philippine conference was critical of the report, but 23 Philippine bishops wrote asking the USCC to testify before Congress. "The decision was made to present the testimony because the USCC has a right to testify before its own government regarding human rights implications of U.S. policies."[23]

The NCCB/USCC leaders also consult with the Vatican before speaking out on international issues. They want to avoid saying anything that would conflict with Vatican foreign policy. The Holy See has its own State Department and diplomatic corps with representatives all over the world.[24] The NCCB/USCC leadership would query the Vatican pro-nuncio in the United States if there were questions about the Vatican position on international issues. They also would visit the Secretariat of State when they traveled to Rome for consultation twice a year.

Archbishop Quinn explains when he was president, "We would get invitations from bodies of bishops to come to their country, and we would consult with the [Vatican] secretary of state about that, and whether it was a wise thing to go at this time." The officers would also report to the Vatican on their visits to other countries. "We always said where we'd been and what visits we'd made and why. Often, before we went, we'd ask their advice."

The chair of the bishops' committee on international policy also keeps in contact with Vatican officials. In 1987-90 this was easy because the chair, Archbishop Roger Mahony, was also a member of the Pontifical Council for Justice and Peace. Likewise, the members of the ad hoc committee on the Middle East stopped in Rome for consultations when returning from their tour of the Middle East.

The Middle East is an area of special concern to the Vatican because of the presence of the holy places and Christian minorities. The Holy See has no diplomatic relations with Jordan or Israel, arguing that international borders and the Palestinian question must be settled first. As a result, the Vatican Secretariat of State is especially interested in what the American bishops say about the Palestinians (their homeland and self-determination), borders, and the Christians in the Middle East.

As long as the bishops stay within the perimeters of Vatican policy, they are encouraged to visit the region and issue statements. For example, the Vatican has asked American and French prelates to visit Lebanon to bring attention to the plight of the Lebanese Christians. When Cardinal O'Connor could not get an American visa to visit Lebanon because the U.S. State Department was terrified at the thought of him being held hostage, he traveled on a Vatican passport.

The USCC statements on the Middle East have been well received by the Vatican. From 1973 on, their statements have routinely been reprinted in *L'Osservatore Romano*, the official newspaper of the Vatican.

Another area of special concern to the Vatican during the pontificate of John Paul II has been Eastern Europe. The Vatican encouraged the American bishops to issue their 1988 statement on religious liberty in Eastern Europe. "Vatican suggestions were enormously helpful," reports a staff person. At times the American bishops were secretly encouraged to take a tougher line than the Vatican itself, which preferred to be more diplomatic. The USCC followed the statement with direct lobbying of Eastern European embassies in Washington.

Often these statements were encouraged by various ethnic groups in the United States. The Poles, Ukrainians, Lithuanians, and Lebanese have been especially successful in getting the American bishops to focus attention on their native lands. They have been helped by the presence of ethnic and Eastern-rite bishops in the conference. But sometimes ethnic groups oppose what the bishops say. Some U.S. Vietnamese were very critical of the 1988 statement on Vietnam. Hungarian Americans were also very angry when the U.S. bishops supported the Carter administration's decision to return the crown of St. Stephen to Hungary. In both cases the bishops stood firm because they knew they were supporting the wishes of the local hierarchies.

Status of Episcopal Conferences

Although social, economic, and political issues have not been points of controversy between the NCCB/USCC and the Vatican, some internal church issues have been. These include the role of the conference itself, the liturgy, the treatment of divorced Catholics, and church finances.

An early disagreement between the NCCB and the Vatican was over who could be a full member of the bishops' conference. The American bishops wanted to include retired bishops as de jure or voting members, while the Vatican insisted that retired bishops could neither vote nor hold office in the conference. The U.S. bishops obtained a temporary exception from the Vatican, but the Vatican argued they should follow the general policy of the church. The Americans finally gave in when revising their statutes in 1975.

Another early controversy was over opening up the assembly meetings to the press. This was controversial within the conference, but ultimately the bishops voted in November 1971 to allow the press to be present at their meetings. Rome was shocked by such openness and wrote Cardinal Krol, the new NCCB/USCC president, expressing dismay that the bishops were going to open their meetings to the press. Ironically, Cardinal Krol, who had opposed opening the sessions, felt obliged to defend the conference decision to Rome and the decision stood.

More important was the debate about the role of episcopal conferences in the church. Some in the Vatican fear that they could become centers of independent power that would foster national churches with theologies and agendas independent of Rome. Dealing with bishops individually placed the Vatican in a more powerful position than in dealing with a united group of bishops. The Vatican found sympathy for its critique of episcopal conferences among some local bishops who felt their authority threatened by episcopal conferences.

This Vatican fear was highlighted by the response of some episcopal conferences to Paul VI's 1968 encyclical, *Humanae Vitae*. By nuancing or qualifying their responses, rather than simply endorsing the encyclical wholeheartedly, these conferences put Rome on notice to the independent character of episcopal conferences. During debate on the 1968 pastoral "Human Life in Our Day," the NCCB response to the encyclical, some bishops said, "We are not first to make a statement following *Humanae Vitae*. How does our proposal parallel or depart from statements made by the French hierarchy, or the Latin American hierarchy?" according to Bishop James Malone.

The response of Roman congregations has been to limit the role of episcopal conferences. Thus the 1983 revised Code of Canon Law severely restricted the legislative authority of episcopal conferences (see Chapter 2) and required actions by the conference be reviewed (*recognitio*) or approved (*approbatio*) by Rome before they could binding. Further interpretations of the code by the Vatican have tightened these restrictions even more. Meanwhile, Cardinal Joseph Ratzinger, prefect of the Congregation for Doctrine of the Faith, has asserted that episcopal conferences have no mandate to teach. He mentioned this explicitly at the 1983 meeting in Rome to discuss the draft of the NCCB peace pastoral.[25]

Early in 1988, in response to a request from the 1985 Synod of Bishops, the Congregation for Bishops issued a draft document (*instrumentum laboris*) that would have severely limited the theological and juridical status of episcopal conferences.[26] The document was severely criticized by scholars and by episcopal conferences for limiting the role of episcopal conferences and for treating open theological issues as if there was a consensus on them.[27] An NCCB ad hoc committee of former NCCB/USCC presidents drafted the U.S. response, which was very critical.[28] After the initial draft of the response was toned down a bit, the NCCB assembly approved it by a vote of 205-59 on November 16, 1988. Scholars also found the Vatican document poorly done, with internal contradictions and incorrect interpretations of Vatican II and canon law. One scholar said that if it were a paper from a graduate student, he would have a hard time giving the student a "C."

In 1990 at the synod of bishops, Cardinal Bernardin Gantin, prefect of the Congregation for Bishops, acknowledged these complaints and said that the document on episcopal conferences would be revised without attempting to settle open theological issues. In his talk he reported that "The bishops truly feel supported, encouraged and sustained by the respective conferences in their pastoral ministry, in the arduous tasks of teaching, supporting and sanctifying that part of the people of God that has been entrusted to their care."[29] He noted in passing that the pastoral ministry of episcopal conferences included teaching. "In reality," he said, "it is unthinkable to have a pastor who does not teach." This contradicts Cardinal Ratzinger's earlier assertion that episcopal conferences have no mandate to teach.

The Vatican has also taken actions that have tended to downgrade the importance of the NCCB/USCC. For example, when the pope decided to meet with some American bishops in 1989, he chose to meet with all the American archbishops rather than the 13 prelates elected by and from the NCCB regions.[30] In fact, only one region elected a prelate (Bishop

James Malone) who was not an archbishop. But the Vatican choice of the archbishops was a signal that ecclesial structures other than the episcopal conference could be used by Rome in dealing with the United States.

Likewise, when the Vatican wanted a study of American seminaries it was conducted by a papal commission of American prelates appointed by the pope and not by an NCCB committee. The same was true of the study of American religious. In both cases the Vatican bypassed official conference committees and structures. There was an attempt by the Vatican to involve the NCCB in its dispute with Archbishop Hunthausen, but it backfired. Shortly before the November 1986 meeting of the NCCB, Archbishop Laghi issued a chronology of the case giving the Vatican side. At the meeting Hunthausen defended himself when the Administrative Committee proposed backing the Vatican actions as "fair and just." The assembled bishops, asked to pass a negative judgment on one of their own, refused to do so without due process. They simply acknowledged that what the Vatican had done was canonically legal and offered their services to bring about a resolution of the conflict. The controversy surrounding Archbishop Hunthausen was eventually resolved by a papal commission, not a conference entity.[31]

The creation of these papal commissions involved informal consultation with conference leaders, but formal structures were ignored. The failure to make Msgr. Daniel Hoye, the former NCCB/USCC general secretary, a bishop was interpreted as another sign of the Vatican's displeasure with the conference. The failure to make former NCCB/USCC president Archbishop John May a cardinal could also be interpreted this way. While none of these is a direct attack on the conference, all of them together suggest a Vatican willingness to ignore the conference without qualms.

Lay Preaching and the Age of Confirmation

Although most Roman actions have downgraded episcopal conferences, in a few cases Rome has stressed the conference's canonical power over local bishops. The American bishops are reluctant to use the NCCB to enact legislation binding on bishops, even when this is allowed by canon law. The American bishops prefer nonbinding guidelines or simply letting each bishop decide for himself, but Rome has at times called for binding norms to establish uniform practice throughout the United States.

For example, the NCCB in 1988 adopted nonbinding guidelines for preaching by lay persons, but Rome has insisted that the NCCB should adopt binding national norms and not simply guidelines. In 1991 the NCCB considered norms for lay preaching drafted by the Committee on Pastoral Practices. Debate over the norms centered on lay preaching after the Gospel during the Eucharist. The Vatican opposed this practice, and some bishops wanted that point emphasized. Others preferred some ambiguity in the norms that would allow them flexibility. A motion by Cardinal Bernard Law eliminating any reference to lay preaching at the Eucharist was approved, but then the norms were defeated (107-141).

Likewise the age of confirmation has also been a controversial issue among the bishops and with the Vatican. A variety of theological opinions on the sacrament exist. Some theologians argue it should take place at baptism as in the Orthodox church, others want it at the age of discretion (around seven) before First Communion, still others say it should be at the beginning of adulthood. The Code of Canon Law states it will be conferred at about the age of discretion unless the conference of bishops determines another age.

The actual practice in the United States has varied among dioceses, but in most dioceses confirmation is given between ages 12 and 16 (between 7th and 10th grades). In 1983 the Committee on Canonical Affairs chaired by Bishop Anthony Bevilacqua recommended that local bishops set the age of confirmation until a study of the issue could be completed. In 1984 the Committee on Pastoral Research and Practices, chaired by Archbishop Bernard Law, recommended conferring confirmation between 8th and 11th grades unless the bishop should decide that pastoral reasons dictate otherwise. First the motion was amended to include the 7th grade since many bishops visit parishes every other year to confirm both 7th and 8th graders. Then the bishops approved a substitute motion by Archbishop Pilarczyk that authorized the local bishop to set the age for confirmation. When Vatican approval (*recognitio*) was requested for this action, Cardinal Bernardin Gantin, prefect of the Congregation for Bishops, replied that the congregation cannot approve a norm that does not specify a particular age, and asked the conference to reconsider the matter. Archbishop Pilarczyk, by then NCCB president, appointed an ad hoc committee to study the issue and prepare a proposal by June of 1993.

Liturgical Issues

At various times liturgical issues have been points of contention between the NCCB and the Vatican. All liturgical texts and rites have to be approved by the Congregation for Divine Worship. English translations of texts done by the International Committee on English in the Liturgy (ICEL) have been approved by Rome with little controversy until recently. For example, the Vatican cabled approval of the 1968 ICEL Eucharistic prayers and prefaces within 24 hours of their passage by the NCCB. Normally texts are approved within a few months. For example, in 1971, the Congregation for Divine Worship confirmed the English translation of the Rite of Holy Week two months after it was submitted by the bishops.

More recently there have been difficulties as the congregation's staff has challenged the choice of words used by ICEL, and even objected to the placement of commas. The NCCB has yet to receive a positive response on its 1980 request for inclusive language in Eucharistic prayers. There were also problems with the ICEL Order of Christian Burial approved by the NCCB in November 1985. The Rev. John Gurrieri, former director of the Office of the Liturgy recalls:

> It had been approved by 11 bishops' conferences unanimously. Ours was almost unanimous. We didn't hear from Rome until June 29, 1987. They took so long to respond, in spite of repeated letters

and meetings when [NCCB president] Bishop Malone went over to Rome. Finally, when we did hear from them we had ten pages of required changes in the text, none of which made any sense. The conference has fought back on this and has not accepted the modifications. No conference [in ICEL] has accepted what Rome wants.

There was some hope that with a new prefect of the congregation the rite would be approved, with a few minor changes made as a face-saving device for Rome.

Likewise, the congregation questioned the conference on the use of "he or she" in referring to non-Catholic ministers in an ecumenical marriage rite approved by the NCCB in 1987. Cardinal Paul Augustin Mayer, then prefect of the congregation, feared that this would be granting jurisdiction to women priests.

Throughout the years, the Vatican has objected to some liturgical proposals from the NCCB. A 1968 proposal simply to leave the issue of Communion under both kinds to the local bishop was "deferred." The Vatican wanted a national policy and not different policies in every diocese. When the conference approved Communion under both kinds on Sundays, Rome argued that this exceeded the authority of the conference. Ultimately, however, Rome granted its approval.

In an attempt to have controlled experimentation in the liturgy, the NCCB requested permission in 1967 to establish centers of liturgical experimentation. Rome responded that this should be "postponed until the revision of the Roman liturgical books is completed." When the NCCB asked again in 1968, Rome said no and recommended "study" at academic centers and not experimentation.

Rome is now adamantly opposed to any significant liturgical changes. "We have been told by Rome that we cannot change anything in the Order of Mass. Period," reports Father Gurrieri. Rome does not want the NCCB to ask for any changes and has made clear that its response will be negative. This has discouraged the NCCB Committee on the Liturgy from doing anything significant other than new translations.

There have also been complaints from the Vatican that the American bishops have been slow to grant permission to priests to celebrate the Tridentine Mass. The American bishops responded that they have no difficulties with the old liturgy, but the people requesting permission are often those who have been divisive in the church on many issues. When the Vatican began giving permission directly to priests to celebrate the Tridentine Mass, European episcopal conferences complained. Swiss, German, and English conference presidents were called to Rome to discuss the issue, but the NCCB president was not invited because he had not complained. He quickly sent a letter complaining.

Often the Vatican complaints are directed at what it considers liturgical abuses. "One time we went to one of our semiannual meetings and I don't know in how many congregations we heard about clown ministries," recalls Archbishop May, "as if it's happening all the time. Somebody had put that bug in their ear."

Marriage Cases

No disagreement between Rome and the American bishops has been as enduring, complex, and pastorally sensitive as the treatment of divorced and remarried Catholics. Catholic families in the United States have experienced divorce at roughly the same rate as other Americans. Since validly married Catholics who get divorced and remarried cannot receive Communion, the bishops have been faced with an enormous pastoral problem.

Although not allowing Catholics in a valid marriage to remarry after divorce, the church does allow a Catholic to marry if the original marriage was invalid from the very beginning. The decision by a church tribunal that an apparently valid marriage was actually invalid from the beginning is called an annulment. Under certain circumstances a convert's marriage to a non-Catholic can be dissolved under the "favor of the faith" rule. Catholic marriage law is technical and complex. Here the discussion must be limited to the points of disagreement between Rome and the American bishops and the role of the conference in this dispute. Any persons interested in an annulment should consult a canon lawyer and not rely on the limited explanation here.

Since about a fourth of the American bishops are canon lawyers and many have worked in diocesan tribunals, they have the expertise and experience to discuss the issues and make recommendations for improving the annulment process.

As early as 1967, the conference requested the authority for local bishops to dissolve certain marriages between a Catholic convert and a non-Catholic. If the Holy See wanted to retain power over these "favor of the faith" cases, then the bishops wanted the paperwork reduced. The bishops authorized the chair of the Canonical Affairs Committee to bring this to the attention of Cardinal Alfredo Ottaviani, prefect of the Holy Office, and, if necessary, to the Holy Father. Their request was denied by Rome. In 1968 the NCCB (by a vote of 210-8) requested the faculty, already delegated to the Holy Office, to prepare these cases for presentation to the Holy Father himself for final judgment, but the request was denied.

In April 1969, the NCCB requested approval of the American Procedural Norms for processing annulments in diocesan tribunals. These norms had been proposed to the bishops by the Canon Law Society of America (CLSA). They streamlined tribunal procedures, making them more efficient and pastoral. For example, the norms allowed the tribunal in the place where the petitioner lives to hear the case if the judicial vicar in the place where the respondent lives approved. More importantly, it eliminated mandatory appeal of affirmative decisions to a higher tribunal.[32]

When the bishops had not heard from Rome by November, they impatiently renewed their request. Approval was forthcoming and the norms became effective in the United States on July 1, 1970. At the same time, American tribunals began using psychological factors more frequently as grounds for judging that one or both of the parties at the time of the marriage were incapable of valid consent and sacramental commitment. Gross immaturity or serious psychological deficiencies affecting the ability to love and fulfill marital obligations became common grounds for an annulment.

Rome soon had second thoughts about these norms as the number of annulments in the United States increased dramatically. As early as 1972 the NCCB was having difficulty getting the indult for the norms extended. Although some American norms found their way into the 1983 Code of Canon Law, mandatory review of affirmative decisions was reinstated by the code, although in a somewhat simplified form. Mandatory review was reinstituted despite intensive lobbying by American canonists and bishops. Rome also began requiring canonical degrees for tribunal officials. Many American canonists saw these moves as Roman attempts to throw procedural obstacles into the annulment process.

The role of the conference in this dispute is difficult to observe because episcopal discussions took place in executive sessions of the NCCB or in the Administrative Committee. Interviews indicate that the issue of annulments was repeatedly brought up in discussions between the NCCB leadership and Roman officials in the Apostolic Signatura and the Roman Rota, the two Vatican tribunals that deal with annulments.

At the 1980 Synod on the Family, Cardinal Pericle Felici complained about the number of annulments. The dispute surfaced again at the 1989 meeting between the American archbishops and the Vatican curia. Cardinal Achille Silvestrini, prefect of the Supreme Tribunal of the Apostolic Signatura, reported that in 1985 there were 36,180 annulments in the United States and only 9,452 in the rest of the world. He accused American tribunals of introducing "their own method, not fully in conformity with the Code of Canon Law." He said there is confusion about the proper meaning of "psychic incapacity" as grounds for declarations of nullity. Cardinal Edouard Gagnon, prefect of the Council for the Family, warned bishops to be careful of women religious working in tribunals so that "their tender hearts do not play tricks on them." Later to the press he said "We have hundreds of cases of tribunals run by nuns and they give declarations of nullity as soon as a woman cries in their presence."

Many archbishops defended the American tribunals, including Cardinal Edmund Szoka of Detroit who accused the

Signatura of really being concerned about numbers and not procedures. The American bishops believe that their tribunals are following the norms and procedures of the code and invited the Signatura to come and inspect them. Cardinal Szoka, the son of divorced parents, will continue to be a significant voice in this debate because he now works in the Vatican.

Alienation of Property

Another canonical disagreement between the NCCB and Rome was over procedures for the "alienation" of church property. To protect the patrimony of a diocese from an incompetent or dishonest bishop, canon law requires a bishop to follow certain procedures before selling or giving away valuable church property. Alienation of church property over a set value requires approval of the Vatican Congregation of Clergy. Some alienations of a lesser amount require the approval of the diocesan finance council, board of consultors, and interested parties. Similar rules apply to borrowing.

Alienation is a canonical term whose technical meaning is debated by canonists. It applies to the transfer of the ownership of property from one person to another. A sale of property is not an alienation unless the proceeds are transferred to another person or institution. In the strict sense, alienation applies to real property and to funds invested for a specific purpose by proper ecclesiastical authority or by the intention of the donor. Money, stocks, bonds, or other securities not designated for a specific purpose do not come under the alienation rules.

The bishops were especially concerned about these rules because failure to conform with canonical requirements for alienation could adversely affect the validity under civil law of the transaction, depending on a state's laws. In addition, one bishop complained that his request took 11 months to get a response from the Vatican and then it was negative. Such delays make the negotiation of contracts very difficult, if not impossible.

In 1967 the NCCB considered several proposals concerning alienation. It rejected $300,000 as too low a figure for the maximum amount that could be alienated without recourse to Rome. Likewise it rejected setting the maximum as a percentage of the annual income of a diocese. It then voted to set no limit, declaring that alienation had no meaning in the United States. Since the alienation rules arose during an agricultural age when church property and investments were mostly in real estate, the bishops had a case. Under the leadership of Cardinal Cooke, the bishops developed uniform accounting principles and reporting practices for dioceses and church-related organizations, but these were only recommended, not mandated.

Rome argued that the alienation rules were still relevant, and the question continued to be debated during the revision of the Code of Canon Law. In 1981, alienations of $1 million or more in the United States required Vatican approval. The 1983 Code of Canon Law retained the alienation rules and left to episcopal conferences the task of proposing maximum figures before approval was needed by the diocesan finance committee or Rome.

In 1985 the NCCB required approval by the diocesan finance committee of any alienation or indebtedness of $500,000 or more. Rather than proposing a fixed maximum before recourse to Rome was necessary, the NCCB proposed a sliding scale of $1 million to $5 million based on the Catholic population of the diocese. The scale was to be set at $5 per capita of the Catholic population of the diocese, although even the smallest diocese could alienate $1 million without Roman approval, and even the largest dioceses would have to get approval for amounts exceeding $5 million.

The Congregation for Clergy denied approval to the sliding scale and kept the maximum at $1 million. It gave no rationale for its rejection. After extended discussions between the NCCB leadership and the congregation, congregation representatives suggested the bishops present two proposals: 1) an increase in the limit to something more realistic and higher than $1 million; and 2) the 1985 sliding scale with a better rationale.

Roman officials stated their preference for the first option but suggested the NCCB present both.

Instead, in 1990, the NCCB ignored the first option and offered two proposals, both of which contained sliding scales. The first was the 1985 proposal. The second was a three-step scale with a maximum of $3 million, $4 million, and $5 million, depending on the size of the diocese. The Canonical Affairs Committee noted that population is an imperfect but workable way of distinguishing among dioceses of different financial size. In April 1991, the Congregation for the Clergy again rejected the proposed sliding scales but approved an interim measure to increase the $1 million limit to $3 million. The NCCB finally gave up and adopted this figure in November 1991.

Terms for Pastors

Another canonical dispute between Rome and the bishops involved limited terms of office for pastors. The NCCB, following the recommendation of its Committee on Canonical Affairs, voted in 1983 to leave determination of terms for pastors to the local bishop. Because of the size of the United States and the variety of pastoral conditions in dioceses, the bishops felt it was impractical to set a definite term for pastors everywhere. They preferred to leave the determination to individual bishops.

When this was sent to Rome for "*recognitio*," the response came back that it was "inappropriate." "The committee again looked at it," reports the Rev. Donald Heintschel, staff to the committee at the time, and decided, "OK, the best we can do is three or four years, no more." The bishops agreed again and sent it back to the Holy See. It came back again: "It is six years, nothing more, nothing less." The conference agreed to this in September 1984. Many canonists find this level of specificity from Rome to be contrary to the whole idea of local implementation of the code.

Doctrine and Discipline

The Vatican and the NCCB/USCC have also had disagreements over doctrinal issues, but these disagreements should not be exaggerated. The U.S. church has never had a serious case of episcopal heresy. Although a few American bishops questioned the definition of papal infallibility at Vatican I, all but one eventually came around after the council.[33] A few were also accused of succumbing to the Americanist heresy, but again under pressure they ultimately conformed.[34] No U.S. bishop has ever led his flock into schism.

Nor has the U.S. bishops' conference ever asked Catholics to believe anything not taught universally in the church, reports the respected theologian Avery Dulles, S.J.[35] On the controversial issues of the day (abortion, birth control, women priests, married priests, sexual ethics), the NCCB has backed papal teaching. This is not surprising since the Vatican uses these issues as litmus tests in the selection of episcopal candidates. Some pastoral practices opposed by the Vatican—general absolution, first Communion before first confession, altar girls—were supported by some bishops, but they eventually toed the Vatican line. These issues were rarely discussed in open session, and often the Vatican communicated directly with local bishops or with the bishops at their *ad limina* visits rather than through the conference.[36] The paucity of theological scholars in the American episcopacy has made the bishops followers, not leaders, in theological issues.

Few doctrinal or moral statements of the NCCB have caused problems with Rome. The 1977 "National Catechetical Directory" was approved with only a few suggested revisions. Archbishop John Whealon of Hartford, who chaired the drafting committee, recalled the issues that caught Rome's attention.

> One of them was the famous revelation question. Back in those days, there was much talk about ongoing revelation and there was a brother [Gabriel Moran] who had written a book[37] that was quite famous at that time. So we thought that we would solve all problems by having a capital R for Revelation that came from God—the Bible, the formal revelation that we know from Scripture and tradi-

tion—as opposed to this ongoing, continuing revelation. The Holy See said, "No, that's not a good idea at all."

The Vatican also wanted it clear that catechesis for the sacrament of reconciliation preceded First Communion and children should normally receive the sacrament of penance before First Communion. Finally, the Vatican wanted the existing norms limiting general absolution stressed. "That was it," reported Archbishop Whealon. "There were three points that they made. They said, 'We approve it and make these changes.'"

Religious education again became an issue at the end of 1990 when a draft *Catechism for the Universal Church* was distributed to the bishops by the Vatican. Although the Vatican-imposed deadline made it impossible for the full NCCB to respond to the draft, an ad hoc NCCB committee composed of the chairs of the committees on doctrine, liturgy, canon law, education, and ecumenism produced a very negative report on the catechism.[38]

In 1991, Cardinal Ratzinger of the Congregation for the Doctrine of the Faith sent a letter to all of the episcopal conferences detailing the role of conference doctrinal committees.[39] While noting that they are advisory to the conferences, he said the committees should compile a list of textbooks approved for teaching and help each bishop monitor and evaluate the theological books and journals published in his territory. Normally, he writes, the other committees of the conference should not publish important documents without first having had the benefit of the doctrinal committee's judgment in what pertains to its competence. The committees also should foster good relations with theologians, he said.

Relations with Theologians

Although not scholars themselves, the American bishops have normally had good relations with the theologians and canonists in their dioceses. The episcopal conference has also used many theologians and canonists as staff and consultants to NCCB/USCC committees. These scholars have helped in writing pastoral letters and statements, in responding to Vatican documents, and in advising the bishops in doctrine, canon law, ecumenism, liturgy, and catechetics. The conference has had a harmonious working relationship with the Catholic Theological Society of America and the Canon Law Society of America, whose committees and scholars have often helped the bishops' conference.

As a result, when the CTSA and the CLSA recommended the adoption of procedures to deal with conflicts between theologians and bishops, the NCCB was sympathetic to their concerns, although Rome was not. The societies' concern began as early as the fall of 1979 when Edward Schillebeeckx, O.P., the famous Dutch theologian, was under investigation in Rome. The CTSA president wrote a private letter to the Congregation for the Doctrine of the Faith to indicate the scandal that would occur if Father Schillebeeckx was condemned. Although Father Schillebeeckx was never condemned, Rome did take away the canonical mission of the Rev. Hans Küng, another famous European theologian. Meanwhile in the United States, the Rev. Charles Curran, a moral theologian at the Catholic University of America, was also under fire.

The leadership of the two societies opposed simply issuing public statements of protest against the treatment of individual theologians. Instead, they appointed a joint committee to do a scholarly study of the relationship between bishops and theologians and to suggest procedures for resolving disputes. Their papers, together with a consensus statement, were published in 1982.[40] At the suggestion of the NCCB/USCC general secretary, Msgr. Daniel Hoye, the joint committee invited three bishops (John Kinney, James Hoffman, and Daniel Pilarczyk) to join them in their deliberations and in drafting procedures for dealing with disputes. Two of the bishops were canonists and the third eventually became NCCB/USCC president.

"It was understood that they were there as consultants," explains Leo O'Donovan, S.J., chair of the joint committee, now president of Georgetown University. "They didn't officially represent the conference, but we looked to them for a bishop's reading of the material, for a reading of what was workable, what might go down with bishops." Key bishops such as Cardinals Bernardin, Cooke, Hickey, and Medeiros, and Archbishop Quinn were also kept informed.

The joint committee developed a three-part statement, "Doctrinal Responsibilities," which was unanimously adopted by both the CTSA and the CLSA in 1983. The first part was a brief description of the responsibilities and rights of bishops and of theologians. The second part described how cooperation was occurring and ways in which it might be promoted. The third part—by far the longest—contained a procedure for resolving doctrinal disputes, which was called "formal doctrinal dialogue."

In the summer of 1986 two members of the joint committee, Father O'Donovan and the Rev. John Boyle, met with the NCCB Committee on Doctrine to explain the document. This was the same summer that Father Curran was disqualified as a theologian at the Catholic University of America. "There was a lot of tension in the air," recalls Father O'Donovan. "Members of the Committee on Doctrine, including the chair [Bishop Raymond Lessard], were very open to any movement that could improve the atmosphere between theologians and bishops."

Fathers O'Donovan and Boyle were made consultants to the Committee on Doctrine which revised and unanimously adopted its own version of "Doctrinal Responsibilities" in March 1987. The committee version made clear the procedures were optional and did not apply to pontifical universities like the Catholic University of America. Meanwhile the Canonical Affairs Committee, chaired by Bishop Adam Maida (then of Green Bay, now of Detroit), gave a negative response to the CTSA-CLSA document. In September the Committee on Doctrine presented its document to the NCCB Administrative Committee which approved it by an overwhelming vote for consideration by the NCCB assembly. Opposition continued from Bishop Maida, who felt the document was unnecessary, untimely, and an insinuation that Roman procedures were insufficient.

When the document came up for discussion as the last item of agenda in November 1987, it was strongly attacked by Archbishop J. Francis Stafford of Denver, who described it as fatally flawed. His move to return the document to committee was defeated, but the vote count showed the absence of a quorum and the assembly adjourned without acting on the document. The Committee on Doctrine went over the draft again and made further revisions and prepared to present the document to the NCCB meeting in November of 1988.

Four days before the meeting began, the Vatican pro-nuncio presented Archbishop May, the NCCB president, with a fax criticizing the document which he had received from Archbishop Alberto Bovone, secretary of the Congregation for the Doctrine of the Faith. The author was "perplexed" that the document "seems to place bishops and theologians on the same level."[41] It is unclear who wrote the memo or what authority it had since it was not on official stationery, was unsigned, and undated. The presumption is that it was a staff memo. In any case, the memo was an unexpected bombshell to the Committee on Doctrine.

Meeting one day before the NCCB session began, the committee decided to postpone its presentation until June so that it could consult with the congregation. The NCCB leadership, the committee's chair and staff met with the Congregation for the Doctrine of the Faith before the March 1989 meeting between the American archbishops and the pope. The congregation appeared embarrassed by the criticism it received for torpedoing the committee's document at the last minute. Archbishop Bovone indicated that there had been no intention of interfering in the ordinary procedures of the American bishops' conference. The pro-nuncio had been told, Archbishop Bovone assured the Americans, that only if he thought it appropriate should the memo be forwarded to Archbishop May. Why the pro-nuncio might consider it inappropriate to forward a memo he received from Rome was not explained.

In any case, the congregation was still concerned that the document put bishops and theologians on an equal footing. Archbishops May, Pilarczyk, and Oscar Lipscomb, the committee's new chair, defended the document. The two staffs met while the archbishops were in Rome and hammered out several emendations in the text that responded to the observations. The goal of the Americans was not to leave Rome until they could tell the rest of the bishops that the concerns of the Congregation for the Doctrine of Faith had been satisfactorily met and the document was ready for a vote. On the other hand, the congregation did not want to say that the document was satisfactory. The congregation may have feared that someone would suggest that it should follow the same procedures for resolving doctrinal disputes. Neither did the congregation want to bear the onus of killing the document.

Ultimately Cardinal Ratzinger gave a letter to Archbishop Lipscomb expressing his "satisfaction with the way in which the Bishops' Conference has chosen to deal with this matter."[42] It was not an endorsement (which would have been inappropriate since the NCCB had not itself acted), but it sufficiently removed any sense of disapproval. The NCCB assembly approved the document on June 7, 1989, by a vote of 214-9.

Father O'Donovan, one of the original authors of the CTSA-CLSA document, believes that the final document of the NCCB retains the spirit and procedures of the original draft.

> There were textual emendations. There came to be some changes in terminology. But it was very substantially the same document. What changed is a clearer insistence on the episcopal office and its teaching authority. That has been underlined repeatedly, that would be the primary shift. In many cases, the changes that were made were clarifying and fortunate. In some cases, they may leave the document redundant or repetitive or clumsy.

The Committee on Doctrine had earlier played a mediating role between theologians and the Congregation for the Doctrine of the Faith. The Rev. Richard McBrien, chair of the theology department at the University of Notre Dame, was under investigation by the congregation for his book *Catholicism*. The Committee on Doctrine under the chairmanships of Archbishops James Hickey and John Quinn investigated the complaints. Several prominent American theologians defended Father McBrien before the committee, and the committee was satisfied when Father McBrien agreed to make revisions in the next edition "regarding theological dissent, the virginal conception of Jesus, baptism, ordination, the papacy and some more issues."[43] He also published an article in *America* qualifying some of his statements in *Catholicism*.

"Everybody was reasonably happy as a result of that," Archbishop Quinn recalls. "The Holy See was happy, McBrien was reasonably happy, everybody seemed to be happy in the end with the way that was dealt with, but it took a lot of time."

The pope and Cardinal Ratzinger have also expressed displeasure to the NCCB leadership about "Do Not Extinguish the Spirit," a statement endorsed by 431 members of the Catholic Theological Society of America.[44] The statement was critical of many recent Vatican actions while saying that relations between bishops and theologians in the United States are good.

Conclusion

The relationship between the Vatican and the NCCB/USCC has varied over time but has never been confrontational to the point of causing a serious breach. "Frequently when the American bishops are perceived as questioning the authority of the Holy See," explained Cardinal O'Connor at the March 1989 meeting of the American archbishops in Rome, "what they are really doing is trying to make things work in our culture—that is, to apply and to integrate into our culture in a meaningful and enduring way those Catholic teachings to which the culture is at least alien, if not hostile."[45]

The Vatican has probably paid special attention to the U.S. bishops' conference because of its size and its high visibility. What the U.S. bishops do has an impact not only in the United States but all over the world. In addition, voicing the concern of many archbishops at their meeting with the Vatican, Archbishop Daniel W. Kucera noted that "So-called traditionalists repeatedly attack the authority of diocesan bishops and the national episcopal conference and encourage disaffected individuals to write to the Supreme Pontiff and to various congregations."[46]

It is a mistake to believe that serious conflicts have occurred over the bishops' teaching on economic and political issues. The relations of the NCCB/USCC with the Vatican Secretariat of State and the Pontifical Council for Justice and Peace have always been cordial. As was made clear in the March 1989 meeting between Vatican officials and the American archbishops, the critical issues have been annulments, liturgy, and the bishops' control over theologians and religious educators.[47] American culture also came under attack for its secularism, hedonism, individualism, and moral relativism. Vatican officials want the bishops to take a stronger hand with American theologians and be more critical of American culture.

The NCCB/USCC leaders and bishops drafting the pastoral letter on women were also called to Rome in May of 1991 to discuss the letter with Vatican officials and with representatives from 12 other episcopal conferences. Three main areas of concern were raised: first, the method and literary form of the document; second, the Christian anthropology in the letter; and third, the treatment of Mary, the mother of God. The non-Americans at the meeting suggested issuing the document, not as a formal pastoral letter, but as something of lesser authority. They also asked that the Americans identify the various levels of authority at which they speak in the letter (something that the Americans had requested the Vatican do in the *Catechism for the Universal Church*).

The dialectic and dialogical relationship between the American bishops and the Vatican can be mutually beneficial. Rome can learn from a vibrant and vital local church, and American views can be critiqued from an external perspective. The positive role of the Vatican can be seen at its best in pushing the American bishops to be more sensitive to race issues. As early as 1904 "curial congregations began to pressure the bishops about the treatment of black Catholics in the United States," including the creation of a bureau to organize and direct the black apostolate in the United States.[48] At their next meeting, the American archbishops, "defensive about Roman meddling in the delicate area of race relations, responded . . . with rheto-ric rather than substantive action." Again in 1914, the Vatican called on the American bishops to train black catechists and to establish more schools, hospitals, and other institutions for blacks.[49]

In 1919 the bishops issued a pastoral letter condemning "all attempts at stirring up racial hatred." This letter responded to an "urgent request from Pietro Gasparri, cardinal secretary of state, that they consider the 'Negro problem' and condemn the lynching of blacks."[50] At the same time, "the Holy See re-sponded to the pleas of black Catholics and of missionaries serving among them in the United States . . . by pressuring the American episcopate to take concrete steps to provide for more black priests, including suggesting that an episcopal vicar with exclusive jurisdiction over black Catholics be ap-pointed."[51] The NCWC leadership, Cardinal James Gibbons and Archbishop George Mundelein, opposed these ideas and they were buried in committee.[52]

After a decade of subtle but increasing pressure on the American episcopate, the Vatican in 1936 sent a letter on the black apostolate to the bishops which Archbishop Amleto Cicognani, the apostolic delegate, summarized as, "More schools, More churches, More Apostles for the Negroes."[53] In this year, the Catholic University of America was reopened to blacks. Despite a 1943 pastoral letter calling on the nation to recognize the political, educational, economic, and social rights of blacks, most Catholic churches were still segregated. Only after the Second World War was progress truly made.

More recently, the Vatican has pushed the American bishops to be more critical of American consumerist and individualistic culture. At the same time, the Vatican has been less than en-thusiastic at the bishops' attempts to reach out to alienated feminists, theologians, divorced Catholics, resigned priests, and homosexuals.

Has the Vatican learned anything from the Americans? Cer-tainly the pope respects American financial acumen as he lis-tened to Cardinal Krol's advice on Vatican finances and brought Cardinal Szoka to Rome to deal with the Vatican budget. But on theological issues, the Americans are considered minor league in comparison with the Europeans. Nor are American concerns for due process and open procedures understood by a bureaucracy for which paternalism is still a good word.

On the other hand, the Vatican under Paul VI developed procedures for prior consultation with the bishops on at least some matters, like the revision of the Code of Canon Law. More recently the Vatican has consulted bishops on drafts of important documents on Catholic universities and on episcopal conferences, as well as on the *Catechism for the Universal Church*. The original documents were all found wanting, but at least they were only drafts. Vatican consultation has tended to be with bishops and selected experts rather than the more inclusive approach taken in drafting the American pastoral letters.

There is no easy formula for easing tension between the NCCB/USCC and the Vatican. Mutual respect and honesty would help, but what Americans consider plain speaking is often considered disrespectful by Vatican standards. And when the Vatican speaks plainly, it sounds authoritarian to Americans. The bishops often assert that their troubles with Rome stem from a failure of communications. One way to improve communications would be to have a permanent NCCB/USCC representative in Rome to look out for its affairs. In the past, this function was sometimes performed by the rector of the North American College.[54] An NCCB/USCC representative in Rome could follow NCCB/USCC business through the various curial offices and report back to Washington. He could be the eyes, ears, and voice of the NCCB/USCC in Rome, just as the American embassy serves that function for the U.S. government.

Some conflict between the Vatican and local episcopal conferences is inevitable and probably good for the church. Conflict forces all sides to see the complexity of issues and to rethink their positions so as to present better arguments. Vatican fears of experimentation and creativity have intensified conflict. Many conflicts would be reduced if the Vatican were willing to trust episcopal conferences to exercise more authority and leadership in responding to local needs without such intensive and detailed oversight. Undoubtedly some conferences would make mistakes, but so too does the Vatican. There is no evidence indicating that conferences cannot be self-correcting institutions.

9. The Shepherds' Purse

Archbishop Romero gave his life but we cut back the budget.
———BISHOP JAMES LYKE[1]

We cannot continue to afford everything, what do you want to put your money in, fellas?
———MSGR. ROBERT LYNCH

Many bishops loath bureaucracy, especially if its in Washington and they have to pay for it.
———BISHOP WILLIAM MCMANUS[2]

The NCCB/USCC, like any other organization, needs money to operate. The conference also attempts to look ahead and plan for the future. Examining how the conference plans, gets money, and spends it, provides an important perspective on the bishops' conference.

The finances of the bishops' conference are complicated because there are several programs, some of which are separately incorporated. Even when not separately incorporated, the finances of the different units are often kept separate for accounting purposes. At least four different financial categories are worth noting.

First, there is the NCCB/USCC budget, which pays for the NCCB/USCC staff but also includes Catholic News Service (CNS) and the Migration and Refugee Services (MRS).

Second, there are two separately incorporated bodies whose boards of directors are elected by the USCC assembly: Catholic Relief Services (CRS) and the Catholic Telecommunications Network of America (CTNA). CRS is a $232 million international relief and development program funded by the bishops ($8.7 million), private sources ($46 million), U.S. Food for Peace ($149 million), U.S. grants ($15 million), and international sources ($14 million, 1989 figures).

CTNA is a wholly-owned subsidiary of the USCC that has been a major financial drain on the conference since its founding in 1981. In 1990 over half its $2.6 million revenues came as a grant from the USCC. CTNA's ability to be self-financing was made nearly impossible when the bishops forbade it to raise money over the air. They feared it would compete with local fund-raising. Distribution of the programs is also limited because its satellite signal is scrambled so that local bishops can control what is broadcast in their dioceses. Dioceses that join the network must pay a fee to CTNA and buy a descrambler and other equipment. In 1988, only 120 dioceses were paying on-line affiliates. This system led one critic to comment that "Only the American bishops could figure out a way to lose money in religious broadcasting." In fact, other denominations have also done poorly, although a few televangelists have done very well.

Third, there are seven NCCB/USCC collections whose funds are distributed by the bishops for special purposes: the Bishops' Welfare and Emergency Relief Fund, the Campaign for Human Development, the Church in Latin America, the Catholic Communication Campaign, the American Board of Catholic Missions, Aid to the Church in Eastern Europe, and the Retirement Fund for Religious. Most of the money from these collections is given out in grants, although a small amount covers the expenses of the collections.

Fourth, there are national collections approved by the bishops whose funds are not administered by the NCCB/USCC: collections for Black and Indian Missions, Operation Rice Bowl (CRS), shrines in the Holy Land, the Holy Father, and the Catholic University of America.

Many of these financial entities are interrelated. The staff that administers the NCCB/USCC collections are USCC employees whose expenses are covered by funds from the collections. Some collections also make grants to the NCCB/USCC or related organizations. For example, the Bishops' Welfare and Emergency Relief Fund gives 90 percent of its collection to CRS and MRS.[3] The Catholic Communication Campaign also makes major grants to CTNA and is planning to give $239,000 to the USCC Office for Film and Broadcasting in 1993. Likewise, both the Bishops' Welfare and Emergency Relief Fund and the Church in Latin America collection help fund the USCC Department of Social Development and World Peace.

NCCB/USCC Budget

The NCCB/USCC adopted a $40 million budget in 1992, up from $34 million in 1991. The NCCB/USCC budget goes from January through December. Of the $6 million increase, $1.5 million was due to an accounting change that put "investment income added to reserve" into the budget. Another $2 million reflected increases in the MRS budget (see Table 9.1 on page 272).

The budget pays salaries and bills for equipment, travel, postage, printing, utilities, building maintenance, office supplies, telephone, and meeting expenses. Since the conference is a labor-intensive service organization, it is not surprising that almost half the budget goes to staff compensation. In the past, salaries at the conference were below those in government or the private sector. This proved to be an embarrassment to the bishops when they preached about economic justice. The salaries for secretaries and support staff are now comparable to others in Washington. Salaries for the top staff are still below what would be paid to equivalent persons in the private sector, but they are comparable or better than those paid by some public interest groups.

Within the NCCB/USCC budget, it is important to distinguish money spent to serve the conference and money financing programs serving others (see Table 9.1). Offices funded in the 1992 budget that directly serve the conference included the General Secretariat and staff offices ($8.2 million), the NCCB secretariats ($4.4 million), and the USCC departments of Education ($1 million), Social Development and World Peace ($1.2 million), and Communications ($6.6 million of which $5.4 million is for publishing, a self-supporting activity through sales and charges to other conference offices). Included in these

Table 9.1
NCCB/USCC Revenue and Expenses

Revenue	1991	1992
General Fund, NCCB/USCC source:		
Diocesan assessment	$8,160,180	$8,315,000
Net royalty income	362,745	380,845
Allocation of administrative costs	1,363,195	1,392,186
Use of investment income	692,292	2,527,779
1989/88 budget variances brought forward	508,762	236,000
	11,087,174	12,851,810
Current Operating Fund:		
BWER funding	536,187	566,019
Grants from affiliated organizations	216,792	493,019
Other grants & contributions	490,443	1,573,557
Publication sales	2,015,092	2,097,423
Service Fees:		
Interconference	2,433,277	2,600,123
Affiliated organizations	2,092,591	2,405,196
Other	1,271,511	1,175,000
	9,055,893	10,910,337
Migration and Refugee Services (MRS):		
BWER funding	1,653,560	1,505,010
MRS expenses funded through government grants	4,842,679	7,235,121
Use of investment income	248,772	740,000
Collection fees-refugee loans	2,100,000	1,750,000
Other	179,154	16,000
Budgeted use of reserves	1,356,491	994,851
Other grants and contributions	-	60,000
	10,380,656	12,300,982
Catholic News Service:		
Newspaper and wire services	2,196,000	2,328,300
Publication sales	1,092,750	1,201,075
Other	2,400	2,200
Administrative overhead: not assessed	398,800	417,396
Budgeted use of (addition to) reserves	(4,384)	(12,738)
	3,685,566	3,936,233
Total Revenues	34,209,289	39,999,362
Expenses		
NCCB Secretaries	3,282,373	4,403,073
Migration & Refugee Services	9,039,184	10,400,982
MRS capital contribution to Catholic		
Legal Immigration Network, Inc.	1,341,472	1,900,000
General Secretariat & Staff Offices	7,681,161	8,172,471
Communication Department:		
Secretary	218,534	221,891
Media Relations/Film & Broadcasting	912,575	952,215
Catholic News Service	3,685,566	3,936,233
Publishing & Promotion Services	5,068,870	5,447,782
Education Department	1,014,436	1,019,559
Social Development & World Peace Department	1,235,534	1,244,337
Other	729,584	733,728
Investment income added to reserve	-	1,567,091
Total Expenses	34,209,289	39,999,362
Excess of Revenue Over Expenses	$ -	$ -

figures are the costs of promoting and administering the NCCB/USCC collections.

Programs in the budget serving others include Catholic News Service (CNS) and Migration and Refugee Services (MRS).[4] CNS, for example, is a wire service founded in 1920 that provides news stories for 160 Catholic newspapers. It is a $3.9 million operation that is mostly self-supporting through sales of services and publications, although the NCCB/USCC subsidizes it by not assessing overhead costs amounting to about $417,000.[5] MRS is a $12.3 million refugee resettlement program funded mostly through government grants, fees, and $1.5 million from the Bishops' Welfare and Emergency Relief Fund.

Both CNS and MRS go back to the days of the NCWC. Both do excellent work, but theoretically both could operate separately from the bishops' conference. For example, it is easy to conceive of MRS operating as a separate corporation, as does Catholic Relief Services. With CNS and MRS subtracted, the NCCB/USCC budget is brought down to about $23.7 million. If MRS was spun off, however, the NCCB/USCC might lose some of the $2 million in reimbursements it receives for administrative costs and program services.

Finally, some expenses of the bishops' conference are borne by the individual bishops. For example, they pay their own travel and living expenses when attending annual meetings.

NCCB/USCC Income

The money to pay for the NCCB/USCC expenses comes from several sources (see Table 9.1). As mentioned above, MRS is funded primarily through government grants, fees, and a BWER grant. CNS is financed through sales of services and publications. The publishing service of the conference brings in $2 million from sales to the public, and the rest of its $5 million budget comes from charges for services to other conference entities.

The remainder of the NCCB/USCC budget is funded by special collections, grants from foundations, investment income, fees for services, royalties (primarily from the *New American Bible*), and an assessment or tax on dioceses. In addition, each conference program not funded by the assessment is charged for its share of overhead—the cost for administrative and support services like the general secretary, general counsel, data processing, human services, and accounting.

The conference's investment portfolio in 1991 had a market value of about $100 million, most of which is held for restricted purposes: pensions, special collections, etc.[6] After paying for its new office building in 1991, the conference had about $19 million in unrestricted reserves earning more than $2 million annually.

Following socially responsible investment guidelines, funds are not invested in companies dealing with nuclear arms, abortion, contraception, or with investments in South Africa.[7] The conference also stays away from leveraged buyouts and junk bonds. These guidelines exclude from investment about 26 percent of the market. The conference has not suffered financially because of these guidelines. According to Merrill Lynch, companies with direct investments in South Africa, manufacturers of birth control devices, and defense contractors performed worse in the 1980s than the S&P 500.

The list of excluded companies is secret since some, or their foundations, are major donors to Catholic causes, including the conference. "It's kind of hard to publicly say we won't buy stock in your company because you make contraceptives or bombs," acknowledged one staffer, "but we can enjoy your foundation's grants." The guidelines also permit the initiation of stockholder resolutions on justice issues.

Assessments

Since assessments and special collections come from the dioceses, it is not surprising that these are the most controversial sources of income for the bishops.

The NCCB/USCC assessment is a per capita tax imposed on dioceses according to their Catholic population as reported in *The Official Catholic Directory*.[8] From 1989-92 the assessment was 15.7 cents per Catholic, which brings in about $8 million annually. A one-penny quota increase is worth about $520,000. The money is not collected directly from each Catholic but from the dioceses. Under this system, large dioceses pay the largest amounts although they are probably helped least by the conference staff since they have their own large staffs. For example, the Los Angeles Archdiocese was assessed $532,000 in 1991.

The NCWC had no canonical authority to impose assessments. It had to depend on voluntary contributions from the bishops, which gave greater power to the richer dioceses. After Vatican II, episcopal conferences received canonical authority to impose assessments. The NCCB/USCC statutes (Article XIV) limit voting on financial matters (assessments, budget, collections) to the diocesan bishops under the theory that they, not the auxiliary bishops, have to come up with the money.[9] The imposition of an assessment requires a two-thirds vote of diocesan bishops.

The assessment is a tax the diocesan bishops impose upon themselves with much reluctance. "You can understand their reluctance because there is a crunch," remarks Francis X. Doyle, associate general secretary, "and they respond to needs at home more than to the national scene." The moaning and groaning that occurs over this vote would warm the heart of any fiscal conservative. Like the U.S. Congress, the NCCB/USCC assembly loves to vote for programs but does not like to pay for them. The bishops have one advantage over members of Congress—they do not have to run for reelection. On the other hand, unlike Congress, which has the power to tax, the bishops cannot compel the laity to donate the money that ultimately pays the assessments.

When an assessment increase is proposed by the Administrative Committee/Board, it usually passes. As Msgr. Daniel Hoye, a former general secretary, recalls:

> So far we have been lucky with the assessment votes. The last time, there were 26 bishops voting against raising it [for 1989]. Some are ideological votes, they don't like what the conference is doing. A couple will vote against any assessment. The bishops are facing tight

budgets in their dioceses. They and their budget people see this sacred cow, the NCCB/USCC assessments, that cannot be cut. That has an effect.

In 1982, the NCCB/USCC assembly decided to set assessments one year before approving the budget. Setting assessments first forces the staff to prepare a budget within the constraints of projected income. The normal pattern from 1976-91 was for the conference to raise assessments once every three years. This proved problematic since deciding the assessment level required projecting conference expenses four years into the future. Also the budget got very tight in the third year.

Some bishops complain that the assessment is constantly going up and that their people cannot afford to give any more. How legitimate are these complaints?

The diocesan assessments have clearly gone up since the NCCB/USCC was established in 1966. As shown in the first column of Table 9.2, the assessments went up from one cent per Catholic in 1967 to 15.7 cents per Catholic in 1989-92. Thus superficially there is evidence to support the complaint that the assessments are constantly going up.

But when the assessments are adjusted for inflation in column two, the increase disappears.[10] Adjusting the assessments for 1982-84 prices shows that assessments peaked in 1971 at 14.8 cents and then steadily declined through 1975. From 1974 through 1991, the assessments varied by no more than 2.3 cents—from a high of 12.66 cents in 1989 to a low of 10.36 cents in 1982. Each time the bishops raised the assessment, its real value declined over the next three years because of inflation. The increases every three years have simply attempted to regain lost ground. The bishops' refusal to raise assessments from 1989 through 1993 (including a cut in 1993) means that the assessment level will continue to fall below inflation. Beginning in 1994, assessments are increased by about 5 percent annually. If this annual increase continues, it will provide some stability to the assessment fund, but it will be below the average funding of the previous two decades, unless the inflation rate is under 5 percent.

Table 9.2
NCCB/USCC Assessments in Cents
per Catholic by Year

Year	Actual	Adjusted (1982-84 cents)
1967	1	2.9
1968	2	5.0
1969	4	10.9
1970	4	10.3
1971	6	14.8
1972	6	14.4
1973	6	13.5
1974	6	12.2
1975	6	11.2
1976	7	12.3
1977	7	11.6
1978	7	10.7
1979	8	11.0
1980	10	12.1
1981	10	11.0
1982	10	10.4
1983	12.3	12.4
1984	12.3	11.8
1985	12.3	11.4
1986	13.3	12.1
1987	13.3	11.7
1988	13.3	11.2
1989	15.7	12.7
1990	15.7	12.0
1991	15.7	11.5
1992	15.7	11.2
1993	15.06	10.4
1994	15.83	10.6
1995	16.61	10.8
1996	17.39	10.9

The bishops have also at times imposed on themselves temporary assessments for special purposes.[11] In 1979, there was a .66 cents per Catholic assessment to help pay for the papal visit. Other special assessments have been voted to pay for lawsuits and for lobbying efforts. For example, the National Committee for Human Life Amendment (NCHLA), a grass-roots lobbying effort to secure a human life amendment to the Constitution, is funded through a one-cent per Catholic assessment each year. A similar assessment funded CREDIT, the Citizens' Relief for Education by Income Tax, a grass-roots lobby for tuition tax credits. For legal reasons, the assessments for CREDIT and NCHLA were paid by the individual bishops directly to these organizations without going through the USCC.

Periodically, complaints arise concerning the regressivity of the assessment system. After passage of the economic pastoral, Bishop William McManus denounced the per capita tax as regressive and said the conference should "practice what it preaches." By taxing each diocese by its number of Catholics, no distinction is made between rich and poor dioceses. Some dioceses are in debt, others have large investment portfolios. Under the current assessment system, a predominantly white middle-class diocese with 100,000 Catholics pays the same as a diocese of 100,000 poor Hispanics. If the U.S. government had such a tax system, the bishops would be outraged.

Public finance economists would agree that a head tax, such as the NCCB/USCC assessment, is inherently regressive. The difficulty is constructing a funding system that would be progressive or at least proportional. Although the NCCB/USCC has recommended a uniform system of diocesan accounting and reporting, the financial books of dioceses are so different that comparisons are difficult.[12] Even if the books were comparable, there is little agreement on what should be compared. For example, should a diocese be punished with higher assessments because it raises more money? Should a diocese that has saved and therefore has an endowment be taxed at a higher rate?

The fairest system might be to tax a diocese according to the income of its Catholics. Unhappily, the U.S. Census does not ask a person's religion, and matching census statistics to diocesan boundaries is problematic. Another method would be to tax total annual offertory collections in each diocese, which is the way the Texas Catholic Conference is funded. When all is said and done, if the assessment is only 15 cents per Catholic, it may not be worth the trouble and administrative expense to make the system progressive (Only two Latin-rite dioceses did not pay their assessments in 1991 because of financial difficulties). In addition, the regressivity of the assessment system could be balanced by the national collections if richer dioceses give more. Also CHD and ABCM grants, described below, can funnel money into poor dioceses and thus redress the regressivity of the assessments. Thus the USCC financial system as a whole could be progressive or proportional, even though the assessments are regressive. In 1991 the bishops voted (182-16) to have an ad hoc committee study the present method of calculating the assessments and make recommendations concerning possible alternatives.

National Collections

The NCCB/USCC also receives money through special collections taken up each year in churches across the nation. Collections are distinguished from assessments in that they normally do not have mandated targets and they are often taken up at Sunday Masses. In some collections, the local diocese can keep a percentage of the collection which acts as an incentive for local fund-raising. There are seven NCCB/USCC national collections bringing in about $55 million annually:[13]

1. The Church in Latin America Collection, begun in 1966, collected $4 million in 1990, most of which was distributed by the NCCB Committee on Latin America to Latin American bishops. Administrative, promotional, and educational costs consumed $329,000, and a grant of $210,000 went to the USCC Department of Social Development and World Peace.

2. Aid to the Church in Central and Eastern Europe and the USSR, a three-year collection begun in 1991, will be distributed by an NCCB ad hoc committee chaired by Archbishop May. The bishops collected more than $6 million the first year of the collection. Requests for funds will be channeled to the NCCB through episcopal conferences in Central and Eastern Europe and the Soviet Union.[14]

3. Bishops' Welfare and Emergency Relief Fund (BWER), more popularly known as the American Bishops' Overseas Appeal, began in 1939 as the Laetare Sunday collection. It collected $12 million in 1990 for distribution by the NCCB Administrative Committee. Ninety percent of this money went to Catholic Relief Services and the USCC Migration and Refugee Services to help the poor abroad. Another $500,000 went to the pope's relief program, $313,000 to the USCC Department of Social Development and World Peace, and $211,000 to promotion and education.

4. Catholic Communication Campaign (CCC), begun in 1979, received $3 million (half the total collection) in 1990 for distribution by the USCC Committee on Communications. Half the receipts stay in the diocese where it is collected. Of the national grants, three-fourths of the money goes to NCCB/USCC activities. In the past, the largest grants have gone to the Catholic Telecommunications Network of America. In 1990 the campaign made $2.3 million in grants, spent $400,000 on education and promotion, and spent $246,000 on administration.

5. Mission Sunday Collection, begun in 1926, is technically not an NCCB/USCC collection but is run by the National Society for the Propagation of the Faith, which retains 51 percent of the receipts for the foreign missions. Another 9 percent goes to the Catholic Near East Welfare Association. Forty percent of the total goes to the NCCB American Board of Catholic Missions (ABCM), which received $5.5 million in 1990 for distribution to needy dioceses in the United States. ABCM made $5.7 million in grants and spent $157,000 on administration. ABCM grants to NCCB/USCC activities have been declining since at least 1987, when they were $366,000. In 1990, they were only $136,000. The decision not to fund the NCCB Office of Hispanic Affairs in 1991 cost the conference another $86,000 annually.

6. Campaign for Human Development (CHD), begun in 1970, received $9 million (75 percent of the total collection) in 1990 that was distributed by the USCC Campaign for Human Development Committee to help impoverished and underprivileged people in the

United States. The other 25 percent of the collection is retained by the dioceses for use in local human development programs. In 1989, CHD made $7.2 million in grants, spent $833,000 on promotion and education, and $1.4 million on administration.

7. Retirement Fund for Religious, a 10-year annual appeal begun in 1988, collected $22 million in 1990. Its first year, it collected $25.9 million, more than any other NCCB/USCC collection in history. In 1990, $21.8 million was distributed to religious communities by Tri-Conference Retirement Project for the care of retired religious. The Tri-Conference Retirement Office spends $332,000 on administration and $418,000 on promotion.

Some NCCB/USCC collections are temporary, such as the one-time collection of $4 million (2.6 cents per Catholic) for Thailand refugees in 1984. The collections for retired religious and the Eastern European churches were approved for limited periods, but what starts as a temporary collection (such as the CUA and CHD collections) sometimes becomes permanent.

The administrative and promotional costs of the collections vary. It is not surprising that BWER, ABCM, and the Tri-Conference Retirement Project have low administrative costs. BWER gives most of its money to conference-controlled agencies (CRS, MRS, and the USCC Department of Social Development and World Peace). There is no need for a BWER staff to review grant proposals or exercise oversight on these agencies. ABCM gives its money to poor U.S. dioceses. The number of grant requests is limited and ABCM expects the local bishop to exercise oversight. In addition, promotion costs are covered by the National Society for the Propagation of the Faith. The Tri-Conference Retirement Project gives its money to religious orders. In addition, since the collection has been so successful, the percentage going to administration and promotion is low.

The collections for Latin America, CHD, and communications have greater administrative costs. The Church in Latin America collection gives money to Latin American dioceses. Distance and the need for greater review increases administrative costs. Not surprisingly, CHD's administrative expenses are high. CHD gives grants to local groups helping the poor. These are not necessarily Catholic organizations, although they do require the approval of the local bishop to get funded. Reviewing these requests is time-consuming. Often these groups are administratively weak and require detailed oversight. CHD has a national staff and field operatives who review grants and monitor the performance of recipients. The Catholic Communication Campaign expenses are more surprising since the grants go primarily to conference entities and the Catholic media.

Besides these seven NCCB/USCC collections, there are five other national collections approved by the bishops that bring in millions of dollars annually. This money is not administered by the conference but goes directly to the proper agency.

1. The Black and Indian Home Mission Collection is the oldest national collection, authorized by the Third Plenary Council of Baltimore in 1884. It collected $6.5 million in 1990 for evangelization programs in needy mission areas in the United States.

2. The Catholic University of America Collection, begun in 1903, received $4.5 million in 1990 for operating expenses of CUA.

3. The collection for the Holy Land is taken up on Good Friday and dates back to about 1888 in the U.S., although its proponents trace its history back to the first century with St. Paul's collection for the relief of the church in Jerusalem. It collected $5.6 million in 1989 for care and maintenance of the Holy Sites.

4. Operation Rice Bowl became a national collection in 1976 and brought in $3.6 million (three fourths of the collection) in 1990. Catholic Relief Services uses this money to fund Third World self-help projects, while the other fourth funds local poverty programs in the diocese where it is collected.

5. Peter's Pence collection is a world-wide collection that assists the pope in his service to the whole church. In 1989, $13.6 million was collected in the United States. This money used to go to the pope's charities but now helps balance the Vatican budget. Cardinal Krol, who has worked to raise money for the Vatican, complains that "they started taking a little from Peter's Pence, then more and more, and then all of it" to balance the budget. The deficits should be covered by alternate sources, he said, "the Peter's Pence money must go back to the pope for the needs of the poor."[15]

One of the few collections ever to be dropped was for the National Office of Black Catholics, which is not part of the NCCB/USCC. In 1972 the collection was authorized to be taken up in black parishes. During his term (1987-90) as chair of the NCCB Committee on Black Catholics, Bishop John H. Ricard informed the conference in an executive session that the black bishops no longer supported the collection. NCCB/USCC backing for the collection was withdrawn without any public announcement. The collection is still taken up in some black parishes.

Although authorized by the conference, not all the collections are taken up in all dioceses. Some bishops send in money without taking up a special collection. Nor is a monetary goal mandated for each diocese, although national staffs encourage percentage increases annually. "None of the collections is mandatory," explains Frank Doyle. "No one can compel a local ordinary to take any collection. So, some are more popular than others."

No bishop is likely to ignore the Peter's Pence collection. Although assessment-paying members of the conference, the Eastern-rite dioceses and the Military Archdiocese do not normally contribute to the NCCB/USCC collections. The ABCM, BWER, CHD, the Retired Religious Fund, and the Black and Indian Home Mission collections are very popular, with no more than four Latin-rite dioceses not contributing (or late) to any of them in 1990.[16] The Catholic Communication Campaign is less popular, with 15 dioceses opting out.

Forty-three (25 percent) of the dioceses do not contribute to the Latin American collection. "Some dioceses support a mission in Latin America themselves," explains Mr. Doyle. "They might be twinning or may actually send several priests to a diocese or parish in Latin America and support them. So, some of those dioceses don't participate in the collection because they do it on their own, so to speak." Some bishops have suggested using some of this collection for Hispanic ministry in the United States, but the proposal was rejected by the bishops in 1990.

The actual administration of the collections in dioceses also varies. Often the collection is a special "second collection" taken up on a specific Sunday of the year. In pre-Vatican II days, the second collection was taken up after Communion.

Today that is liturgically unacceptable and parishioners are asked to use special envelopes, mark their checks, or the second collection is taken up immediately after the first during the presentation of gifts.

Some bishops take up the collection on a Sunday different from the date set nationally. Some consolidate national collections with each other or with local collections. Others send a donation in without having taken up a collection.[17] Such variety in dates and modes for taking up the collections has frustrated attempts at national promotion campaigns. The amount of money raised through the five traditional NCCB collections has declined steadily since 1977 when adjusted for inflation. The Bishops' Overseas Appeal and the Mission Sunday Collection have been declining steadily since 1968 and 1977 respectively. The Latin America Collection declined from 1967 until 1984 when it began to hold its own against inflation. After peaking in the mid-1970s, the Campaign for Human Development has declined. The take from the Catholic Communication Campaign has been erratic, but on average keeping up with inflation. All but the last collection help poor people and poor churches either here or abroad.[18]

Besides these national collections, there are also special local collections. As a result, many bishops, pastors, and laity complain that there are too many special collections. In 1977 the NCCB/USCC Advisory Committee had unanimously voted that "all present collections be evaluated, some continued, some consolidated, some dropped." Around the same time, a survey of diocesan bishops found that 64 of the 80 responding wanted a consolidation or combination of collections.

Despite support for consolidation in theory, in practice it proved difficult because the bishops and constituencies supporting a particular collection oppose merging their collection with anyone else's. "On the national collections, you've got vested interests, which I respect," explains Archbishop Daniel Pilarczyk. "If I've got this collection every year, and you want to put my collection with his collection, there's no way."

In 1978, an ad hoc committee on national collections chaired by Archbishop Thomas McDonough recommended consolidating the collections. The committee proposed a new "Mission Collection" that would include the old Mission Sunday Collection, the Church in Latin America Collection, and the Black and Indian Home Mission Collection. In fact, the traditional mission collection was already a consolidated collection for the Propagation of the Faith, the Catholic Near East Welfare Association, and the American Board of Catholic Missions. The ad hoc committee saw these "mission"-oriented collections coming together in a natural and unified way. The committee also recommended consolidating the Campaign for Human Development and the National Office for Black Catholics collections into a single Human Development Collection. The Communication Collection and the collection for the Catholic University of America were to be combined into a Communication and Evangelization Collection.

The consolidation proposal came under heavy criticism. Cardinal John Carberry asked if people who gave $5 in four collections could be expected to give $20 in one collection. Bishop James Hickey also feared fewer collections would collect less money. Bishop William Connare, a former missionary, feared that support for missionary activity would suffer. Bishop James Rausch and Archbishop John Whealon wanted to know why there was no collection for Hispanics. Archbishop Philip Hannan, a member of the board of trustees of CUA, spoke for retaining a separate collection for the Catholic University of America. Bishop John Sullivan noted that 87 dioceses receive help from the Black and Indian Mission collection and that the ABCM could not assume those commitments. Cardinal John Krol called the proposal "highly impractical and practically impossible." As chair of the Black and Indian Mission Board, he did not see the logic of the combination. Cardinal Terence Cooke summed up the criticism by saying that with consolidated collections less money will be received, poor people will be neglected, some dioceses may be in trouble, and the home and overseas missions will get less.

No one is recorded in the minutes as speaking in favor of the proposal. Archbishop Roach joked that Archbishop McDonough, "on advice of his doctor," withdrew the proposal from the floor.[19] Only when Archbishop McDonough offered to withdraw his proposal did a few bishops speak about there being too many collections and ask what would happen if the proposal was withdrawn. Further study was promised, but nothing happened.

In 1991 a new ad hoc committee began to look at the national collections again, and it may propose another consolidation. A Committee on Stewardship was also appointed to examine ways to increase giving to the church by Catholics who give less to their denomination than do Protestants or Jews.[20]

Of the national collections, the most controversial outside the conference has been the Campaign for Human Development, which has come under attack from conservatives. "CHD's commitment is not to Christian charity but to a brand of radical politics . . . alien to our historic political consensus," charged a report of the Capital Research Center. CHD funds "'community organizing' and other causes central to the operation of the American radical left."[21] One author had served as a research analyst to the House Committee on Un-American Activities.

In 1989 William E. Simon, a conservative Catholic, distributed this report to the membership of the Knights of Malta, an organization of Catholic donors, with a letter stating that the report "documents how this program of the U.S. Catholic Conference is a funding mechanism for radical left political activism in the United States, rather than for traditional types of Catholic charities." Mr. Simon had earlier co-chaired with Michael Novak the Lay Commission on Catholic Social Teaching that had critiqued the bishops' views on economic justice.[22] The use of the Knights' mailing list to circulate a vicious attack on the American bishops, which was authorized by the Knights' president J. Peter Grace, so upset former Ohio governor John J. Gilligan that he resigned in protest from the Knights of Malta.

The conservatives especially object to CHD funding grassroots organizing groups. "When CHD leaders speak about developing the self-help skills of the poor," charged the *National*

Review, "it's not the ability to earn a living, to educate their children, or to fix up dilapidated housing that they mean. The only skill that seems to impress CHD is the ability to wheedle money out of the Federal Government."[23]

These attacks, which came from the same people who had attacked the bishops' economic and peace pastorals, did not deter the bishops. Bishop Joseph A. Fiorenza of Galveston-Houston, chair of CHD at the time, responded that the attacks were "baseless and scurrilous accusations." He said that CHD was founded because the bishops "felt that no longer was it enough to give poor people food, clothing and shelter, the time had come to also assist the poorest among us to 'break the hellish cycle of poverty' and build a better life for themselves and their children."[24]

The accusation to which the bishops were most sensitive was that CHD was funding organizations that supported abortion. CHD had given $20,000 to the National Health Care Campaign, a Washington-based organization providing information and help to groups supporting expansion of health care to uncovered needy people. The NHCC has 160 members, including the USCC, National Catholic Charities, and the Catholic Health Association. Some member groups do support government funding of abortions, but everyone was aware of the Catholic organizations' opposition to abortion. The CHD funds helped create statewide networks of poor and low-income people working for accessible and affordable health care services in their communities. Because of the criticism of this grant and others, CHD has to be especially careful in helping groups in the health care field.

Episcopal support for CHD was reiterated in 1988 when, following a two-year study, the bishops voted to continue the collection and to raise CHD from an ad hoc to a standing committee of the USCC. Survey data in 1991 showed the bishops would rank CHD first or second in importance among four of their collections (CHD, ABCM, Latin America collection, and Communication Campaign).[25]

The ranking of ABCM collection was undoubtedly helped by the fact that many bishops receive money from this collection and have a vested interest in its continuance. The future of this collection, however, is in question. The Congregation for the Evangelization of Peoples is insisting that all of the Mission Sunday collection go to the foreign missions.

Conference Priorities and Plans

As the conference budget and staff grew, better management and planning were instituted to control programs and finances. Today the NCCB/USCC has 450 employees, and the accounting office processes 20,000 checks and $100 million in revenues a year. The finances of the NCWC were more informal. "The finance office was one or two maiden ladies, practically writing the checks out by hand," recalls Russell Shaw. The episcopal treasurer, Cardinal John Cody, did some of the finances out of his chancery in Chicago. Conference offices were operating on different fiscal years with separate bank accounts that were not audited. Finances were gradually centralized in Washington, and the first audited financial report was done in 1971. In the early years, the conference budget only included programs funded by the assessments and the BWER. The implication was that if an office raised its own money, it could spend it however the staff and its committee wanted. In the late 1970s, the budget began to include all conference income and expenses. And in 1980 the conference switched from cash basis accounting to accrual.

More professional management was instituted by Msgr. Daniel Hoye as general secretary with strong backing from Bishop James Malone when he was vice president and president and from Archbishop Edmund Szoka when he was treasurer. An associate general secretary was added to deal with finances, accounting, personnel, archives, library, and general services (housekeeping, maintenance, purchasing of supplies, parking).

Monsignor Hoye appointed Francis X. Doyle, the first lay associate general secretary, to head this office. Mr. Doyle, a lawyer, also oversees the staffs of three collections: the Campaign for Human Development, the American Board of Catholic Missions, and the Latin American Secretariat. These offices are primarily involved in grant-making. He also gets ad hoc assignments, like supervising the construction of the new USCC office building,[26] doing a study of portability of pensions for lay employees of the church, and staffing the NCCB ad hoc Committee on Stewardship and the ad hoc Committee on National Collections.

The planning process developed in the early 1980s increased financial control, but it also helped make sure that the staff was doing what the whole conference wanted it to do and not simply what a committee, chair, or the staff itself wanted.

"There was a sense in the conference that the committees had heretofore crafted their own agenda, and thereby crafted the direction of the conference," explains Bishop Malone who, as vice president and president, was chair of the Committee on Priorities and Plans.

> What we needed was some larger process by which we could drive the conference by goals and objectives and strategies. We worked closely with the management consultants and came up with what has remained to the present time a very workable method of saying to the conference periodically, "These are the five objectives that you have set, given us. We in our review, seeing the work the committee has done in the last three years, we feel that there is this adjustment [needed] to your goals."

The planning process begins with each staff working with its committee to draw up goals and objectives for the staff and the committee. These are reviewed internally by the associate general secretaries and the general secretary. This work is then reviewed and modified by the Committee on Priorities and Plans, chaired by the NCCB/USCC president with the former president, the vice president, treasurer, general secretary, and two other bishops as members.

"Priorities and Plans really does review them thoroughly," reports Associate General Secretary Sharon Euart, R.S.M., who is also in charge of planning. Over a three-year cycle, key office directors appear before the committee to describe their programs and plans. "They are subject to rather close scrutiny," says Sister Euart. Also subject to close review would be offices "that have been reorganized, have new directors, or have been the result of mergers or expansions—to see how all of that is working."

In recent years, offices getting close attention included the Secretariat for Laity and Family (a merger of several offices including laity, family life, women, and youth in 1987), the Social Development and World Peace Department (a new secretary in 1988, whose committee was split into international and domestic sections in 1987), the Secretariat for Black Catholics (a new secretariat in 1987), the Communications Department (the result of a major reorganization in 1989), and the Education Department (reorganized and given a new secretary in 1990). "They have come in and been interviewed by Priorities and Plans," reports Sister Euart.

In 1981 the assembly unanimously adopted a four-sentence mission statement (see appendix A). The statement was so general it did little to direct the conference. The planning process also calls for the adoption and revision of conference goals and objectives on a three-year cycle. For 1988-90 there were seven conference-wide goals taken from the *Directory for the Pastoral Ministry of Bishops*. These are rather general, admits Sister Euart. "In one sense, they are the goals of a bishop in his local church and I'm not sure they are the most appropriate goals for a body of bishops at a national level," she says. "However, they at least help to categorize what happens."

Under the seven goals were 36 objectives for 1988-90 that attempted to provide some direction to the conference. These were slightly revised with two additions for 1991-96 (see appendix B).[27] Again, the objectives were often sweeping in extent, but they did provide some focus. In addition, six objectives were selected for special emphasis during the planning cycle. These objectives dealt with catechesis, vocations, respect for human life, Catholic social teaching, multi-cultural evangelization, and the role of parents and pastors in Catholic education.

Before adopting the revised goals and objectives in 1989, the committee chairs were asked to review the goals pertinent to their committees. They were also asked if any other areas needed to be addressed by the conference. Finally, they were asked "Were there any areas that are adequately being addressed, institutionalized, or were appropriately addressed at the local level that should be dropped?"

"We didn't get any recommendations [for dropping things]," reports Sister Euart. "That's a typical aspect of church planning, whether it's parish, diocese, or the national church. We're very hesitant to say something is no longer necessary." Despite the flaws in the system, "We have an adequate set of directives for directing the conference at this point," says Sister Euart. "However I think we have too many objectives because we will be facing a question on resources, what can we do? My hunch is that in the future we will have to identify fewer of these directions that are the responsibility of the national level."

Using the planning process to set priorities has been difficult. "I'm not sure it's even possible," admits Sister Euart, "because the leaders, the bishops, come from different parts of the country, from churches with different needs and different resources. To determine what is a priority at the national level—to come to any consensus or agreement on that with 300 people who have the final say—is difficult."

"When we first did it [priorities and plans]," recalls Monsignor Hoye, "we simply described goals that fit the work that the staff and committee were [already] doing. Then when we changed the goals, we put what the staff and committees were doing as subordinate clauses to the goals. I told them that if we were not doing those goals, then we should cut the staffs."

By and large, the recommendations of the Priorities and Plans Committee have been accepted by the assembly with little consideration. "They're approved by the full body of bishops, often with very little attention," admits Msgr. Robert Lynch, the general secretary. "It passes automatically, and it's a huge and overwhelming document."

"When the plans contain activities like a teleconference, a research study, a specific program, theoretically the full body is knowledgeable about all of those activities," explains Sister Euart. "Realistically, what happens is that the bishops know very well what their own committee is doing, but depend on the recommendations of Priorities and Plans as to whether they approve the others."

The process does in theory give the assembly control. "It gives the bishops a chance to have a say on what goes on in the conference," explains Archbishop Pilarczyk.

> Whether they are always aware of that chance, whether they take advantage of it is another question. This lump [the priorities and plans document] comes, and if you really want to be up on what's going on, you have to sit down for a long time and go through that stuff. But it's there, and it's amendable. "And you, bishop, vote on it. So that you can't say that the staff controls the conference, you can't say the committee chairmen control the conference." They may in fact do that, but structurally, it's the bishops who tell the chairs and the staff people what they want done.

As a result of this process, NCCB/USCC chairs and committees are accountable to the conference, because anything that is proposed by them must go through the planning process and be voted on by the conference. "A staff person and a committee chairman cannot just go off half-cocked way down some country road with some project that they decide is important," explains Archbishop Pilarczyk. "They have to abide by the priorities and plans. Obviously, the suggestions for plans come through the staff and committee, and the committee has to approve the plans that are submitted to the process." Since these plans have to be approved by the whole conference, "It's a check and balance type of thing, which is only as effective as people choose to make it." Most of the bishops appear to recognize that the planning process allows them to set priorities. Only 26 percent of the bishops feel that the bishops do not set the direction and establish the agenda of the conference.[28]

The assembly almost never changes these plans which means that the Administrative Committee/Board plays the key role. In 1991 Bishop William K. Weigand got the assembly to amend the Priorities and Plans document to include more concern for families in crisis and for the sacrament of penance. How this will work out in practice is unclear. What is clear is that a determined bishop can intervene and change the priorities and plans if he can swing the assembly behind him.

Both Monsignors Hoye and Lynch agree on the importance of the planning process for the general secretary. "The process is in place to make sure that the general secretary knows and understands the plans and programs of the individual committees," said Monsignor Lynch. "He evaluates the performance of the staff and he is responsible for their continuation, their advancement, their promotion. He basically administers the conference." The plans, once approved, also protect the general secretary from pressure from bishops who want the conference doing something else.

Budgetary Process

The planning process ultimately must be linked to the budgetary process if it is to have real consequences, but this has not occurred, in the view of the top staff. "The planning process, in my judgment, will never work adequately until bishops make hard choices about where they want to put their diminishing resources," remarks Monsignor Lynch. "As long as they have to play 'Which of my favorite children will I murder this meeting?' they simply don't want to make those decisions."

Mr. Doyle agrees that the planning process has "enhanced collaboration among conference units, but there has not been progress in the area of priorities. If you were funded at a certain level, you will probably get funded at that level. There haven't really been any reductions or eliminations of any conference activities. Those are the hard questions."

The Budget and Finance Committee came to the same conclusion in 1988. Attempts to establish priorities "have had very little, if any, impact on the allocation of General Fund resources," the committee reported to the Administrative Committee/Board. "Although more attention has been given to collaboration among NCCB/USCC entities, such efforts may, at times, result in the development of new programs and additional costs."[29]

From year to year, there are few changes in the NCCB/USCC budget. Like budgets everywhere, it increases incrementally every year, but most increases are simply responding to inflation and keeping the old programs operating at the same level. "The budget process is long," explains Monsignor Hoye. "It starts in March with the staff drawing up budgets. Usually I tell them to present their budgets with increases for salaries and benefits but to hold the line on projects. Last year [1987] we gave them a whopping 2 percent increase for projects after having held the line for a couple of years." In 1989, the project budget was frozen.

Since the assessment is set at least a year ahead of the budget, "We know what the pie is from the assessments and the budget has to fit within that," explains Monsignor Hoye. When the bishops only raised the assessments every three years, the budget would get tight toward the end of the three-year cycle. As inflation cuts into the value of the NCCB/USCC assessments, parts of the budget must be cut to provide inflationary adjustments for salaries and fringe benefits. With about $5.6 million in salaries, a 5 percent increase costs $280,000.

In the first year of the three-year cycle, the conference attempted to run a budget surplus that could be carried forward to cover future deficits. "Where it becomes most difficult is the third year," reports Mr. Doyle. "Costs rise and you have no more income from that source. As a matter of fact, the budget for 1990 is really going to be a deficit budget." In 1989 Monsignor Lynch was forced by the budget to institute a hiring freeze. The decision in 1991 to increase assessments by 5 percent a year beginning in 1994 will provide more stable funding since assessment income will increase each year.

Although the Committee on Budget and Finances puts together the final budget proposal, the general secretary plays an important role in reviewing the staff and committee budgets. "Sometimes committee chairmen feel that the general secretary is exercising more, let's say, budgetary discretion than he should by holding the chairman to an accountability that he doesn't want to be held to," explains Archbishop Roach. He recalls when he was president,

. . . a committee chair, very charismatic guy, coming in with a very elaborate proposal to which was attached just the vaguest budget. Well, he snowed enough members of the Administrative Committee to almost forget that that was true, and the general secretary had to move in. The chair got very angry at the general secretary. The chair called me and he was angry, and I said "The general secretary did exactly what he was supposed to do. He did his job, and you didn't do yours."

Some changes in the budget do reflect changes in the conference priorities and plans. For example, when the conference is working on a major document (pastoral letter, pastoral program, directory, etc.), money will be needed for extra staff, printing, and implementation. But new programs or expansion of old programs without outside funding must fight an uphill battle for approval in the budget. "Much closer scrutiny is given to new positions or projects," admits Monsignor Hoye.

Programs that are self-financing or that can be funded with foundation grants have fewer problems getting approval in the budgetary process. The NCCB Secretariat for Family Life, Laity, Women, and Youth has been very successful in getting funding for workshops, conferences, and teleconferences. The NCCB Secretariat for Pro Life Activities received $3 to $5 million from the Knights of Columbus. These activities would not have been approved without outside funding.

Cutting the Budget

No one has found it very easy to cut the NCCB/USCC budget. "I tried to cut a few things and was unsuccessful," says Monsignor Hoye. Many bishops, like members of Congress, complain about the size of the budget and the size of the NCCB/USCC bureaucracy. But whenever the general secretary, the president, or the budget committee recommends eliminating a staff position, many people come to its defense.

When reviewing the budget as president, Archbishop John Quinn tried to cut from the budget an office occupied by Msgr. George Higgins. Monsignor Higgins had been with the conference since 1944 and was well known for his work for social justice, especially with labor unions. When the conference was reorganized after Vatican II, he was offered the position of executive director of the Office of Peace and Justice. He declined, but continued to have an office in the conference. Although Archbishop Quinn considers Monsignor Higgins "an outstanding priest, and a very intelligent, able, gifted man," the archbishop felt his work was not directly related to the conference anymore. "It seemed to me in principle unjustifiable to maintain an office and staff for Justice and Peace and then, separate from that, maintain another office and budget with the same purview," explains Archbishop Quinn. Monsignor Higgins himself admits that "By the time Quinn came along, I was pretty well doing my own thing."

The cut immediately took on symbolic importance way beyond its monetary value (about $50,000). "You have no idea the pressures that were placed on me from all over the United States," recalls Archbishop Quinn. Monsignor Higgins was widely known and respected among bishops, social activists, labor unionists, and politicians. Archbishop Quinn was inundated by people trying to reverse the decision, including Arthur Goldberg, the Rev. Theodore Hesburgh, and many bishops. The Rev. Andrew Greeley said that Archbishop Quinn would go down in history with Benedict Arnold.

The issue was further complicated since Monsignor Higgins would have reached retirement age in another year. People wondered why he was being pushed out a year early. Monsignor Higgins now says that, if he had simply been asked for budgetary reasons to retire a year early, he would have. In any case, Archbishop Quinn felt it was a matter of principle. "I could not go back to my own archdiocese and defend the NCCB assessment if we were duplicating functions in our NCCB offices," he said. After a lengthy discussion, he was overruled by the Administrative Board/Committee.

"I never again raised any question about the budget," says Archbishop Quinn. "I said, 'they want to take care of it, that is their responsibility.' I for the last time put my neck on the block for the budget. I regarded it as a matter of principle, and as an unjustifiable expense when we were raising dioceses' rates. But the bishops caved in to the pressures." Because of this fracas, the Administrative Committee/Board added an elected member to the Executive Committee as a check on the officers to keep them from doing such things. Ironically, Archbishop Quinn later was elected to the position.

Archbishop Quinn is not the only one to have difficulties cutting staff. In 1987 Monsignor Hoye and Father Lynch reorganized the education department to concentrate on two areas: religious education and schools. They wanted to move the responsibility for youth ministry out of education and into family ministry. This was opposed by some, especially those involved with student groups, who wanted a full-time staff person for youth in education. Monsignor Hoye and Father Lynch were supported by the Priorities and Plans Committee, the Budget Committee, and the Administrative Committee/Board.

They ran into trouble in the assembly when Auxiliary Bishop Robert A. Carlson of St. Paul complained that the bishops' commitment to youth was being dropped. "Our young people are hurting," he said. "Today's Church and our future Church is our responsibility. We cannot fall short or abdicate this responsibility. We cannot let these concerns take a minor place in the conference."[30] Bishop Carlson won on the issue of a full-time person for youth, but he lost in his attempt to keep it in the education department.

"My intention was to move out peripheral things that were in education, such as youth ministry and family life ministry, and put them in NCCB under a combined secretariat for lay activities," recalls Monsignor Lynch. "I did it, but in the process of going from one to the other, there's now a youth position that was never planned or programmed or budgeted."

"I tried several times to cut, but every time I tried I lost," explains Monsignor Hoye. "I tried to cut the Human Values Committee, but someone complained that we have to dialogue with atheists. It has nothing to do with dialogue with atheists, but it was kept by the assembly."

Besides the youth position, there was also an office for non-Christian religions (Muslims, Buddhists, etc.) proposed by

Bishop Keeler, chair of the Committee on Ecumenical and Interreligious Affairs. This office was opposed by the general secretary, the Priorities and Plans Committee, and the Budget Committee. But the Administrative Committee/Board approved it.

Those two new offices plus a reduction in ABCM funding for the Hispanic Affairs Secretariat cost one additional cent to the bishops, according to Monsignor Lynch. "In so far as the two offices were concerned," he says, "we would have said it wasn't necessary. But someone gets up and demagogues on the floor and you can't say on the floor what you really think or what you said behind closed doors. It's not fair. So you just have to sit back and watch them slap you around a little bit."

"It is contradictory to be reluctant to increase the support of the conference and at the same time to ask the conference to do more things and to put back things that were taken out by competent committees or were not approved by competent committees," concludes Mr. Doyle. "You can't have it both ways, but we try to."

Archbishop Pilarczyk agrees:

> This is part of the dynamic of the conference, that everybody says, "It costs too much, and I'm not going to pay any more." But, "Do you want to cut out something that I'm interested in? You'll never get away with it, and I've got a lot of friends. I can get up on the floor and say this is a slap in the face to the Catholic youth of our country." You can say that about any office. Take one, and I'll give you a speech about it, because I've heard them.

Ideally, the priorities and planning process should feed into and direct the budgetary process. In reality it often works in the opposite direction. "Actually, what happens," admits Sister Euart, "is your planning becomes reactive rather than proactive. The priorities should direct your budget, rather than the budget direct your priorities. The priorities have to be realistic, but at the same time they can't be totally directed by finances."

Faced with declining resources, the conference may be forced to make more hard choices. "It's very easy to say yes," explains Sister Euart. "It's much harder to say no. What is going to happen, I believe, is that every time we say yes to something, we're going to have to simultaneously say no to something else. Those are hard decisions."

"They will move something up in priority without dropping anything," points out Monsignor Hoye. "I gave a speech to the Administrative Committee that they are going to have to decide priorities, which also means deciding what you are not going to do, or they are going to have to raise assessments." Since committee chairs are members of the Administrative Committee/Board, conflicts can occur. "Committee chairmen will fight to keep their staff. We have to get them to forget their positions as chairmen and think about the goals of the conference as a whole over the next three to five years," he says.

Often in this process, the treasurer has to play the bad guy. "The treasurer serves as the financial conscience of the body," explains Mr. Doyle. "When proposals come up to do this or to do that, the treasurer says, 'Where is the money coming from? Let me see the budget.'"

In June 1991, the conference met for three days in executive session to evaluate NCCB/USCC programs and reduce expenditures in order to control the increase in assessments.[31] According to Bishop William E. McManus, the gathered bishops were:

> . . . armed with knives, hatchets, and axes to bring down their diocesan assessments for NCCB and USCC. "Cut the Washington bureaucracy," was the war cry. "Slash away," some bishops chanted, "we have to cut at home and we should do it here, too."[32]

Despite these general attacks on "bureaucracy," the bishops could not focus on what office budgets to cut. Before the meeting the bishops were surveyed to see what they wanted cut. "We surveyed everybody and they all said we've got to do less," explains Archbishop Keeler, "but when you got down the specifics, almost everybody liked everything that we were doing." For no NCCB/USCC office did a majority of the bishops call for cuts. Forty-one percent wanted to cut the funding to the National Advisory Council. Thirty-seven percent also wanted to cut the budget of the Film and Broadcasting Office that reviews and rates movies and TV shows. Since the budgets of these programs were $77,000 and $249,000 respectively, not much money would be saved, short of eliminating them entirely. Support for cuts fell below 30 percent before major budgets were reached. About 28 percent of the bishops wanted cuts in the budgets of the offices of Social Development and World Peace, of Education, of Media Relations, and of the secretary for communications.[33]

A committee chaired by President Pilarczyk called for deep cuts in the Social Development and World Peace Department ($140,000), the Education Department ($100,000), and the Communication Department ($300,000 to $500,000), although only 28 percent of the bishops wanted cuts in these departments. Archbishop Pilarczyk admitted that those units with the largest budgets seemed to be the foremost candidates for budget reductions. Cardinal James Hickey came to their rescue by proposing to spread the cuts more widely through the conference, especially in the administrative offices, including the budgets of the general secretary, general counsel, and government liaison office. The bishops agreed to a $1.1 million cut in 1993 programs funded by assessments, while allowing for a growth of 5 percent from 1993 through 1996. But $239,000 of the cut simply shifted the cost of the Office for Film and Broadcasting (in the Department of Communications) from the assessment to the Communication Campaign Collection.

Following Cardinal Hickey's proposal, the bishops approved a 10 percent reduction in administrative operations and a 6 percent cut in offices with two or more professionals. The general secretary was told to work out the details. In November he came back with a $60,000 cut in the Permanent Diaconate Office, a budget only 22 percent of the bishops favored reducing in the survey. The proposal caused a furor among deacons around the country. The chair of the Committee on the Permanent Diaconate (Archbishop Patrick Flores) and former chairs objected, but the cut was approved by the bishops.

The cuts allowed the bishops to lower the assessments from 15.7 cents per Catholic in 1991 to 15.06 in 1992. "For about 30 bishops with low Catholic populations (under 50,000)," explains Bishop McManus, "the one-year reduction of their diocesan tax was an amount less than their travel, hotel and incidental expenses to attend the June meeting."[34] Although the bishops did not make major changes in the conference, perhaps they understood it better after the three-day meeting.

Conclusion

Despite the spiritual nature of the church, there is very little that the NCCB/USCC can do without money. Money pays for staff and programs. The more the bishops want their conference to do, the more they will have to find money to pay for it. Normally this means increasing assessments or raising more money through national collections.

The assessments and most collections have not kept up with inflation, so the conference has less real money today than it did in the past. At the same time that real contributions to the conference were declining, real costs were increasing. No longer is the conference staffed primarily by low-salaried priests and religious. Nor can the church any longer get away with paying the laity low salaries as it did in the past. The bishops' conference must practice what it preaches and pay just wages. Without an increase in assessments or other sources of income, the conference must reduce its staff and programs.

The American bishops are reluctant to accept that an essential part of the episcopal vocation is fund-raising. American theologians tell the bishops they should be pastors. European theologians, who pontificate from state-supported theological chairs, tell the bishops that they are supposed to be teachers. This is easy to say when the state pays the church's bills, as it does in Germany, Italy, and other countries.

No one can possibly be against having pastoral and teaching bishops, but in the United States the bishops also have to pay the bills, which means they have to raise money from the laity. St. Paul proved that a bishop could teach, be pastoral, and raise money. In American Catholic mythology, the old Irish pastor only preached about sex and money. In reaction to this myth, today's clergy does not want to preach on either. The bishops still talk about sex, but unlike their predecessors they are very reluctant fund-raisers.

Conclusion

We need a good conference. We have a good conference. As our legacy to those who follow us, let us keep our conference strong and vital.[1]

——CARDINAL JOSEPH BERNARDIN

[The conference], it's a trade organization.

——ARCHBISHOP DANIEL PILARCZYK

Bishops, just like the very poor and uneducated, should be treated with a special prudence.

——MONSIGNOR QUIXOTE[2]

The NCCB/USCC is an assembly of bishops operating within an American context. This chapter will compare the conference with other legislative bodies, examine its strengths and weaknesses, and make recommendations for improving it.

When social scientists look at the National Conference of Catholic Bishops, they see a legislative assembly that meets periodically, follows parliamentary procedures, elects officers, works through committees, and has a staff.[3] A legislature "has more than one member and they meet, deliberate, and vote as equals as a way of doing their business," explains Nelson Polsby. "Multimemberedness, formal equality, collective decision making, deliberativeness" are characteristics of legislatures.[4] As official bodies, their formal enactments are binding on some population and their legitimacy comes from their relationship to that population. Comparing the conference to other legislative bodies provides insight into its operations.

Despite some similarities, the NCCB/USCC is different from the U.S. Congress and state legislatures: its members are appointed, not elected, it meets fewer than ten days a year, it has no organized political parties, and it has no police power to

302

enforce its decisions. Using Professor Polsby's terminology, the NCCB/USCC operates in a "closed regime," a category that includes corporate boards, since its members are appointed and not elected.

Professor Polsby also distinguishes between "arenas," exemplified by the British parliament, and "transformative legislatures," exemplified by the U.S. Congress.[5] The conference is somewhere between the two. In a transformative legislature, power is decentralized, members specialize by topic, committees and internal procedures are important, and the legislature can actually determine outcomes on specific issues. In an arena, power is more centralized in the party leaders, debate and appeals to public opinion are important, staff is limited or nonexistent, and legislative power is limited to making or breaking governments.

Although these categories are more appropriate for open regimens, comparing the NCCB/USCC to parliament and Congress is instructive. As in the Congress, NCCB/USCC committees and internal procedures are important and power is decentralized. On the other hand, because of limited terms for chairs, NCCB/USCC members do not specialize as much as do congressional members. Despite its size, the NCCB/USCC assembly tries to act more like the U.S. Senate than the House, where strict limits are placed on amendments and debate.

In other respects the NCCB/USCC is like a parliament: the Administrative Committee/Board is like a cabinet and the NCCB/USCC president is like the prime minister, although neither has the power granted under the British model. The lack of political parties, the desire for consensus, and the reluctance to appeal to public opinion make the NCCB/USCC unlike other arenas.

The powers of the NCCB/USCC are so circumscribed that it is difficult to recognize it as a supradiocesan legislature. Because of its limited power and the members' local concerns, the conference often looks more like a convention of mayors or governors than a legislature. "People think that we're the holding company for the church," reports Mark E. Chopko, chief counsel for the conference. "We're not." Bishops are less like stockholders than independent barons whose primary concerns are local, but who devote a limited amount of time each year to national concerns. "We're a convener in terms of our legal status vis-à-vis the dioceses," says Mr. Chopko. "The bishops are members, and we convene them into a national assembly." Diocesan autonomy is a highly-valued principle. "It's a states' rights operation," explains John Carr, secretary for Social Development and World Peace. "Anybody that doesn't understand that isn't going to make it."

While the NCCB/USCC looks like a legislative body in the church, within the American political scene the NCCB/USCC is like any other interest group trying to influence public opinion and government policy. "The analog that I use often when I talk to people about the conference is that it's a trade organization," explains Archbishop Daniel Pilarczyk. "It's like the National Independent Grocers' Association. They've got their various things that they're interested in." As in any trade association, Archbishop Pilarczyk reports, the bishops "don't want the association to be doing stuff that's going to cause trouble at home, although the bishops are willing to go along with a certain amount of that."

The interests of the conference are wide-ranging, far beyond the self-interest of the bishops and the church as an institution. "We can't become just a trade association, protecting our institutional concerns," says Mr. Carr. The church's concern for social morality, justice, and peace means that its agenda goes beyond its own self-interest.

Strengths

Despite its limitations, the NCCB/USCC has been very successful as an organization.

Managing Church Reform

Most importantly, it managed the reforms following the Second Vatican Council so that the American church did not experience a schism. Despite the divisions in the church and despite those who would like to see them divided, the bishops stuck together and kept their flocks together. They put the liturgy into English, turned around the altars, allowed Communion in the hand, and encouraged singing and lay participation. They instituted a diaconate program, RCIA, produced the National Catechetical Directory, eliminated meatless Fridays, made the annulment process easier, spoke out on social justice issues, and initiated a strong program of ecumenical dialogue. All of this was done while alienating only a small fraction of the laity. In fact, there is wide approval of these actions by American Catholics.

Monday-morning quarterbacks can legitimately argue that the reforms could have been managed better. This should not distract from the fact that, except for the exodus of tens of thousands of priests and religious and the decline in vocations, the bishops were able to avoid a major disaster during this period of reform. What they could have done to limit the exodus or to foster new vocations is not clear.

The bishops have also performed an unusually good balancing act between Rome and their people. They have refused to take as hard a line with dissenters as Rome would like, nor have they been willing to be as independent of Rome as most Americans would like. For example, despite public opinion polls showing Catholic rejection of papal teaching on birth control, the bishops have tried to support papal teaching without driving the people out of the church. This has not been easy since birth control, according to the Rev. Andrew Greeley, has negatively affected church attendance.[6] Likewise, the conference has tried to listen sensitively to the concerns of American women while still affirming Vatican positions on birth control and women priests.

An American Conference

The bishops have also been very successful adapting episcopal conference structures to the American political and cultural context. This can be easily seen by comparing the NCCB/USCC with episcopal conferences in other parts of the world. The NCCB/USCC is the only conference that is open to the press (including live television), follows *Robert's Rules of*

Order, has a large staff and committee structure, and has followed a widely consultative process in drafting pastoral letters. These adaptations clearly have an American flavor to them, reflecting the American experience in open government, strong legislative committees, and legislative staffs. The bishops do not see themselves in any way as "representing" the views of their people—as teachers they speak "to" their people rather than "for" their people. On the other hand, by meeting openly they have made themselves accountable for their actions to public opinion, more accountable than they would be if they worked behind closed doors.

Public Presence

The NCCB/USCC has also been successful in catching the attention of the American media and through them the American public. Religion is a difficult subject for the American press to cover. But what the conference does on abortion, AIDS, child care, economic justice, peace, and women makes headlines. For example, actions by the NCCB/USCC have frequently been listed among the top ten stories of the year by the Religion Newswriters Association: the decision to support the Hatch Amendment in 1981; drafting of peace pastoral 1982; first draft of economic pastoral in 1984; visit of U.S. bishops to Nicaragua and Cuba in 1985; hiring of Hill & Knowlton in 1990.[7] The bishops may not always like this coverage, but they are not ignored.

The NCCB/USCC has also been able to maintain its independence and uniqueness within the American political environment because of its adherence to the church's social teaching. "Anybody who watches us closely knows that neither political party likes us at all," says Mr. Carr. "They shouldn't." The conference has areas of agreement and disagreement with both Republicans and Democrats, and has avoided identifying itself with either political party. It is allied with each group on some issues and opposed on others.

Many political observers cannot understand how the bishops can be conservative on one issue and liberal on another. "We are very unpredictable," asserts Mr. Carr. "Reporters can't make head nor tail of this outfit. That is the way it should be because our agenda is not ideological or political, it comes from the teaching." The NCCB/USCC draws on a long tradition of social teaching in the church that developed independently of American partisan politics.

"This body can't be typecast," explains Mr. Carr.

> We're the peace pastoral, but we're also the religious liberty [for Eastern Europe] statement. We have the great advantage of having an old, consistent, deep tradition. We can't trim to meet the ideological or media needs of the time. So we are for human rights, whether it's in the Soviet Union or El Salvador or, for that matter, Nicaragua. There are a lot of organizations who are [concerned about human rights in] the Philippines or Poland, but not both. By vocation, by tradition, and by heritage, we've got to stand for a single standard.

Catholic People

Nor have the bishops been out of step with American Catholics on most political and social issues. After reviewing the opinion research literature on Catholic voters, Henry C. Kenski and William Lockwood conclude:

> On social issues. . . . they are slightly more conservative than both the nation overall and white Protestants on issues like legalized abortion. . . .
>
> Catholics approximate the nation's conservatism on other social issues like capital punishment, school prayer, pornography, and busing. They are more liberal than the nation and Protestants generally on other social issues like women's rights, gun control, civil rights for minorities and homosexuals, and decriminalization of marijuana. . . .
>
> Catholics are also more liberal on foreign policy questions than the nation and white Protestants. . . . They strongly favor arms control and weapons reduction, as well as reduced military spending, and are also opposed to the Reagan administration policy in Central America.[8]

Although the bishops would like to see more of the laity opposed to abortion and capital punishment, the general orientation of Catholic voters is in line with positions taken by the bishops' conference. Certainly the bishops are more united on these issues than the laity, but the majority of Catholic voters back the bishops on most issues. In comparison with many religious lobbies in Washington that are out of step with their members, Allen D. Hertzke found, "The U.S. Catholic Conference, intriguingly, appears well supported in both its conservative anti-abortion lobbying and its liberal economic and military positions."[9]

The congruence of the bishops and the laity on many issues raises the question whether the laity are following the bishops or the bishops are following the laity. This of course is not an either/or choice. The bishops consult the laity before taking positions and the laity listen to the bishops. It is noteworthy that on capital punishment—an issue that sharply divided the bishops—the bishops have had little impact on Catholic views. Now that the bishops are more united on this question it will be interesting to see if Catholic voters change.

There is some evidence that the bishops can affect Catholic opinions. Following the debate and passage of the 1983 peace pastoral, Catholic views on military spending underwent a dramatic shift. "By comparison with both their 1983 attitudes and the 1984 Protestant preferences, Catholics in 1984 had moved significantly toward the view that the United States was devoting too many resources to military purposes," reports Kenneth D. Wald.[10] The reaction, however, was short-lived. By 1985 Protestants and Catholic attitudes toward military spending coincided.[11]

Helping Dioceses

Finally, a less visible role of the conference is helping bishops in their local dioceses. Often when a bishop or a member of his staff has a problem or a question, the conference is the first places he calls, whether it be about liturgy, civil law, canon law, finances, lay ministry, social concerns, or pastoral programs.

For the larger and richer dioceses, the conference staff is not important because they have local experts and resources to deal with these issues. Thus large dioceses, which pay the most assessments, probably benefit least from conference services. For the smaller and poorer dioceses, the expertise of the conference is very helpful. The staff at the conference can either answer their question or refer them to an appropriate person or organization. In addition, the conference has run many workshops and conferences for diocesan personnel and provided speakers at others. Poor dioceses also receive financial help from the ABCM and CHD.

"The vast majority of the bishops are proud of the conference," reports Cardinal Joseph Bernardin, "and even though they may have difficulties with a particular issue and the way it was dealt with, I think there will be quite a bit of support for the conference as we have known it."

Weaknesses

Even its ardent supporters admit that the NCCB/USCC has problems and weaknesses.

Clericalism

Liberal and conservative lay critics of the conference agree in accusing the conference of clericalism. Liberals complain that the bishops do not reflect their views on internal church issues; conservatives complain that the bishops do not reflect their views on social and political issues. Historically, the American Catholic church has not suffered from anticlericalism (except during the dispute over trusteeism) as has the church in many other parts of the world. Today anticlericalism is on the rise among conservative Catholics over political and economic issues; among women over birth control and the role of women in the church; and among theologians over academic freedom. The bishops do listen to lay people and employ lay experts, but the bishops see the conference as their agent and voice. As teachers, they are not speaking for the people of God but to it and the world.

Institutionally, the problem is not so much with the episcopal conference as with the absence of a national pastoral council that could reflect a wider perspective in the church, including a lay perspective. Vatican opposition to such a council means that the bishops will not even consider the idea.

No Follow-Through

A frequently-cited fault is the conference's inability to follow through on major documents. This may be one reason for the short-lived impact of the peace pastoral on Catholic opinion mentioned above. "We spend so much time drawing up documents and then they fly off into a sort of a limbo," complained Archbishop John Whealon, who chaired the committee that developed the National Catechetical Directory. "No one knows quite what to do with them once they're there. They're on the record. They might be pulled out to guide someone in later years and they do help. But when I think of that whole array of documents in past years—I've got them, but I never look at them."

"The fundamental flaw wasn't in the process and the creation of a document," says Richard Hirsch, who advised the bishops on communications, "it was the follow-through afterwards. I don't think the conference has yet determined what it needs to do to make a teaching document a truly teaching moment." For example, one rarely hears about an action of the NCCB/USCC from the parish pulpit. If it is a priority for the local bishop, he will write a letter to the parish priests asking them to preach on it. The priests can easily ignore the request or execute it weakly.

Part of the conference's focus on documents comes from the bishops' demand that the staff not do anything without formal approval. "It was just impossible to do anything unless you had those documents lined up on the shelf," explains Ronald Krietemyer, who worked on economic issues.

> There was so much effort in getting the statements, to create the kind of charter for the work of the conference, that nobody got around to seriously saying, "How can we commit some resources to implementing this, really helping the dioceses implement it?" The bishops can't really implement anything at the national level except the work on [national] legislation, which they were doing. But they didn't devote any energy, except distributing the documents, to helping dioceses figure out how to use them in their evangelization or in adult ed and whatever else they were doing.

Because of this experience, the bishops included a follow-up program for the pastoral letter on the economy. "There were large plans and more modest plans," reports Mr. Krietemyer, who worked on the letter. "The more modest plans got implemented because they cost a lot less money. They basically said we're going to be a catalyst and a resource, but we're not going to be a major producer of items." With limited funding, the results were modest. The conference convened educators, publishers of Catholic textbooks, media producers, and drew up lists of available resources for implementation coordinators in each diocese. The very nature of the pastoral letters, their length and complex content, makes it unreasonable to think that they will have a very wide audience. Rather the follow-up targeted those who could integrate ideas from the letters into their work of education and social and pastoral ministry.

Even on earlier documents, some follow-through and implementation had been attempted. Five years after the peace pastoral, for example, the conference received a report examining whether its conditional acceptance of deterrence was still valid in changed circumstances. The national pastoral plans for black and Hispanic Catholics were also followed by significant programs aimed at helping dioceses implement the plans. Other documents, like the National Catechetical Directory, had local and national groups and agencies that took over implementation.

Implementing pastoral letters and other conference documents on the local level is also hampered by the conference's lack of legal authority over local dioceses and institutions. The bishops get very nervous about infringements on their local authority. While developing a document to implement the pastoral letter on the economy, the committee consulted with bishops, finance directors, and personnel directors. "They said what this thing really needs are some models," reports Mr. Carr. The committee and staff developed models for dealing with salaries, collective bargaining, and other financial issues.

When the document was brought to the Administrative Committee/Board, "people focused only on the models," recalls Mr. Carr. "People felt that we were mandating programs.

Lengthy discussion. Big trouble. Pull it back. The question was whether you'd get out of that meeting alive." A group of bishops, including some leading opponents of this document, redid it. "Everything went in the conditional tense," reports Mr. Carr. "One thing you always have to be clear on—the conference doesn't tell any bishop to do anything." The revised document passed.

Non-Participation

Another complaint is that the conference is run by a few activists while most of the bishops do not speak at meetings or participate on committees. Although participation varies from meeting to meeting, most bishops are silent. "One former president said that when he became president he was afraid that he was going to have a hard time calling on the bishops because there are so many of them," recalls Archbishop Pilarczyk. "Then he realized that there are only 30 or 40 that talk anyway."

Actually, more than 40 speak at a typical meeting. For example, of the approximately 270 members present at the November 1991 meeting, 98, more than a third, spoke at least once. Of the 98, about 20 spoke from the podium presenting material on the agenda. Some of these 20 also spoke from the floor on other issues. Prelates who took the floor five or more times included Cardinals Anthony J. Bevilacqua and James Hickey, Archbishops Francis T. Hurley, Oscar H. Lipscomb, and John R. Quinn, and Bishops Anthony Bosco, Norbert F. Gaughan, Enrique San Pedro, Austin B. Vaughan, and William K. Weigand. Bishop Vaughan is so well known for frequently giving his opinions on issues that a group of bishops had a, pool betting on how many interventions he would make.

Although they are silent, the other bishops appear to listen and make up their own minds. If they all decided to speak on every issue, the result would be chaos since the conference meets for such a limited time. In any case, under conference procedures the silent majority determines the outcome of votes on amendments and action items.

More problematic is non-participation on committees. In 1991, 97 bishops, or almost one-third of the membership, were not members of any NCCB/USCC committees.[12] Since much of the work of the conference is done in committees, a third of the conference is not actively involved. Auxiliaries are more likely to be nonparticipants than diocesan bishops. About 42 percent of the auxiliaries do not serve on committees, as compared with 25 percent of the diocesan bishops who are not on committees.

Non-participation can have many causes: apathy, alienation, satisfaction with current policies, other priorities for time and energy, or being closed out. Before 1993, the cost of traveling to committee meetings could have been a restraint, but beginning in 1993 the conference will reimburse travel expenses of those bishops who request it.

How many bishops want to be on a committee but are not invited is unclear. In appointments to committees, chairs probably prefer diocesan bishops to auxiliaries. Most observers believe that the diocesan bishops who are not on committees simply do not volunteer because they do not want to take time from diocesan concerns to work on national issues. Supporting this thesis is the fact that only 15 percent of the bishops return the forms asking them to express their interest in serving on the committees as chairs or elected members.[13] In June 1991, the bishops voted (168-27) to have an ad hoc committee to study and make recommendations on the selection process for committee members.

Although this vote indicates some dissatisfaction with the process for selecting committee members, there is little evidence to support the notion that the nonparticipants are unhappy. If this third of the conference were truly unhappy, they could be very disruptive by registering large negative votes on action items. More likely they are simply uninterested, or the conference does not act against their preferences to the degree that would motivate them to act. As long as the activists pay attention to the preferences of the silent third, the conference can function peacefully without their active participation.

This non-participation is more easily understood if the NCCB/USCC is compared to the British Parliament where half the members are not members of committees. The NCCB/USCC non-participants are like backbenchers—they are not actively involved in the running of the conference, but without their support the leaders cannot act. These "backbenchers" are not uninformed. "I think most of them do their homework," says Archbishop Thomas Kelly. "I would not accuse any of them of having an uninformed vote. Now, that doesn't mean that you read every word of the agenda material. I don't either, but I know what is in there. Sometimes, I have come without my mind made up on several questions, and have been very capably instructed [by the presentations and discussions]."

No Priorities

Some bishops and staff complain that the conference is involved in too many things and its activities are unfocused. Too many items are on the agenda of the assembly, so that bishops are supposed to read 700 or 800 pages of documents before the meeting. "I still remember the sense of helplessness and confusion that came over me the first time I sat down with the documentation for a general meeting and realized that I was supposed to read and digest all that stuff and be ready to vote on much of it more or less intelligently," recalled Archbishop Pilarczyk in his address to the bishops in November 1991.

Some critics would like to see the bishops decide priorities and stick to them. They emphasize the importance of planning, setting goals, and management by objectives. The application of management principles is helpful to many aspects of the conference, but such criticisms often ignore political reality. The conference is not a business with a bottom-line criterion of success. It is more like a political institution than a business. Achieving consensus requires inefficiencies that would sink a business. Symbolic issues have an importance to members far beyond their practical impact. Members seek multiple and sometimes conflicting goals. The conference has multiple priorities because the bishops have multiple priorities. More planning, a better mission statement, or more specific goals may not help that much. There are simply many things the bishops want the conference to do, but they do not want to pay for them.

Lack of Power

The conference is a small center of power squeezed by Roman authority on one side and by diocesan authority on the other. Many of those most active in the conference see its limited power as a major problem. The canonical authority of the conference is limited, and even in those areas where the conference has power, the bishops often do not want it to make decisions that are binding on dioceses. Conference decisions can often be ignored on the local level. The need to get Roman approval for a multitude of decisions reduces the influence of the conference, especially when Vatican offices insist on changes before granting approval.

Bishops often speak eloquently in favor of national leadership by the conference in one area while vocally opposing it in another. It usually depends on whether one's preferences are advanced or blocked in the conference. Bishops want the conference to do things that help them in their local areas, but they oppose action if they feel it will cause them troubles in their diocese. Which bishops oppose or support conference action switches depending on the issues. At the spring 1989 meeting, "those of us who wanted help on AIDS didn't want any help at all on general absolution," admits one archbishop. Those who wanted guidelines on general absolution did not want advice from the Administrative Board on AIDS.

Also lacking is clear agreement of how the principle of subsidiarity applies to the church, not only on the theoretical level but also on the practical level.[14] The principle of subsidiarity was first applied by the church to the social realm. Against totalitarianism, the principle argued that issues should be dealt with at the lowest level possible in society. Individuals, families, and voluntary associations should have the freedom and resources to work for their own interests and the common good. Against liberal individualism, it argued that government and even international agencies have an obligation to help (*subsidium*) lower-level entities solve problems and to deal with issues that individuals and voluntary associations cannot.[15]

When applied to the church, subsidiarity would call for more local autonomy and more freedom to respond to diverse cultural and religious circumstances. Although a study of subsidiarity in the church was requested by the 1985 Synod of Bishops, no report has been issued by Rome. Most observers feel that Rome fears that application of the principle of subsidiarity will undercut its authority by calling for more autonomy for local and national churches. While no Catholic would deny the importance of Rome as a sign and agent of unity, many feel that there is a need for greater decentralization in the church.

The application of the principle of subsidiarity might also force the conference to acknowledge that certain issues should be dealt with on the local rather than national level. Each time something is put before the conference, the bishops need to ask: Is the conference the only organization that can deal with it, is the conference the best agent to deal with it, and what can the conference realistically do about it?

Rubber-Stamp Legislature

As mentioned earlier, from a political science perspective, the NCCB/USCC operates in a "closed regime" since the members are appointed and not elected. Their legitimacy within the church comes from the fact that they are bishops, not from their method of selection. There have been periods in church history when bishops were elected by their people or their clergy. When this role was usurped by local lords and kings, it was disastrous for the church because they turned episcopal offices into political plums to be handed out to relatives and political supporters. Church reform became possible only when the papacy was able to wrest this power away from the state. Whether it should now be returned to the people and the local clergy is a debated question within the Catholic church.

The current system keeps dioceses from becoming divided into factions who back one candidate or another. At the same time it puts the appointments into the hands of a small group of prelates who have the ear of the pope. Political scientists tell us that the danger of closed regimes is that only those supporting the executive are appointed to the legislature that then rubber-stamps executive decisions. Such legislatures can then fail to perform "one of their most important functions," which "is to criticize the executive."[16] The reluctance of the NCCB/USCC to criticize the Vatican fits this pattern.

It should be noted, however, that it is almost impossible for the Vatican to remove a bishop before he turns 75, the age of retirement. This makes bishops much more independent than the typical member of a legislature in a closed regime, who can be removed at will by the executive. Once he is appointed, a bishop has wide discretion in what he does and says. That is why the Vatican takes the screening of candidates so seriously.

Some observers feel that there is a lack of honesty on the floor of the NCCB/USCC assembly. Bishops do not like to disagree among themselves in public. Nor do they want to disagree with Rome in public. Without knowing the innermost thoughts of the bishops, it is difficult to measure how serious a problem this is. Certainly there are some topics (married clergy, women priests, birth control) that are not debated in public, but whether this reflects consensus or secret divisions is unclear. There have been disagreements publicly expressed among the bishops on other issues. The bishops were also willing to respond negatively to the Vatican draft on episcopal conferences. But these actions were taken reluctantly with much difficulty. Executive sessions are the preferred forum for airing such disagreements.

Irrelevancy

Some critics argue that because of its limited power and because of the absence of honest debate, the NCCB/USCC is irrelevant to the life of the church. The conference is an adequate instrument for the church's social agenda, but it is unable to solve internal church issues. "You quickly learn that these public meetings [of the NCCB/USCC] are not the place to make policy," says Archbishop Rembert Weakland. "You make policy at home, quietly. You try to move things there, not in Washington."[17]

In this view, major problems of the church—fewer priests and religious, declining resources, closing schools, religious illiteracy, divorced and remarried Catholics, ideological and theological divisions, conflicts with Rome, the slowing of renewal, a growing anticlericalism among women, birth control, sexual ethics, declining church attendance, pro-choice Catholic politicians—are not being dealt with in the conference. Some of these issues are avoided because they are divisive among the bishops. Others are not discussed because the Vatican has made clear that they are closed topics for which official answers have already been given.

Since liberals are not getting their way in Rome, they hope that the bishops' conferences would be more responsive to their views if given more power. It is not clear that, if the NCCB had authority to deal with these issues, it would respond in a very liberal way. Nor is it clear that any action by the NCCB/USCC could solve these problems.

Limited Liaison

One conservative complaint against the NCCB/USCC is that it focuses on the federal government as the solution to all social-economic problems. There is some truth to this complaint. But the problem is not the focus on governmental solutions to grave problems, but the lack of focus on other national but nongovernmental organizations. Dialogical outreach to the voluntary sector, to the business sector, and to labor unions on the national level is limited or nonexistent. For more than 30 years, Msgr. George Higgins was the de facto liaison between the bishops and the American labor movement. In his retirement he has continued this role, most recently by convincing the AFL-CIO leadership not to endorse abortion rights. Once he passes from the scene there will be no one to replace him.

The bishops do have an extensive and professional liaison with non-Catholic religious leaders through the NCCB Office of Ecumenical and Interreligious Affairs. They have a minor outreach to scientists through the NCCB Committee on Science and Human Values. Outreach to national associations of lawyers, doctors, teachers, and the business community is practically nonexistent. Attempts to establish a relationship with the television and film industry were supported by the Communications Committee, but most of the other bishops never understood the importance of this work and considered it a waste of money. "It did the church a lot of good, by putting us into dialogue with the media," recalls Mr. Hirsch, "but there's no immediate payoff." All most bishops wanted was an office that would attack pornography and do public relations.

If the bishops want to have an impact on American society and culture, the NCCB/USCC must influence not just government officials but also national leaders in education, business, finance, labor, media, philanthropy, law, medicine, and other fields. The national leaders of professional associations, of businesses, ethnic groups, and labor unions make decisions that shape American society and culture as much as does the national government, but they are being ignored by the bishops' conference. It is insufficient to say that the Catholic laity is responsible for influencing these aspects of American life if there is no leadership or guidance from the bishops. Nor can this be done effectively on the diocesan level.

Some liaison could be done through national Catholic organizations of lawyers, doctors, educators, and others where they exist. Here a bishop would need to be designated as contact person with the group, just as certain bishops specialize in dialogue with specific Protestant denominations. Where such national organizations exist, there would be less need for additional staff at the NCCB/USCC. But episcopal liaison should not be limited to Catholic leaders in a profession if the bishops want to impact American culture.

As chair of the Committee on Pro-life Activities, Cardinal O'Connor saw the need for establishing liaison with pro-life groups which were often at odds with each other. "I've had meetings with the various major pro-life leaders, Jack Wilke of the National Right to Life, Judy Brown [Americans United for

Life], a number of others," he explained. "I've asked them to come together with me to discuss how we can resolve differences and function in a united form."[18] Ultimately, he looked forward to a loose federation of all pro-life organizations, Jewish, Protestant, Catholic, and Muslim that could work together.

Communications

One of the biggest failures of the NCCB/USCC has been its inability to use the electronic media as an effective instrument of evangelization, despite the expenditure of millions of dollars. The conference failed because diocesan bishops feared the creation of a Catholic television network that would be beyond their individual control when it operated in their dioceses. Some feared that the network would broadcast programs they disagreed with. Others feared a network would take money out of their diocese through fund-raising over the air.

Whether any strategy would have been successful is debatable, but because of these fears, the Catholic Telecommunications Network of America (CTNA) was created with two strikes against it. First, it had to scramble its message so that each diocesan bishop could control its broadcast in his diocese. Second, it could not raise funds over the air, and therefore had to depend on the bishops for funding. Since membership was voluntary, not enough bishops signed up to make the system viable.

A more effective strategy would have been to trust the episcopal board of directors of CTNA, who are elected by the USCC, to control the content of the broadcasts. CTNA could then have provided its signal free and unscrambled to cable networks who, in the early days of cable, were desperate for programs. After initial seed money from the conference, CTNA should have become self-supporting through advertising and fund-raising. CTNA could have also raised funds for conference collections. By noting zip codes on checks, money could have been easily credited to diocesan accounts for these collections so that each diocese would receive credit for donations from that diocese.

On the other hand, Catholic News Service has been a conference success story. "There is no corporation in this country that harbors within its bosom an independent newsgathering agency," marvels Mr. Hirsch. "Corporations do not do that. They have a public relations office or media relations office, whose job it is to make them look good." Catholic News Service has played an important role in advancing the conference's agenda, but it has done it in a way that protects its credibility as an independent news agency. The service is close to self-supporting through sales to diocesan newspapers. In addition, it is available on-line through Newsnet, and this on-line service will undoubtedly grow in the future.

What to do?

It is not my intention to recommend a radical restructuring of the NCCB/USCC and its place in the church. At heart I am an incrementalist because institutions and people have difficulties adapting to change. Nor do I think radicals are smart enough to understand both the negative and positive consequences of their reforms. On the other hand, refusal to experiment and to make small changes builds up pressure over time until an explosion occurs.

Selection of Bishops

The NCCB/USCC is an episcopal organization. Who becomes a bishop determines to a great extent what the NCCB/USCC does. While the hierarchy is not ready to return to the more ancient and traditional mode of electing bishops, steps could be taken to increase the role of bishops in the selection process. For example, the bishops from an NCCB/USCC region could be made responsible for drawing up the *ternus* for a vacant see from their region. The NCCB/USCC Committee on the Selection of Bishops could review this *ternus*. The committee also could be responsible for drawing up the *ternus* for a vacant archdiocese. The pope could, of course, reject the *ternus*. This proposal is similar to the practice common in the United States in the 19th century before the arrival of the apostolic delegate.

Lay Input

Since its reorganization in 1966, there have been many suggestions for further changes in the structure and procedures of the conference. The most far-reaching suggestion would be the creation of a national pastoral council that would include among its members priests, religious, and laity along with the bishops. Such a council would be more representative of the American Catholic church than the NCCB/USCC. Since Rome opposes such an assembly, it is not likely to happen any time soon.

Those who recommend such a council need to think through how the lay members will be chosen so that they are truly representative of the people in the pews and not just of the lay activists. The most likely format would be to have the lay representatives elected by diocesan pastoral councils.[19] Since the success with diocesan pastoral councils has been limited and since in the minds of the hierarchy the Detroit Call to Action was a disaster, planning a national pastoral council would have to be extensive and careful. In the meantime, the National Advisory Council should make recommendations not only to the Administrative Committee/Board but to the NCCB/USCC assembly. In addition, as mentioned above, ways are needed to improve liaison with national, nongovernmental organizations.

People have frequently recommended merging the USCC and the NCCB so that there would be only one organization. This is unlikely to happen because the USCC committees have lay, religious, and clerical members besides the bishops. If the two organizations were merged, the nonepiscopal members would have to be kicked off the committees, something that would send a very negative signal to the laity. As a result, both organizations will continue to exist until some better way is found for lay input.

Administrative Committee/Board

With 53 members, the Administrative Committee/Board is bigger than most episcopal conferences. One proposal would have made it even larger by having representatives from each of the 33 ecclesiastical provinces replace the 13 regional representatives. This proposal was defeated (13-190) in June 1991. Most bishops felt such a change would make the Administrative Committee/Board too large.[20]

Some critics complain that each chair on the Administrative Committee/Board looks out for his committee's interests rather than the common good of the conference. Bishop McManus would like to limit membership on the Administrative Committee/Board to regional or geographical representatives. But most people involved in the conference believe that it is very useful to have the chairs of major standing committees on the Administrative Committee/Board so that when issues or questions arise, the chairs are present to give a variety of perspectives.

If the Administrative Committee/Board is too large, the chairs of some less important committees might be dropped from the committee/board. It is difficult to see why the chairs of the American College Louvain Committee and the North American College Rome Committee need to be on the Administrative Committee/Board. Nor do the chairs of grant-making committees, like ABCM, CHD, and Church in Latin America, need to be on the Administrative Committee/Board. For the same reason, the chairs of CRS and CTNA could be dropped. These chairs could be invited when topics of concern to their committees are up for discussion. Nor do elected members of USCC committees need to be on the Administrative Committee/Board. This is an anachronism from the NCWC days.

On the other hand, it might be worthwhile to improve representation on the Administrative Committee/Board for auxiliaries who are underrepresented. Although auxiliaries make up about 36 percent of the conference, they have only 17 percent of the positions on the Administrative Committee/Board. Since most of them will eventually become diocesan bishops, this is a temporary problem not unusual in any organization. Special efforts should be made to include the auxiliaries in the policy-making process. For example, the conference might limit to auxiliaries the nominees for the elected members of the USCC committees who sit on the Administrative Committee/Board. Or these elected members might be dropped in favor of simply electing some auxiliaries to the committee/board. Such a procedure would ensure that auxiliary bishops have a chance to participate more fully in the conference.

NCCB/USCC Committees

One weakness of the NCCB/USCC is that chairs change so frequently, every three years. A chair has little opportunity to develop expertise in his committee's area of responsibility before his term expires. He can be, therefore, very dependent on staff. For some committees, the bishops have decided to elect the chairs a year before they take office. The chair-elect then has a year to learn about the committee before taking charge. This reform should be applied to all committees.

Some observers, like Russell Shaw, believe that the need is for a more adaptable structure composed of fewer but larger committees to address ad hoc needs via task forces and working groups. This would also call for a smaller and less departmentalized staff. "What you have now is an organization—committees and staff—suffering from ossification," he says. "It's locked into doing the same things, over and over, while failing to respond to new needs as they arise." Such a structure could fall into the trap of dealing with today's relevant topics while failing to provide the institutional base for professional attention to ongoing concerns such as ecumenism, seminaries, Catholic education, liturgy, federal legislation, pro-life activities, etc.

Assembly Debate

Many bishops and observers complain that the discussion in the assembly is superficial and frequently off target because anyone can get up to say anything. On the other hand, attempts to limit debate are frowned upon. Various procedures (including small group discussions at round tables) have been tried for improving the discussion in the assembly. Without political parties to organize the debate, each member is free to make his own intervention. With almost 300 members present, this can be chaotic. Perhaps it would be helpful for the bishops to discuss the agenda on the first morning in regional groups. Chairs, officers, and staff could circulate among the regions and answer questions.

More importantly, the bishops need to discover a way that they can have honest debate on church issues without "scandalizing" the faithful or upsetting Rome. On several issues, the hierarchy has adopted a siege mentality that forbids the discussion of various sides of certain issues. Rome has even forbidden the bishops to have contact with organized groups of Catholics—Dignity (an organization of Catholic homosexuals), CORPUS (Corps of Reserve Priests United for Service), and the Women's Ordination Conference—who want to change certain church teachings or disciplines. Talking to such groups, Rome fears, would give them credibility and support.

"Anything that looks as if it might be weakening the deposit of faith, the bishops become very nervous about, very defensive about, and very hostile about," explains Archbishop John Roach.

> At a [NCCB] meeting you have people just sitting there, sometimes overwhelmed with boredom; but bring up a doctrinal issue and everybody fires up.
>
> We see ourselves living in a world where the faith-life is threatened from a whole variety of quarters. We are determined that one of our jobs is to defend the faith-life of the church, especially if there is any inkling that it is being attacked or even criticized internally.
>
> That is very unfortunate. We have to get to a point of maturity where we can articulate critical positions on issues that are not *de fide* but are somewhere within the province of faith, and where we can recognize pluriform theological positions, and be able to do that comfortably and respectfully and not feel that somehow we are disloyal.
>
> We are not at that point and that may be our greatest weakness right now.

Perhaps it would be useful for the bishops to spend a spring session discussing two fundamental issues in systematic theology: the development of doctrine and the hierarchy of truths. The first explains how church doctrines evolve over time and the second shows that all church teachings do not carry the same weight. Developing a pastoral letter on these topics would be instructive for both the bishops and the faithful.

Regional Conferences

Because of the size of the United States and the NCCB/USCC, it would be appropriate for NCCB/USCC to leave some decisions to its 13 regions acting as regional episcopal conferences. Some NCCB regional groups have more bishops than many episcopal conferences. These regions might, for example, determine policy on holy days, the age of confirmation, or other issues where the conference has found it difficult to establish a national norm.

Research and Experimentation

Parishes and most dioceses lack the resources to research critical issues facing the church. For example, extensive research is needed to find out the extent of religious illiteracy, its causes, and possible solutions. The Catholic church devotes a smaller percentage of its resources to research than any large institution in the world. Church officials often look upon researchers as the cause of problems because they frequently report bad news. For example, the bishops did not like projections on seminary enrollments that were based on collected data.

Some research is done by Catholic universities, but it does not always have practical applications.[21] The NCCB/USCC has encouraged some research, most notably the 1971-72 study of Catholic priests in the United States.[22] More research is needed on many topics, and the conference should do it or support other organizations doing research. More work is needed in stimulating interest in research among Catholic foundations and in focusing research efforts on the real needs of the church.

Horror stories about episcopal manipulation or suppression of research abound. A questionnaire for seminarians had to be revised because some bishops objected to the inclusion of questions that would uncover the incidence of homosexual orientation among seminarians. A study, with many negative conclusions, on morale of priests, intended for limited distribution to an approved audience, drew considerable flak when it reached a wider audience. A sociologist who authored an extensive demographic study on the priest shortage was blackballed from future research under NCCB/USCC auspices because bishops did not like his vocal support for a married clergy. Ignoring facts, suppressing research results, and blackballing scholars have never been useful ways of finding the truth.

Nor do parishes and most dioceses have the resources to develop new programs. A few programs like Renew were developed locally and then successfully marketed nationally. The conference needs to do more in discovering and publicizing successful programs and techniques that have been created on the local level. It should also help in the development of local programs that can be used nationally. The conference should not run programs, it should help create them and then be a wholesaler, not a retailer.

In developing programs, there needs to be an openness to error and failure. Few programs are perfect at conception. Fear of experimentation—what one observer referred to as the "E" word—is widespread at every level of the church, from the parish to the Vatican. Although the bishops asked the Vatican for permission to have controlled experimentation in the liturgy in 1967, approval was denied. With many church programs, especially liturgy and religious education, there is no way of knowing what will work without experimentation and testing. Authorizing experimentation under controlled circumstances is necessary for the development of new programs.

Caring for Bishops

A principal responsibility of a bishop is to minister to his priests, but no one is responsible for ministering to the bishops.[23] Like other priests, some bishops find themselves suffering from loneliness, stress, alcoholism, overwork, or unrealistic expectations from their people. Like managers of other major corporations, they sometimes face failure and their inability to do the job they have been given. Except for a sympathetic metropolitan, there are few systems in place to come to the aid of troubled bishops. This responsibility cannot be fulfilled by the pope since there are thousands of bishops around the world.

The NCCB needs to have staff and structure to respond to the spiritual and human needs of bishops: retreats, sabbaticals, workshops, spiritual directors, psychologists, financial and management consultants, etc. While it is unlikely the bishops would give the NCCB the authority to intervene in dioceses, it should have staff and systems for coming to the help of a bishop who requests it. This could be a fulfilling ministry for retired bishops who are still able to be active.

An Office in Rome

To improve communications with Rome, the bishops need a permanent NCCB/USCC staff person in Rome. In the past, the rector of the North American College often acted as the American bishops' man in Rome, but this is no longer the case. Such a person could keep the NCCB/USCC officers informed of what is going on in Rome, could visit Vatican offices to inquire about American concerns, and argue the NCCB/USCC case when necessary. When Vatican officials had questions, these could be directed to this person.

Funding

Since I argue that the conference should do more not less, it is necessary for the bishops to find more revenues. Research has shown that Catholics on average give less to their church than do Protestants and Jews.[24] The NCCB has an ad hoc Committee on Stewardship that is looking into this problem. The bishops must accept that part of their episcopal vocation is to be fund-raisers. They need to examine ways that the conference can do better fund-raising on the national level. Their 1991 vote against (61-141) establishing a conference development office was not fiscally responsible.

The bishops also need to be more creative in managing church resources on a national scale. For example, the conference could save the church millions of dollars by acting as a negotiating agent in dealing with suppliers of certain goods and services. Having telephone companies, insurance companies, financial institutions, credit card companies, and others bid for the business of the U.S. Catholic church would allow the church to reap the benefits of its national size, just as other large corporations have. For example, the Catholic church is the third-largest user of the telephones in this country, preceded by the federal government and General Motors. When Executone approached the conference with a proposal on telephones, it was rejected by the Administrative Committee/Board because the conference had never acted for the dioceses in that way.

Common sense and good business practice demands that the church exercise stewardship appropriate to its size and financial clout. The NCCB/USCC might become self-financing if it retained a fraction of the money it would save the church through such common business practices.

Conclusion

The NCCB/USCC is not the Catholic church. It is a human institution created to serve the church on the national level. The church is the entire people of God. One would be foolish to place all one's hopes for the Catholic church in the NCCB/USCC or to expect too much from it. The same, of course, could be said of the Vatican curia.

The NCCB/USCC has proved to be an important and useful instrument of the American bishops who ultimately are the NCCB/USCC. Their preferences and values imbue and direct the conference. Their votes decide policy. The leaders they choose are followers and consensus builders rather than charismatic prophets. The staff person who fails to realize this either becomes frustrated or gets in trouble. In fact, the NCCB/USCC staff has been hard working and loyal to the bishops.

The NCCB/USCC is not all-powerful. It cannot act independently of its ecclesial, political, or economic environment. It must defer to Catholic tradition, theology, and canon law. It must operate within a pluralistic democratic society while remaining true to its Catholic character. What it can do is also limited by what it can afford.

Often the NCCB/USCC cannot even set its own agenda but is forced to react to agenda set by others. What Bishop Malone said of the NCCB/USCC presidency applies to the entire conference: "It is almost like someone who is working in the emergency room of a hospital. You can't predict what is going to come through the door. It is not as if the conference could make its own agenda. There is initiative taken at the level of the Holy See. Or there is some bishop who unexpectedly rises to do something that you wouldn't expect him to do. Suddenly, you are not in a position of leadership, but you are trying to react, or trying to put the best face on whatever happens." Likewise, actions in the political environment (wars, Supreme Court decisions, actions of Congress or the president) or economic environment (recession, inflation) force their attention on the bishops.

Despite its weaknesses, the NCCB/USCC functions amazingly well. The norm of consensus decision-making is always sought if not always achieved. Its committee system, although not perfect, functions well. The conference has never done anything that has permanently or severely damaged the church. It has done a credible job managing the American church since Vatican II. It has usually spoken prudently, if slowly, on many social and political issues of national concern. Its sins are often more of omission than commission since it must operate within ecclesial, political, and economic constraints. With more resources and fewer constraints the conference could undoubtedly do more, but not everyone wants it to. To function better as an institution it needs more resources and greater authority. Having reached its 25th year of operation since its reorganization in 1966, the NCCB/USCC is ready to perform its role as a mature actor in the church and the world.

Appendix A

NCCB/USCC Mission Statement Adopted November 1981

The National Conference of Catholic Bishops and the United States Catholic Conference are a permanent institute (Cf. Canon 447) composed of Catholic bishops of the United States of America in and through which the bishops exercise in a communal or collegial manner the pastoral mission entrusted to them by the Lord Jesus of sanctification, teaching, and leadership (Cf. *Lumen Gentium* 21), especially by devising forms and methods of apostolate suitably adapted to the circumstances of the times (Cf. *Christus Dominus* 38.1). Such exercise is intended to offer appropriate assistance to each bishop in fulfilling his particular ministry in the local Church, to effect a commonality of ministry addressed to the people of the United States of America, and to foster and express communion with the Church in other nations within the Church universal, under the leadership of its chief pastor, the Pope.

The National Conference of Catholic Bishops deals principally with matters connected with the internal life of the Church.

The United States Catholic Conference deals principally with affairs involving the general public, including social concerns, education, and communications, on the national level and in support of efforts at the regional and diocesan levels.

Appendix B

NCCB/USCC Goals and Objectives 1991-96

Major Goal #1: To foster unity and collegiality between the bishops of the United States and the Roman Pontiff.

Objectives:

1.1 To support and promote the Pope's universal teaching authority and leadership. Lead Agent: Doctrine

1.2 To be a voice for the U.S. bishops in an ongoing dialogue with the Holy See on matters of mutual concern. Lead Agent: General Secretariat

1.3 To assist the U.S. bishop delegates in preparing for participation in the Synod of bishops. Lead Agent: Pastoral Research & Practices and General Secretariat

Major Goal #2: To foster collegial collaboration among the bishops of the United States and between them and the whole episcopal college.

Objectives:

2.1 To plan and develop effective means of communication, deliberation and decision making which promote collegial action and the fraternal support among bishops of the U.S. and unity among dioceses. Lead Agent: General Secretariat

2.2 To continue informal relations with other episcopal conferences. Lead Agent: General Secretariat

Major Goal #3: To assist the bishops individually and collectively in fulfilling their roles as teachers in the faith community.

Objectives:

3.1 (Special Emphasis Objective): To teach Catholic doctrine where collective teaching by the bishops is needed and to offer to the bishops evaluations of theological trends and individual theological positions. Lead Agent: Doctrine

3.2 To seek the active collaboration of theologians as bishops exercise their teaching mission individually in their dioceses, collectively in the Episcopal Conference and as they participate in synods of bishops or ecumenical councils. Lead Agent: Doctrine

3.3 To provide ongoing doctrinal and theological orientation and theological programs for the bishops. Lead Agent: Doctrine

3.4 To initiate, encourage and support programs for the conversion of individual and collective consciences and for the transformation of people's lives, activities and cultures in which they live through the divine power of the Gospel the Church proclaims. Co-lead Agents: Evangelization, Missions, ABCM.

3.5 To initiate, encourage and support programs to improve the quality of liturgical preaching and mystagogical catechesis. Lead Agent: Priestly Life & Ministry

3.6 (Special Emphasis Objective): To provide leadership in collaboration with national and professional Catholic organizations for the betterment of Catholic educational institutions and for the promotion of ongoing faith formation for youth, young adults and adults through catechesis and related ministries. Lead Agent: Education

3.7 To foster maximum participation of parents, teachers and students served by Catholic educational institutions in programs of federal assistance, to represent the Catholic voice in the educational community of this country, to encourage the continued Catholic identity of institutions of higher education and to provide guidance on issues of public policy. Lead Agent: Education

3.8 To support the catechetical ministry of the Church in the United States by developing guidelines for the creation of doctrinally sound textbooks and by providing for their implementation. Lead Agent: Education

3.9 To foster programs which encourage an enlightened understanding of the role of the media—print, film, and electronic—in transmitting values within society, and to promote the efficient use of these media in service to the many fields of the apostolate. Lead Agent: Communication

3.10 To provide leadership for actualizing the vital role of parents, as primary educators and pastors in the enterprise of Catholic education. Lead Agent: Education

Major Goal #4: To assist the bishops individually and collectively in fulfilling their roles as priests and leaders of the worshipping community.

Objectives:

4.1 To provide leadership to clergy, religious and laity in liturgical formation, sacramental (mystagogical) catechesis, and liturgical celebration. Lead Agent: Liturgy

4.2 To approve, adapt, and authorize liturgical rites, texts, and books. Lead Agent: Liturgy

Major Goal #5: To assist the bishops individually and collectively in fulfilling their roles as fathers and shepherds in the Church and administering of the Church's resources.

Objectives:

5.1 To organize interdisciplinary research and analysis of perceived pastoral needs and to recommend solutions to pastoral issues. Lead Agent: Pastoral Research & Practices

5.2 To study the trends affecting the sacramental life of the parish community and to suggest effective responses to these trends. Co-Lead Agents: Pastoral Research & Practices, Liturgy

5.3 To study and promote the role of the laity in the mission of the Church and in the world. Lead Agent: Laity

5.4 To assist dioceses, seminaries and educational institutions in the education and formation of priests, deacons and non-ordained Church ministers and to respond to their continuing needs and concerns. Co-Lead Agents: Priestly Life & Ministry, Permanent Diaconate, Priestly Formation

5.5 To promote collaboration in the Church in the United States among the bishops, clergy and men and women religious and laity. Lead Agent: General Secretariat and Religious Life & Ministry

5.6 To encourage vocations to the priesthood, diaconate and religious life and to collaborate with national Catholic organizations concerned with vocations. Lead Agent: Vocations

5.7 To engage in ecumenical and interreligious dialogue and cooperation. Co-Lead Agents: Education, BCEIA

5.8 To respond to the contemporary issues facing marriage and family life by seeking to strengthen and develop pastoral reflection on and care for marriage and family life at the various levels of the Church. Lead Agent: Laity

5.9 To advocate and promote the dignity of women and to foster their just treatment by society and in the Church. Lead Agent: Women in Society and the Church

5.10 To assist in promoting an integrated and comprehensive approach to ministerial development while at the same time clarifying the distinct identity and function of the ordained and the non-ordained minister. Co-Lead Agents: Priestly Life & Ministry, Vocations, Permanent Diaconate, Laity

5.11 To initiate, promote, and engage in dialogue and cooperation with the scientific community. Lead Agent: Human Values

Major Goal #6: To assist the bishops individually and collectively in fulfilling their roles as models to and guardians of the communion of justice and charity.

Objectives:

6.1 To teach respect for all human life and organize for its protection, especially in behalf of the unborn, the elderly, and handicapped. Lead Agent: Pro-Life Activities

6.2 To foster and communicate Catholic social teaching and to build the capacity of the Church to act effectively on that teaching as a constitutive dimension of Catholic faith and Church life. Lead Agent: Social Development & World Peace

6.3   To foster and support collaborative efforts in the Church's health apostolate and to advocate greater access for health care for the poor and underserved. Lead Agent: Social Development & World Peace

6.4   To set policy on domestic and international issues and to advocate social justice programs and structural reform in society for the poor and vulnerable, for genuine justice and peace in the public arena. Lead Agent: Social Development & World Peace

6.5   To carry out the Church's option for and with the poor through the empowerment of poor people, especially minorities, to raise the consciousness of members of society regarding the varying causes of poverty and social injustice, and to build solidarity by providing ways for people to engage in the empowerment process. Lead Agent: Campaign for Human Development

6.6   To encourage the development and assist in the implementation of pastoral programs in relation to evangelization and incorporation into the local church of racial, ethnic, cultural and language groups and people on the move. Co-Lead Agents: Pastoral Care of Migrants and Refugees (PCMR) division of MRS, Black Catholics, Hispanic Affairs, Evangelization

6.7   To develop Conference policy on immigration, migration, and refugee issues and to provide both national and international coordination and program support for diocesan migration and refugee programs. Lead Agent: Migration & Refugee Services

6.8   To provide pastoral, educational and advocacy resources for the Church regarding special needs arising from changing social and economic conditions; in particular, with respect to racism, sexism, rural life concerns, family life, human rights, poverty and economic injustice. Co-Lead Agents: Social Development & World Peace, Latin America, Campaign for Human Development

Major Goal #7: To provide representation and coordination of effort for the bishops in relation to the federal government.

Objectives:

7.1 (a) To monitor and disseminate policies and activities of the federal government and national voluntary organizations and (b) To serve as a source of information about the Church and about the bishops' views and policies to these agencies. Co-Lead Agents: Government Liaison, General Counsel

7.2 To provide legal services at the national level and to furnish appropriate legal guidance to the dioceses and other Church organizations. Lead Agent: General Counsel

Appendix C

Major NCCB/USCC Statements

Statement[1]	Vote[2]
On the Government and Birth Control (1966)	Vu
Peace and Vietnam (1966)	B 169-5
Statement On Penance and Abstinence (1966)	B 159-32
On Race Relations and Poverty (1966)	B 172-0
Resolution On Antipoverty Legislation (1967)	Vu
Resolution on Peace (1967)	V
Statement on Clerical Celibacy (1967)	V
Statement on Catholic Schools (1967)	V
The Church in Our Day (1967)	u[3]
On the *Dutch Catechism* (1967)	Vu
Statement on National Race Crisis (1968)	V
Resolution on Peace (1968)	V
Statement on Due Process (1968)	V
Human Life in Our Day (1968)	B 180-8
Statement on Farm Labor (1968)	V
Statement on Abortion (1969)	V
Resolution on Celibacy (April 1969)	V
Statement on Celibacy (Nov. 1969)	B 145-68
In Protest of US Government Programs against the Right to Life (1969)	B 143-20
On Crusade against Poverty (1969)	V
Statement on Prisoners of War (1969)	V
Ecumenism (1970)	V
Christians in Our Time (1970)	Vu
Statement on Abortion (1970)	B 114-52
On Welfare Reform Legislation (1970)	V
Catholic Press (1970)	V
On 25th Anniversary of the UN (1970)	V
On the Implementation of Apostolic Letter on Mixed Marriages (1970)	B[4]
Declaration on Abortion (1970)	B 224-8
Birth Control Laws (1970)	V
On the Campaign for Human Development (1970)	Vu

On Conscientious Objection and Selective Conscientious Objection (1971)	M 2/3[5]
Ethical and Religious Directives for Catholic Health Facilities (1971)	B 232-7-2
On Parental Rights and the Free Exercise of Religion (1971)	V ???-2
Christian Concern for the Environment (1971)	Vu
Statement on the Missions (1971)	Vu
Population and the American Future: A Response (1972)	Vu
Where Shall the People Live? (1972)	B 206-9-1
To Teach as Jesus Did (1972)	B 187-30-4
Resolution on Imperatives of Peace (1972)	B 186-4
Basic Teachings for Catholic Religious Education (1973)	M 2/3
Statement on Population (1973)	Vu
On the Pro-Life Constitutional Amendment (1973)	Vu
On the 25th Anniversary of the Universal Declaration of Human Rights (1973)	V[6]
Towards Peace in the Middle East (1973)	Vu
The Reform of Correctional Institutions (1973)	V
Resolution on Farm Labor (1973)	Vu
Behold Your Mother: Woman of Faith (1973)	M
Resolution against Capital Punishment (1974)	B 108-63
On Farm Labor Legislation (1974)	Hu
Statement on World Food Crisis (1974)	V
Concerning the 10th Anniversary of the Decree on Ecumenism (1974)	V
The Eucharist and the Hungers of the Human Family (1975)	B 177-0
Pastoral Plan for Pro-Life Activities (1975)	Vu
The Economy: Human Dimensions (1975)	Vu
The Right to a Decent Home (1975)	Vu
On Catholic-Jewish Relations (1975)	B 190-6
Resolution on Farm Labor (1975)	Vu
Resolution on Human Life Foundation (1975)	Vu
Society and the Aged (1976)	B 211-8
Political Responsibility (1976)	B 176-5
Teach Them (1976)	B 153-30
Let the Little Children Come to Me (1976)	B 201-23
U.S.-Panama Relations (1976)	B 170-61
On the Pastoral Concern of the Church for People on the Move (1976)	Su
To Live in Christ Jesus (1976)	B 172-25
Resolution in Honor of Cardinal Krol (1976)	Vu
On American Indians (1977)	B 254-8-3
Religious Liberty in Eastern Europe (1977)	B 252-2-1

The Bicentennial Consultation:
A Response to the Call to Action (1977)	B 179-7-1
Resolution on *Jesus of Nazareth* (1977)	Vu
Principals and Guidelines for Fund-Raising (1977)	V
To Do the Work of Justice (1978)	B 236-6
The Plan of Pastoral Action for Family Ministry (1978)	V
On Handicapped People (1978)	B 216-2
Statement on the Middle East (1978)	B 213-8
On Conciliation and Arbitration (1979)	Vu
Brothers and Sisters to Us (1979)	B 215-30-2
Resolution on Cambodia (1979)	V
Resolution on Iran (1979)	V
Resolution on the Papal Visit (1979)	Vu
Resolution on the Iranian Crisis (1980)	V
Resolution on Cuban and Haitian Refugees (1980)	Vu
Pastoral Letter on Marxist Communism (1980)	B 236-17
Catholic Higher Education (1980)	B ???
Called and Gifted (1980)	Vu
Statement on Capital Punishment (1980)	B 145-31-41
Resolution on the Hostages in Iran (1980)	Vu
Statement on Central America (1981)	S ???-10
Health and Health Care (1981)	Vu
NCCB/USCC Mission Statement (1981)	Vu
The Challenge of Peace (1983)	B 238-9
Hispanic Presence: Challenge and Commitment (1983)	Vu
Resolution on Central America (1983)	V
Pastoral on Liturgy (1983)	Vu
Statement on the Ukraine (1985)	Vu
Pastoral Plan for Pro-Life Activities (1985)	Vu
Resolution on Immigration Reform (1985)	Vu
Statement on Lithuania (1985)	So
Pastoral on Campus Ministry (1985)	B 176-4
Statement on Food and Agriculture (1985)	Vu
Resolution on Aguilar Decision (1985)	Su
Statement on Evangelization (1985)	Vu
Resolution on Lebanon (1986)	Vo
Resolution on Lithuania (1986)	Vo
Statement on World Mission (1986)	Vu
Economic Justice for All (1986)	B 225-9
Pastoral Plan for Hispanic Ministry (1987)	Vu
Resolution on Korea (1987)	Vu
Resolution on Lebanon (1987)	Vu
Priests in Third Age (1987)	Vu

Statement on School-based Clinics (1987)   Vu
Statement on Central America (1987)   Vo

Reflection on Peace Pastoral (1988)   Vu
Report on Peace Pastoral (1988)   Vo
Report on Agriculture (1988)   Vu
Resolution on Handicapped Pastoral (1988)   Vu
Statement on Employer Sanctions (1988)   Vu
Statement on Religious Freedom in E. Europe (1987)   Vu

Appendix D

NCCB/USCC Legislative Priorities: 102nd Congress (1991-92)[1]

Communications Department

Priority One

- **Cable Television**: support legislation which serves to regulate the industry to provide greater protection to consumers from unreasonable or abusive rates; greater public, educational and governmental access; equal access to programming for all competitors; carriage of public and commercial broadcast signals; standards for consumer protection, customer service, and minimum technical quality; and stringent safeguards in light of proposed telephone company entry into video services.
- **Fairness Doctrine**: support Congressional mandate of the policy which requires broadcasters to afford reasonable opportunity for the discussion of conflicting views on issues of public importance.

Priority Two

- **Comparative Renewal Process**: support legislation which requires that instead of broadcasters having their licenses automatically renewed, they must compete with challengers pledging to better meet the needs of the community.
- **Telephone Life-Line Service**: support legislation assisting those segments of the population whose lives would be endangered without access to a phone; and maintaining affordable telephone service for the public.

- **Sunset of Must Carry**: support legislation to require cable companies to carry the signals of local television stations, particularly independent and public television within the cable system's coverage area.

Priority Three

- **Reducing the Amount of Violence and Drug Abuse on Television**: support new legislation.
- **Anti-trafficking Policies**: support legislation to require broadcast stations to be held for three years before being sold, in order to prevent broadcast stations from becoming just commodities to be bought and sold, rather than facilities intended to render a long term service to the community.

Important

- **Children's Television**: support legislation which further reduces commercialization and improves educational and informational quality of children's television programming.
- **Cross Ownership**: support legislation to prevent the common ownership of a daily newspaper and a television station in the same community.
- **Curtailing Pornography**: support new legislation.
- **Maintaining the Number of Television Channels for Non-commercial Use**: preventing any decrease in the number of such VHF channels; in effect, preventing the trading of commercial VHF stations for the more valuable educational VHF stations.
- **Broadcasters Ties to Community**: require broadcasters to provide programming regarding local matters, permit access to their public files and access to station personnel.

Domestic Social Development Office

Priority One

- **Civil Rights Bill**: (Reconsideration of employment discrimination legislation) support congressional enactment of a new Civil Rights bill dealing with employment discrimination.

- **Family and Medical Leave Act**: support legislation to require employers to offer limited unpaid leave to workers with serious health conditions, newborn or ill dependents.
- **Housing Appropriations**: support new and increased funding for low-income housing development by community based organizations.
- **Comprehensive Substance Abuse Treatment and Rehabilitation**: support funding and new legislative initiatives to provide services for pregnant women and other mothers and treatment and care for their children. This could include proposed changes in medicaid coverage and reimbursement as well as new legislation to authorize and fund programs for alcohol, drug abuse and mental health and a comprehensive overhaul of child welfare law.

Priority Two

- **Anti-Hunger Initiative**: support increased funding for and the expansion of the food stamp program; support increased funding for the nutrition subsidy program for women, infants and children (WIC).
- **Crime Control and Racial Justice Act**: oppose expansion of death penalty—support gun control legislation.
- **Tax Relief for Families with Children**: support significant expansion of "Young Child Tax Credit" for lower income families.
- **Worker Replacement**: general support for legislation which outlaws "permanent replacement workers," practices that effectively deny workers the right to strike.

Priority Three

- **Medicaid**: support mandate for states to expand coverage for low-income pregnant women and children.
- **AIDS Care**: support funding for "Ryan White Bill" which is designed to help cities and states cope with the growing number of patients with AIDS; funds would go: in targeted cities directly to hospitals, nursing homes and other acute care facilities; as well

as to states to help develop comprehensive AIDS care programs and to build or renovate facilities.

- **SSI Reform**: support increased federal benefits and improvement of eligibility for disabled children.
- **Farm Subsidies (GATT Agreement)**: support policies to protect interest of small and moderate sized farms.
- **Federal Budget**: support increased funding for programs affecting low-income persons.

Important

- **"Violence Against Women Act"**: monitor proposed legislation which would: create new penalties for sex crimes; provide funding in local law enforcement against sex crimes; double funding for battered women's shelters; make gender-motivated crimes a violation of federal civil rights laws.

Education Department

Priority One

- **Chapter 1 Funding**: support fully authorized funding ($40 million) for "Capital Expenses," to restore compensatory educational services to pre-*Felton* levels and quality for low-income/educationally disadvantaged, Catholic school students.
- **School Asbestos Abatement, Loans/Grants**: support funding at $200 million as authorized in the new Asbestos School Hazard Abatement Act.
- **Child Care Block Grant**: support full funding as authorized in the new child care legislation.
- **Higher Education Act Reauthorization**: insure programs which affect elementary and secondary education such as loan forgiveness for teachers, teacher recruitment, training and retention; provide for fair treatment of nonpublic school teachers and students.

Priority Two:

- **"Bush" Education Initiatives**: proposed legislation likely to include programs: to implement national education goals; to reward excellent schools, teachers and students; to reduce illiteracy; to improve math/science education; to address teacher certification and professional standards; to expand magnet schools; to promote a national education test and report card; to enlarge early childhood development; to deregulate federal education programs; to demonstrate parental choices; etc.—possibly seek amendments to insure fair treatment of nonpublic school teachers and students.

- **Improvement of American Urban Schools:** proposed legislation to fund strategies to raise academic achievement, ensure urban children begin school ready to learn and are well nourished, increase graduation rates, provide qualified, racially sensitive teachers and ensure that all urban schools are well maintained and drug-free; possibly seek amendments to insure fair treatment of nonpublic school teachers and students.

- **In-Door Air Quality—in Public and Commercial Buildings:** proposed legislation to create national program to reduce the threat to human health posed by exposure to contaminants in the air, indoors. Schools, child care facilities and parish buildings would be required to conduct exposure assessments and perform response actions; seek amendments related to impact on nonpublic schools (and possibly the church buildings).

- **Mandated Radon Testing/Remediation in schools—loan/grants:** proposed legislation to require radon testing and remediation in public and private schools; support inclusion of federal financial assistance to assist in compliance with these requirements.

Priority Three:

- **Teaching Values in Public Schools:** creates a national commission to address the issue of how to deal with teaching values in public schools; monitor and possibly support new legislation.

Important

- **Education of the Handicapped Act—Part H**: Reauthorization of programs for disabled infants and young children.
- **Office of Education Research and Improvement Reauthorization**: will extend all programs in educational research and statistics under the jurisdiction of this agency.
- **Job Training Partnership Act**: will amend federal employment and training programs to better target economically disadvantaged youth and adults.
- **Institutional Conservation Program (ICP) Energy Grants**: matching grants to public and private schools and hospitals to analyze and implement energy conservation measures to reduce energy use and costs.

General Counsel (Tax Legislation)

Priority Two

- **Pension Simplification**: support revision of pension laws to reduce administrative burdens on churches.

Important

- **Charitable Giving**: support legislation to strengthen incentives for giving.
- **Reporting Requirements for Churches**: oppose possible removal of the churches' exemption from annual information returns.
- **Unrelated Business Income (UBIT)**: monitor possible excise tax on passive income and other possible changes in UBIT affecting Catholic organizations.

International Justice and Peace

Priority One

- **Central American & Caribbean Issues:**
  El Salvador: support diplomatic solutions and a just peace in El Salvador; continue insistence on conditioning U.S. aid on human rights progress and

progress on the investigation and prosecution of those who have murdered church people; **Panama**: support provision of promised post-invasion U.S. assistance to Panama; **Nicaragua**: support provision of promised U.S. assistance to Nicaragua; **Guatemala**: support human rights in Guatemala; **Haiti**: support congressional action to promote human rights and support democracy and economic justice in Haiti.

- **Middle East Regional Issues**:
  Persian Gulf War: pursue an early, just and stable peace in the Persian Gulf; **Israeli-Palestinian Issues**: support efforts to achieve a just and stable peace in the Middle East.

Priority Two
- **African Regional Issues**: oppose military and support diplomatic solutions to regional conflict in southern Africa, support appropriate sanctions and progress toward a peaceful end to apartheid in South Africa; support congressional efforts to limit covert military aid programs in Angola and support a just and peaceful end to civil war there; support a just and peaceful end to civil strife in Liberia.
- **Eastern European and USSR Regional Issues**: support dialogue, self-determination and non-violence in the dispute between the Baltic republics and the Soviet Union; support continued and increased U.S. assistance to help assist the people of Eastern Europe.

Priority Three
- **Defense Spending and Arms Control**: address possible ratification of the Strategic Arms Reduction Treaty (START) agreement, ratification of conventional arms control treaty and broader defense spending issues.
- **Third World Debt and Development**: support appropriate legislative or executive initiatives to relieve the debt burden for poor countries, support for programs of U.S. development assistance and U.S. funding for the United Nations.

- **Third World Militarization Issues**: support for conversion of military assistance to development aid in the Third World.

Important

- **U.S. International Drug Policy**: closely follow U.S. international drug policy, especially Administration's Andean Initiative in close collaboration with Latin American episcopates.
- **Other Regional Issues**: support human rights and advocate for human needs in the Philippines, in East Timor, and throughout Latin America as well as human rights in China and Vietnam.

Migration and Refugee Services

Priority One

- **Refugee Funding**: work to increase appropriations for refugee admissions and for refugee assistance overseas. Effort will focus on the following appropriations measures: Department of Labor and Health and Human Services Appropriation; Foreign Aid Appropriation; and Department of State, Department of Commerce and Department of Justice Appropriation; pursue changes in Migration and Refugee Assistance program including obtaining funding for non-refugee cases; monitor proposed changes to the refugee travel loan fund, and attempt to limit increase of costly reporting requirements for diocesan affiliates.
- **Refugee Consultation**: pursue increased numbers for refugee admissions, with particular attention to regional allocations; urge the Congress to reexamine the priority categories for refugees so that they can be made more flexible.
- **Implementation of the Refugee Act of 1980**: seek affirmation or expansion of current scope of refugee definition; urge that alternative forms of admission be examined, particularly with regard to the parole authority; support the re-evaluation and revision of the refugee resettlement process in light of the federal government's increasing reluctance to appro-

priately fund programs: pursue adjustments to the refugee consultation process and support efforts to establish a commission to examine U.S. refugee policy.

Priority Two

- **Haiti**: seek to end the interdiction of Haitian boat people through the establishment of U.S. consular processing office in Haiti and other countries in the region to take Haitian applications for refugee status.
- **Employer Sanctions**: support measures calling for the repeal of employer sanctions as part of long-term effort to repeal sanctions.

Priority Three

- **Alternatives to Detention**: seek legislation to provide the Immigration and Naturalization Service with guidance on alternatives to detaining undocumented aliens while their asylum applications are being adjudicated.
- **Unaccompanied Refugee Minors**: press Congress to explore alternatives to the Immigration and Naturalization's current policy of detention of undocumented minors and mandate that the United Nations High Commissioner for Refugees improve its services to this population.
- **Political Asylum**: pursue changes to asylum definition and process. (Issues to monitor include effects of the Immigration Act of 1990 on the political asylum process, the effectiveness of the new asylum officers, the role of attorneys, and the reduction of backlogs).

Pro-Life Office

Priority One

- **Hyde Amendment**: support legislation to prohibit the federal funding of abortions under the Labor/HHS Appropriation Bill.
- **Dornan Amendment**: support legislation to prevent any public funds (federal or local tax revenues) from being used for abortions in D.C.

- **Foreign Aid for Abortions**: oppose any Congressional action to change the policy of denying U.S. foreign aid funds to private "family planning" organizations which promote abortion, or which support programs of coerced abortion or involuntary sterilization.

Priority Two

- **Abortions in Military Hospitals**: oppose efforts in Congress to overturn existing policy of prohibiting abortions in military hospitals.
- **Title X Reauthorization (the federal family planning program)**: oppose reauthorization, focusing on provisions for development of new abortifacient drugs and for establishment of school-based contraceptive clinics.
- **Title XX Reauthorization (the Adolescent Family Life program)**: support simple reauthorization and oppose efforts to change the program by eliminating parental rights and adding abortion counseling.
- **NIH Reauthorization**: oppose efforts to provide federal support for harmful fetal research, fetal tissue transplants, in-vitro fertilization and abortifacient research (RU 486).

Important

- **"Freedom of Choice Act"**: oppose legislation designed to create a federal "right" to abortion.
- **Legal Services Corporation**: oppose any legislation to remove the prohibition on participating in any litigation with respect to abortion.
- **Preventing prison abortion funding**: oppose efforts in Congress to overturn existing policy of prohibiting abortions in federal prisons.
- **Federal Employee Health Benefit Program**: support the continuation of the exclusion of abortion coverage.
- **"Fetal Protection" Policies**: monitor the possible effects of civil rights legislation on protection of unborn children in the workplace.

Miscellaneous

Important:

- **Postal Rates:** monitor possible changes to the non-profit postal subsidy program.

Appendix E

Canons Mentioning Episcopal Conferences[1]

Canons Authorizing or Requiring General Decrees

1. qualifications for installation as a lector or acolyte (c. 230, 1);

2. norms for the formation of candidates for the permanent diaconate (c. 236);

3. norms on presbyteral councils (c. 496);

4. authorization for cathedral chapters to take the place of the college of consultors (c. 502, 3);

5. sacramental books to be maintained by parishes (c. 535, 1);

6. determination of standards for the care of retired pastors (c. 538, 3); [in 1987 approved Norms for Priests and Their Third Age]

7. norms for preaching by lay persons in churches (c. 766);

8. norms for preaching on radio and television (c. 772, 2); [in 1984 authorized, until study completed, guidelines from diocesan bishop]

9. regulations on the catechumenate (c. 788, 3); [in 1986 established National Statutes for the Catechumenate]

10. norms on religious education in schools and on the media (c. 804, 1);

11. norms for clergy and religious appearing on radio and television (c. 831, 2); [in 1984 authorized, until study completed, guidelines by diocesan bishop]

12. adaptation of the adult catechumenate and norms for conducting it (c. 851, 1);

13. norms on the administration of baptism (c. 854);

14. norms on recording the baptism of adopted children (c. 877, 3); [in 1984 authorized, until study completed, guidelines by diocesan bishop]

15. decision to require parishes to keep a record of confirmations in addition to the diocesan record (c. 895);

16. norms concerning the arrangement of confessionals (c. 964, 2);

17. setting an older age for ordination to the diaconate or presbyterate (c. 1031, 3); [in 1984 set minimum age for ordination to diaconate at 35]

18. particular law governing the promise to marry or engagements (c. 1062, 1);

19. norms on pre-nuptial investigation and banns (c. 1067); [in 1984 authorized, until study completed, diocesan bishop to establish norms]

20. setting an older age to enter marriage licitly (c. 1083, 2);

21. determination of how marriages are to be noted in parish registers (c. 1121, 1);

22. decision to abolish or transfer the observance of a holy day (c. 1246, 2); [in 1983 decided to retain traditional holy days]

23. determination of a different food besides meat from which faithful are to abstain on days of penance (c. 1251);

24. norms on contributions given to the church (c. 1262); [in 1984 authorized diocesan bishop to establish norms]

25. norms on fund-raising (c. 1265, 2);

26. regulations on benefices where benefices are still in effect (c. 1272);

27. norms on leasing church property (c. 1297); [defined as extraordinary act when lease is for more than nine years and amount exceeds minimum]

28. norms for conciliation and arbitration of disputes (c. 1714);

29. decision to require each diocese to have an office of mediation (c. 1733, 2).

Other Canons Mentioning Conferences

1. establishing interdiocesan seminaries, with the approval of the Apostolic See (c. 237, 2);

2. setting a program of priestly formation, with the approval of the Apostolic See (c. 242, 1);

3. determining the participation expected of permanent deacons in the liturgy of the hours (c. 276, 2, 3); [in 1984 encouraged deacons to pray morning and evening prayer]

4. specifying clerical garb for the area (c. 284);

5. being consulted before the Apostolic See erects a personal prelature in the area (c. 294);

6. erecting public associations for the area (c. 312, 1, 2; cc. 313, 314, 316, 318, 319 are included in this authority);

7. suppressing public associations erected by the conference (c. 320, 2);

8. granting juridic personality to private associations (c. 322);

9. suppressing private associations erected by the conference (c. 326, 1);

10. electing representatives to the synod of bishops (c. 346, 1);

11. being consulted by and receiving cooperation on the papal legate (c. 364, 3);

12. being consulted before the Apostolic See erects a particular church for a special rite or group of persons in the territory (c. 372, 2);

13. cooperating in drafting lists of potential candidates for the episcopacy (c. 377, 2);

14. seeing to support of retired bishops (c. 402, 2);

15. proposing erection by the Apostolic See of regions within the conference (c. 433, 1) which have canonical status even though not the same power as a conference of bishops (c. 434);

16. calling a plenary council, with the approval of the Apostolic See (c. 439);

17. determining the place for a plenary council; setting the rules of order, agenda, and meetings, and with the approval of the Apostolic See, selecting the council's president (c. 441);

18. determining certain numbers of participants at a plenary council (c. 443);

19. receiving copies of decrees from diocesan synods (c. 467);

20. authorizing bishops to set a limited term in the appointment of pastors (c. 522); [in 1984 set six-year term, renewal at discretion of diocesan bishop]

21. cooperating with conferences of major religious superiors (c. 708);

22. exercising authentic magisterium (c. 753);

23. promoting Christian unity (c. 755, 2);

24. issuing catechisms for their territory, with the prior approval of the Apostolic See (c. 755, 2);

25. establishing catechetical office for the conference (c. 755, 3);

26. providing for the care of visitors from missionary areas (c. 792);

27. providing for Catholic universities and faculties (c. 809);

28. exercising vigilance over doctrine in the territory (c. 810, 2);

29. establishing higher institutes for religious studies (c. 821);

30. exercising vigilance, passing judgment, and even taking corrective action concerning publications and media (c. 823, 2);

31. permitting ecumenical translations of the Sacred Scriptures (c. 825, 2);

32. permitting ecumenical translations of the Sacred Scriptures with notes (c. 825, 1);

33. developing a list of censors for books or even establishing a commission of censors (c. 830, 1);

34. preparing adaptations and translations of liturgical books and, with prior approval from the Apostolic See, publishing them (c. 838, 3);

35. determining cases of "other grave necessity" when baptized non-Catholics may receive Catholic sacraments of Eucharist, penance, and anointing (c. 844, 4);

36. developing norms on such sacramental sharing after consulting the appropriate authorities of other churches (c. 844, 5);

37. determining another age for confirmation than the age of discretion (c. 891); [in 1984 authorized determination by diocesan bishop]

38. determining whether it is acceptable for lay persons to assist at marriages (for which individual bishops must seek permission from the Apostolic See) (c. 1112, 2); [in 1989 authorized individual bishops to request permission]

39. drawing up a marriage ritual for the area, to be approved by the Apostolic See (c. 1120);

40. determining how the declaration and promises for a mixed marriage are to be made (c. 1126); [in 1983 decided 1970 norms to remain in effect]

41. establishing common norms for dispensation from canonical form (c. 1127, 2); [in 1983 decided 1970 norms remain in effect except diocesan bishop can no longer grant dispensation from form]

42. approval for a shrine to be called "national" (c. 1231);

43. approving statutes of a national shrine (c. 1232, 1);

44. permitting use of materials other than stone for altars (c. 1236, 1);

45. determining the laws of fast and abstinence more precisely or substituting other penitential practices (c. 1253); [in 1983 decided to retain 1966 norms on penance and abstinence]

46. where social security does not care for the clergy, seeing that some institute does provide for this (c. 1274, 2);

47. defining acts of extraordinary administration for dioceses (c. 1277); [defined acts of extraordinary administration in 1985]

48. defining minimums and maximums on values for alienation of church goods (c. 1292, 1); [set at $3 million in 1991]

49. permitting lay persons to serve as judges (c. 1421, 2); [in 1983 authorized diocesan bishops to appoint lay judges]

50. permitting bishops to use single-judge courts if collegiate tribunals cannot be formed (c. 1425, 4); [in 1983 authorized diocesan bishop to permit single-judge court]

51. forming a tribunal of second instance with the approval of the Apostolic See, if the Apostolic See has allowed an interdiocesan tribunal of first instance (c. 1439, 1); [in 1983 expressed willingness to establish tribunal when petition is submitted]

52. establishing tribunals of second instance in other situations, with the approval of the Apostolic See (c. 1439, 2); [in 1983 expressed willingness to establish tribunal when petition is submitted]

53. exercising certain powers relative to interdiocesan tribunals of second instance (c. 1439, 3).

Notes

Introduction: A Conspiracy of Bishops

1. James A. Hickey, "The Bishop as Teacher," *The Ministry of Bishops: Papers from the Collegeville Assembly* (Washington, D.C.: U.S. Catholic Conference, 1982), 17.

2. Cited in Robert J. Hutchinson, "Are the U.S. Bishops Out of Step with the Laity?" *Wanderer*, July 17, 1988.

3. Joseph Bernardin, "Los Angeles Meeting of the Pope and U.S. Bishops," *Origins* 17 (October 1, 1987): 256.

4. The head of a diocese or an archdiocese used to be called an "ordinary," but under the 1983 Code of Canon Law the proper term is a "diocesan bishop" who can be either a bishop or an archbishop. The broader term "ordinary" refers also to other leadership figures, such as some religious superiors.

5. The other bishops are called "suffragans." See Thomas J. Reese, *Archbishop: Inside the Power Structure of the American Catholic Church* (San Francisco: Harper & Row, 1989), 307-309.

6. For a description of diocesan governance, see Thomas J. Reese, *Archbishop: Inside the Power Structure of the American Catholic Church* (San Francisco: Harper & Row, 1989).

7. The NCCB/USCC includes the Virgin Islands but not Puerto Rico which is a separate conference.

8. The USCC is often inaccurately identified with the staff of the bishops' conference. To avoid confusing it with the body of bishops organized as the USCC, I will refer to the staff as the NCCB/USCC secretariat. Scholars who have identified the USCC with the staff include: Timothy A. Byrnes, *Catholic Bishops in American Politics* (Princeton, N.J.: Princeton University Press, 1991), 49; Mary Hanna, "The Dance of Legislation," in *Religion and U.S. Political Behavior* ed. Ted G. Jelen (New York: Praeger, 1989), 214; Mary Hanna, "Bishops as Political Leaders," *Religion in American Politics*, ed. Charles W. Dunn (Washington, D.C.: Congressional Quarterly, 1989), 78.

9. See my reports in *America*, January 16, 1982; December 18, 1982; December 25, 1982; April 23, 1983; May 21, 1983; December 17, 1983; November 3, 1984; December 8, 1984; February 2, 1985; April 27, 1985; July 13, 1985; November 30, 1985; November 29, 1986; July 16, 1988; December 3, 1988; July 1, 1989; November 4, 1989; November 25, 1989; June 15, 1991; November 30, 1991.

Chapter 1: A Flock of Shepherds

1. T.S. Eliot, "Murder in the Cathedral," *The Complete Poems and Plays 1909-1950* (New York: Harcourt, Brace & World, 1952), 203.

2. *Code of Canon Law, Latin-English Edition* (Washington, D.C.: Canon Law Society of America Press, 1983), Canon 378 §1.

3. For a detailed examination of the appointment process, see Thomas J. Reese, *Archbishop: Inside the Power Structure of the American Catholic Church* (San Francisco: Harper & Row, 1989), 1-52.

4. Cover letter (1984) from apostolic delegate requesting information on candidate for the office of bishop. All caps and bold in original. See also "Instruction on the Pontifical Secret," February 4, 1974, *Origins* 4 (May 30, 1974): 9-11.

5. For the text of the questionnaire, see Reese, *Archbishop*, 31-34, or Thomas J. Reese, "The Selection of Bishops," *America* 151 (August 18-25, 1984).

6. A bishop must submit his resignation at age 75; it is up to the pope whether the resignation is accepted, but in the United States they normally are. Cardinal John Krol's retirement was postponed the longest of any Latin-rite bishop in the United States, 27 months after his 75th birthday.

7. The Vatican believes there are too many auxiliary bishops in the United States and is not replacing all those who die or retire. See Anthony Pilla, "Vatican Denies Request for Auxiliary Bishop." *Origins* 21 (January 30, 1992): 556.

8. An assistant bishop with the right of succession is a coadjutor. Recently, the Vatican appears to be giving coadjutor bishops to diocesan bishops over 70 years of age if they ask for an auxiliary.

9. Canon 377 §3. *Terna* is the Italian word in common use by the participants, but *ternus* is the English term used in *Code of Canon Law, Latin-English Edition* (Washington, D.C.: Canon Law Society of America Press, 1983).

10. "Minutes of the Second General Meeting of the National Conference of Catholic Bishops and the U.S. Catholic Conference," April 11-13, 1967, pp. 4-8. Also on the committee were Bishop Thomas Donnellan and Bishop Gerald V. McDevitt. The minutes were not detailed and in places were unclear, and I was refused access to the committee report. In any case, the committee report was amended to continue having province meetings and to have them on an annual rather than the current biennial basis. They also voted to include auxiliary bishops in the meetings (this recommendation was accepted by the Vatican in its norms for the selection of bishops in 1972). It is not clear whether the NCCB voted also to include retired bishops in the meeting. The bishops of the province were to prepare a report on the episcopal candidates that would be given to both the apostolic delegate and to the NCCB Committee on the Selection of Bishops. A motion to have the NCCB president chair the committee, consisting of six additional members appointed by him from the Administrative Committee with attention to geographical representation, was approved. The report as amended and approved was presented to the Vatican as a recommendation since the conference could not change the process without approval.

11. "Minutes of the Ninth General Meeting of the National Conference of Catholic Bishops," November 16-20, 1970. The bishops first discussed the norms in regional meetings. The reports from the regional discussions indicated division within the conference over group consultation (five yes, six no), sending lists of candidates to NCCB president for his review and suggestions (seven no, four yes), to the NCCB Committee on the Selection of Bishops (four yes, seven no), expanding the role of the conference to include responsibility for drawing up a *terna* for filling vacant sees (five yes, five no, one abstained), and having an ordinary consult with metropolitan and members of province when nominating for auxiliary a priest not on the province list (seven yes, four no). Bishop Begin pointed "out that the results of voting in the regional groups could be somewhat misleading since it frequently involved a split vote."

After the debate, the bishops voted 105-90 in favor of allowing a collective consultation process, although the norms permitted a bishop to consult people only individually. They also voted 175-83 that an ordinary requesting the appointment of an auxiliary whose name is not on the provincial list should consult with the metropolitan and bishops of the province. Requiring him to consult with the NCCB Committee on the Selection of Bishops was defeated 61-98 with 30 abstentions. Other votes are given in the text.

12. Letter of Bishop Francis J. Mugavero to Archbishop John Quinn, December 20, 1979. In 1979 there were 12 regions and 20 provinces. In 1991, there are 13 regions and 31 Latin-rite provinces.

13. Before the reestablishment of formal diplomatic relations between the United States and the Holy See in 1984, the pope's representative to the American hierarchy was an apostolic delegate.

14. Before 1980, the NCCB president was asked by the papal representative for suggestions when a see became vacant, but was not consulted again. In December 1979, Archbishop John Quinn requested and received the permission for the president to be consulted a second time, this time on the names that had surfaced.

15. "Ad quosdam episcopos e Statibus Foederatis Americae Septentrionalis occasione oblata 'ad Limina' visitationis coram admissos" (September 5, 1983), *Acta Apostolicae Sedis* 76:103-104, italics in original.

16. See Thomas J. Reese, "The Laghi Legacy," *America* 162 (June 16, 1990): 605-608.

17. Paul Wilkes, "Profiles: The Education of an Archbishop—I," *New Yorker* (July 15, 1991), 56. See also Scrutator, "Moderates Need Not Apply," *The Tablet* [London] 245 (October 19, 1991): 1,278.

18. E. J. Dionne, Jr., *New York Times* (January 30, 1987).

19. Richard J. Gelm, "The United States Catholic Bishops: A Survey Research Perspective" (Paper delivered at Annual Meeting of the American Political Science Association, San Francisco, August 30-September 2, 1990), p. 38. His data is based on a 1989 survey of active and retired bishops, 40 percent of whom responded. "Recent" appointees were those appointed within four years of the survey. See also

his "Religion and Politics in Transition: American Catholics since the Second Vatican Council" (Ph. D. diss., University of California, Davis, 1991).

20. "Pio Laghi Years Uphold Vatican Orthodoxy," *National Catholic Reporter*, April 20, 1990.

21. Richard P. McBrien, "A Papal Attack on Vatican II," *New York Times*, March 12, 1990.

22. *National Catholic Reporter* (September 18, 1987)

23. For suggested reforms in the appointment of bishops, see Reese, *Archbishop*, 49-52.

24. John Tracy Ellis, "On Selecting American Bishops," *Commonweal* 85 (March 10, 1967): 643-9; John Tracy Ellis, "On Selecting Catholic Bishops for the United States," *The Critic* 26 (June-July 1969): 42-48; John Tracy Ellis, "The Selection of Bishops," *American Benedictine Review* 35 (June 1984): 111-127; James Hennesey, "'To Chuse a Bishop': An American Way," *America* 127 (September 2, 1972): 115-18; Robert Trisco, "Democratic Influence on the Election of Bishops and Pastors and on the Administration of Dioceses and Parishes in the U.S.A.," *Concilium* 77 (1972): 132-38.

Chapter 2: Corralling the Shepherds

1. Jan Schotte, "A Vatican Synthesis," *Origins* 12 (April 7, 1983): 692.

2. "Draft Statement on Episcopal Conferences," *Origins* 17 (April 7, 1988): 736.

3. Thomas J. Reese, S.J., ed., *Episcopal Conferences: Historical, Canonical, and Theological Studies* (Washington, D.C.: Georgetown University Press, 1989).

4. National Conference of Catholic Bishops, "Response to Vatican Working Paper on Bishops' Conferences," *Origins* 18 (December 1, 1988): 397-402.

5. Cardinal Bernardin Gantin, "An Update on the Bishops' Conference Study," *Origins* 20 (November 8, 1990): 355-56.

6. See "Church Order 1990: Collegiality Put to the Test," ed. James Provost and K. Walf in *Concilium* 1990.

7. For more on the role of bishops in their dioceses, see Thomas J. Reese, *Archbishop: Inside the Power Structure of the American Catholic Church* (San Francisco: Harper and Row, 1989).

8. Brian E. Daley, S.J., "Structures of Charity: Bishops' Gatherings and the See of Rome in the Early Church," in *Episcopal Conferences: Historical, Canonical, and Theological Studies*, ed. Thomas J. Reese, S.J. (Washington, D.C.: Georgetown University Press, 1989), 25-58; Hermann-Josef Sieben, S.J., "Episcopal Conferences in Light of Particular Councils During the First Millennium," in *The Nature and Future of Episcopal Conferences*, ed. Hervé Legrand, Julio Manzanares, and Antonio García y García (Washington, D.C.: Catholic University of America Press, 1988), 30-56.

9. Daley, "Structures of Charity," 29.

10. Joseph Komonchak, "Introduction," in *Episcopal Conferences: Historical, Canonical, and Theological Studies*, 1-2.

11. Ibid., 2.

12. James Hennesey, S.J., "Councils in America," in *A National Pastoral Council: Pro and Con* (Washington, D.C.: USCC, 1971), 39. From 1829 to 1849, the bishops held seven provincial councils under the archbishop of Baltimore. After the creation of new provinces, they held plenary councils in 1852, 1866, and 1884. All these councils were held in Baltimore. Two councils were postponed because of wars, first in 1812 and later in 1862.

13. Hennesey, "Councils in America," 47. He cites Thomas T. McAvoy, *The Great Crisis in American Catholic History, 1895-1900* (Chicago: Regency, 1957), 33-35.

14. For examination of bishops and blacks, see Stephen J. Ochs, *Desegregating the Altar: The Josephites and the Struggle for Black Priests 1871-1960* (Baton Rouge: Louisiana State University Press, 1990).

15. See Hugh J. Nolan, ed., *Pastoral Letters of the United States Bishops*, vol. 1 (Washington, D.C.: U.S. Catholic Conference, 1983). James Hennesey, S.J., "Councils of Baltimore," *The New Catholic Encyclopedia* (New York: McGraw-Hill, 1967) 2:38-43.

16. Thomas T. McAvoy, *A History of the Catholic Church in the United States* (Notre Dame: University of Notre Dame, 1969), 264, as cited by Hennesey, "Councils in America," 47.

17. William Keeler, "Tracing the Development of a Bishops' Conference," *Origins* 21 (July 18, 1991): 150.

18. Elizabeth McKeown, *War and Welfare: American Catholics and World War I* (New York: Garland Publishing, 1988). Francis T. Hurley, "National Catholic Welfare Conference (NCWC)," *The New Catholic Encyclopedia* 10:225-29.

19. Elizabeth McKeown, "The National Bishops' Conference: An Analysis of its Origins," *Catholic Historical Review* 66 (October 1980), 567.

20. Ibid., 575.

21. "The National Catholic Welfare Council," *National Catholic War Council Bulletin* 2 (September 1920), 2.

22. William Keeler, "Tracing the Development of a Bishops' Conference," *Origins* 21 (July 18, 1991): 151.

23. Elizabeth McKeown, "The National Idea," in *Episcopal Conferences: Historical, Canonical, and Theological Studies*, 67.

24. McKeown, "The National Bishops' Conference: An Analysis of its Origins," 580.

25. John B. Sheerin, C.S.P., *Never Look Back: The Career and Concerns of John J. Burke* (New York: Paulist Press, 1975), 78. Sheerin has a fascinating and detailed description of the American bishops' efforts to reverse the Vatican decision.

26. Elizabeth McKeown, "Apologia for An American Catholicism: The Petition and Report of the National Catholic Welfare Council to Pius XI, April 25, 1922," *Church History* 43 (December 1974): 514-28.

27. McKeown, *War and Welfare*, 185. Sheerin cites a letter from James H. Ryan saying 80 bishops, representing 90 percent of hierarchy, signed the petition. *Never Look Back*, 74.

28. John Dearden, "Universality and Collegiality," *The Ministry of Bishops: Papers from the Collegeville Assembly* (Washington, D.C.: U.S. Catholic Conference, 1982), 10.

29. See Hugh J. Nolan, ed., *Pastoral Letters of the United States Bishops*, vol. 1-2 (Washington, D.C.: U.S. Catholic Conference, 1983).

30. Ibid., 2:41.

31. "Virtually the entire bishops' program of 1919 was eventually enacted into law during Roosevelt's presidency." Timothy A. Byrnes, *Catholic Bishops in American Politics* (Princeton, N.J.: Princeton University Press, 1991), 28.

32. Ibid., 2:111-25.

33. Lawrence J. McAndrews, "A Closer Look: The NCWC and the Elementary and Secondary Education Act," *Records* 102 (Spring 1991): 45-65.

34. This debate, which is still going on, is too complex and extensive for treatment here. See articles by Joseph A. Komonchak, Avery Dulles, S.J., Ladislas Orsy, S.J., Michael A. Fahey, S.J., and James H. Provost in *Episcopal Conferences: Historical, Canonical, and Theological Studies*, ed. Thomas J. Reese, S.J. (Washington, D.C.: Georgetown University Press, 1989).

35. "Decree on the Bishops' Pastoral Office in the Church," in *The Documents of Vatican II*, ed. Walter M. Abbot, S.J., and trans. Joseph Gallagher (New York: America Press, 1966), 425.

36. Ibid., 425-26.

37. Congregation for Bishops, *Directory on the Pastoral Ministry of Bishops* (Ottawa, Ontario: Canadian Catholic Conference, 1974), article 212, p. 113.

38. Ibid.

39. In reorganizing their conference, the bishops were also guided by the August 6, 1966, *motu proprio Ecclesiae sanctae* (I, 41) of Paul VI which implemented *Christus Dominus*.

40. Before the 1983 code, legal specifics on episcopal conferences were given in the 1966 *motu proprio Ecclesiae sanctae* (I, 41).

41. Thomas J. Green, "The Normative Role of Episcopal Conferences in the 1983 Code," in *Episcopal Conferences: Historical, Canonical, and Theological Studies*, ed. Reese, 143.

42. Green, "Normative Role," 139.

43. James A. Coriden, Thomas J. Green, and Donald E. Heintschel, eds., *The Code of Canon Law: A Text and Commentary* (New York: Paulist Press, 1985), 368.

44. Coriden et al., 369.

45. "Review" (*recognitio*) has a technical meaning when applied to general decrees of councils and conferences. It implies a less significant Roman intervention than the papal approval (*approbatio*) required for a program of seminary studies or a conference catechism.

46. Coriden et al., 362.

47. *Complementary Norms: Implementation of the 1983 Code of Canon Law* (Washington, D.C.: USCC, 1991) says that the 1983 code contains 84 canons that call for or permit legislative action by episcopal conferences. The CLSA Commentary lists only 82. See Coriden et al., 370-72. See Appendix D.

48. For a complete list of actions of the NCCB implementing the code, see *Complementary Norms: Implementation of the 1983 Code of Canon Law* (Washington, D.C.: USCC, 1991).

Chapter 3: Shepherding the Shepherds

1. Joseph Bernardin, "The Bishops and Their Conference," *Origins* 20 (July 19, 1990): 147.

2. Archbishop Dearden was elected on the third ballot against Archbishop Krol (121-88).

3. Also on the committee were Cardinal Meyer, Archbishop Alter, Archbishop Krol, Archbishop James Byrne of Dubuque, and Bishop Unterkoefler.

4. Jerry Filteau, "Cardinal Dearden Called 'The Key Figure' in U.S. Church Renewal," NC News, August 3, 1988.

5. NC News, "Cardinal Dearden Dead at 80; Led U.S. Church after Council," August 3, 1988.

6. Ten members of the NCWC Administrative Board were elected annually for one-year terms. After five successive terms, a member had to go off the board for at least one year. The cardinals were ex officio members of the board. Francis T. Hurley, "National Catholic Welfare Conference (NCWC)," *The New Catholic Encyclopedia* (New York: McGraw-Hill, 1967) 10:227.

7. Many of the presidential statements and speeches referred to in this chapter are available in *Origins*, which began publication in May 1971.

8. Hugh J. Nolan, ed., *Pastoral Letters of the United States Bishops* (Washington, D.C.: USCC, 1983) 3:69-297.

9. John Tracy Ellis, ed., *The Catholic Priest in the United States: Historical Investigations* (Collegeville, Minn.: St. John's University Press, 1971); Eugene Kennedy and Victor J. Heckler, *The Catholic Priest in the United States: Psychological Investigations* (Washington, D.C.: USCC, 1972); Andrew M. Greeley, *The Catholic Priest in the United States: Sociological Investigations* (Washington, D.C.: USCC, 1972).

10. Jerry Filteau, "Cardinal Krol Retirement Ends Era of Vatican II Leaders," NC News, December 8, 1987.

11. Archbishop Krol was the only vice president elected by a plurality, 101 of the 205 votes cast. Procedures later adopted by the conference would have required a second or third ballot until he received a majority vote. The other votes went to Archbishop John Cody, 24; Bishop John Wright, 20; Bishop Primeau, 18; Bishop

McNulty, 13; Archbishop McGucken, 9; Archbishop Cousins, 8; Archbishop Binz, 6; Archbishop Hannan, 6.

12. Cardinal Krol was elected on the second ballot with 130 votes. Other bishops on the second ballot included the general secretary, Auxiliary Bishop Joseph Bernardin, with 89, Cardinal Terence Cooke 22, Cardinal John Carberry 4, Archbishop Leo Byrne 4, Archbishop Humberto Medeiros 1.

13. Nolan, *Pastoral Letters* 3:232.

14. Nolan, *Pastoral Letters* 3:298-457.

15. John Krol, "Testimony on Salt II," *Origins* 9 (September 13, 1979): 195-99; "Salt II and the American Bishops," *America* 142 (March 8, 1980): 183-85.

16. For a sympathetic biography, see Eugene Kennedy, *Cardinal Bernardin* (Chicago: Bonus Books, 1989). See also Robert J. McClory, "Bernardin's Chicago adrift in a sea of malaise," *National Catholic Reporter* (February 14, 1992), 6-11.

17. Archbishop Bernardin was elected on the second ballot with 143 votes. Other candidates were Cardinal John Carberry 60, Archbishop Thomas Donnellan 13, Cardinal Terence Cooke 8, Cardinal Timothy Manning 8, Archbishop John Quinn 5, Archbishop William Borders 3, Bishop George Guilfoyle 3, Archbishop John Whealon 2, Archbishop Peter Gerety 0. On the third ballot, Cardinal Carberry defeated Archbishop Borders (133-107) for vice president.

18. Eugene Kennedy, *The Now and Future Church* (Garden City, N.Y.: Doubleday, 1984), 24.

19. Nolan, *Pastoral Letters* 4:39, citing Cardinal Krol.

20. Kennedy, *The Now and Future Church*, 24-25.

21. Kennedy, *The Now and Future Church*, 23-24.

22. Nolan, *Pastoral Letters* 4:44-237.

23. For more on the 1976 election, see Chapter 7. See also Timothy A. Byrnes, "The Bishops and Electoral Politics: A Case Study," in *Church Polity and American Politics: Issues in Contemporary American Catholicism*, ed. Mary C. Segers (New York: Garland Publishing, 1990), 121-41.

24. For more on the Hunthausen crisis, see Thomas J. Reese, *Archbishop: Inside the Power Structure of the American Catholic Church* (San Francisco: Harper & Row, 1989), 337-44.

25. Joseph Bernardin, *The Consistent Ethic of Life* (Sheed & Ward, 1988); "The Consistent Ethic of Life after Webster," *Commonweal* (April 1990).

26. Archbishop Quinn was elected on the third ballot against Archbishop Roach (146-112). Roach was then elected vice president on the second ballot with 168 votes. The next highest candidate was Cardinal Cooke with 55 votes.

27. Nolan, *Pastoral Letters* 4:238-436.

28. Richard P. McBrien came under attack from the Vatican for his two-volume book, *Catholicism* (Minneapolis, Minn.: Winston Press, 1980). As part of a deal to settle the issue, he published a clarification, "The Pastoral Dimensions of Theology Today," *America* 151 (July 28, 1984): 25-28.

29. Archbishop Roach won on the second ballot with 135 votes. The next highest candidate was Bishop Malone with 47, who went on to win the vice presidency on the second ballot with 152 votes. Other candidates for vice president were Archbishop Donnellan 65, Archbishop May 16, Archbishop Whealon 5, Bishop McNicholas 2, Archbishop Bernardin and Cardinal Cooke 1 each.

30. *The Ministry of Bishops: Papers from the Collegeville Assembly* (Washington, D.C.: USCC, 1982).

31. Nolan, *Pastoral Letters* 4:438-5:82.

32. Bishop Malone won on the first ballot with 150 votes. The next highest candidate was Archbishop James Hickey with 25 votes, followed by Archbishop John May and Archbishop John Whealon with 19 each. Archbishop May won the vice presidency on the third ballot against Archbishop Hickey 156-82.

33. Nolan, *Pastoral Letters* 5:83-492.

34. Archbishop May was elected president on the second ballot with 164 votes. The next highest candidate was Cardinal Law with 90 votes, followed by Archbishop Weakland 13, Archbishop Pilarczyk 6, Archbishop Hickey 3, Archbishop Kelly 2, Archbishop Mahony 2. Archbishop Pilarczyk won the vice presidency on the third ballot against Cardinal Law (159-116).

35. Nolan, *Pastoral Letters* 5:492-764.

36. Archbishop Pilarczyk was elected on the first ballot with 186 votes, followed by Archbishop Keeler with 27.

37. Daniel E. Pilarczyk, *Twelve Tough Issues: What the Church Teaches and Why* (St. Anthony Messenger Press, 1988). For his statements while president, see *Origins* 1989-92.

38. "Ad Hoc Committee Report on the Universal Catechism," *Origins* 19 (April 26, 1990): 773-84.

39. Archbishop Keeler was elected vice president on the second ballot with 189 votes, followed by Archbishop Mahony with 47.

40. In 1987 the Bishops' Committee on Ecumenical and Interreligious Affairs published a collection of the pope's writings on the Jews and Judaism. The pope used the occasion of receiving this collection from Archbishop May as an excuse to mention in his thank you letter that he was going to have a major statement on the Holocaust. By doing this in a letter to Archbishop May rather than to a Jewish leader, he responded to Jewish concerns without appearing to give in to pressure. See Bishops' Committee on Ecumenical and Interreligious Affairs, *John Paul II: On Jews and Judaism, 1979-1986* (Washington, D.C.: USCC, 1987).

41. As priests, Cardinals Dearden, Krol, and Carberry, and Archbishops Quinn, Roach, and Pilarczyk were seminary professors or rectors.

42. In the first step of the presidential election, nomination, neither the most senior nor the most junior bishops make the list. Among those nominated, seniority (how long a man has been a bishop) is of little importance for the outcome. Cardinal Krol (1971), Archbishop Leo Byrne (1971), Bishop Malone (1980 and 1983), and Archbishop May (1986) won elections when they were the most senior bishop in the

race. Cardinal Carberry (1974) and Archbishop May (1983) were elected vice president with only one man more senior in the race. On the other hand, Archbishops Bernardin (1974) and Quinn (1977) outpolled six more senior bishops and became president. Archbishop Pilarczyk defeated three more senior bishops for vice president (1986). Archbishop Roach was elected vice president (1977) and president (1980) when he was the least senior bishop nominated.

43. Cardinal Baum in 1977; Cardinal Cooke in 1971, 1974, 1977, and 1980; Cardinal Manning in 1974; Cardinal Law in 1986.

44. In 1967, the entire body acted as a nominating committee to nominate 12 bishops. A total of 146 names appeared on the first ballot. Then the top 12 were voted on until four delegates and two alternates were chosen.

In 1971, each bishop was given a list of the entire membership of NCCB before balloting began. On the first ballot for each election, each bishop was asked to write one name on a plain ballot. If no one received an absolute majority on the first ballot, a second ballot would be provided on which would be listed the names of the ten bishops receiving the highest number of votes in the order in which they ranked by vote. It was understood that voting on the second ballot would not be limited to the ten listed. If no one received an absolute majority on the second ballot, on the third and final ballot there would be a run-off between the two bishops receiving the highest number of votes on the second ballot. If there was a tie on the third ballot, the procedure outlined in canon 101, 1, would be followed.

In 1973 and 1976, the conference selected synod delegates using a procedure similar to its procedure for electing the NCCB president. In 1973 each bishop submitted six names in a "dry run" to serve as possible synod delegates and the top 15 were put on the ballot. Similarly in 1976, a "straw ballot" was taken and the top ten were placed on the ballot with additional write-in candidates permitted. These "straw ballots" or "dry runs" were used as a way of getting around the election procedures in the "*Ordo Synodi*" that were more appropriate for smaller conferences. If no one received a majority in the first or second ballot after the "straw vote," there would be a run-off between the top two candidates.

In 1979, 1981, 1986, and 1989, regional meetings took place to nominate delegates. The bishop nominated need not have been from the region, but he usually was. Other candidates could be put forward by a nominator with five "seconds."

45. All dates refer to the date of the election, not the synod.

46. These statistics do not include synod alternates. Midwest here includes Illinois, Missouri, Michigan, Ohio, Minnesota, and Wisconsin.

47. Three out of four delegates elected in 1971 and 1973 were cardinals. Half were cardinals in 1967, 1976, and 1989; one in 1986; and none in 1979 and 1981.

48. NC News, "U.S. Synod Delegates Elected," April 29, 1971.

49. Daniel Pilarczyk, "The Changing Image of the Priest," *Origins* 16 (July 3, 1986): 137-46.

50. Cardinal Law ended up attending the synod as a papal appointee, where he called for the establishment of a compendium of faith and morals or catechism for the universal church.

Chapter 4: The Shepherds' Staff

1. *Catholic Eye*, November 10, 1986.

2. Electing the general secretary by the entire assembly for a five-year term will strengthen his power. Through the election he has a mandate equal to that of the NCCB/USCC president or committee chairs. Nor are there any procedures for removing him from office before the expiration of his term. If the proposers were intending to weaken the general secretary, their change accomplished exactly the opposite.

3. A committee of bishops examined the charges of unorthodoxy against Father Buckley and gave him a clean bill of health. They noted that the letter he signed did not support the ordination of women but merely said that the theological arguments given in the Vatican document were not persuasive.

4. Elizabeth McKeown, *War and Welfare: American Catholics and World War I* (New York: Garland Publishing, 1988); John B. Sheerin, C.S.P., *Never Look Back: The Career and Concerns of John J. Burke* (New York: Paulist Press, 1975).

5. Sheerin, *Never Look Back*, 85.

6. Sheerin, *Never Look Back*, 89-90.

7. Sheerin, *Never Look Back*, 72.

8. Many of the statements and speeches by the general secretaries referred to in this chapter are available in *Origins*, which began publication in May 1971.

9. These statements are all printed in *Origins* 1973-77.

10. NC News, "Bishop Rausch, Former NCCB General Secretary Dies," May 18, 1981.

11. A. J. Matt, Jr., "The Rausch Double Standard," *Wanderer*, October 14, 1976.

12. *Catholic Eye*, November 10, 1986. After leaving the conference, Father Buckley taught theology at the University of Notre Dame and was elected president of the Catholic Theological Society of America.

13. For more on the 1976 election, see Chapter 7. Also see Timothy A. Byrnes, "The Bishops and Electoral Politics: A Case Study," in *Church Polity and American Politics: Issues in Contemporary American Catholicism*, ed. Mary C. Segers (New York: Garland Publishing, 1990), 121-41.

14. Kenneth A. Briggs, "James S. Rausch, 52, Bishop of Phoenix," *New York Times*, May 19, 1981.

15. These statements appear in *Origins* 1977-81.

16. These statements appear in *Origins* 1982-89.

17. The second general secretary, Michael J. Ready (1936-44), was made bishop of Columbus, Ohio, in 1944. The third, Howard J. Carroll (1945-57), became bishop

of Altoona-Johnstown, Penn. The fourth, Paul F. Tanner (1958-68), was made a bishop while general secretary in 1965. In 1968 he became bishop of St. Augustine, Fla. Bernardin was already a bishop when appointed general secretary. Rausch and Kelly were also made bishops while general secretary.

18. See Robert N. Lynch, "The National Committee for a Human Life Amendment, Inc.: Its Goals and Origins," *Catholic Lawyer* 20 (Winter 1974): 303-308.

19. These statements appear in *Origins* 1989-91.

20. I use the generic term "office" to refer to entities under the NCCB and USCC associate general secretaries. The terms used in NCCB/USCC have varied over time and are currently confusing. Thus the main divisions under the USCC are called departments (education, communications, and social development and world peace) and are headed by secretaries while the NCCB has secretariats headed by directors.

21. J. Brian Benestad, *The Pursuit of a Just Social Order* (Washington, D.C.: Ethics and Public Policy Center, 1982), 98.

22. Mr. Quigley dealt with Latin American issues and was heavily criticized by conservative Catholics. A Mr. Cyril Quigly appeared as "a mysterious, less-than-endearing Englishman" and spy in *The Captain and the Enemy*, a novel by Graham Greene, situated in Panama (Viking, 1988). See Mr. Quigley's review of the book in the *National Catholic Reporter*, December 9, 1988.

23. "CAP-92 Supplemental Questionnaire," Booklet #3, June 13-15, 1991, p. 1.

24. "Conference Assessment Project Questionnaire," Booklet #2, June 13-15, 1991, pp. 152-55. A differently phrased question asking the bishops to rank the top ten offices produced a very similarly ranked list of offices: general secretary, general counsel, liturgy, pro-life, education, priestly life and ministry, Catholic News Service, social development and world peace, doctrine and pastoral practices, vocations and priestly formation, government liaison, laity and family life, Hispanic affairs, evangelization, ecumenism, black Catholics, communications, migration and refugee services, publishing and promotion services, media relations, missions, research, communications policy, Campaign for Human Development, American Board of Catholic Missions (collection), film and broadcasting, permanent diaconate, science and human values, Latin American secretariat (collection), and communications campaign (collection).

Chapter 5: Shepherds in Committees

1. *Membership Directory: National Conference of Catholic Bishops, United States Catholic Conference* (Washington, D.C.: USCC, April 1991).

2. According to Archbishop Keeler, the committees were established: in 1884 the Committee for the American College at Louvain, the Committee for the North American College in Rome, the American Board of Catholic Missions; in 1940 the Bishops' Welfare Emergency and Relief Committee; in 1943 the War Relief Services which became Catholic Relief Services; in 1958 the Commission on the Liturgical Apostolate, which became the Committee on the Liturgy; in 1964 the Ecumenical

and Interreligious Affairs Committee, the Religious Life and Ministry Committee; in 1966 committees for Canonical Affairs, Doctrine, Priestly Formation, Missions, and Selection of Bishops; in 1967 the Pastoral Research and Practices Committee; in 1968 the Committee on Vocations and the Committee on Permanent Diaconate; in 1969 the Committee on Priestly Life and Ministry; in 1970 the Committee on the Laity; in 1971 the Committee on Migration and Committee on Women in Society and the Church; in 1972 the Committee on Hispanic Affairs and the Committee on Pro-Life Affairs; in 1973 the Committee on Science and Human Values; in 1975 the Committee on Marriage and Family Life; in 1976 the Committee on Evangelization; in 1986 the Committee on Black Catholics. See William Keeler, "Tracing the Development of a Bishops' Conference," *Origins* 21 (July 18, 1991): 151.

3. The membership of the Bishops' Welfare and Emergency Relief Committee is the same as the Administrative Committee/Board. The BWER Committee does not meet separately since the Administrative Committee/Board deals with the BWER fund as part of the NCCB/USCC budget.

4. The conference also has an ad hoc Liaison Committee with Catholic New Service, whose function is to review complaints from bishops about CNS.

5. Some bishops disliked these studies, especially *Reflections on Priestly Morale* (Washington, D.C.: USCC, 1988). In June 1989 the conference adopted the policy that any publication about priests had to be reviewed by the assembly.

6. "Conference Assessment Project Questionnaire," Booklet #4, June 13-14, 1991, p. 96.

7. There is evidence supporting the complaint of the southern bishops. For the years 1968-91, Region 5 (from Kentucky to New Orleans) has 6.8 percent of the bishops but its bishops were nominated for chairs only 5.1 percent of the time and were elected only 5.2 percent of the time. Doing even worse was Region 1 (New England) with 9 percent of the bishops and only 6 percent of the nominations and 5.2 percent of the elections. Region 12 (Northwest) also had fewer chairs than bishops (2.8 percent versus 4.8 percent).

Region 9 (Nebraska, Iowa, Kansas, and Missouri) did well in nominations, with 10 percent of the nominees for 7 percent of the bishops. But it translated these nominations into only 7.1 percent of the chairs. Region 10 (Texas, Oklahoma, and Arkansas) did well with 6.5 percent of the bishops getting 7.4 percent of the nominations and winning 8.5 percent of the elections. Likewise Region 4 (from Maryland to Florida), with 11.5 percent of the bishops, got 12.3 percent of the nominations and 13.3 percent of the chairs.

Getting nominated is the important thing. Only Region 7 (Wisconsin, Illinois, and Indiana) had a lower percentage of nominees (10 percent) than of bishops (10.5 percent) and still ended up with a higher percentage of the committee chairs (11.8 percent).

Nominees from most states have a 50-50 chance of getting elected once they are nominated, but some states consistently win or lose. The District of Columbia won five out of five times from 1968 through 1991. Kansas, on the other hand, lost six for six. Illinois won 13 out of 18 races while Minnesota lost 14 out of 19. Texas and

Ohio have also done well, each winning 16 out of 26. But these are the exceptions, with most states coming close to breaking even.

8. In 115 chair elections from 1968-91 when bishops of different rank were nominated, 69 percent of the winners were of higher rank. On the other hand, seniority does not appear to have any effect on the elections. Half the time the man who has been the bishop longest wins, and half the time he does not.

9. Auxiliary bishops who won seats on USCC committees against higher-ranking bishops and later became archbishops include: Flores (1972), McCarrick (1979 and 1980), Schulte (1983), and Lyke (1987).

10. Electing members to USCC committees has its historical roots in the NCWC. The NCWC Administrative Board was composed of ten elected members: the chair, vice chair, treasurer, and episcopal chairs of the seven departments of the NCWC. These ten members "with portfolios" selected 20 other bishops to serve as assistants and advisors for different areas of concern. These were designated "without portfolio" because they served under the 10 elected members and had no right to vote at board meetings.

In the 1966 reorganization, the number of bishops without portfolios was raised to 30 and they became elected by the assembly. From the 30 members "without portfolio," 20 were chosen by the bishops "with portfolio" to become assistant and advisor bishops to the various departments of the secretariat. In 1969 "assistants" were replaced by two members directly elected to the USCC committees by all the bishops. In 1988 the bylaws were amended to reduce the number of elected members to one for each USCC committee.

11. Bishops Cummins (1974 and 1975), Pilarczyk (1975), Marino (1976), Stafford (1977), DuMaine (1979), McCarrick (1979 and 1980), Bosco (1982), Schulte (1983), and E. O'Donnell (1984) won seats on USCC committees as auxiliary bishops and later went on to be elected chairs.

12. The following cardinals defeated lower-ranking prelates in chair elections: Cardinal Timothy Manning for the Committee on Missions in 1974; Cardinal Baum for the Committee on Doctrine in 1976; Cardinal Bernardin for the Committee on Pro-Life Activities in 1986 and the Committee on Marriage and Family Life in 1990; Cardinal Law for the Committee on Migration in 1989; Cardinal O'Connor for the Committee on Pro-Life Activities in 1989; Cardinal Bevilacqua for Canonical Affairs in 1991. In a move that bypassed the procedures of the bylaws, the bishops elected Cardinal Hickey chair of the Committee on the North American College "by acclamation" with no other candidate in 1988.

13. The only prelates reelected to the same position are: William G. Connare for Missions (1969 and 1977), Thomas A. Donnellan as treasurer (1972 and 1978), William E. McManus for Education (1969 and 1975), John J. Maguire as treasurer (1969 and 1975), Roger Mahony for Arbitration (1976 and 1982), John Quinn for Pastoral Research and Practices (1971 and 1986), Ernest Unterkoefler for Permanent Diaconate (1968, 1969, and 1974), and Anthony Bevilacqua for Canonical Affairs (1981 and 1991).

14. Bishops who have been elected to two chairs: Archbishop Thomas A. Donnellan, Liaison with Religious Men and treasurer (twice); Bishop Mark Hurley for Human Values, and Social Development and World Peace; Archbishop Thomas Kelly for secretary and Religious Life and Ministry; Archbishop Oscar Lipscomb for North American College and Doctrine; Archbishop Daniel Kucera for Liaison with LCWR and treasurer; Bishop Raymond Lessard for Pastoral Research and Practices and Doctrine; Archbishop Roger Mahony for Arbitration (twice) and Social Development and World Peace (International); Archbishop Eugene Marino for Diaconate and secretary; Archbishop John May for Communications and Liaison with CMSM; Cardinal John O'Connor for Social Development and World Peace and Pro-Life Activities; Archbishop Daniel Pilarczyk for Education and Liturgy; Archbishop Robert F. Sanchez for American Board of Catholic Missions and secretary; Ernest Unterkoefler for Permanent Diaconate (three times) and Ecumenical and Interreligious Affairs; Archbishop Rembert Weakland for Liturgy and Ecumenical and Interreligious Affairs.

15. Standing committees that were first ad hoc committees include: Campaign for Human Development Committee, Vocations Committee, Committee on Laity, Committee on Priestly Life and Ministry, Committee on Science and Human Values, Committee on Pro-Life Activities, Committee on Marriage and Family Life, and Committee on Women in Society and in the Church.

16. Jim Castelli, *The Bishops and the Bomb* (New York: Image, 1983), 68.

17. *Membership Directory: National Conference of Catholic Bishops, United States Catholic Conference* (Washington, D.C.: USCC, April 1991).

18. "Appendix II: Questions to be Considered in Drafting NCCB/USCC Statements," in *Minutes of the 13th General Meeting of the National Conference of Catholic Bishops,* November 12-16, 1973, p. 100. Also in *National Conference of Catholic Bishops United States Catholic Conference Handbook* (Washington, D.C.: USCC, February 1989), 61. To improve readability, this quotation was broken into three paragraphs.

19. See William E. McManus, "To Teach as Jesus Did: A Chronicle," *Living Light* 10 (1973): 282. For consultation on another education document, see Charles C. McDonald, "The Background and Development of 'The Basic Teachings' Document," *Living Light* 10 (1973): 264-77.

20. See Berard L. Marthaler, *An Official Commentary on Sharing the Light of Faith* (Washington, D.C.: U.S. Catholic Conference, 1981), 4-7. Mary Charles Bryce, OSB, *Pride of Place: The Role of the Bishops in the Development of Catechesis in the United States* (Washington, D.C.: Catholic University Press, 1984), 147-53.

21. Raymond Lucker, "The Bishops and the Catechism," in *The Universal Catechism Reader,* ed. Thomas J. Reese, S.J. (San Francisco: HarperCollins, 1990).

22. For a description of the consultation on the peace pastoral, see Jim Castelli, *The Bishops and the Bomb* (New York: Image, 1983).

23. Thomas J. Reese, *Archbishop: Inside the Power Structure of the American Catholic Church* (San Francisco: Harper & Row, 1989), 120-23.

24. The selection process for the NCCB Administrative Committee and the USCC Administrative Board has varied over time. The selection process described in the text is that in the bylaws approved June 25, 1989 (and amended in November 1991).

Originally, as reorganized in November 1966, the Administrative Committee/Board members included all the cardinals plus the elected president, vice president, eight bishops with portfolios (treasurer and seven "department" chairs), and 30 bishops without portfolios. "Committee" chairs were not automatically members.

In April 1969, the bishops approved a motion by Cardinal James McIntyre to drop cardinals as ex officio members of the Administrative Committee. The NCCB Administrative Committee would be composed of 40 members: the immediate past president, conference officers (president, vice president, treasurer, and secretary), standing NCCB committee chairs, USCC department chairs, and at-large members. The USCC Administrative Board would be composed of 25 members: the immediate past president, conference officers, chairs and two elected members of USCC department chairs, and at-large members. All these bishops were elected by all the bishops.

In 1972, the bylaws were changed to have one representative elected by and from the members of each NCCB geographical region (then 12) rather than at-large members elected by the general membership.

In 1975, the membership of the USCC Administrative Board was made the same as that for the NCCB Administrative Committee: the former president, conference officers, chairs of NCCB standing committees, chairs and two elected members of USCC committees, and one representative from each NCCB region.

In 1979, the chair of the Board of Directors of Catholic Relief Services was added. Beginning in 1979, the members of the CRS board were elected by the USCC. Until that time it had been a self-perpetuating board.

In 1988, the number of elected members from each USCC committee was reduced to one.

In 1991, the chair of the board of CTNA was added to the Administrative Committee/Board. Members of the CTNA board have been elected by the USCC since 1989.

25. "CAP-92 Supplemental Questionnaire," Booklet #3, June 13-15, 1991, p. 1.

26. *Reflections on Priestly Morale* (Washington, D.C.: USCC, 1988).

27. In a few instances, the Administrative Committee has acted on canonical issues for the conference. In 1983, after the revision of the code of canon law, the Administrative Committee voted to continue most of the norms previously established by the conference on marriage, fast and abstinence. It also approved the establishment of courts of second instance. In 1985 it slightly modified norms on the daily recitation of morning and evening prayer by deacons. *Complementary Norms: Implementation of the 1983 Code of Canon Law* (Washington, D.C.: USCC, 1991), 4, 16-17, 19, 27. For text of Administrative Committee/Board statements, see *Origins*.

28. "CAP-92 Supplemental Questionnaire," Booklet 3, June 13-15, 1991, p. 1.

29. Since the Administrative Committee/Board minutes were not made available to me, I cannot give a detailed description of what occurs during the meetings. Some of the minutes were made available to the Rev. Walter J. Woods. See Walter J. Woods, "Pastoral Care, Moral Issues, Basic Approaches: The National Pastoral Texts of the American Bishops from the Perspective of Fundamental Moral Theology," (S.T.D. diss., Gregorian University, 1979).

30. Although the NAC is authorized to have 63 members, because of budget constraints the actual number is less. In April 1991 there were 51 members: four bishops, six diocesan priests, three religious men, two religious women, 26 lay regional representatives, and ten at-large members (one bishop, three priests, one religious women, and five lay persons).

31. Mary P. Burke and Eugene Hemrick, *Building the Local Church* (Washington, D.C.: USCC, September 1984).

32. Conference Assessment Project Questionnaire," Booklet #2, June 13-15, 1991, p. 8.

33. William E. McManus, "Did the Bishops Crunch the Budget, or Vice-Versa?" *America* 165 (September 21, 1991): 156-57.

34. *A National Pastoral Council: Pro and Con* (Washington, D.C.: USCC, 1971).

35. One archbishop believes that Dearden hoped that the USCC, which has lay people on its committees, would eventually allow lay people into the assembly. Thus the USCC would evolve into a national pastoral council while the NCCB would be the episcopal conference.

36. Membership of the Administrative Committee and the Administrative Board was the same except for the period from November 1969 to February 1975. For this period, the table includes membership on either committee.

Chapter 6: A United or Divided Flock

1. John Dearden, "Universality and Collegiality," *The Ministry of Bishops: Papers from the Collegeville Assembly* (Washington, D.C.: U.S. Catholic Conference, 1982), 12.

2. For an earlier version of this section, see Thomas J. Reese, S.J., "Conflict and Consensus in the NCCB/USCC" in *Episcopal Conferences: Historical, Canonical, and Theological Studies*, ed. Thomas J. Reese, S.J., (Washington, D.C.: Georgetown University Press, 1989), 107-136.

3. I use here the translation by Rev. Joseph Komonchak. The Vatican translation reads: "possibly, the indication of an aim to pursue a morally unanimous consensus, without however making this a juridical norm, which would be too paralyzing. . . ." See "Theological and Juridical Status of Episcopal Conferences" (Vatican City: Congregation for Bishops, July 1, 1987, photocopy), 20. Also see Congregation for Bishops, "Draft Statement on Episcopal Conferences," *Origins* 17 (April 7, 1988): 736.

4. *The Code of Canon Law: Latin-English Edition* (Washington, D.C.: Canon Law Society of America, 1983), Canon 119, 1º.

5. Ellsworth Kneal, "Title VI: Physical and Juridic Persons," in James A. Coriden, Thomas J. Green and Donald E. Heintschel, eds., *The Code of Canon Law: A Text and Commentary* (New York: Paulist Press, 1985), 84.

6. Canon 119, 2º.

7. Canon 455 §2. What is required is a two-thirds vote of the de jure members, which in the NCCB include active diocesan bishops and auxiliaries, but not retired bishops. American bishops working outside the United States are not members of the conference, except for the bishop of the Virgin Islands.

8. General decrees are laws properly speaking (general decrees) or determinations of how to observe laws (general executory decrees). See canons 29 and 31.

9. In 1968, the regulations said a joint pastoral letter or statement "shall be adopted only by a two-thirds vote." See *Minutes of the Fourth General Meeting of the National Conference of Catholic Bishops,* April 23-25, 1968, pp. 50-56.

Revised versions of these regulations were approved in November 1971 and November 1981. The 1971 version reads: joint pastorals and formal statements "must be approved by two-thirds of the Conference membership. If this becomes impractical owing to limited attendance at the general meeting, the Conference President may rule that two-thirds approval of all de jure members is sufficient." See *Minutes of the Eleventh General Meeting of the National Conference of Catholic Bishops,* November 15-19, 1971, p. 81.

Because the Holy See objected to the American custom of allowing retired bishops to vote, the statutes and bylaws were revised. The 1981 version of the regulations read: joint pastorals and formal statements of the NCCB "require the approval of two-thirds of the membership," but formal statements of the USCC "require the votes of two-thirds of the members present and voting for approval." *Handbook: National Conference of Catholic Bishops, United States Catholic Conference* (Washington, D.C.: USCC, March 1982), 57-58.

10. "Revised Regulations Regarding NCCB/USCC Statements," in *Minutes of the Eleventh General Meeting of the National Conference of Catholic Bishops,* November 15-19, 1971, pp. 80-85. Also see, "Appendix: Revised Regulations Regarding NCCB/USCC Statements," in *National Conference of Catholic Bishops: Statutes and Bylaws* (Washington, D.C.: USCC, July 1976), 41-48.

11. "National Conference of Catholic Bishops, Monday, November 16, [1981], Morning Session, First Part" (USCC Press Release, Washington, D.C., November 16, 1981, photocopy), 6.

12. "Revised Regulations Regarding NCCB/USCC Statements," in *Minutes of the 11th General Meeting of the National Conference of Catholic Bishops,* November 15-19, 1971, pp. 81. Also see, "Appendix: Revised Regulations Regarding NCCB/USCC Statements" in *National Conference of Catholic Bishops: Statutes and Bylaws* (Washington, D.C.: USCC, July 1976), 43; and "Regulations Regarding NCCB/USCC Statements," in *National Conference of Catholic Bishops/United States Catholic Conference Handbook* (Washington, D.C.: USCC, February 1989), 47-63.

13. Ibid. This rule was not applied to the 1988 "Policy Statement on Employer Sanctions" (see *Agenda Report Documentation, Action Items 2-19*, November 1988, p. 331). Since it passed overwhelmingly, there is no question of its validity.

14. Likewise, an 80-page "report" (June 1988) on the "Challenge of Peace" needed only a majority vote, although it would provide a basis for conference policy.

15. Walter J. Woods, "Pastoral Care, Moral Issues, Basic Approaches: The National Pastoral Texts of the American Bishops from the Perspective of Fundamental Moral Theology," (S.T.D. diss., Gregorian University, 1979), 222 n.24.

16. Ibid., 225.

17. *Minutes of the Fourth General Meeting of the National Conference of Catholic Bishops*, April 23-25, 1968, p. 51.

18. See William E. McManus, "To Teach as Jesus Did: A Chronicle," *Living Light* 10 (1973): 278-83.

19. For purposes of this study, I define pastoral letters and statements as those printed in Hugh J. Nolan, ed., *Pastoral Letters of the United States Bishops*, vol. 3-5 (Washington, D.C.: U.S. Catholic Conference, 1983, 1989). Volumes 1 and 2 contain statements of the American bishops before the creation of the NCCB/USCC in 1966.

20. Ibid. Volumes 3-5 contain 191 NCCB/USCC statements since 1966, but only 121 were passed by the full assembly. The others were by NCCB/USCC officers or committees.

Of the 121 approved by the full assembly, the final vote on five is unrecorded: "The Church in Our Day" (November 1967), "Declaration on Conscientious Objection and Selective Conscientious Objection" (1971), "Basic Teachings for Catholic Religious Education" (1973), "Behold Your Mother" (1973), and "Catholic Higher Education and the Pastoral Mission of the Church" (1980). The 1973 statements were approved on a mail ballot and received at least a two-thirds vote.

Father Nolan says that the 1971 "Declaration on Conscientious Objection and Selective Conscientious Objection" was by the USCC Division of World Justice and Peace (vol. 3, pp. 61 and 228). Father Woods, who examined the minutes of the Administrative Committee/Board, indicates that the declaration was approved by a two-thirds vote in a mail ballot. See Woods, "Pastoral Care," 291. I therefore count it as an assembly statement.

21. The official minutes of the NCCB/USCC assemblies from November 1966 through November 1988 were examined, except those held in executive (closed) session beginning in 1972, when most meetings became open to the press. Also examined were the press releases issued by the USCC press office that summarized the meetings.

22. See note 20 above.

23. Not included in volume 5 of *Pastoral Letters* is the November 16, 1988, conference response to the Vatican draft on episcopal conferences which passed 205-59.

Since the publication of volume 5, the conference has continued to act on pastoral letters and statements. In 1989 the conference approved documents on doctrinal responsibilities, Vietnam, priests' retreats, abortion, the black Catholic pastoral plan, Middle East, HIV/AIDS, and food and agriculture. These were approved by unanimous or nearly unanimous votes.

In 1990 the conference passed a pastoral letter on evangelization in America, a statement in support of Catholic schools, a pastoral message on substance abuse, a pastoral message on the 100th anniversary of *Rerum Novarum*, a resolution reaffirming the pastoral plan for family ministry, and a document on the promotion of the spirituality of priests. Of these, the statement on schools received the most negative votes: ten. In 1990 the conference also approved guidelines for doctrinally sound textbooks, guidelines for teaching about human sexuality, criteria for inclusive language in the lectionary, and principles for translating Scripture for the lectionary. The issue of inclusive language proved the most controversial, passing by a vote of 183-35. The others passed on voice votes.

In 1991 the conference adopted statements on children (221-4), Native American concerns (165-5), and the environment (voice). Also adopted by voice vote were two "reflections" on the teaching ministry of bishops and on presbyteral councils.

24. "That the USCC goes on record in opposition to capital punishment." See "Thursday - P.M. Session, NCCB/USCC Annual Meeting, November 21, 1974" (USCC Press Release, Washington, D.C., November 21, 1974, Mimeographed), 1 and 4.

25. The resolution may not have even received a majority vote of those "present" since at one point at least 236 bishops were attending the meeting. On November 19, 1974, 236 bishops voted on whether there should be province consultations on the issue of general absolution. The capital punishment motion was approved on November 21, 1974, the second to the last day of the meeting with only 108 yes votes, less than half of 236.

26. Having a resolution on abortion in April 1967 was tabled. A statement on conscientious objection was tabled in November 1970.

27. "Thursday - P.M. Session, NCCB/USCC Annual Meeting, November 21, 1974" (USCC Press Release, Washington, D.C., November 21, 1974, Photocopy), 1.

28. The general secretary, Bishop Thomas Kelly, O.P., announced that in computations "we don't count abstentions, and so the document has a 2/3 vote and is accepted as a conference statement." See "NCCB/USCC General Meeting, A.M. Session, Thursday, November 13 [1980]" (USCC Press Release, Washington, D.C., November 13, 1980), 7.

Bishop Kelly appears to have miscalculated and believed that the motion did not receive a two-thirds vote of those handing in ballots. The statement just barely received two-thirds approval from those voting or abstaining: 145/217 = 66.8 percent. As will be seen below, his interpretation of the rules appears to have also been inaccurate.

29. "Revised Regulations Regarding NCCB/USCC Statements," in *Minutes of the 11th General Meeting of the National Conference of Catholic Bishops*, November 15-19, 1971, p. 81. Also see, "Appendix: Revised Regulations Regarding NCCB/USCC

Statements," in *National Conference of Catholic Bishops: Statutes and Bylaws* (Washington, D.C.: USCC, July 1976), 43. The regulations were changed in November 1981 so that a formal statement by the USCC could be approved by a two-thirds vote of those present and voting. See "Regulations Regarding NCCB/USCC Statements," in *National Conference of Catholic Bishops/United States Catholic Conference Handbook* (Washington, D.C.: USCC, February 1989), 47-63.

The statement on capital punishment was voted on the last day of the meeting, November 13, 1980. If this 3,000-word document is considered a "formal statement," it required a two-thirds approval of the entire membership, not two-thirds of those casting votes.

If the document is simply a "resolution or brief statement," then it only required a two-thirds approval of those "present and attending the general meeting." If only those voting or casting abstentions are considered "present," then as a "brief statement" the document squeaked by.

If there were others "present" who did not cast ballots, the motion would have required more yes votes. On an earlier vote (November 12, 1980), 37 more bishops (254) voted on the "Pastoral Letter on Marxist Communism." If even one of them was still "present and attending the general meeting" but did not hand in a ballot, then the statement did not receive a two-thirds vote of those "present."

It is difficult to believe that the "Statement on Capital Punishment" can be considered a "brief statement." Woods notes that "resolutions and other brief statements . . . are generally regarded as less momentous than the other three categories [joint pastorals, formal statements, and special messages]." Woods, "Pastoral Care," 224.

30. *Minutes Annual Meeting, National Conference of Catholic Bishops,* November 14-18, 1966, p. 208.

31. Only one archbishop during the debate said that one should not rule out the possibility of change or the ordination of mature, stable married men. The chair of the drafting committee answered that in his opinion the statement did not preclude such a possibility. See Minutes of the *Seventh General Meeting of the National Conference of Catholic Bishops,* November 10-14, 1969, p. 53.

32. Nolan, *Pastoral Letters* 4:26.

33. Later in the meeting, after many bishops had left, the assembly declared the existence of a quorum (despite visual evidence to the contrary) and then approved their statement on population control.

34. On five of the 121 statements, the votes are unrecorded (see note 20 above). Of the 116 statements for which we have a record, 103 passed with fewer than 20 negative votes: 103/116 = 89 percent.

35. Other than the official minutes and the USCC press releases, there are few sources of information on the legislative history of the statements issued by the NCCB/USCC. Father Nolan has an introduction to each collection of statements in *Pastoral Letters.* Another excellent source is Walter J. Woods, "Pastoral Care, Moral Issues, Basic Approaches: The National Pastoral Texts of the American Bishops from

the Perspective of Fundamental Moral Theology" (S.T.D. diss., Gregorian University, 1979). Finally, there are the news stories by the Catholic News Service (formerly NC News).

36. For an excellent analysis of conciliar procedures and consensus building, see Richard T. Lawrence, "The Building of Consensus: The Conciliar Rules of Procedure and the Evolution of *Dei Verbum*," *Jurist* 46 (1986): 474-510.

37. Woods, "Pastoral Care," 338. The official minutes are almost totally silent about the 1967 pastoral letter "Church in Our Day," which Cardinal Krol and Father Nolan call the bishops' "first purely doctrinal pastoral." Nolan, *Pastoral Letters* 3:1 and 54. "Behold Your Mother" (1973) is also referred to by Nolan as "one of their rare, completely doctrinal statements." Nolan, *Pastoral Letters* 3:243.

38. From the minutes it is unclear what was the position of the Farm Labor Committee, which drafted the statement, on this amendment. It appears that the committee supported the boycott and was overturned by the assembly. If so, this is the first indication of a committee being overruled by an assembly vote.

39. See William E. McManus, "To Teach as Jesus Did: A Chronicle," *Living Light* 10 (1973): 278-83.

40. The conference has adopted five "Special Rules of Order Relating to Debate." See *National Conference of Catholic Bishops/United States Catholic Conference Handbook* (Washington, D.C.: USCC, February 1989), 45-46. Rule one deals with recognizing bishops to speak in the order in which they raise their hands. Rule two allows the chair, at his discretion, to terminate debate subject to appeal, which requires a two-thirds vote to sustain the chair. Rule three limits each speaker to ten minutes unless the speaker has permission of the assembly (in 1991 this was changed to five minutes). Rule four applies these rules to both the NCCB and the USCC. Rule five allows the grouping of amendments for consideration in one vote.

41. The committee's position on amendments was unclear in the minutes for better than half the amendments. When the minutes and press releases are silent, it probably can be presumed that the committee did not object to the amendment.

42. Of the 61 amendments offered, the minutes indicated the position of the task force on 37. In every case but one, the assembly followed the task force's recommendation in approving or rejecting the amendments. Archbishop Peter L. Gerety's amendment to have an ad hoc committee to respond to the recommendations passed over the objections of the task force.

43. Thomas J. Reese, "Archbishops Go to Rome," *America* 160 (March 4, 1989): 187-88; "Discussions in Rome," *America* 160 (March 25, 1989): 260-61.

44. *Sharing the Light of Faith: The National Catechetical Directory for Catholics of the United States* (Washington, D.C.: U.S. Catholic Conference, 1977). Although not a pastoral letter or statement, the "National Catechetical Directory" is treated here because of its impact on procedures dealing with future letters and statements. For a history of the directory, see Berard L. Marthaler, *An Official Commentary on Sharing the Light of Faith* (Washington, D.C.: USCC, 1981), 4-7.

45. Interestingly, although the "Statement on the Handicapped" was noncontroversial, whether the bishops should spend money to have a national office for the handicapped was.

46. See Jim Castelli, *The Bishops and the Bomb* (Garden City, N.Y.: Doubleday, 1983).

47. On each amendment, unless the president ruled otherwise, the ad hoc committee chair, Cardinal Bernardin, was given half a minute to give the committee's recommendation. The mover of the amendment was given two minutes. Four additional speakers, two on each side, were limited to two minutes each.

48. "Not only the use of strategic nuclear weapons, but also the declared intent to use them involved in our deterrence policy, are both wrong." John Krol, "Testimony on Salt II," *Origins* 9 (September 13, 1979): 197; "Salt II and the American Bishops," *America* 142 (March 8, 1980): 183-85.

49. Nolan, *Pastoral Letters* 4:170.

50. Frederick R. McManus, ed., *Thirty Years of Liturgical Renewal: Statements of the Bishops' Committee on the Liturgy* (Washington, D.C.: U.S. Catholic Conference, 1987).

51. ICEL has 11 episcopal conferences that are full members and 15 conferences, mostly in Africa and Asia, that are associate members.

52. The Vatican did not approve the assembly's recommendation.

53. McManus, *Thirty Years*, 64.

54. For a complete list of actions of the NCCB implementing the code, see *Complementary Norms: Implementation of the 1983 Code of Canon Law* (Washington, D.C.: USCC, 1991). According to this pamphlet, the NCCB has acted on 23 of the 84 canons that call for or permit legislative action by episcopal conferences.

55. The conference also has a Committee on Pastoral Research and Practices which originally included as members the chairs of Liturgy, Canonical Affairs, and Doctrine. The idea was to have a super committee that could deal with issues of concern to more than one committee. The chairs, however, complained that they had too much work in their own committees and did not want to sit on another committee. The Committee on Pastoral Research and Practices has been given a number of issues by the president, but often it appears to depend on the president's confidence in the chair rather than on any strict jurisdictional grounds.

Pastoral Research and Practices, for example, dealt with mixed marriages in 1970, general absolution in 1974 and the age of confirmation in 1972 and 1984. The last two issues have been hotly debated in the conference and have been areas of controversy with Rome (see Chapter 8). In 1990 a proposal to have Pastoral Research and Practices responsible for granting imprimaturs to Scripture translations was sent back to committee when the chair of the Committee on Canonical Affairs complained they were not consulted. In the meantime, the Administrative Committee was given authority to grant imprimaturs.

56. Thomas J. Reese, "Bishops and Theologians," *America* 161 (July 8, 1989): 4-6.

57. See *Complementary Norms*.

58. National Conference of Catholic Bishops, "Response to the Vatican Working Paper on Bishops' Conferences," *Origins* 18 (December 1, 1988): 397-402. For an analysis of the issues, see Thomas J. Reese, S.J., ed., *Episcopal Conferences: Historical, Canonical, and Theological Studies* (Washington, D.C.: Georgetown University Press, 1989). Also see Thomas J. Reese, "Communication and Confrontation: A Report on the U.S. Bishops' Meeting," *America* 159 (December 3, 1988): 451-3.

59. Joseph Bernardin, "The Bishops and Their Conference," *Origins* 20 (July 19, 1990): 147.

60. I was denied access to the minutes of executive sessions, so what follows is based on information gathered through interviews and press reports.

61. All of the documents since 1972 in Hugh J. Nolan, ed., *Pastoral Letters of the United States Bishops*, vol. 3-5, were adopted in open session.

62. USCC Administrative Board, "Statement on Sterilization Procedures in Catholic Hospitals," *Origins* 7 (November 22, 1977): 399. "Statement on Tubal Ligation" (July 3, 1980), *Pastoral Letters* 4:379.

63. *Human Sexuality* (New York: Paulist Press, 1977) was written by a committee of the Catholic Theological Society of America but never endorsed by the full society.

64. Mark Chopko, "USCC Pedophilia Statement," *Origins* 17 (February 18, 1988): 624.

65. In 1989, the Religion News Writers Association selected the NCCB/USCC as first winner of the "Into the Darkness Award" for meeting in executive session for an afternoon during their November meeting. In 1990 the NCCB/USCC was runner-up for the award for holding its debate on the Persian Gulf in executive session.

66. William E. McManus, "Did the Bishops Crunch the Budget, or Vice-Versa?" *America* 165 (September 21, 1991): 156.

67. Ibid.

68. L. Bruce van Voorst, "The Churches and Nuclear Deterrence," in *The Political Role of Religion in the United States*, ed. Stephen D. Johnson and Joseph B. Tamney (Boulder: Westview Press, 1986), 305.

69. For a comparison of the bishops appointed under Archbishop Pio Laghi and Archbishop Jean Jadot, see Thomas J. Reese, "The Laghi Legacy," *America* 162 (June 16, 1990): 605-608. An interesting research project would be to examine the video tapes of the NCCB/USCC meetings that show how bishops voted in standing votes.

70. John Dearden, "Universality and Collegiality," *The Ministry of Bishops: Papers from the Collegeville Assembly* (Washington, D.C.: U.S. Catholic Conference, 1982), 12.

71. "CAP-92 Supplemental Questionnaire," Booklet #3, June 13-15, 1991, p. 1.

Chapter 7: Shepherds Among the Wolves

1. T.S. Eliot, "Murder in the Cathedral," *The Complete Poems and Plays 1909-1950* (New York: Harcourt, Brace & World, 1952), 187.

2. Stephen D. Johnson and Joseph B. Tamney, eds., *The Political Role of Religion in the United States* (Boulder: Westview Press, 1986), 223.

3. Thomas J. Reese, "Nuclear Weapons: The Bishops' Debate," *America* 147 (December 18, 1982): 386. Jim Castelli, *The Bishops and the Bomb* (New York: Doubleday Image Book, 1983), 117-8.

4. Catholic organizations are granted 501(c)3 (tax-exempt) status through a group ruling from the Internal Revenue Service. All organizations listed in *The Official Catholic Directory* (Wilmette, Ill.: P. J. Kenedy & Sons, annually) are covered by the ruling. The USCC controls what groups can be listed in the directory. Organizations denied inclusion in the directory can request an individual ruling from the IRS.

5. The 1976 Tax Reform Act attempted to clarify this ambiguity by providing safe-haven rules, which could be elected by tax-exempt organizations, setting the amount of money that could be devoted to lobbying without being challenged by the IRS. The churches requested and received an exemption from this provision.

6. *Regan v. Taxation with Representation*, 461 U.S. 540 (1983).

7. *Abortion Rights Mobilization, Inc. v. United States Catholic Conference*, 110 S.Ct. 1946 (1990). The prohibition against endorsing candidates is even stricter than that against lobbying. A tax-exempt organization under section 501(c)(3) may "not participate in, or intervene in (including the publishing or distribution of statements), any political campaign on behalf of (or in opposition to) any candidate for public office." For a discussion of the tax issues, see Ellin Rosenthal, "Prelates and Politics: Current Views on the Prohibition Against Campaign Activity," *Tax Notes* 52 (September 2, 1991): 1122-28; D. Benson Tesdahl, "Intervention in Political Compaigns by Religious Organizations after the Pickle Hearings—A Proposal for the 1990s," *Exempt Organization Tax Review* 4 (November 1991): 1165-84; Deirdre Dessingue Halloran, "Reaction to Tesdahl Proposal for Political Intervention by Religious Organizations," *Exempt Organization Tax Review* 5 (February 1992): 217; Paul Streckfus, "Swaggart Settlement Drawing Comments," *Exempt Organization Tax Review* 5 (February 1992): 205-207.

8. USCC General Counsel, "Political Campaign Activities and Tax-Exempt Groups," *Origins* 18 (September 1, 1988): 181-86.

9. Hugh Nolan, ed., *Pastoral Letters of the United States Bishops* (Washington, D.C.: USCC, 1989), vol. 4, p. 89.

10. Nolan, *Pastoral Letters* 4:129-37.

11. Sooner or later the farm-belt bishops will catch on and demand that the title of their issue be changed from "Food and Agricultural Policy" to "Agricultural and Food Policy" in order to move it up in the list.

12. Jerry Filteau, "Many Significant Shifts in Bishops' New Election-Year Statement," *CNS*, October 15, 1991. Every four years, Mr. Filteau has done an excellent analysis of the political responsibility statements.

13. Nolan, *Pastoral Letters* 4:317-29.

14. Nolan, *Pastoral Letters* 5:95-108.

15. Nolan, *Pastoral Letters* 5:526-39.

16. USCC Administrative Board, "Political Responsibility: Revitalizing American Democracy," *Origins* 21 (October 24, 1991): 313-23.

17. Nolan, *Pastoral Letters* 5:645-56; "Testimony Before Democratic and Republican Platform Committees," *Origins* 10:65; "Testimony Submitted to Democratic and Republican Platform Committee," *Origins* 14:116. According to Archbishop Francis Hurley, laymen with political influence were asked in the 1960s to speak on behalf of Catholics and as representatives of the NCWC and the USCC.

18. "Presidential Candidates: Responses to USCC Questionnaire," *Origins* 18 (October 20, 1988): 311-15.

19. In 1976, when Jim Castelli of NC News got Mr. Carter to agree to come to the NC News office for an interview, Bishop Rausch objected and told Mr. Castelli not to bring any presidential candidate into the NCCB/USCC building.

20. For an excellent examination of the role of the bishops in the 1976-88 presidential elections, see Timothy A. Byrnes, *Catholic Bishops in American Politics* (Princeton, N.J.: Princeton University Press, 1991), 68-146; for the 1976 election, see Timothy A. Byrnes, "The Bishops and Electoral Politics: A Case Study," in *Church Polity and American Politics: Issues in Contemporary American Catholicism*, ed. Mary C. Segers (New York: Garland Publishing, 1990), 121-41. Also see Robert N. Lynch, "'Abortion' and 1976 Politics," *America* 134 (March 6, 1976): 177-78.

21. Eugene Kennedy, *Cardinal Bernardin: Easing Conflicts—and Battling for the Soul of American Catholicism* (Chicago: Bonus Books, 1989), 157. See this book for an interpretation of the meetings sympathetic to Archbishop Bernardin.

22. "I was so traumatized by the whole thing that without even wanting to, I turned it into fiction," says Russell Shaw, author of the novel *Church and State* (Huntington, Ind.: Our Sunday Visitor, 1979) which describes conflict within the NCCB/USCC during a presidential election in which euthanasia is a major issue.

23. Nolan, *Pastoral Letters* 5:157-8.

24. For the 1980 election see Byrnes, *Catholic Bishops in American Politics*, 82-91.

25. For the 1984 election, see Byrnes, *Catholic Bishops in American Politics*, 108-126; Mary C. Segers, "Ferraro, the Bishops, and the 1984 Elections," in *Shaping New Vision: Gender and Values in American Culture*, ed. C. W. Atkinson, C. H. Buchanan, and M. R. Miles (Ann Arbor: UMI Research Press, 1987), 143-67.

26. Byrnes, *Catholic Bishops in American Politics*, 127-35.

27. For a description of other Catholic lobbies in Washington, see Thomas J. O'Hara, "The Multifaceted Catholic Lobby," in *Religion in American Politics*, ed. Charles W. Dunn (Washington, D.C.: Congressional Quarterly, 1989), 137-44; Thomas J. O'Hara, "The Catholic Lobby in Washington: Pluralism and Diversity Among U.S. Catholics," in *Church Polity and American Politics: Issues in Contemporary American Catholicism*, ed. Mary C. Segers (New York: Garland Publishing, 1990), 143-56.

28. Francis T. Hurley, "National Catholic Welfare Conference (NCWC)," *The New Catholic Encyclopedia* (New York: McGraw-Hill, 1967) 10:227.

29. For an excellent study of lobbying by church groups, see Allen D. Hertzke, *Representing God in Washington: The Role of Religious Lobbies in the American Polity* (Knoxville: University of Tennessee Press, 1988). See also his "The Role of Religious Lobbies," in *Religion in American Politics*, ed. Charles W. Dunn (Washington, D.C.: Congressional Quarterly, 1989), 123-36. Also see Denise Shannon, "The Bishops Lobby," (Washington, D.C.: Catholics for a Free Choice, 1991).

30. "Memorandum Re: Legislative Program: 101st Congress," March 1989 (Washington, D.C.: USCC Office of Government Liaison), 1. Exact wording was repeated in "Memorandum Re: Legislative Program: 102nd Congress," February 1991 (Washington, D.C.: USCC Office of Government Liaison), 1.

31. "Memorandum Re: Legislative Program: 101st Congress," March 1989, pp. 1-2. In the quotations that follow, the italic was underlining in the original. Exact wording was repeated in "Memorandum Re: Legislative Program: 102nd Congress," February 1991 (Washington, D.C.: USCC Office of Government Liaison), 1.

32. From the 101st to the 102nd Congress the number of items for Priority One increased from 13 to 19, for Priority Two from 19 to 20, and for Priority Three from 11 to 14. Only the number of items under "important" decreased, from 31 to 21.

33. "Memorandum Re: Legislative Program: 102nd Congress," February 1991 (Washington, D.C.: USCC Office of Government Liaison).

34. "Memorandum Re: NCCB/USCC Legislative Priorities for the 101st Congress," from Frank J. Monahan, May 4, 1989, (Washington, D.C.: USCC Office of Government Liaison).

35. There are 34 entries under "U.S. Catholic Conference—Testimony" in *Origins Index: Volumes 1-20* (Washington, D.C.: Catholic News Service, 1991), 202-203. There was other testimony during this 20-year-period that the editor of *Origins* decided not to publish.

For a list of more than 90 USCC testimonies or statements to Congress between 1969-79, see J. Brian Benestad and Francis J. Butler, eds., *Quest for Justice: A Compendium of Statements of the United States Bishops on the Political and Social Order 1966-1980* (Washington, D.C.: USCC, 1981), 433-56.

36. There are 11 cases listed under "U.S. Catholic Conference—Amicus Curiae" in *Origins Index: Volumes 1-20*, 200.

37. "Legislative Final Report: 101st Congress," Office of Government Liaison, December 1990.

38. Ibid., 5.

39. For an analysis showing the ineffectiveness of the NCWC lobbying effort for aid to Catholic schools, see Lawrence J. McAndrews, "A Closer Look: The NCWC and the Elementary and Secondary Education Act," *Records* 102 (Spring 1991): 45-65.

40. Allen D. Hertzke, *Representing God in Washington: The Role of Religious Lobbies in the American Polity* (Knoxville: University of Tennessee Press, 1988), 94-101.

41. Stephen D. Johnson and Joseph B. Tamney, eds., *The Political Role of Religion in the United States* (Boulder: Westview Press, 1986), 223 and 339.

42. Allen D. Hertzke, *Representing God in Washington: The Role of Religious Lobbies in the American Polity* (Knoxville: University of Tennessee Press, 1988).

43. Hertzke, *Representing God in Washington*, 81.

44. Colman McCarthy, "Catholic Charities is now U.S.'s Largest Charity," *National Catholic Reporter*, December 6, 1991, p. 24.

45. Robert N. Lynch, "The National Committee for a Human Life Amendment, Inc.: Its Goals and Origins," *Catholic Lawyer 20* (Winter 1974): 303-308.

46. "Project Life 1990: Final Report," National Committee for a Human Life Amendment, Washington, D.C., December 17, 1990.

47. These included the Hyde Amendment, the Kemp-Kasten Amendment, the Mexico City Policy, the D.C. abortion funding prohibition, the Department of Defense regulation prohibiting the use of military health facilities for abortion, restriction on the use of Legal Services funds in abortion cases, prohibition of fetal experimentation, Title X regulations, and abortion-neutral language in child care legislation.

48. "Project Life 1990: Final Report," National Committee for a Human Life Amendment, Washington, D.C., December 17, 1990.

49. Byrnes, *Catholic Bishops in American Politics*, 53.

50. Byrnes, *Catholic Bishops in American Politics*, 119.

Chapter 8: The Shepherds and the Chief Shepherd

1. John B. Sheerin, C.S.P., *Never Look Back: The Career and Concerns of John J. Burke* (New York: Paulist Press, 1975), 78.

2. John Roach, "Presidential Address," NCCB meeting, November 14, 1983.

3. Reported by Archbishop John May at a Washington, D.C., press conference Nov. 17, 1988. He said that this meeting with the pope took place three weeks earlier.

4. Gerald P. Fogarty, *The Vatican and the American Hierarchy from 1870-1965* (Stuttgart, Germany: Anton Hiersemann, 1982; Wilmington: Michael Glazier, 1985). See especially "Romanization of the Hierarchy," 195-206.

5. For a discussion of the relations between Rome and diocesan bishops, see Thomas J. Reese, *Archbishop: Inside the Power Structure of the American Catholic Church* (San Francisco: Harper & Row, 1989), 316-48.

6. Richard A. McCormick, S.J., *The Critical Calling: Reflections on Moral Dilemmas Since Vatican II* (Washington, D.C.: Georgetown University Press, 1989), 82.

7. The Congregation for the Doctrine of the Faith, which at that time dealt with laicization of priests, asked the NCCB to send staff over to help write a document explaining the laicization process. NCCB associate general secretary Rev. Donald Heintschel and the Rev. John Alesandro were sent. They worked for a week with the congregation, drafting a document explaining how a bishop would go about applying for the laicization of one of his priests. "It got kind of quasi-approval"

from the congregation, explains Monsignor Heintschel. "They never put their final say on anything. But it had kind of quasi-approval. We published it here as a document—a confidential document—to all the bishops in the United States. It took the whole thing on laicization and laid out the issues and laid out how the dossier is prepared for application and things like that."

8. McCormick, *The Critical Calling*, 281-85.

9. See also Daniel Pilarczyk, "Domestic Manners of the American People," *America* 152 (May 25, 1985): 425-29.

10. I have nothing against people criticizing these letters. I did it myself. See Thomas J. Reese, "The Bishops on the Economy: What Next?" *America* 152 (February 2, 1985): 78.

11. Jim Castelli, *The Bishops and the Bomb* (New York: Image, 1984), 111-12, 130-34.

12. Jan Schotte, "A Vatican Synthesis," *Origins* 12 (April 7, 1983): 692. See also "Memorandum to NCCB Ad-Hoc Committee on War and Peace" from Archbishop John R. Roach and Cardinal Joseph L. Bernardin (January 25, 1983).

13. *Bishops' Pastoral Letters: Out of Justice, Peace, and Winning the Peace*, ed. James V. Schall, S.J. (San Francisco: Ignatius Press, 1984). There were differences of view between the NCCB and some European conferences over the morality of the first use of nuclear weapons by NATO.

14. John Finis, Joseph M. Boyle, and Germain Grisez, *Nuclear Deterrence, Morality, and Realism* (New York: Oxford University Press, 1987) argues for unilateral nuclear disarmament because of the immorality of deterrence. For a critique of this view, see book review by David Hollenbach, S.J., in *Theological Studies* 49:766-68.

15. Thomas J. Reese, S.J., "The Bishops' 'Challenge of Peace,'" *America* 148 (May 21, 1983): 393.

16. Pontifical Justice and Peace Commission, "An Ethical Approach to the International Debt Question," *Origins* 16 (February 5, 1987): 601ff.

17. USCC Administrative Board, "Statement on Relieving Third World Debt," *Origins* 19 (October 12, 1989): 305-314.

18. "Concerns Expressed About U.S. Bishops' Draft Pastoral on Women," *Origins* 21 (June 13, 1991): 73-75.

19. Paul Wilkes, "Profiles: The Education of an Archbishop—I," *New Yorker* (July 15, 1991), 56.

20. Peter Steinfels, "Policy on Women Hits Vatican Snags," *New York Times*, May 30, 1991, p. A18.

21. For more information on this meeting, see Thomas J. Reese, "The U.S. Archbishops Go to Rome," *America* 160 (March 4, 1989): 187-88; "Discussions in Rome," *America* 160 (March 25, 1989): 260-61; and *Origins* 18 (March 23, 1989): 677-96; *Origins* 18 (March 30, 1989): 697-728; Joseph McNeal, "Report from Rome: Audition for Tragedy," *Commonweal* 116 (April 21, 1989): 228-31.

22. For an examination of the bishops' role in debate over American policy in Central America, see Ronald T. Libby, "Listen to the Bishops," *Foreign Policy* 52 (Fall 1983), reprinted in *The Political Role of Religion in the United States*, ed. Stephen D. Johnson and Joseph B. Tamney (Boulder: Westview Press, 1986), 263-78.

23. "NCCB/USCC Morning Session, May 3, 1978," USCC Press Office.

24. See Robert A. Graham, S.J., *Vatican Diplomacy* (Princeton: Princeton University Press, 1959); Thomas J. Reese, "Diplomatic Relations with the Vatican," *America* 152 (March 16, 1985); and Thomas J. Reese, "Three Years Later: U.S. Relations with the Holy See," *America* 156 (January 17, 1987).

25. Jan Schotte, "A Vatican Synthesis," *Origins* 12 (April 7, 1983): 692.

26. "Draft Statement on Episcopal Conferences," *Origins* 17 (April 7, 1988): 736.

27. Thomas J. Reese, S.J., ed., *Episcopal Conferences: Historical, Canonical, and Theological Studies* (Washington, D.C.: Georgetown University Press, 1989).

28. For the NCCB response, see National Conference of Catholic Bishops, "Response to Vatican Working Paper on Bishops Conferences," *Origins* 18 (December 1, 1988): 397-402.

29. Cardinal Bernardin Gantin, "An Update on the Bishops' Conferences Study," *Origins* 20 (November 8, 1990): 355-56.

30. Along with the archbishops were invited the four NCCB/USCC officers, all of whom were archbishops except the secretary, Bishop William Keeler. He was later made an archbishop.

31. For more on the Hunthausen crisis see Thomas J. Reese, *Archbishop: Inside the Power Structure of the American Catholic Church* (San Francisco: Harper & Row, 1989), 337-44. Also see special issue of *Jurist* 49 (1989): 339-739.

32. In November 1970, the NCCB considered a proposal to request from the Holy See delegated power for all U.S. diocesan bishops to grant a dispensation from the non-consummated marriage. The resolution was replaced by one asking Rome to keep the NCCB informed on developments in this area.

33. Fogarty, *The Vatican and the American Hierarchy from 1870-1965*, 1-9.

34. Fogarty, *The Vatican and the American Hierarchy from 1870-1965*, 177-94.

35. Joseph Kenny, "Fr. Dulles Backs Bishops' Position," *St. Louis Review* (April 14, 1989), 1.

36. Thomas J. Reese, *Archbishop: Inside the Power Structure of the American Catholic Church* (San Francisco: Harper & Row, 1989), 316-45.

37. Gabriel Moran, *Theology of Revelation* (New York: Herder & Herder, 1966) and *Catechesis of Revelation* (New York: Herder & Herder, 1966).

38. "Ad Hoc Committee Report on the Universal Catechism," *Origins* 19 (April 26, 1990): 773-84. For a similarly negative response from scholars, see Thomas J. Reese, S.J., ed., *The Universal Catechism Reader: Reflections and Responses* (San Francisco: HarperCollins, 1990).

39. Joseph Ratzinger, "Bishops' Conferences and Their Doctrinal Commission," *Origins* 21 (June 6, 1991): 71-72.

40. *Cooperation Between Theologians and the Ecclesiastical Magisterium: A Report of the Joint Committee of the Canon Law Society of America and the Catholic Theological Society of America* (Washington, D.C.: Canon Law Society of America, Catholic University of America, 1982).

41. "Text on Bishops and Theologians Deferred," *Origins* 18 (November 24, 1988), 390.

42. "Documentation Action Item #1: Doctrinal Responsibilities," National Conference of Catholic Bishops, United States Catholic Conference Documentation, June 1989, page ii.

43. Richard McBrien, *Catholicism* (Minneapolis, Minn.: Winston Press, 1980). Richard McBrien, "The Pastoral Dimensions of Theology Today," *America* 151 (July 28, 1984): 27.

44. "Statement of Catholic Theological Society of America Members," *Origins* 20 (December 27, 1990): 461-67. For responses by Archbishops Oscar Lipscomb and John Quinn see *Origins* 20 (December 27, 1990): 467.

45. John O'Connor, "The Bishop as Teacher of the Faith," *Origins* 18 (March 23, 1989), 686.

46. Daniel Kucera, "Liturgy and the Sacraments," *Origins* 18 (March 23, 1989), 696.

47. Thomas J. Reese, "Discussions in Rome," *America* 160 (March 25, 1989): 260-61.

48. Stephen J. Ochs, *Desegregating the Altar: The Josephites and the Struggle for Black Priests 1871-1960* (Baton Rouge: Louisiana State University Press, 1990), 140.

49. Ibid., 179.

50. Ibid., 228.

51. Ibid., 5.

52. Ibid., 261-63.

53. Ibid. 352.

54. See references to Denis J. O'Connell in Fogarty, *The Vatican and the American Hierarchy from 1870-1965*, 35-44, 115-16.

Chapter 9: The Shepherds' Purse

1. "National Conference of Catholic Bishops/United States Catholic Conference: Spring 1980 Meeting, Chicago, April 29, Morning Session," (Washington, D.C.: USCC Press Office, April 29, 1980), 3. Bishop James Lyke, now archbishop of Atlanta, was opposing cuts in Campaign for Human Development.

2. William E. McManus, "Did the Bishops Crunch the Budget, or Vice-Versa?" *America* 165 (September 21, 1991): 157. Quotation is from original manuscript before changes made by *America* editors.

3. Interest from the money collected for the BWER fund had been used for operating expenses of the NCCB/USCC, but the bishops voted in June 1991 to have the

interest given to CRS and MRS. Since the money was donated for the poor, some bishops felt using the interest for the NCCB/USCC was inappropriate and against the intention of the donors.

4. Not included in MRS expenses funded through grants are approximately $13.1 million and $16.7 million in 1991 and 1992 respectively, representing reimbursements to dioceses for both direct aid to refugees and administrative and support cost reimbursements.

5. CNS has always fought this overhead charge that is over and above charges for rent and utilities. According to the USCC Finance Office, this charge is an equitable share of the cost of administrative services and supporting services of the conference, for example the general secretariat, the general counsel, Human Services, planning, accounting, etc. CNS argues it could get the services it needs cheaper if it were independent. Since CNS gets most of its money from diocesan newspapers, the bishops realize if they forced CNS to pay the overhead, it would have to raise the price for its services to dioceses.

6. The conference temporarily invests money from the collections for religious retirement, Campaign for Human Development, the Bishops' Welfare and Relief Fund, and the Catholic Communications Campaign. The investment income goes to the collections.

7. The guidelines were originally established by the Administrative Board, and in November 12, 1991, they were adopted without debate by the assembly. On South Africa, the guidelines say the conference will take its direction from the South African bishops. "Socially Responsible Investment Guidelines," *Origins* 21 (November 28, 1991): 405-408.

8. *The Official Catholic Directory* (Wilmette, Ill.: P. J. Kenedy & Sons, annually). In the past there was some evidence that the directory, which gets its figures from dioceses, underreported the Catholic population. Gallup and other surveys indicated that the Catholic population was a higher percentage of the population than reported in the directory. The U.S. Census Bureau does not collect statistics on religion.

Many believe that parishes underreport the number of Catholics they serve in order to reduce their diocesan tax burden. For more on diocesan finances see Thomas J. Reese, *Archbishop: Inside the Power Structure of the American Catholic Church* (San Francisco: Harper & Row, 1989), 150-91. Similarly, some dioceses do not rush to update their statistics in the directory. Chicago, for example, reported the exact same statistics for five years in a row.

More recently, Gallup has reported a decline in the percentage of Catholics to 25 percent in 1991, which brings his number closer to the 24 percent figure in the directory.

9. Theoretically this system also strengthens the hand of smaller dioceses that do not have auxiliary bishops, but there is no evidence to indicate this has had an effect.

10. I am grateful to Allen Manvel of *Tax Notes* for adjusting these figures for inflation. The 1967-91 adjustments are based on the "Survey of Current Business," while the 1992-96 adjustments are based on projections in President Bush's budget for FY 1993.

11. Sometimes it is unclear whether a fund-raising project is an assessment or a collection. For example, the 1981 collection for Thailand refugees had a target of $4 million (2.6 cents per Catholic). In 1968 the yearly collection for the Catholic University of America was set at five cents per Catholic. It no longer has a target.

12. Thomas M. Rowe and Gary A. Giroux, "Diocesan Financial Disclosure: A Quality Assessment," *Journal of Accounting and Public Policy* 5 (1986): 57-75. National Conference of Catholic Bishops, *Diocesan Accounting and Financial Reporting* (Washington, D.C.: NCCB, 1971) and *Accounting Principles and Reporting Practices for Churches and Church-Related Organizations* (Washington, D.C.: NCCB, 1983; revised 1990).

13. Includes only contributions from dioceses. Collection statistics are from "NCCB/USCC Including Campaign for Human Development National Office and Committee for the Church in Latin America National Office and Catholic Communication Campaign National Office and American Board of Catholic Missions: Financial Statements and Supplementary Information and Reports Thereon, Years Ended December 31, 1990 and 1989," (Washington, D.C.: Coopers & Lybrand, May 10, 1991).

14. By requiring that funding requests be cleared by episcopal conferences, the NCCB/USCC has stimulated Eastern European bishops to take their conferences seriously and use them to set national priorities.

15. Jerry Filteau, "Philadelphia Cardinal Says Pope Needs Money," Catholic News Service, November 13, 1990. For more on Vatican finances see Edmund Szoka, "A Presentation to the National Conference of Catholic Bishops of the United States of America on the Financial Situation of the Holy See," (Washington, D.C.: USCC photocopy, November 12, 1991).

16. Diocesan breakdowns for Peter's Pence, NOBC, CUA, Holy Land, and Rice Bowl collections were unavailable. Nineteen dioceses had initiated programs for retired religious prior to the Retirement Fund for Religious. Since distribution of these funds is coordinated with the Tri-Conference Retirement Office, these dioceses are counted as participating in the collection.

In 1990, the Eastern-rite dioceses and the Military Archdiocese did not contribute to the BWER or the Latin America collections. The Eastern-rite dioceses did not contribute to CCC. The Military Archdiocese did not contribute to CHD, and only one Eastern-rite diocese contributed.

The Eastern-rite dioceses and the Military Archdiocese do contribute to ABCM, probably because they sometimes receive grants from it. Dioceses from Puerto Rico, Virgin Islands, Guam, and the Caroline and Marshall Islands also contribute to ABCM and CHD from whom they have also received grants.

17. Some dioceses have given the same amount in consecutive years or have given amounts ending in three zeroes, which indicates that the figures do not reflect the actual take from a Sunday collection.

18. The receipts from the Black and Indian Home Missions declined faster than inflation from 1968 to 1983 and then began to increase slightly. The take from the Holy Land collection kept up with inflation from 1977 through 1987 and increased faster than inflation in 1988 and 1989. After a good start in 1976 and 1977, the Rice Bowl collection dropped steadily until 1983. It has been erratic since. Peter's Pence statistics are only available since 1983, but it appears to be increasing slightly faster than inflation. Data on collections were provided by the USCC Finance Office, the USCC Archives, and offices administering the collections.

19. "NCCB/USCC Morning Session, May 3, 1978," USCC Press Office.

20. The average Catholic contributes $320 to the church each year, or 1.1 percent of his or her annual income. Protestants give 2.2 percent of their income or $580 a year. Andrew Greeley and William E. McManus, *Catholic Contributions, Sociology and Policy* (Chicago: Thomas More Press, 1987), 2.

21. William T. Poole and Thomas W. Pauken, *Campaign for Human Development: Christian Charity or Political Activism* (Washington, D.C.: Capital Research Center, 1989). For more positive reviews of CHD see John D. McCarthy, Joseph J. Shields, and Ann Patrick Conrad, *The Campaign for Human Development: Strategic Planning Process Research Reports* (Washington, D.C.: Life Cycle Institute, Catholic University of America, 1988); Joseph J. Shields, "The Church and Social Justice Activities: A Case Study of the Campaign for Human Development," *Social Thought* 17 (1991): 22-31; William J. Byron, "Empowerment and Progress in the Campaign for Human Development," *America* (April 15, 1989): 350-52.

22. Lay Commission on Catholic Social Teaching, *Toward the Future* (Lanham, Md.: University Press of America, 1984).

23. Charlotte Hays, "'And the Greatest of These is Social Justice,'" *National Review* (December 31, 1987): 38.

24. Liz Schevtchuk, "Bishops Dispute Claims CHD Program Supports Inappropriate Causes," Catholic News Service, February 7, 1990.

25. "Conference Assessment Project Questionnaire," Booklet #2, June 13-15, 1991, pp. 152-53. The question actually dealt with the importance of the "office" that administers these collections rather than the collection themselves, but without the office to distribute the money it is hard to see how the collection would be administered. When the question was phrased differently, ABCM was ranked first and CHD second.

26. According to Mr. Francis Doyle, the five acres of land for the building, near the Catholic University of America, cost $1.1 million. The five-story building cost "$17.6 million, which is slightly over $100 a square foot, and that is a very usual cost in this area to build a building," he said. In addition, there was about $600,000 worth of electronic equipment for teleconferencing, etc. "Then there is furniture, landscaping, attorney's fees, architect's fees, and the cost of the zoning—just going

before the zoning commission was very costly—because the zoning commission, you have attorney's fees there, and the zoning commission turned down the first design. So you have to start from scratch and go back again, and that delayed the project for six months as well as increasing the costs. So, the budget for the whole project was $26.9 million. That includes everything from paying the attorneys to start the zoning process, to cleaning the building before we occupied it on June 12, 1989, and everything in between. . . . We'll exceed the budget by about 8 percent or slightly more. That actually is not bad considering all the problems that have been encountered."

The building was paid for with $9.9 million from the sale of the old building (1312 Massachusetts Ave.) "which was cramped, dreary, and in desperate need of repair," according to the *National Catholic Reporter* (June 30, 1989). Another $7.2 million came from gifts, and the rest came from the unrestricted fund balance the conference had built up over several years. The dedication of the building was picketed by demonstrators who said the money should have gone to help the poor and homeless.

Mr. Doyle reported to the bishops that the cost of operating the old building in the last full fiscal year of operation was $420,000. The cost of operating the new building in the first full year of occupancy was $1,188,000. Monsignor Lynch pointed out that the square footage of the new building was double the old and that little was spent on the old building for the last several years of occupancy. In addition, the new on-site food service is subsidized because of the building's location.

Soon after the staff moved into their new offices, the Washington office building market suffered a depression. If the conference had waited it could have purchased an existing office building at a bargain price. On the other hand, the USCC sold its 48-year-old building in 1989 at the top of the market. At the beginning of 1992 it was still empty and unrenovated.

27. In 1991 the conference voted to extend the 1991-93 goals and objectives for three more years while it conducted a study of the conference.

28. "CAP-92 Supplemental Questionnaire," Booklet 3, June 13-15, 1991, p. 1.

29. Budget and Finance Committee, "NCCB/USCC General Fund Allocation of Resources and Designation of Priorities," Administrative Committee/Board Meeting, September 13-15, 1988, page 40.

30. "NCCB/USCC General Meeting, November 17, 1987, Tuesday Afternoon, Part I," (Washington, D.C.: USCC Media Office, November 17, 1987), appendix "Intervention by Bishop Carlson, Offering an Amendment to Action Item #11 (Priorities and Plans)," 3.

31. Thomas J. Reese, S.J., "The Bishops and the Almighty Dollar," *America* 164 (June 15, 1991): 636-64.

32. William E. McManus, "Did the Bishops Crunch the Budget, or Vice-Versa?" *America* 165 (September 21, 1991): 156.

33. "Conference Assessment Project Questionnaire," Booklet #2, June 13-15, 1991, pp. 1-146.

34. McManus, "Did the Bishops Crunch the Budget, or Vice-Versa?" 157.

Conclusion

1. Joseph Bernardin, "The Bishops and Their Conference," *Origins* 20 (July 19, 1990): 148.

2. Graham Greene, *Monsignor Quixote* (New York: Simon & Schuster, 1982), 169.

3. For one political scientist's analysis of the NCCB as a legislature, see Mary T. Hanna, "The Dance of Legislation: Church Style," *Religion and Political Behavior in the United States*, ed. Ted G. Jelen (New York: Praeger, 1989), 209-21. See also her "Bishops as Political Leaders," in *Religion in American Politics*, ed., Charles Dunn (Washington, D.C.: Congressional Quarterly, 1989), 75-86.

4. Nelson W. Polsby, "Legislatures," *Handbook of Political Science 5: Governmental Institutions and Processes*, ed. Fred I. Greenstein and Nelson W. Polsby (Reading, Mass.: Addison-Wesley Publishing Co., 1975), 260.

5. Polsby, "Legislatures," 277-92.

6. The Rev. Andrew Greeley argues that the 16 percent decline in church attendance from 1969 to 1975 is due to the laity's rejection of the teaching on birth control. Andrew M. Greeley, *American Catholics Since the Council* (Chicago: Thomas More Press, 1985), 54-58. See also George Gallup, Jr., and Jim Castelli, *The American Catholic People* (New York: Doubleday, 1987).

7. Reported by Religious News Service in December of the years cited. Sometimes, stories listed were general topics like AIDS or Central America that the bishops and other religious leaders were involved in. Listed as runner-up stories were approval of the economic pastoral in 1986; the ARM suit against the Catholic church in 1986; adoption of guidelines on human sexuality and delay of vote on women's pastoral in 1990. In 1989, the Religion Newswriters Association selected the NCCB/USCC as first winner of the "Into the Darkness Award" for meeting in executive session for an afternoon during their November meeting. In 1990 the NCCB/USCC was runner-up for the award for holding its debate on the Persian Gulf in executive session.

8. Henry C. Kenski and William Lockwood, "The Catholic Vote from 1980 to 1986: Continuity or Change?" in *Religion and Political Behavior in the United States*, ed. Ted G. Jelen (New York: Praeger, 1989), 114-15. See George Gallup, Jr., and Jim Castelli, *The American Catholic People* (New York: Doubleday, 1987); Andrew M. Greeley, *The American Catholic: A Social Portrait* (New York: Basic Books, 1977), 90-111; Andrew M. Greeley, *American Catholics Since the Council* (Chicago: Thomas More Press, 1985), 35-48.

9. Allen D. Hertzke, "The Role of Religious Lobbies," in *Religion in American Politics*, ed. Charles W. Dunn (Washington, D.C.: Congressional Quarterly, 1989), 123-36.

10. Kenneth D. Wald, *Religion and Politics in the United States* (New York: St. Martin's Press, 1987), 228. See also Andrew M. Greeley, "Why the Peace Pastoral Did Not Bomb," *National Catholic Reporter* (April 12, 1985), 11.

11. Kenneth D. Wald, "From the Word of God to the Voice of God: The Impact of the Peace Pastoral on Public Opinion," paper delivered at the Catholic University of America conference on "The Challenge of Peace: The Catholic Church in Public Debate," October 27-28, 1989.

12. *Membership Directory: National Conference of Catholic Bishops, United States Catholic Conference* (Washington, D.C.: USCC, April 1991). Another 57 were members of only one committee.

13. "Conference Assessment Project Questionnaire," Booklet #4, June 13-14, 1991, p. 96.

14. Joseph A. Komonchak, "Subsidiarity in the Church: The State of the Question," *The Nature and Future of Episcopal Conferences*, ed. Hervé Legrand, Julio Manzanares, and Antonio García y García (Washington, D.C.: Catholic University of America Press, 1988), 298-349.

15. *Quadragesimo Anno*, 79.

16. Polsby, "Legislatures," 258, citing K. C. Wheare, *Legislatures* (New York: Oxford University Press, 1963), 1.

17. Paul Wilkes, "Profiles: The Education of an Archbishop--II," *New Yorker* (July 22, 1991), 53.

18. Michael A. Russo, *The Church, the Press and Abortion: Catholic Leadership and Public Communication* (Cambridge, Mass.: John F. Kennedy School of Government, Harvard University, December 1991), 26.

19. *A National Pastoral Council: Pro and Con* (Washington, D.C.: USCC, 1971). Thomas J. Reese, *Archbishop: Inside the Power Structure of the American Catholic Church* (San Francisco: Harper & Row, 1989), 120-27.

20. "Conference Assessment Project Questionnaire," Booklet #2, June 13-14, 1991, p. 156.

21. Good research is done by the Life Cycle Institute at the Catholic University of America and by the Center for the Study of Contemporary Values at Notre Dame University. Both have been supported by grants from the Lilly Endowment, one of the few foundations that supports research on religious topics.

22. John Tracy Ellis, ed., *The Catholic Priest in the United States: Historical Investigations* (Collegeville, Minn.: St. John's University Press, 1971); Eugene Kennedy and Victor J. Heckler, *The Catholic Priest in the United States: Psychological Investigations* (Washington, D.C.: USCC, 1972); Andrew M. Greeley, *The Catholic Priest in the United States: Sociological Investigations* (Washington, D.C.: USCC, 1972).

23. Reese, *Archbishop*, 306-309, 364-65.

24. The average Catholic contributes $320 to the church each year, or 1.1 percent of his or her annual income. Protestants give 2.2 percent of their income or $580 a

year. Andrew Greeley and William E. McManus, *Catholic Contributions, Sociology and Policy* (Chicago: Thomas More Press, 1987), 2.

Appendix C: Major NCCB/USCC Statements

1. Based on statements printed in Hugh J. Nolan, ed., *Pastoral Letters of the United States Bishops* (Washington, D.C.: USCC, 1983; 1989), vol. 3-5.

2. "Vote" indicates how the motion passed: "V" means a voice vote, "B" a written ballot, "H" a show of hands, "M" a mailed ballot, "S" a standing vote. A "u" following any of these letters means the minutes say the vote was unanimous; an "o" means the minutes say the vote was overwhelming. When the minutes do not indicate the method of voting, it is presumed to be a voice vote. Question marks mean the actual vote count is unknown.

3. There is no record in the minutes of a vote on this document. Bishop Jim Wright said no one voted against it. A. E. P. Wall, "Pastoral Meets Today's Faith Problems: Wright," *National Catholic Reporter* 4 (Jan. 24, 1968), 2.

4. Separate votes on 8 sections, from 214-9 to 172-49 (conclusion).

5. Father Nolan says that this was a statement by the USCC Division of World Justice and Peace (Nolan, *Pastoral Letters* 3:61 and 228). Father Woods, who examined the minutes of the Administrative Committee and Administrative Board, indicates that the declaration was approved by a two-thirds vote in a mail ballot (Woods, "Pastoral Care," 291).

6. Passed easily according to press release.

Appendix D: NCCB/USCC Legislative Priorities

1. "Memorandum Re: Legislative Program: 102nd Congress," February 1991 (Washington, D.C.: USCC Office of Government Liaison).

Appendix E: Canons Mentioning Episcopal Conferences

1. James A. Coriden, Thomas J. Green, and Donald E. Heintschel, eds., *The Code of Canon Law: A Text and Commentary* (New York: Paulist Press, 1985), 370-72. Information in brackets from *Complementary Norms: Implementation of the 1983 Code of Canon Law* (Washington, D.C.: USCC, 1991). Although the CLSA *Commentary* indicates there are 82 Canons mentioning conferences, *Complementary Norms* states there are 84. To the CLSA list should be added canon 961, 2, the criteria for general absolution [in 1988 the NCCB determined the meaning of *diu* is one month].

Index